Prevention
of Delinquency

Edited by

JOHN R. STRATTON *The University of Iowa*

and

ROBERT M. TERRY *The University of Iowa*

Prevention
of Delinquency:
Problems
and Programs

THE MACMILLAN COMPANY, NEW YORK
COLLIER-MACMILLAN LIMITED, LONDON

Library of Congress catalog card number: 68–15271

THE MACMILLAN COMPANY, NEW YORK
COLLIER-MACMILLAN CANADA, LTD., TORONTO, ONTARIO

Printed in the United States of America

To our wives, Elizabeth and Irene

Preface

This book is designed to provide the student of juvenile delinquency with a comprehensive overview of the nature of prevention and an illustration of issues and problems confronting those concerned with the control and prevention of delinquency. Work in this area is widely scattered throughout a variety of professional journals, special reports, pamphlets, and books, and is often relatively inaccessible. Although a number of excellent summaries of the prevention literature as it relates to specific programs or to the problem in general are available, they are not adequate substitutes for the articles themselves. The reading of primary sources can provide insights and understandings that are often lost in the process of distillation and summarization.

In selecting articles for inclusion in this volume we have attempted to limit our choices to those that treat basic issues, illustrate noteworthy programs, or provide research findings relevant to current prevention orientations. This decision was partially influenced by the availability of materials, because uniformity of quality and depth of coverage are not characteristic in the prevention literature. Also relevant for our decision was the desire to present writings that are primarily analytical and evaluative rather than descriptive. A number of excellent articles were excluded because of space limitations, overlapping content, or because they were already easily accessible.

We are grateful to the authors and publishers who granted us permission to reprint their materials, and to our colleagues who encouraged our efforts during the preparation of this volume. We also wish to express our appreciation for the assistance and cooperation we received from Mr. John D. Moore of The Macmillan Company during all phases of the preparation of this book.

J. R. S.
R. M. T.

Contents

Prevention
of Delinquency

General Introduction

The problem of juvenile delinquency has at one time or another captured the attention of many different types of citizens, from the man on the street to the President and other governmental officials. Statistical evidence (or purported evidence) that the incidence of delinquency is consistently increasing and that increasing proportions of American youth are engaging in the more serious forms of delinquency such as burglary and auto theft has converted this attention into concern and distress. Generally, however, the concern and distress tend to remain unexpressed and unorganized until they are crystallized by some new and spectacular episodes of misbehavior that are brought to the attention of the public.

In recent years two basic questions have been raised to greater prominence: (1) What causes juvenile delinquency? (2) How can it be prevented? The present state of knowledge on this subject unfortunately does not permit the resolution of either of these questions. At best, there are available tentative explanations that are sometimes useful in organizing the established facts about delinquency and in making researchers and practitioners aware of specific areas that warrant concentration of their efforts. The day when complete answers to all questions pertaining to delinquency are available remains in the distant future.

The state of knowledge regarding the problems of delinquency causation and prevention is best illustrated by reviewing the writings of individuals who are supposedly the most knowledgeable about these issues. Experts offer an almost limitless variety of perspectives on these subjects. These individuals, who have often invested considerable time and energy in the study of delinquency, are generally very cautious in presenting their viewpoints. They seldom offer simple or complete solutions and frequently qualify their statements and findings, often giving the impression that they know almost nothing about delinquency. Although there is considerable divergence between representatives of different disciplines, similar divergences also exist within disciplines. The variety of explanations offered view delinquency as a result of learning experiences, early childhood training practices, extreme poverty, defective character structures, disorganized social structures, physical defects, emotional disturbances, and many other characteristics and conditions. The techniques suggested for effectively preventing delinquency are equally varied, although the literature dealing with prevention is less abundant than that dealing with causation, which perhaps reflects the complexity of the prevention problem as well as the social scientist's general lack of emphasis upon practical problems.

This volume focuses upon the issues raised by the second of the two questions stated before: How can delinquency be prevented? Although this question is often considered separately from that of causation, the two are interrelated. Theories of causation contain implications for preventive techniques, and effective preventive techniques give clues to the causes of delinquency. Although the answers to one question do not automatically yield answers to the other, there is a logical connection that suggests that prevention programs would be strengthened if they were based on the most accurate explanations of delinquency available. Although causation theory does not necessarily provide practical solutions to problems of policy and social engineering, it does identify the salient variables. An orientation to theory as a prerequisite for practice also helps to avoid the "isms" fallacy.

In the area of social problems in general the public seems to have adopted an "ism" orientation as a way of dealing with these problems. "Doism" and "newism" are two examples. "Doism" refers to the belief that it is better to do something than to do nothing—a somewhat naive and over-optimistic view. It assumes that well-intentioned efforts, regardless of what they are, will produce desirable results and seldom, if ever, have deleterious consequences. It leads to alleviation of public concern for the problems because "something is being done" (that is, social workers are visiting deprived families, slum housing is being removed, or recreation facilities are being built to keep children off the streets). Humanitarian programs are especially applauded by persons with this orientation, despite the questionable utility of the program for delinquency prevention.

Newism is a term for the belief that an approach or a program must be worthwhile because it is new. This orientation is reinforced by the failure of older programs and the continuing rise of delinquency rates. Persons who develop "new" approaches to prevention tend to set fashions and are eagerly supported by others. This results in the bandwagon effect of implementing new programs and policies without carefully assessing their validity or reviewing the history of similar types of programs that preceded them.

It is our view that current knowledge regarding delinquency prevention is very limited. This state of affairs is a result of many factors, but it is in part caused by the ad hoc nature of many prevention efforts and the reluctance to impartially and critically evaluate existing theories and practices. Although we do not wish to imply that nothing is known about prevention, we maintain that adequate knowledge can only be developed through careful and critical thinking and research. We have in fact progressed a long way from a state of complete ignorance. Information has been slowly accumulating through the processes of theorizing, experimenting, criticizing, and describing. More systematic and coordinated efforts, however, would accelerate the progress that is being made. Some of the recent governmental efforts in this area provide an example of actions that may facilitate this goal.

Within the limits of available materials, we have attempted to assemble a collection of articles that provide a comprehensive review of delinquency prevention. These articles serve a variety of functions. Some can be termed theoretical and descriptive; these writings delineate problems, provide hunches, set forth theories, and generally inform the reader about currently existing orientations. Others are empirical studies that illustrate research techniques and procedures as well as provide "facts" about delinquency prevention. Another type of article is basically evaluative, dealing essentially with the evaluation of prevention programs and perspectives. Some of the articles included deal with several of these aspects simultaneously. It is hoped that they will provide an inclusive and representative view of the current state of knowledge. As more knowledge becomes available, these articles will lose their representative nature.

In order to make the book as adaptable as possible, the readings have been arranged in six sections that are believed to comprise two basic divisions of the subject matter: problems and programs.

The first three sections deal with the problems involved in formulating and implementing prevention programs. Articles presenting divergent points of view have been selected, and representatives of different disciplines have been included. It is hoped that this arrangement will not only make the reader aware of the lack of consensus and information at basic levels, but will also make him aware of the need for carefully planned and evaluated programs.

The last three sections present reports of specific programs and problems. Section IV contains articles dealing with the efforts of three basic institutions (law, family, and education) to cope with delinquency on a more or less day-to-day basis. These institutions consist of groups and individuals directly concerned with the problem of delinquency, who are commonly thought to constitute the first line of defense against it. It should be noted that not a great deal of information is available regarding the efforts of law, family, and education, in these areas, and even less is known about their effectiveness. This is important to note because of the general consensus that they possess special significance.

Section V is organized around reports of programs specifically developed to cope with delinquency problems. These programs are in the schools and other agencies and are variously directed toward individuals as individuals, or toward individuals in group situations. Their distinguishing characteristic, however, is that they have been developed specifically because of an awareness of and a concern for reducing delinquency. Their existence suggests a perceived breakdown in the community institutions normally concerned with the control of deviant behavior.

Section VI is concerned with efforts to prevent delinquency through changes in the social structure of the community. These are attempts to reach and modify communal and societal conditions believed to be responsible for producing delinquents, rather than manipulating behavior on an individualistic basis.

Prerequisites for Successful Prevention

Programs designed to reduce delinquency have been many and varied in approach. This diversity has not overshadowed the notable lack of success that has characterized them, however. Failures have been attributed to such factors as inadequate funds, lack of community support, insufficient time, and inadequate and/or insufficient personnel. Seldom have evaluators of these programs suggested that failure was caused by an inadequate understanding of the problem or the use of procedures unrelated to the causes of delinquency. It is probable that in many instances these kinds of deficiencies were responsible for the failures experienced. Too often the desire to take immediate action on a pressing problem leads to adoption and implementation of procedures without adequate assessment of their relevance to that problem. Thus many programs have been based on "theories" that are naive or already proven inadequate.

If they are to be successfully conceived and executed, delinquency prevention programs must be based on a thorough understanding of the particular problem at hand and the technique and procedures that will effectively resolve it. This should be the case whether the program is to encompass a total community or a small neighborhood, and whether a limited or a comprehensive program is envisioned.

An adequate understanding of the problem requires the examination of two kinds of issues: (1) the nature and extent of the problem and (2) the etiological processes relevant to the problem. Once these issues have been at least tentatively resolved, the question of prevention strategies can be raised. The first of these issues raises a series of questions directly relevant for prevention programs: How big is the problem? Is it really a problem? What kinds of deviance are involved? Are they serious or minor violations? Information concerning the social and geographical distribution of the delinquency is also necessary: What areas of the city have the highest incidence? What age groups are involved? What is the distribution in terms of sex, race,

5

ethnicity, religion, and so on? This information must be available
before the problem can be put in its proper perspective and
prevention strategies developed.

Reliable delinquency statistics, however, are often not readily
available. The official statistics of the police and the courts frequently do not accurately reflect the extent and nature of delinquency in a community but the policies of these agencies. A more
comprehensive view of the delinquency situation may be obtained
by supplementing official statistics with information from other
agencies that deal with deviant children, such as private and
public welfare and youth agencies, counseling clinics, and the
schools. Even this does not insure a completely accurate assessment of the situation, because some delinquencies will not be
known to any agencies and some agency information will be
overlapping. A statistical center for delinquency information that
draws from all agencies dealing with juveniles would facilitate
the gaining of insight into delinquency, but very few communities have this kind of facility. The development of an organization
for this purpose might be a logical first step in the development
of a long-range delinquency prevention program.

Agencies dealing with juveniles are not the only sources of
information on delinquency. Supplementary data can be obtained
in a variety of other ways. For example, commercial concerns
and other organizations that are frequently victims of certain
kinds of delinquent activities (for example, shoplifting) often
keep records of these activities. A survey of the community's youth
by means of self-report questionnaires could also provide useful
information.

In his article, "Juvenile Delinquency: Myth or Threat," Herbert A. Bloch develops some of the points outlined. Bloch points
out that statistics of delinquency must be cautiously interpreted,
taking into account not only the care with which they were
gathered and recorded, but also general conditions that affect
their nature, such as public temper and morality. He maintains
that official statistics are useful for indicating changes in the
policy and procedures of legal authorities even though they may
be misleading with respect to the extent and nature of actual
delinquency. Bloch sensitizes the reader to some of the structural reasons for variations in the policies of the police and the
courts. He points out the variety of behavior encompassed under
the concept *delinquency* and implies that figures on youth crime
are better indicators of the extent to which delinquency constitutes a serious problem than are figures on other types of juvenile
misconduct.

Once the nature and extent of delinquency in a community

have been determined, information regarding etiology becomes essential to provide the criteria for the development of programs and practices, that is, criteria for decision-making. Although it can be argued that theories of causation do not contain within them mandates regarding the specifics of prevention techniques, it must be admitted that they do embody implications as to what kinds of activities might be expected to be fruitful and what kind might be expected to lead to failure.

Even a casual review of the literature dealing with delinquency causation reveals a plenitude of theories. Many explanations have been offered for delinquency in general and for the delinquencies of selected categories of juveniles. These explanations come from a variety of traditions and often conflict in their assumptions and implications. Obviously, it is desirable to utilize the orientation most likely to lead to a solution of the problems at hand. In the article, "The Problem of Competence to Help," Lyle W. Shannon offers some guidelines for selecting among competing orientations. His focus is primarily upon professional orientations and their accompanying theories rather than upon competing theories within an orientation, but his points can be generalized for this problem.

Walter A. Lunden argues that the contribution of theory to prevention efforts is limited, emphasizing the difficulty of abstracting prevention principles from theories of causation. He suggests that theoretical formulations do not take into account many of the contingencies of real life situations, which can and do subvert prevention efforts. He calls for the development of a theory of crime prevention.

Eva Rosenfeld, like Lunden, is interested in the strategies of prevention. She expresses concern with the limited contribution research has made to the problems of delinquency prevention in the last thirty years and registers distress that we still formulate solutions on premises "which common sense, logic, and available knowledge would declare to be naive." She attempts to detail those factors that interfere with the development and utilization of knowledge in prevention by describing the difficulties encountered in a program designed to control juvenile narcotic usage. Eva Rosenfeld concludes by calling for less emphasis on causation research and more emphasis on a "carefully recorded, analyzed, and evaluated trial-and-error method, using various approaches in various combinations in various conditions, learning all the while—unlearning and learning."

James C. Hackler, in the final article in the section, maintains that evaluation is a necessary aspect of delinquency prevention programs and discusses several forms that evaluation may take.

Because each of these forms poses difficulties for the researcher, idealized evaluation procedures must be modified in order to meet the political and practical demands of communities and existing agencies and personnel.

1   Juvenile Delinquency: Myth or Threat

HERBERT A. BLOCH

What Is the Problem of Juvenile Delinquency?

The problem to which I address myself is that of the reality of a phenomenon. The question, in effect, is whether or not there is an actual problem of juvenile delinquency. Certainly, on the basis of the agitated concern by the public at large and its delegated authorities, the problem is real and unmistakably clear. Further, if we examine the statistical data purporting to give us some insight into the index or frequency of delinquency—without examining the validity of the data for the moment—the actual numerical indexes would strongly suggest a striking increase in the volume of youthful offenses over the last two decades, and particularly since the end of the Second World War.

Certainly, both of the following facts are dramatic and translucently clear —the extent and degree of public concern, and secondly, the marked upward trend of official statistics concerning delinquency during the past two decades. The fundamental question, however, and the one which is being constantly overlooked, is the question as to what do the figures *and* the aroused public concern represent. In the case of the latter—the matter of public concern—is the problem actually one of the inability of the older generation to control effectively the behavior of our children or is it, rather, a modification in attitude as to what we can reasonably expect of children? In the case of the statistical reports—the mounting public record of youthful offenses— does the increasing demonstration of youthful offenses, misdemeanours, sexual escapades, vandalism, youthful intransigence and reported anti-social behavior constitute a genuine index of anti-social behavior, or is it an emotional protest on the part of the public in the form of a moral judgment upon our young?

Thus, you see, unlike the relatively simple problem of our fellow scientists

Reprinted from the *Journal of Criminal Law, Criminology and Police Science* Copyright © 1958 by the Northwestern University School of Law, Volume 49, Number 4, November–December, 1958, pp. 303–309, with permission of The Northwestern University School of Law.

in the natural and biological fields, where the data they are asked to examine is relatively stable and subject to precise formulation and measurement, we are being asked to examine a composite problem (many, if not most of the elements of which, lie beyond the possibility of measurement) involving the behavior of the young, the nature of community attitudes (which are hardly common or generic), the state of the public morality, and the degree of public resentment and pique. This is a far cry from the observed reaction of a single or unitary form of behavior within a highly limited and narrowly prescribed frame of reference. In a very real sense, the question I am posing demands an assessment of the public temper and the public morality.

The Duplicity of Statistics

Examples of the ambiguousness with which we tend to examine the problem of delinquency are innumerable. The duplicity of statistics in this area is almost too well known to bear repetition. In 1931, the National Commission on Law Enforcement and Observance made its famous pronouncement: "The eagerness with which the unsystematic, often inaccurate, and more often incomplete statistics available for this country are taken up by text writers, writers in the periodicals, newspaper writers, and public speakers, speaks for itself. . . . Actual data are the beginning of wisdom in such a subject, and no such data can be had for the country as a whole." There has been very little since this time to cause us to change our opinion concerning the unreliability of most of our current statistical compilations of delinquent and criminal data.

Thomas Huxley in the nineteenth century made an eloquent plea for the rising place of the natural sciences when he said that we must be humble and silent before what he called the "little facts," and that our perspectives and judgments must be rigorously controlled by such facts. Although the public has tended to become somewhat wary concerning the frequent statistical excursions and alarums describing, one crisis after another, there exists nevertheless a peculiar disposition among large sections of the public to look for statistical reinforcement for what it would like to believe. Statistical evidence, in this respect, appears to satisfy a psychological need. Francis Bacon, in another reference, said many centuries ago that the average man tends to believe what he would like to believe. Apparently modern man displays the same propensity reinforced with the support of statistics. The consequence is that regardless of the understandable suspicion with which the public has come to regard what is referred to as "hard" statistical facts, the use of numbers has become satisfyingly effective in attempting to prove the rise and fall of delinquency.

Let me cite a recent example. When the late Frank Flynn and myself were attempting to arrive at some conclusions concerning the control of delinquency in certain communities, as reported in our volume on delinquency,[1] we came across a number of communities in which the rates of

[1] Bloch, Herbert A., and Flynn, Frank T., *Delinquency: The Juvenile Offender in America Today*, New York, Random House, 1956.

delinquency seemed to have drastically declined as a result of the development of a new agency. To those of us who have become painfully aware of the complex and ramifying nature of delinquency, the issuance of such a report is sufficient to arouse one's deepest suspicions.

In one community, thus, where the overall rate of delinquency was reported to have been cut in half at the end of a given year, presumably as a result of the institution of a new youth bureau associated with the police department, we found an interesting fact. By arrangement with the local children's court, and the newly established police agency, cases ordinarily handled by the court, except in those instances where certain forms of recidivism occurred, were automatically referred to the youth bureau for special handling. Such cases, unofficially handled, were actually removed from the official rolls and consequently never appeared in the annual reports. The result was a minor miracle, a sharp decrease in the incidence of delinquency by means of a limited agency consisting of three full-time police officers. Indeed, as we examined the community, we found that the active delinquency rate had increased appreciably during the same period—by about 33⅓ percent—but the public was able to feel pleasantly reassured and smugly satisfied, particularly in view of the fact that the total budgetary allocation for the new agency was somewhat less than $20,000 per annum. I suppose that this is a small price to pay for the euphoric satisfaction of peace of mind and peace of soul. If personal salvation can be obtained by statistical self-deception, there may be in such a use of statistics a new therapeutic tool for the psychiatrists to allay public anxiety and doubt. The sad fact remained, however, that the delinquency rate in this community kept on going higher and, to my best knowledge, shows no prospect of abatement. For a great many years, Thorsten Sellin has pointed to similar shortcomings in our methods of compiling statistical data, and the late Professor Sutherland indicated how "miraculous cures" were effected in certain states during the thirties by healthy dosages of statistical barbiturates administered to an unwitting public.

What Do the Statistics Really Mean?

The interesting fact about such disclosures, however, is not that the statistical data are themselves misleading but the fact that, when honestly compiled, they still register something. What they indicate, however, is not a rise or decline in delinquency, but a change in official public policy and, as such, they merit our careful consideration and examination. What we should be concerned with here, providing the data are honestly and conscientiously compiled, is the issue as to what do the data actually represent and why? Certainly, during the past ten years, we have witnessed a more sustained and intelligent effort to get at the facts by public and private agencies than at any time during the preceding forty years. Further, just as the public is slowly becoming educated in this respect, and possibly as a corollary to this public enlightenment, our public agencies have become considerably more sophisticated in their handling of statistical data. The fact remains, however, that a vast amount of our data concerning delinquency is not so much a measurement of what transpires on the national scene concerning the misbehavior of the young, *but rather a description of the volume of traffic through selected children's courts.*

The data, therefore, represents, perhaps, the zeal and conscientiousness, and especially the working philosophy, of a given court, rather than an accurate portrayal of the amount of delinquency in the area in which the court functions. Despite the painstaking efforts and honesty of the federal Children's Bureau in its periodic compilations of data concerning court-reported delinquency, the character of the data can really tell us very little. This, incidentally, is not intended in any way to be a reflection upon the Children's Bureau or this phase of its work. Indeed, the Bureau is to be strongly commended for its efforts since 1946 to change the method of its reporting and for its valiant efforts to have the several states report juvenile data through central coordinating state agencies.

The issue under discussion is of another type. Since the Bureau is concerned essentially with adjudicated cases, and since the reasons for adjudication and the resultant court process are highly variable from community to community, the Bureau can only record, in a very real sense, what the local community wants it to report. In this respect, the fingerprint arrest records of the Federal Bureau of Investigation are considerably better as an index since they concentrate upon crimes known to the police as they pertain to youths under 21 years of age. Although the F.B.I. can also tell us very little about the actual state of delinquency for the country as a whole, the limited data compiled by this agency for the youthful age categories gives us some limited insight concerning the criminal activities of some of our youth.

The Variable Nature of the Courts' Business

Before examining some of the official and unofficial data which has been compiled during the past decade, it may be helpful to direct our attention to a few more instances of the variable activities of the courts and the highly variable nature of the courts' business. The common belief of the public, for example, that the adjudication of a child provides an instance of the severity of his behavior or offense has actually no basis in fact. Unless under specific mandate by law or the pressure of public opinion, courts will only handle those cases they are best equipped to handle. Such handling not only represents very frequently the attitude of the presiding judge but, in the case of the children's courts, the professional philosophy of the court staff (particularly the "in-take" department), the nature of community standards, the number of available agencies (both public and private) for disposition and treatment, and the public temper.

In assessing a rate of delinquency as reported by the courts, consequently, all of these variables—reflective of different values and points of view—must be carefully considered. Thus, in 1954, Presiding Justice John Warren Hill of the New York City Domestic Relations Court made it perfectly clear that a large number of delinquent boys—he referred to them as being "in the hundreds"—were not being adjudicated because of the lack of institutional facilities for their commitment.[2] It is easy to see, therefore, that an official court rate for such an area as Manhattan gives very little evidence of the actual incidence of delinquency. Certainly, the severity or gravity of the child's behavior is no ultimate guarantee of his adjudication in a great many areas. Thus, the rates that are reported do not even represent the serious cases of maladjustment since the criteria for court-handling may be, as in Justice Hill's pronouncement, the capacity of the court to handle the child in the light of institutional facilities. In effect, therefore, when such conditions prevail, the data do not represent the volume of delinquency in an area but the public's unwillingness or inability to provide training schools. This constitutes the measurement of an attitude and not the measurement of a problem, except in a very limited way.

Let us indicate another example of how statistics purporting to measure delinquency actually measure a phase of the public's attitude towards this problem. The rates of Negro children adjudicated by the courts are considerably higher in most communities where there are large Negro populations than the rates for white children of the same class and economic background. Reported rates in various parts of the country range from two to five times as high as for white children. Sidney Axelrod, reporting in 1952, showed that Negro children are apt to be committed far more frequently than white children for far less serious offenses and with far fewer previous court commitments.[3] Further, this is not necessarily a result of the more obvious processes of discrimination. Frequently this occurs because of the absence of private agencies to which such Negro children may have access. In this case, therefore, the statistical discrepancy is reflective of an economic condition far more than the waywardness of a particular segment of our youthful population.

The end-results of such investigation reveal that it is rare for the children's courts or the police to be aware at any given time of as much as one-half of the total volume of delinquency within a given area. In the well known study undertaken by the District of Columbia Council of Social Agencies in 1943–44, and in the similar study carried on in New York City in 1950–51, these facts were graphically portrayed.[4] Further, as the District of Columbia study showed, many commonplace delinquencies, such as truancy and running away, hardly ever were brought to the courts, while "traffic violation" offenses were invariably brought before the courts. Are we to ascertain from this that traffic violation is a serious offense in the federal district while it is of no consequence in New York City, Philadelphia

[2] New York Times, Sept. 16, 1954.

[3] Axelrod, Sidney, Negro and White Institutionalized Delinquents, American Journal of Sociology, 57 (1952), pp. 569–74.

[4] Schwartz, Edward E., A Community Experiment in the Measurement of Delinquency, Yearbook of the National Probation and Parole Association (1945), pp. 157–82. See also Deardorff, Neva, Central Registration of Delinquents, Probation, 13 (June, 1945), pp. 141–7.

or Boston, while in these latter cities we are only concerned with property offenses and sexual disorders?

By this time, it is apparent that the statistics are not only hopelessly confused and inadequate, but indicate very little of what is actually transpiring in the United States in respect to this overwhelming problem which is so disturbing to the American public.

The Extent of Youthful Criminal Activity

If we care to use the official figures for what they are worth, however, certain rather striking facts emerge. Using 1940 as a base year, and upon the basis of the Children's Bureau figures, approximately one percent of the youthful population of ten through seventeen years of age appeared before our courts—approximately 190,000 young people. By 1955, this figure had risen to approximately two percent—a doubling of our rate—while the same age-group (ten through seventeen years of age) had risen to approximately 20,000,000, giving an estimated total of approximately 400,000 children. More recently, our estimates are about 2.2 percent of approximately 20.5 million young people in the 10–17 year old category, indicating that our courts presently handle about 480,000 cases annually. More significant, perhaps, is the fact that while our juvenile population increased by less than eight percent since 1940 (7.7 percent), the volume of delinquency handled by our courts more than doubled during the same period.

Contrary to popular opinion, however, offenses which bring our youth before the courts are rarely homicides, serious sexual assaults, and public intoxication with which the popular press arouses and titillates the public. The offenses are largely in the nature of property thefts and acts of vandalism. It seems to me that in this respect delinquency and youthful offenses constitute a genuine "threat" and not a myth, viz., that the hard cores of some of our classical crimes appear to have become concentrated among our youthful age categories.

But even here we have to exercise more than a modicum of caution. For example, approximately 54 percent of our automobile thefts are committed by youths under 21 years of age, but if we examine the nature of automobile theft—as I have done in a forthcoming book on adolescent youth [5]—it is hardly the problem that the public is apt to envisage. The youth who takes a car for the purpose of a short joy-ride is a completely different type of individual from the person who steals a car for purposes of personal gain. The former type of offense, comprising a large volume of typical automobile thefts by the young, actually represents a form of youthful prankishness and it is dubious as to whether it may actually be considered a criminal act in the normal sense, despite strict definition by the law. Even robbery, which is a serious offense among our youth, accounting for more than 43 percent of all robberies committed in the United States during 1956, must be examined with caution. It is not unlikely, for example, that the reason for

[5] The Gang: A Study of Adolescent Behavior, New York, Philosophical Library, 1958, in collaboration with Arthur Niederhoffer.

the high percentage of the young appearing in our national bookkeeping is that the young, immature individual is apprehended while the more mature offender has learned how to escape detection. However, it does appear likely that many forms of hard-core crimes have settled among our youthful age-categories.

The Ambiguous Nature of Non-Criminal Delinquency

We must remember, however, that the delinquent, under the law, is not to be considered merely as a "junior criminal." Actually, statutory violations of the criminal codes constitute only a limited aspect of the phenomenon we call delinquency. In virtually all states, the behavior which can bring a child before the courts may only be construed in terms of certain moral judgments of the community, which are derived from the older laws of chancery of the British common law courts. Thus, children may be adjudicated for a wide variety of behaviors such as incorrigibility, truancy, the habitual use of obscene language, absenting themselves from their homes, or associating themselves with vicious persons, and the like, which are fundamentally matters of community taste, standards, and discretion. The question which we must really ask ourselves is whether or not these evidences of social immaturity and poor self-judgment—for this is what they essentially are—have actually increased or not. Although it appears almost impossible to give a definitive answer to this question, it would appear, according to the best judgment that we can muster, that although there may have been an increase in what we may refer to as youthful infractiousness, the increase has not been considerable and may, in fact, be rather negligible.

Fundamentally, the problem is one of our greater liberality in social standards generally, and secondly, our inability to define with any degree of adequacy the role of the adolescent in contemporary society. There is not necessarily, thus, a substantial change in the forms of behavior in which the modern youth indulges as compared to the behavior of his father, but rather a shift in the public's reaction to such behavior. An incidental by-product of this reaction is the seeming upward climb in the number of cases brought before the courts. It also accounts for the greater sensitivity of our police, particularly within the impersonal context of our increasingly urbanized way of life, to matters which formerly might have been resolved out of court—and frequently with far better results.

Conjointly, however, this dual pressure tends to create a problem as a concomitant of social change in which our attitudes have not kept pace with the changing facts of family and community life. Some proof of this can be seen in the widespread motivations towards unsocial and antisocial behavior which seems so characteristic of our youth in general on all social levels today. It is difficult to determine whether these acts of youthful protest and dissidence are considerably different or more extensive than the adolescent protests of their father's day. What is essentially quite different is the capacity that existed in the past, because of different community and family structures, to resolve and to contain such upsurges of youthful protest and misbehavior.

Partial confirmation for this opinion may be obtained by examining the data of the studies which have been done with college youth, presumably coming from economically privileged and stable families, in which the reporting of frequent delinquencies emerges as a matter of course. In the well-known Porterfield study of 437 college students,[6] and in the study conducted by the writer,[7] such youths admitted freely to the commission of offenses and delinquent acts, many of them quite serious. In the Porterfield study, all of the respondents admitted to having committed one or more of the 55 items appearing on the check-sheet, producing an average in excess of eleven offenses for each student reporting. In my own study, 91 percent of the students admitted having committed delinquent acts, with an average yield of nine offenses for each individual examined. Such facts are well known and simply indicate that the differences in reported and adjudicated delinquency among youths of different social classes are largely matters of the kinds of protection afforded to youths of different social background. It seems quite reasonable that the apparent increase in the amount of "noncriminal" delinquency has resulted from the inability of many modern family types—such as the increasing type in which both parents are employed—to cope with a problem which was formerly resolved in family situations where close supervision of the child was possible. This is a change in forms of family control and not necessarily a change in the forms and quantity of common youthful misbehavior.

Adolescent Motivations and Non-Criminal Delinquency

What we are saying in effect here is that the motivations towards behavior which might be termed delinquent, in strict conformity with the ambiguous definitions of the law, are virtually coextensive with the entire adolescent age group in our society and on all social levels. Further, these motivations have been deeply rooted within the American social structure for a considerable time and, very likely, since the period of the mid-nineteenth century. Such behavior has become in part an aspect of a rapidly changing industrial society with its marked trend towards urban dominance. An examination of our presently rapidly moving patterns of social change would suggest that adolescent motivations towards what the public might regard as delinquent misbehavior tend to become intensified during periods of extreme population mobility and exaggerated urban and suburban concentration.

[6] Porterfield, Austin L., *Youth in Trouble*, Texas, Leo Potishman Foundation, 1946.
[7] Bloch, Herbert A., *Disorganization: Personal and Social*, New York, Alfred Knopf, 1952, p. 260.

The Prolongation of Adolescence

There is, moreover, in a rapidly changing and highly complex society such as ours, an inevitable factor which must be considered in attempting to understand the tensions of contemporary adolescent life. This is the enormous prolongation of infancy in our society, with its enhanced dependence of the young, and the extension of schooling and consequent postponement of entrance into adult status. In a forthcoming study on adolescence in which I have participated,[8] it is conspicuous that, under such conditions, the adolescent youth attempts to assume the symbolic equivalents of adult status without its substance and responsibility. In other words, we prolong the period in which adolescent protests may ordinarily take place. That this may be a genuine contributory factor towards the seemingly high rates of youthful delinquency which we observe today seems quite reasonable and supported by most current investigations.

Environmental Opportunity and Community Attitude

In assessing youthful maladjustment and misbehavior, however, we are confronted with variables other than the motivations induced by a given type of social structure. We must take into consideration as well as the factors of environmental opportunity and community attitude. In the language of the research technician, motivation functions as an independent variable while the factors of environmental opportunity and community attitude serve as dependent variables. It is, in fact, the last two factors which will ultimately determine whether a child is adjudged delinquent or not. If the motivations towards youthful protest have seemed to remain relatively constant, have we increased the possibilities of youthful misbehavior through facilitating environmental opportunities and predisposing community attitudes?

In the case of the former—the matter of facilitating environmental opportunities—our congested urban areas, increased permissiveness towards the young, and less sustained parental supervision have tended to induce greater opportunities for adolescent disorder and tension. In the case of community attitudes, it is a well known fact that if delinquency occurs in many cases, it is because the community itself is more highly aware of the problem, and is ready to acknowledge it and to deal with it. But this is a highly variable condition. The tolerance rates of communities are highly different in this respect. Some communities are immediately prone to react to a series of youthful disturbances which would hardly create a ripple of excitement in others.

If we are to appraise the increase or decrease of delinquent behavior in the United States today, thus, we must take into account such variable community standards and certain general trends concerning community at-

8 Bloch and Niederhoffer, *op. cit.*

titudes and goals. In view of the general tendency for most communities to aspire towards what may be referred to as "middle class" standards, and the broad increase in living standards generally, we may observe an increasing tendency to be far less tolerant towards youthful disorders and a greater propensity towards restrictions upon what a previous generation regarded as the normal self-assertiveness of youth. This is a part of the previously mentioned inability to come to grips realistically with the definition of adolescent status in our culture. That it tends to increase the public's awareness of delinquency and the felt need to deal with such problems of youthful waywardness there seems to be little doubt.

Delinquency and the Growing Middle Class Attitude

If we take a long and sober look at the problem of delinquency in the light of what has been said—particularly in the wayward expressions of non-criminal delinquency—delinquency must be regarded as that type of continuing misbehavior of the young which impairs the efficiency of those fundamental groups (family, school, community) with which the child comes into continuing contact. Viewed from this vantage point, American communities are remarkably flexible in their attitudes of tolerance or rejection of the young. However, when this flexibility tends to disappear and a uniform pattern begins to emerge—as is slowly happening in American life through the impersonal logic of modern technology and urbanism—our attitudes tend to become uniform. Under such conditions, the recognition of what might ordinarily be considered the normal intransigence of the young seems to become a universal problem. Since this uniformity has as yet not taken place, however, our reactions to the problem and our public recognition of its prevalence become diffuse and confused. Parenthetically, I would like to add, it would be helpful in dealing with maladjusted and wayward children described as delinquents if modern psychiatrists recognized fully the variations in such community attitudes and, more specifically, the variable structures of family and community life.

Conclusions

To summarize briefly what we may learn concerning the reality of delinquency as a myth or threat, we might tentatively come to the following conclusions. (1) In respect to certain "hardcore" crimes such as the property theft variety, including such offenses as automobile theft, robbery, larceny and burglary, there seems to have been a substantial increase among the youthful segments of the population, especially for the age group ranging from sixteen to twenty-one years of age. (2) In respect to the "non-criminal" type of delinquency, involving a good deal of what may be referred to as youthful intransigence and infractiousness upon which moral judgments are imposed, much of the increase may be attributed to modern conditions of family life, in which sustained parental supervision is lacking, and to the increase of police activity. (3) Whereas during the latter decades of the nineteenth century and the early decades of the present, the status of the adolescent was more clearly articulated, the current trends toward prolongation of schooling and the deferment of adult status seem to have provided greater opportunity and a longer period for adolescent protests to make their impact upon society. In a real sense, the problems of "non-criminal" delinquency which we witness may be due to a prolongation of the period of adolescence. (4) Finally, whereas delinquency in the past was frequently a function of variable community attitudes and standards, the growing tendency towards a middle-class sense of normalcy and uniformity have tended to make us far more sensitive to the manifestations of such youthful disorders than we were, very likely, in the past. This sensitivity registers itself in higher statistical rates of delinquent disorders.

BIBLIOGRAPHY

BLOCH, HERBERT A. AND FLYNN, FRANK T., DELINQUENCY: THE JUVENILE OFFENDER IN AMERICA TODAY (Random House, New York, 1956), Chaps. 1 and 2.

CARR, LOWELL J., *The Extent and Significance of Youthful Law Breaking*, ALABAMA CORRECTIONAL RESEARCH, Vol. 4 (October 1957), pp. 1–5.

DAVIS, KINGSLEY, *The Sociology of Parent-Youth Conflict*, AMERICAN SOCIOLOGICAL REVIEW, V (Aug. 1940), pp. 523–35.

PERLMAN, I. RICHARD, *Reporting Juvenile Delinquency*, NPPA JOURNAL, 3 (July 1957), pp. 242–49.

ROBISON, SOPHIA M., CAN DELINQUENCY BE MEASURED? (New York, 1936).

SCHWARTZ, EDWARD E., *Statistics of Juvenile Delinquency in the U. S.*, THE ANNALS OF THE AMERICAN ACADEMY OF POLITICAL AND SOCIAL SCIENCE, 261 (January 1949), pp. 9–20.

SELLIN, THORSTEN, *The Uniform Criminal Statistics Act*, JOURNAL OF CRIMINAL LAW AND CRIMINOLOGY, Vol. 40 (March–April 1950), pp. 678–700.

TAPPAN, PAUL W., COMPARATIVE SURVEY ON JUVENILE DELINQUENCY, PART I: NORTH AMERICA (United Nations, Division of Social Welfare, New York, 1952).

2   The Problem of Competence to Help

LYLE W. SHANNON

No more than a generation ago in many, if not most, parts of the United States a person might have engaged in behavior that would have resulted in classification or definition by society as deviant or problem behavior,

Reprinted from *Federal Probation*, 25 (Mar. 1961), 32–39, with permission of *Federal Probation* and the author.

but unfortunately neither appropriate institutional facilities nor professional assistance might have been available. Even the layman is aware today of the attitudes that prevailed toward certain types of deviant persons only a generation or so ago. Aside from the grimmest custodial approach, and perhaps a general attitude of condemnation, the community often had little to offer, much less an understanding of the process whereby the person engaging in deviant behavior happened to become that way. This is not entirely untrue today, as witnessed by some explanations of deviant behavior suggested by the layman.[1]

On the other hand, the present situation is quite different in many respects. In our large metropolitan areas we may find that there are various professional and nonprofessional groups competing for the privilege of helping the less fortunate, those who have been defined as deviants or persons with a problem by the larger society. Not only are they anxious to help, but they no longer condemn the deviant, they may even consider him to be normal rather than abnormal.[2]

But still, these competing groups, so willing to help, have one thing in common with those who did not appear as anxious to help at an earlier period—they remain without an adequate explanation of the process whereby deviants have acquired the patterns of behavior about which everyone is so concerned and how they should be treated.[3]

You may say that the professional who wishes to help does understand the behavior with which he is confronted, otherwise he would be unwilling to assume the responsibility of helping. The fact that there are so many competing explanations and conflicting approaches to treatment for a specific form of deviant behavior is evidence to the contrary and cause for concern.[4] Since there are competing groups of persons claiming competence

[1] A New York mechanical engineer contends that "juvenile delinquency can be eliminated completely with the aid of corrective shoes and eye glasses." He states, "If the human body is properly balanced, that is, if a person has both mental and physical balance, that person is not apt to be badly behaved or commit a crime." At the same time a Milwaukee pigeon raiser wishes to join the fight against juvenile delinquency . . . . "If we could encourage young men to take an interest in pigeon racing there would be less juvenile delinquency because they wouldn't have as much time to get into trouble."

[2] See Marshall B. Clinard, "Criminal Behavior is Human Behavior," Federal Probation, March 1949, pp. 21–27.

[3] See: Francis A. Allen, "The Borderland of the Criminal Laws: Problems 'of Socializing' Criminal Justice," The Social Service Review, June 1958, pp. 107–119. On page 114, Allen states, "Ignorance, of itself, is disgraceful only as far as it is avoidable. But when, in our eagerness to find 'better ways' of handling old problems, we rush to measures affecting human liberty and human personality, on the assumption that we have knowledge which, in fact, we do not possess, then the problem of ignorance takes on a more sinister hue. One of the most alarming aspects of the current agitation for reform of criminal justice and related areas is the apparent willingness of some proponents of reform to substitute action for knowledge, action of the sort that often results in the most serious consequences to the affected individuals. Unfortunately, this is a tendency found too frequently among lawyers of the more 'progressive' variety."

[4] No one has portrayed the situation more lucidly than has Percival Bailey in, "The Great Psychiatric Revolution," The American Journal of Psychiatry, November 1956, pp. 387–406. This is one of the most authoritative and well documented articles that can be found on this issue.

to help and competing explanations of deviant behavior, the question of determining competence arises; this is a thorny question and not readily settled.

Although the less fortunate persons in our society have some freedom of choice, they are restricted in many ways as soon as they are defined as deviants and thus are relatively powerless to decide to what extent they will be helped and who will help them.[5]

Criteria of Competence

What are the criteria of competence? How may we decide which groups or professions are competent to deal with the various types of deviant behavior with which we are concerned, with the behavioral types whom the larger society defines as in need of help? The following criteria are suggested:

Positive Criteria. 1. *The ability to predict human behavior*. Can the group claiming competence predict what people will do under certain circumstances? Can they make "if, then" statements with any high degree of accuracy about the behavior with which they claim themselves competent to deal?[6] If these questions can be answered in the affirmative, then there is some evidence of competence.[7]

What must we conclude if a group contends that predictions of human behavior cannot be made? What would we say about an engineer who refused to predict whether or not a bridge constructed in a specified fashion could withstand a specified load? What would we say if a medical doctor claimed the competence to treat persons with a certain type of disease and refused to make predictive statements about the likelihood of recovery for persons treated in the manner *specified*? If the chance of recovery is minimal, the doctor states that it is. If the chance of recovery is almost 100 percent, he states that fact.

But is the ability to predict sufficient? It is necessary, but not sufficient.

2. *The ability to modify or control human behavior*. If a particular professional group has the ability to modify the behavior of deviant persons

[5] There is a possibility that eagerness to help may have as its consequence certain types of action without due process. This has been of concern to many persons who are just as interested in effectively dealing with the problem behavior but aware of the desirability of judicious procedures. See Paul W. Tappan, "The Adolescent in Court," *The Journal of Criminal Law and Criminology*, September–October 1946, pp. 216–229 and "Treatment Without Trial," *Social Forces*, March 1946, pp. 306–311.

[6] A vast literature exists on parole prediction in criminology. Several representative articles are cited as examples of the research that has been conducted on this decision-making problem: Lloyd E. Ohlin and Otis Dudley Duncan, "The Efficiency of Prediction in Criminology," *The American Journal of Sociology*, March 1949, pp. 441–452; Otis Dudley Duncan, Lloyd E. Ohlin, Albert J. Reiss, Jr., and Howard R. Stanton, "Formal Devices for Making Selection Decisions," *The American Journal of Sociology*, May 1953, pp. 573–584; and Daniel Glaser, "The Efficacy of Alternative Approaches to Parole Prediction," *American Sociological Review*, January 1955, pp. 283–287.

[7] The ability to make value judgments, i.e., "ought" statements, must not be confused with scientific generalizations to which we refer as "if, then" statements. Everyone is capable of making value judgments and professional or scientific status gives one no special competence in this respect.

so that they conform to the norms of the society of which they are a part, does that group meet the test of competence? This may be answered with a "perhaps."

       .   .   .

It is possible to appear to modify behavior without actually being the change agent. First of all we must be sure that change in the desirable direction has been due to the efforts of the professional persons involved. This is not an easy task and we shall say more about it in another part of this article. Assuming that the desired change is brought about by the therapy of the professional persons involved, is it related to or derived from the explanation of the deviant behavior accepted by that professional group? That is, is the treatment or therapeutic activity of professional persons consistent with their explanation of the process whereby deviant persons become the way that they are? If not, then why are members of this professional group with this particular explanation of the deviant behavior those whom we entrust with the responsibility of helping? Wouldn't an effective therapy be even more effective if it was derived from an explanation of the behavior in question? It would appear that the success of the therapy employed was probably related to the fact that it contained in some cases or to some extent the elements of a more appropriate therapy that would be derived from a better, in the scientific sense, explanation of the behavior in question.

3. *The existence of a body of scientific research that tends to support the explanation of the professional group in question and with which the therapy in question appears to be consistent.* A scientific discipline in the behavioral sciences has a theory or theories of behavior based on its conception of man. From this theory of human or deviant behavior, or specific types of deviant behavior, is derived a set of interrelated hypotheses. Predictions are made of what will happen under certain circumstances or what will be found under certain circumstances. The test of the hypothesis involves observing, measuring, recording and statistically manipulating the relevant data.[8]

If a body of research exists that is supportive of hypotheses that could be derived from the theory of behavior held by a particular professional group, then we may be inclined to accept that group as competent to work in the field. This is close to the already-suggested criteria, but is not the same. External evidence supportive of the group's explanation is not the same as evidence of the ability of members of the group to make predictions or the same as evidence of ability to modify or control behavior. What is called for here is research that tests hypotheses that could be derived from the theory or theories of human behavior held by a particular professional group.

Negative Criteria. 1. *Existence of a body of research indicating that a group has not been able to effectively deal with the behavior in question*

---

[8] For a discussion of procedures mentioned herein see: Roy G. Francis, "The Relation of Data to Theory," *Rural Sociology*, September 1957, pp. 258–266.

although it may purport to have such ability. If scientific research shows, for example, that those who have received a given therapy from a given professional group improve no more than those who have not, then there is a question as to the competence of the professional group contending that the approach in question is appropriate.[9]

2. *Existence of a body of evidence that the group is so torn by dissension that it cannot be considered to have a unitary approach to the problem behavior.* There are such a multitude of approaches and explanations within the discipline that no particular approach can be called the "....
........". explanation and approach to such and such behavior.[10] That is not to say that individuals or subcategories of individuals within a particular profession may not have a theory of human behavior from which may be derived hypotheses that have been or are testable by scientific research and which serve as a basis for an effective program of treatment or therapy.

Most important of all the criteria listed is the ability to move from a theory of deviant behavior to verified hypotheses and a program of training, therapy, treatment, or re-education with a tested effectiveness on a large proportion of those to whom it is directed.[11]

The ability to effectively modify human behavior comes from research and experimentation. It is one thing to say, let us try this out and see what happens, but it is quite another thing to be able to say, if we do this, such and such is likely to happen a given percent of the time.

---

[9] There have been a number of pioneering efforts in this regard. Persons who conduct research leading to such conclusions are not often well received by members of their professions following publication of the findings. If the research is conducted by a group defined as competitors, the reaction may be even less favorable. As examples of such studies see: LaMay Adamson and H. Warren Dunham, "Clinical Treatment of Male Delinquents: A Case Study in Effort and Result," *American Sociological Review,* June 1956, pp. 312–320; Edwin Powers and Helen Witmer, *An Experiment in the Prevention of Delinquency,* New York: Columbia University Press, 1951, p. 337.

[10] For a penetrating criticism of the psychiatric approach see: Michael Hakeem, "A Critique of the Psychiatric Approach to Crime and Correction," *Law and Contemporary Problems,* Autumn 1958, pp. 650–682. This is a most detailed exposition of the conflicts within psychiatry. Professor Hakeem cites the leading psychiatrists of the country chapter and verse in his contention that the profession is torn over basic issues in reference to various forms of deviant behavior. The author has seen no evidence to contradict Professor Hakeem's charges.

In the same journal see: Frank E. Hartung, "A Critique of the Sociological Approach to Crime and Correction," *Law and Contemporary Problems,* Autumn 1958, pp. 703–734. Professor Hartung points out that sociology is not a unitary discipline and that "sociologists hardly seem to agree on anything." He goes on to say that, "Criminologists are so free in destroying and rejecting each other's theories and hypotheses that criminology must appear nihilistic to the outsider." Lest it seem that sociology and psychiatry are in the same boat, it should be noted that sociologists are more than reluctant to claim that they are in basic agreement and that sociology as such has the answer to the problem of dealing with the deviants in our society. Some of the important controversies in sociology are described with detailed references to the pertinent sociological literature.

[11] See: Donald R. Cressey, "Application and Verification of the Differential Association Theory," *Journal of Criminal Law, Criminology and Police Science,* May–June 1952, pp. 43–52 and "Contradictory Theories in Correctional Group Programs," *Federal Probation,* June 1954, pp. 20–26.

Possible Conclusions

If the choice had to be made today, we could make one by evaluating available studies. This should be done by an independent group not attached to any particular theory of human behavior or program for dealing with the deviants in our society.

Unfortunately, they would probably end up by saying that no one is now competent to claim the ability to deal effectively with various problem areas. The various alternative conclusions might be as follows:

1. Research indicates that a particular professional group has an explanation of either human behavior or some specific deviant behavior that has been verified by research. This group has also developed a program for dealing with the behavior that grows out of their explanation. Research has also shown that the treatment or training is effective. We have already indicated that this will probably not be the conclusion that any independent team of evaluators would reach.

2. Research indicates that there are competing explanations of human behavior or specific deviant behavior and that prevention and control programs based on them have about the same effectiveness. Therefore, each explanation contains an element of the complete explanation of the behavior and each program built on an incomplete explanation has less efficiency than it would have if built upon a fuller explanation of the behavior in question.

Which explanation and which program would we select under such circumstances? From the standpoint of the taxpayer, we should select the program that is least expensive and from the humanitarian viewpoint that which is most readily available, particularly if the short-run view is taken.

If the long-run view is taken, then further research and experimentation would be called for at the same time that some application of existing knowledge was made.

3. Research indicates that no group or profession has demonstrated the ability to effectively deal with deviant behavior; research shows that treatment results in no greater improvement than that which accrues by simply leaving persons with a behavioral problem alone. In this case the cry for more money, for a saturation approach, is indeed uncalled for.[12]

In the case of either of the latter two conclusions, we might wish to carefully examine the training of persons dealing with deviant behavior. It may well be that it is unreasonable to expect them to have much success

---

[12] Cressey has pointed out that no matter how a program works out, personnel maintaining either theoretical or practical interests in the control of crime and delinquency, for example, develop a vocabulary of motives for justifying what they are doing. This entire article demonstrates an unusual degree of perceptivity on the part of the author. Donald R. Cressey, "The Nature and Effectiveness of Correctional Techniques," *Law and Contemporary Problems*, Autumn 1958, pp. 754–771. The obstacles to and difficulties involved in evaluating programs are discussed at length in this particularly thought-provoking article.

in developing theories of human behavior or corrective or treatment programs considering the training they have had and the nature of the problem
with which they are confronted.

The sociologist, for example, is not trained to administer drugs in the
fight against disease. The medical doctor is usually not trained in the structure of social organizations and in the functioning of social systems, and
is thus ill-equipped to deal with human behavior.

.   .   .

3   The Theory of Crime Prevention

WALTER A. LUNDEN

With all the brilliant advances in the field of technology of space flight
there still remains the down-to-earth question: why have not social scientists applied the same skills to the prevention of crime? Why have theoreticians and technologists been so successful in the biological and physical
areas but not in the field of human behaviour? Why is it that the countless
crime prevention programmes, begun with glowing promises, almost invariably end in some kind of cynical defeat or with a summary, "More needs
to be done in other fields," or "The programme is still in progress and future developments may show results"?

In the past fifty years or more, successive theories have been "created"
which were supposed to have "solved crime." At one time the solution
centred on environmental manipulations (bad housing causes crime; therefore, clear the slums and build better houses). Then came the psychological
protagonists (mental deficiency is the cause; therefore, develop clinics to
deal with the antisocial people). Hard upon the heels of these rode the
physical education champions who advocated more and better sports and
recreation. Then came the special contingent of psychiatrists who did battle
with the problem of deep personality conflicts, ego suppression, and "frac-
tured chunks of unorganised conscience." These demanded more and better
psychiatric clinics to uncover the personality disorders of offenders. Latest
to arrive on the field of battle are the "total child approach" groups who
have found the cause and the cure of crime in improved child-rearing
formulae. Now, just coming over the horizon, appears still another brigade
of researchers in shining armour (with unlimited funds) to enter the lists,
flying the banner of psychosomatic involvements, searching out the delin-

Reprinted from British Journal of Criminology, 2 (Jan. 1962), 213–228, with permission
of the publisher.

quency-prone individuals in society. In addition there are a number of auxiliary groups under various flags of "group dynamics," "group therapy" and "child-parent revitalisation approaches." Each and all of these "warriors against crime" represent noble and laudable ambitions and efforts to prevent crime, but the fact remains that we already know more about the causes of delinquency than we do about the means of controlling it. Furthermore, it does appear that crime is more of a "hydra" than a fire-breathing dragon which may be killed by one well-directed thrust of the Siegfriedian sword. In addition it seems that crime has begun to change its habitat, moving into the upper or higher echelons of society with serious results at this level.

Preliminary Considerations

Prior to any discussion of the subject it should be made clear that any theory of crime prevention is not one and the same as a theory of criminality or crime causation. Both deal with the problem of crime but from quite different approaches. The observer must, therefore, exercise caution in order to avoid confusing one with the other. A theory of criminality is a *why* question, whereas the issues in prevention are *how* questions. Hence there is a vast difference between a *why* and a *how* problem. Some analysts might disagree with this distinction and maintain that any theory of crime causation should be the starting-point for any theory of prevention. Others may assume that a theory of prevention could establish a theory of crime causation by working in what may be called the backward approach. Even though there may be some plausible relationship between the two, causation and prevention, the situation is improbable because there is no valid theory of crime causation, and crime prevention is not a theoretical pursuit.

Theoretical criminality, as any theory, is based upon clearly defined and consistent abstractions or sets of propositions which may be substantiated or verified. Beyond this, a theory must be useful or applicable to a given situation or set of circumstances in understanding the *why*. If this is true of a theory of criminality it is equally true of any theory relative to prevention. Crime prevention is distinct from causality because it transcends aetiology and proceeds into the field of strategy and tactics. The theoretician in crime deals with concepts and abstractions deduced from observations; the strategist, on the other hand, must work with methods of controlling human conduct in the arena of reality. Miscalculations for the theoretician may be disconcerting, but errors in dealing with the lives of people bear incalculable consequences. Theoretical considerations in a military classroom involve problems of logic, but military strategy and tactics must operate under fire where casualties often run high. Theoretically, a sprinter should be able to run a distance in nine seconds, but actually it may take him nine and a half or ten seconds. The sprinter may know his theory of physics, but he is confronted with the weather, the track, opponents, the spectators and many other factors. All this leads to the primary consideration that much of the erudition which the theoretician may have gathered has often

"been stood on its head" when applied to life. This is especially true when
there is a time-lag between the formation of the theory and the changes
immanent in society. The reality which was there yesterday may no longer
be present today. Life has a way of proceeding faster than theory, much as
the horizon advances before the traveller. Basically, therefore, any theoretical
consideration of prevention must be cast in the framework of strategy or
tactics of the present and not in the laboratory or in the calculations of
the IBM machine. Any sound procedure in strategy operates from three
well-established considerations: (i) the objectives or goals to be attained;
(ii) the means available to attain the objectives; and (iii) the strength or
potential of the enemy or the opposing forces.

Barriers to Crime Prevention

In the main, considerations of objectives or goals of crime prevention
are generally agreed upon to prevent crime before it occurs and to prevent
persons who have already committed crime from committing more offences.
The goals may be stated in other ways but these may serve for the present.
It is the second and the third parts of the proposition which cause serious
concern because the "available means" and the "strength of the enemy"
are often miscalculated or not understood. There are, therefore, certain
barriers which confront those who would prevent crime.

Relativity vs. Certitude. One of the first barriers to crime prevention is
that the theory of crime causation has often been confused with crime-
prevention procedures, and this has resulted in much fruitless effort. Who-
ever deals with social theory encounters probabilities and fallibilities. Even
the rigid determinism in the physical sciences, assumed to be sound in the
past, is no longer tenable. "In its place there now stand the shadow of
probability and the shade of what is perhaps never to be known" (Thomson,
1959, p. 105). Instead of a theory of light there are now "three theories of
light" which strangely enough produce the paradox that scientific principles
can be something other than true or false. Theories are, therefore, relatively
true or *untrue*, depending on the field of approach. Whether we deal with
physical happenings or forces affecting human behaviour, we are forced to
deal with probabilities and incertitude. As a collateral consideration it appears that in either area, physical or social, as scientific investigations advance the knowable world becomes smaller and the unknowable world
much larger.

Herein lies the first barrier to crime prevention—the incertitude and
highly unpredictable nature of human conduct. Caution, therefore, is a
prime prerequisite for the serious student in any field and especially in
attempting to control human beings.

Validity of Punishment. Another barrier to crime prevention arises from
the present tendency for theoreticians to discount punishment as a factor
in crime prevention. They contend that punishment follows after the crime,
and that crimes are committed with the hope of concealment which nullifies
fear of punishment. Punishment is considered as an outworn factor in

history which "neither improves the criminals nor does it deter them." This tends to support the ultra-Freudian advocates who maintain that "punishment does not deter the criminal, but unconsciously drives him to the forbidden deed." Punishment is "under certain psychological extremely common conditions in our culture, the most dangerous unconscious stimulus for crime because it serves the gratification of the unconscious feeling of guilt, which presses toward a forbidden act" (Reik, 1959). In other words, punishment is an inducement to crime.

Intriguing as may be the psychiatric explanation of crime and punishment, the theoretical framework rests on very shaky ground because of the frequent use of inferences and unsubstantiated experiments. Basically, a crime is an act in which society as a totality is seriously concerned. Whether in primitive or contemporary societies the act offends the strong cohesive conscience of the people. Durkheim (1933, p. 86) has pointed out that in spite of certain crudeness punishment is a "veritable act of defence" and that it is a "defence weapon which has its worth." Society punishes the offender in order to make certain that the act may be considered abhorrent to the minds of men. This preserves the moral ideal, for without punishment no man would know whether an act were "good or bad." Hegel has put the same thought in other words: "Punishment is negation of the negation of law, hence positing restoration of law." This leads to the oft neglected fact in penal theory that any consideration of prevention must be directly concerned with the moral structure of society. No matter how intricate a theory may become, the fact remains that, if there is no social or moral force behind efforts to keep criminals from doing wrong, how can the social order be preserved? If or when theoreticians advance some means of maintaining social solidarity other than by punishment then it may be discarded as an outmoded principle of control or prevention. Though it may seem brutal, as long as man remains a non-rational being it appears that society will have to protect itself. Here, then, is another barrier to crime prevention—the failure to understand that the basic issue in crime prevention is a moral issue and that the bonds which hold society together are moral bonds.

Two Theoretical Approaches

Beyond these preliminary considerations, two broad theories of prevention have been advanced out of which arise other barriers that defeat the best plans of strategy. The goals may be clear but the means employed to attain these objectives are often impracticable. The first of these explanations holds to the theory that crime arises from the environment, which may be the community, group relations or the total habitat of the individual. The individual, therefore, is but the product of the culture in which he lives and to which he must relate himself. The other explanation follows from the theory of personality. Crime is the result of a disorganised personality caused by deep emotional conflicts or ego involvements.

Is There a Community? First let us examine the environmental or community prevention considerations. Out of the theoretical considerations of the academicians and field workers have developed innumerable theories of the community as a breeder of crime. These cover a wide range from area programmes to community reconstruction, community group approaches and similar plans. In general, all of these hold that the community is responsible for behaviour, therefore the task of crime prevention rests with the community. Here, in this theoretical framework, rests one of the many operational barriers to crime prevention because strategists and tacticians have unknowingly accepted the theory of criminal causation without being aware of reality. Today there is no social substance as a community in the proper sense of the word. If it does not exist, how can that which does not exist be a proper approach to crime prevention? There are, it is true, countless numbers of people living in geographical proximity. They may have their mail addressed to a given zone within a city, but beyond this numerical designation there is only a social vacuum. Today people live in mechanised, segmented and isolated relationships in which there is a minimum of community concern, common consciousness or agreement on values or standards. Some few may know each other but not the man who lives across the street; and no one wants to know too much about anybody because others may find out too much about the inquirer. Furthermore, people move around so much that no one has the time or the concern to become attached to any place or group. There was a day when "Home on the Range," "My Old Kentucky Home," "Indiana Moon" and similar songs had a real meaning to those who sang them because people had a sense of belonging. The writers of popular songs today understand society better than many social theoreticians. Today people sing such songs as, "The Big City Blues" or "I am a Stranger in Paradise" or "Why Was I Born?" with a sense of longing for something they cannot find. Even stage productions that have a long run reveal the tremendous psychosocial isolation of present-day society. (Auntie Mame describes the situation when she says, "Life is a banquet and the guests are starving to death from loneliness.") How, therefore, can a community-oriented crime-prevention programme be applied when there is no community? A half century ago E. Durkheim foresaw the present segmented society when he said we have become "a disorganised dust" of many particles without cohesive conscience. Today people live not only in an Atomic Age but in an atomised society.

Where does such a condition lead to if the community theory of crime prevention is to be accepted? Strategically you cannot make something out of "disorganised dust" unless some miracle can bring the lifeless "bones" together into a living, breathing entity. Without a community there is little or no uniformity and no common standards of behaviour. Segmentation has advanced so far as to make community thinking almost improbable. Suppose a plan of action were to be devised for some geographical area. Who would programme it? Whose programme would it be? Outside the force of a police state how could any system be imposed upon a divided and segmented aggregate of people?

The segmentation of a community has further ramifications which add to the barriers. Should an attempt be made to prevent crime in a given area there is frequently a minimum of co-operation among respective groups and sometimes unsuspected opposition. There are those who talk about preventing crime, others who are actively engaged in dealing with crime on a day-to-day basis, and finally the so-called "egghead" research people. The talkers are often so busy talking that they have little time for anything else. The action people—the police, probation officers and others—are so submerged in case-loads that they have little time for co-operation. Finally the "eggheads" are often too far removed from either group to deal realistically with the task. Again, there is a fourth group—those who control the purse-strings in or out of government—with another set of values. This fracturing of groups in a community makes co-ordination on a united "front" very difficult. Any theory or plan of strategy for crime prevention must consider these conditions. The observer need only to turn to various crime investigations to verify these facts.

Reform vs. Status Quo. There is another barrier to any theory of crime control. Crime prevention implies some kind of change or reform from a present situation to something new. Reformers are persons who try to make innovations. People often rush to obtain the newest in cars or hi-fi sets but rarely will they give serious consideration to new methods of dealing with basic social conditions. It has been rightly said that changing behaviour patterns or methods of human relations is more difficult than relocating a cemetery that has been in existence for years. Nobody wants to be reformed and, more than likely, most people distrust reformers. H. Thoreau once said, "If I knew that a man were coming to my front door to reform me I would run out the back door as fast as I could." Changing conditions or suggesting reforms implies a certain amount of criticism about present conditions, and very few persons will tolerate criticism of their community or methods of dealing with offenders. A theory of crime prevention must, therefore, understand the theory of human nature which in most instances is *status-quo* minded unless threatened with serious disaster.

Crime and the Disorganised Personality. After considering crime prevention from the community approach, let us next turn to the second main theoretical phase—that crime is due to a disorganised personality caused by emotional imbalance, psychiatric disorders, asocial drives or some type of conflict between the ego and the super-ego arising from the Freudian or neo-Freudian libido.

The theoretical approach to crime prevention in this field of endeavour implies a number of phases or elements. Basically antisocial behaviour is the resultant of certain complexes, repressions, libidinal or sexual instincts, primordial drives, destructive sadistic urges, Oedipus or Narcissus involvements, all of which lead to criminal behaviour. A second element in this theory implies that practitioners through certain kinds of tests, Rorschach, T.A.T. and others, can determine the degree or type of personality disorders present in an individual. After these have been uncovered, individual or group psycho-analytical procedures or treatments may be used to re-establish the person and to correct his antisocial behaviour.

Group Therapy

In spite of the intricate involvements and the great potentials of this theory, most attempts to prevent crime by these methods have proved to be unsatisfactory up to the present. Here and there a limited number of celebrated cases have been used as special examples to substantiate the theory but at no time has the programme been applied or been able to deal with crime prevention on a broad front. A recent report on "An Experiment in Reaching Asocial Adolescents Through Group Therapy" initiated by the New York City Youth Board showed only very meagre results. For a period of three years the Group Therapy Project treatment was applied to a selected number of asocial children. The report concludes by saying: "No matter how much healthier and better functioning they are, they still need individual therapy of a special character. . . . They still need help to become independent, successful citizens" (Stranahan & Schwartzma, 1959).

The Cambridge-Somerville Project

Another report has just been made on one of the better planned and organised crime-prevention programmes yet developed in the country. With the aid of a $500,000 grant, a group of well-selected specialists established the Cambridge and Somerville Youth Project. After considerable planning, the programme became operative in 1939 with the selection of 650 boys, 325 in a control group who were given a wide range of treatments and 325 who remained in the area with no supervision other than that given the average youth. In 1956 Joan and William McCord made a final assessment of the programme after it had been in operation for seventeen years. Although the boys in the control group were assisted for an average of five years they committed approximately as many crimes as those with no supervision. "Thus, using the standard of 'official' criminal behaviour, we must conclude that the Cambridge-Somerville Youth Study was largely a failure. Some individuals undoubtedly benefited from the programme, but the group as a whole did not" (McCord & McCord, 1959a).[1]

In spite of the great potential of the personality-disorganisation approach to the prevention of crime, as yet there is no sound, practical and workable method which has shown results. It holds great hope for the future but the problem is current. Those in authority are interested in stopping crime rather than in studying more about it.

The Normality of Crime

Beyond these general theoretical approaches to the problem of crime prevention there are other factors which must be considered. Present-day social scientists have, in the main, held that criminality is something abnormal

---

[1] For a complete report on the project see McCord & McCord (1959b).

or pathological to society. They often forgot what A. Prins pointed out years ago, "Criminality proceeds from the very nature of humanity itself, it is not transcendent, but immanent" (1886). Not long after Prins, E. Durkheim made the point even clearer when he indicated that criminality is a "normal" factor and not pathological. "Crime is normal because a society exempt from it is utterly impossible." The "fundamental conditions of social organisation . . . logically imply it." Crime is not due to any imperfection of human nature or society any more than birth or death. "A society exempt from it [crime] would necessitate a standardisation of the moral concepts of all individuals which is neither possible nor desirable" (Durkheim, 1938, p. xxxviii). Durkheim maintained that crime is not only normal for society but that it is necessary. Without crime there could be no evolution in law. If society is to progress each person must be able to express himself. "The opportunity for the genius to carry out his work affords the criminal his originality at a lower level." "Aside from this indirect utility, it happens that crime itself plays a useful role." "According to Athenian Law, Socrates was a criminal, and his condemnation was no more than just. However, his crime, namely, the independence of his thought, rendered a service not only to humanity but to his country." Crime, therefore, "must no longer be conceived as an evil that cannot be too much suppressed" (Durkheim, 1938, p. 71). All this does not mean that crime should be condoned, but it does indicate that if people are to be controlled to the point where no crime exists serious consequences may result to the whole society. If people are to be controlled by some one person or agency of government to such a degree as to inspect or check every action such a regimented society would become unbearable. Nobody wants to live in a police state of Big Brothers watching every act. Actually, therefore, there are limits placed upon any attempt to control or prevent crime.

A Society Without Crime

All of these considerations lead to two elemental questions: Can crime be prevented? Is it possible to have a society with a minimum of crime? The only possible answer to the first question is "no." [Crime cannot be prevented, but it is possible to decrease the amount.] The answer to the second question is "yes." There are and there have been societies with no crime or a minimum of criminality. It is very probable, however, that most people would not desire to live in these societies.

The well-known Arctic explorer V. Stefansson at various times reported that as he travelled away from the civilisation of Western society into the farthermost regions of the Eskimo society crime decreased almost to a minimum. More recently S. D. Porteus of the Juvenile Court of Hawaii (1951, pp. 6–7) reported his experiences during the time he lived with the Australian aborigines where there is very little or no criminality.

> The Australian aborigines, with whom I lived for some time, allow their children to grow up as the most uninhibited youngsters in the world. Up to the age of ten or eleven years, the child is never chastised, seldom if ever

scolded, and never denied anything in the gift of the parents. He learns by example some important tribal conventions, such as avoiding his future mother-in-law and keeping a respectful distance from the campfire of the old men when in council. From dawn to dusk, he does what he likes. No school, no family discipline, no duties, no cares other than those which nature imposes. He is Alexander and Staub's typical socially unadjusted individual. His mother indulges him, his father makes him toy spears.

Suddenly, one evening, two old men approach the family campfire and seize the boy. His father grabs his spears and puts up a vain show of resistance; his mother and all the women weep violently and put up a pathetic outcry. From the moment he is led away, scared out of his wits by the sudden withdrawal of all the customary props that family and associates provide, he is subjected to the most uncompromising social pressures. He is beaten, starved, famished by thirst, taken on long journeys to strange tribes, subjected to body scarring and circumcision with a blunt stone knife. At the same time, he is ceaselessly impressed with the fact that he is now a member of the tribe, a guardian of and participant in the secret tribal rites, a man in a man's world. The result? A member of a race that breeds no rebels, a rigid social conformist accepting the 'tribal line'—a more successful educational product than any religious or political state can possibly turn out. This statement includes both communist and fascist regimes.

Obviously present-day society cannot be "time machined" backward to a society similar to that of the Australian aborigines. Also it is very unlikely that anyone would desire to return to conditions where there were no radios, no TV sets, no bathtubs and no space ships, but the practical organisation of that society does have considerable significance. When people are bound together by strong cohesive bonds of community consciousness, well-accepted and internalised values and governed by established family or tribal traditions, crime can be reduced to a minimum.

.   .   .

Finally, where does all this fit into the statement outlined at the beginning of the discussion—the theory of crime prevention? Here it should be restated that [there may be a number of theories of crime causation but there is no theory of crime prevention.] The issues do not lie in the realm of theory but in the field of strategy. There is an objective to be attained—the prevention or lessening of crime—and all possible resources must be marshalled to gain that objective. At present the strength of the opposition or the forces of crime may not be fully known, but it does now appear that to date the present systems of corrections have not "gotten off the ground" and have certainly not gained a beachhead in the attack. The time has come for less theory and more strategy in the struggle against the rebels in society.

REFERENCES

Annual Report, The Juvenile Court, Honolulu, First Judicial District, T.H. (1951).

DURKHEIM, É. (1933). *The division of labor*. Trans. G. Simpson. New York: Macmillan.

DURKHEIM, E. (1938). *The rules of sociological method*. Ed. G. E. Gatlin. Chicago: Chicago Univ. Press.

KROPOTKIN, P. (1902). *Mutual aid*. New York: Extending Horizon Books (1955).

McCORD, JOAN & McCORD, W. (1959a). A follow-up report on the Cambridge Somerville Youth Study. *The Annals*. 322, 89–96.

McCORD, JOAN & McCORD, W. (1959b). *Origins of crime*. New York: Columbia Univ. Press.

REIK, T. (1959) *The compulsion to confess*. New York: Farrar, Straus & Cudahy.

STRANAHAN, M. & SCHWARTZMA, C. (1959). An experiment in reaching asocial adolescents through group therapy. *The Annals*. 322, 117–125.

THOMSON, G. (1959). What you should know about physics. *Sat. Ev. Post*. 231, 105.

4   Social Research and Social Action in Prevention of Juvenile Delinquency

EVA ROSENFELD

Most workers in the field of juvenile delinquency are painfully aware of the wide gap between the amount of past and ongoing research in this area and the difficulty in translating our knowledge into effective preventive action. No doubt there are many reasons for this difficulty, some of them inherent in the very complexity and scope of the problem. But it is becoming increasingly clear that some, and perhaps major, reasons are methodological: the tradition of our research approach seems to be remarkably sterile.

The following discussion concerns itself primarily with these methodological reasons for the notorious deficiency in our knowledge of how to prevent juvenile delinquency. The analysis of the problem will be illustrated by a case study, the problem of prevention of narcotics use among juveniles.

To begin with, let us briefly consider how much have we learned about the problem of juvenile delinquency in the past thirty years of empirical study.

.   .   .

Writing 30 years ago, Cyril Burt recommended the following six basic pillars of a prevention and rehabilitation program (2, pp. 584–587):

Reprinted from *Social Problems*, 4 (Fall 1956), 138–148, with permission of the Society for the Study of Social Problems and the author.

This article is based on a paper read at the Conference of the American Association of Public Opinion Research, May 25, 1956.

1. All young persons who show delinquent tendencies should be dealt with at the earliest possible stage. Parents should be taught that the pre-school period is a period vitally decisive. . . . Teachers should be urged to watch, and when necessary to report, all who show antisocial inclinations. . . . When the school period is over, after-care workers should be persuaded to extend their supervision to the social conduct, as well as the industrial efficiency, of children who have just left; and, above all, special efforts should be made to meet the transitional phase of adolescence.

2. The problem of delinquency in the young must be envisaged as but one inseparable portion of the larger enterprise for child welfare. Crime in children is not a unique, well-marked, or self-contained phenomenon, to be handled solely by the policeman and the children's court. It touches every side of social work. The teacher, the care committee worker, the magistrate, the probation officer, all who come into official contact with the child, should be working hand in hand not only with each other, but with all the clubs, societies, and agencies, voluntary as well as public, that seek to better the day-to-day life of the child.

3. The delinquent himself must be approached individually as a unique human being with a peculiar constitution, peculiar difficulties, and peculiar problems of his own. . . . The court, therefore, and whatever authority has to grapple with such cases must at all times regard not the offense, but the offender. The aim must not be punishment, but treatment; and the target not isolated actions, but their causes. . . . Such authorities must have access to all available information and possess means to make for every case intensive investigations of their own. . . . A social investigator must report upon home circumstances; a medical officer must inspect the child for physical defects; a psychologist must be at hand to apply mental tests, to assess temperamental qualities, and to analyze unconscious motives. A psychological clinic embodying all these different workers studying the same cases scientifically, side by side, is the most pressing need of all.

4. The remedies, in the same way, will be adapted, not to the nature of the offense, but to the nature of the factors provoking it. Probation should be employed with a larger freedom, and at the same time with finer discrimination; it should include, for each separate case, not merely passive surveillance, but active and constructive efforts. . . . After-care, in particular, calls for further extension; to lavish a hundred pounds upon the intensive training of a youth in an institution and then suddenly to fling him loose into the old environment, sparing neither time nor trouble for further aid and following-up, is not economy but waste.

5. Fuller knowledge is urgently wanted: it is wanted both in regard to the causation of crime and in respect of the relative efficacy of different remedial measures. Only from the organization of research can this fuller knowledge come, and organized research means an established criminological department. The fruits of such research should be made immediately accessible to the practical officer, and courses of instruction should be arranged where all who have to deal with the young offender may learn the latest and best accredited results of modern criminal psychology.

6. Finally, society must aim at prevention as well as at cure. Housing, medical treatment, continued education, the psychological study of children in schools, improved industrial conditions, increased facilities for recreation, the cautious adoption of practicable eugenic measures, and above all, sustained investigation into all the problems of childhood—these are but a few of the countless needs to be supplied, if delinquency in the young is to be not merely cured as it arises, but diverted, forestalled, and so far as possible wiped out.

This, let us remember, was said on the basis of the available research evidence of over 30 years ago. Let us now take a look at our current accomplishments in the field of preventive action.

We have very few studies on *what* can be done to arrest the rising tide of juvenile delinquency, *how* it might be done, and *how effective* the efforts are. Consider research reported in the *Current Sociological Research* series for the past three years. About 30 to 40 studies on criminology and sociology of law are studied each year. Most of these studies deal with the description of the ongoing practices in criminal procedure, or statistical description of crime rates and areas of high delinquency, or a refinement of analysis of background factors. Of the over one hundred studies reported in the past three years, only 10 have anything to do with the evaluation of some way of handling some aspect of the problem, and of these, eight deal with evaluation of treatment in correctional institutions, that is, at the end of the line, after the crime has been committed. Only one research project dealt with an evaluation of a preventive program in the community.

Neither was there much activity in this area in the past years. We have available a survey of delinquency prevention programs in this country and of the measure of their success. The survey was recently prepared by Helen Witmer and Edith Tufts of the Children's Bureau. (8) There have been a number of preventive programs in various parts of the country, some of them carried on over a period of many years and evaluated—in a manner. One striking characteristic of all these programs is that each is focused on *one* simple aspect of the supposed multiple causal factors: better recreational facilities *or* detached group workers *or* better community facilities *or* friendly counselling *or* child guidance treatment *or* an "area" approach stimulating grass-roots responsibility and neighborhood feeling. We may add that not even the New York City Youth Board, which includes many approaches in its program, pursues any of these in an integrated fashion in any one area of the city; in effect, its program consists of a congeries of programs rather than of one program.

Another characteristic of these programs is that those who had set them up truly believed that their particular program would make a significant difference in delinquency rates, and were genuinely disappointed when evaluation in those terms showed no results whatsoever. The authors of the survey sum up by asking, "What does it all add up to in knowledge about how to prevent or reduce delinquency?"—and their answer is, "With certainty, rather little."

When we compare this sad state of affairs with Cyril Burt's six points, we are faced with a most embarrassing situation. Not only have we not learned anything in the past 30 years, but we seem to have proceeded on premises which common sense, logic, and available knowledge would declare to be most naive. What, then, interferes with the progress of applied and applicable knowledge in this field?

Let us take a case in point: the problem of understanding and controlling narcotics use among juveniles. By looking at it, we will obtain a clear picture of most of the difficulties in the general field of delinquency prevention.

A Case Study: How to Prevent Narcotics Use by Juveniles

1. *The first step: understanding the nature of the problem.* When the most recent wave of juvenile drug use hit the headlines some five years ago and the staff of the Research Center for Human Relations started its investigations at the request of the National Institute of Mental Health,[1] we were exploring a virtually unknown territory. Available information was for the most part unsystematic or unreliable or both. Consequently, in planning a series of studies, we felt compelled to obtain first, a bird's-eye view of each of the many aspects of this phenomenon which might be likely to play a role as a contributing factor. Using the customary methods, we pinpointed the New York City areas where the greatest juvenile users live and investigated the distinguishing characteristics of these neighborhoods; we looked into the backgrounds and past histories of the juvenile drug users; we studied their family situations and their relations with peers; we tried to understand the general climate of values and attitudes which is hospitable to a favorable attitude to drug use; we studied the role of the street gang in the spread of drug use and the relation between drug use and other forms of delinquency. We worked closely with a psychiatrist who had done studies of the personality of juvenile addicts and is currently engaged in therapeutic work with addicts.

Thus, we arrived, after several years of research, at a general understanding concerning the social and psychic dynamics behind the problem. The picture that emerged is, briefly, as follows:

The adolescent boy who becomes involved with drugs, continues to use them regularly, and eventually reaches the stage of being "hooked" is, usually, a member of a deprived racial or ethnic group, often a native-born son of immigrant parents, whose family lives in one of the poorest and most disorganized areas of the city, though their own social and financial standing is often higher than what is typical for the area. His family is a source of special strain and deprivation. Relations between parents are seriously disturbed. The father is absent or hostile or weak. The mother's attitude to the son is extreme: either passionate and consuming, or cool and distant. Parental discipline is either overindulging or extremely harsh. Parental standards and expectations are unclear and unrealistic—too high or too low. Their general attitude to life and to society is pessimistic and distrustful.

The boy's personality is seriously damaged. He might be suffering from overt or incipient schizophrenia. Whatever the form of his disturbance, however, he is almost certain to have a weak, inadequate ego and a poorly

---

[1] A series of studies have been conducted since 1952 by Donald L. Gerard, Robert S. Lee, Eva Rosenfeld, and Daniel M. Wilner, under the general direction of Isidor Chein. See (3), (4), and (6).

functioning superego. He also has serious problems in sexual identification, distrusts authority and has a poor sense of reality, especially regarding his own future. As he reaches young adulthood at the age of 16, 17, or 18, he enters situations with which he cannot cope. He faces failure and loneliness of which he is deeply afraid.

He is likely to be more or less loosely attached to one of the street gangs in the neighborhood. Unlike his well-adjusted neighbor, he has made no efforts to stay away from the aggressive, delinquent "cats," though their violent "hell-raising" may not be quite to his taste. But he stays in their orbit. He gains some measure of support from a sense of belonging to a group. In this group, he becomes exposed to drugs, marijuana, and heroin, taken at parties for a kick, in a spirit of experimenting with danger. The drug has a pacifying effect—his sadness, loneliness, anxiety seem to vanish, and he experiences a pleasurable relief from unbearable tension. The gang frowns upon uncontrolled use of drugs which leads to addiction. For a year, or even two, he may use the drug irregularly. But the time comes when the gang loses its cohesiveness, hell-raising becomes "kid stuff," and some of the less disturbed youngsters turn their minds to growing up in a man's world, going "steady," finding a good job. It is at this point that, having to face life alone, as a man, the anxious and inadequately functioning boy falls back on the pacifying and engrossing life of a habitual user. Enmeshed in the pattern of activities revolving around the purchase, sale, and use of heroin, and the delinquent efforts to get money to meet the exorbitant cost of the drug, the young user can comfortably forget about girls, careers, status, and recognition in the society at large. His sexual drive is diminished, he is able to maintain a sense of belonging to the immature, limited world of the addict. He can remain a child forever. He can give up all sense of responsibility for his life and conveniently project the blame for his shiftless existence on his "habit."

His chances for a cure are very small. Physical withdrawal does not take away the psychic need for some relief from inner tension, nor does it erase the memory of the relief brought by opiates. The road from the hospital or jail to the drug peddler is short, indeed. His resistance to psychotherapy is great; he feels that it offers nothing but increased anxiety and his tolerance of anxiety is, as we said, very low.

This is a bare outline of our knowledge. It satisfied our need for understanding and we took a pause for reflection.

2. *The second step: drawing implications for action.* Our investigation was started with the general idea of learning something of relevance to the *solution* of a social problem. On the basis of our data, we regretfully find ourselves unable to recommend any specific action. Knowing the forces that *contribute* to a social evil tells us nothing about how to eradicate the evil. In fact, why should it? There is no logical reason why the weapon most effective in destroying a social phenomenon should be in a direct way related to the forces that make it grow. The general purpose of the type of exploratory studies we did is not so much to discover how to eradicate the

evil but, rather, how *not* to try to eradicate it. For, by highlighting the enormous complexity of interdependent factors of which drug use is a symptom, our studies in fact taught us that there is no simple and easy way of doing away with the symptom.

So far, we have not committed any methodological sins. What we did had to be done. We now had a general picture of our target area. What next?

3. *The third step: creating a framework for preventive action.* Clearly the next step was research on specific measures aimed at a reduction of drug use by forestalling the pressures that appear to lead to it. And since so many of the pressures overlapped with those which had been discovered by experts in juvenile delinquency, we expected to profit from their experience. But in examining available research in the prevention of delinquency, we discovered—as I had mentioned—that very little had been done. There is, in fact, no conceptual framework for preventive action.

It is not difficult to understand why such a framework was slow in developing. Research in the causes of delinquency, as well as our own research in the causes of drug addiction, pointed, as we said, to a complex maze of interrelated personal and environmental pressures and deprivations. And theories based on empirical investigations stressed the fact that only a *convergence* of pressures and deprivations led to delinquency. It was difficult, in fact impossible, to derive from this complex picture, by a process of reasoning, some reasonably manageable, manipulable prescription for effective prevention. A variety of things were to be recommended for the great variety of contributing factors: more financial help to deprived families, child guidance for the emotionally disturbed, recreation for the street gangs, a substitute father figure for the fatherless, grass-root participation, and so on. The multiplicity of these services adds up to a task which it is difficult for many an individual mind to grasp. And, as preventive programs were initiated as a rule by well meaning individuals with limited funds at their disposal and acting in a framework of a single local agency, it would appear that good will and an urge to some action led them to substitute what was feasible for what reason and knowledge indicated was *necessary*. And in evaluating their one-pronged programs, it would seem that they were led by irrational hope: maybe it will make a difference.

Well, it did *not* make a difference. Profiting from their disillusion, we decided that in approaching the task of devising a preventive and rehabilitative program for youths in trouble, we will honestly consider all measures that, on the basis of our knowledge, appeared to be important, without worrying for the time being about the practicability of such a program. We consequently put down on paper all the measures that either available knowledge or, in its absence, common sense and intelligent guesswork suggested as remedies for the wide variety of personal and environmental deficiencies which appear to be at the root of the problem.

This task was not particularly difficult. Soon we had a list of preventive and rehabilitative measures, each backed by a specific rationale.

The general rationale of the project is to modify the youths' experience in their school and street environment so that it will counteract (rather than, as is now the case, reinforce) the early family experience of emotional deprivation, by giving multiple proof that the society *cares* about them and their future. More specifically, the aim is to: (a) expand their reference groups to include ever larger circles of people and, by thus giving them a more broadly based sense of *belonging*, make it more difficult for them to deny guilt for hostile acts against persons perceived as strangers; (b) provide *constructive channels* for the expression of "free-floating energy" and, in general, to satisfy the adolescent need for new experience, exploration, and learning; and (c) offer special *help and support* to individuals who need it.[2]

4. *The fourth step: from social theory to social engineering.* The chief difficulty in envisaging the program on a community basis was the nature and extent of coordination of all those efforts directed at youth, at their families, and at adults working with youth, such as teachers, police, recreation workers, parole officers, and the like.

We could say *what* we thought should be done, but when we started thinking about the *how*, we found that it was impossible to predict in advance what approach would be successful. It was, in fact, impossible to make safe guesses about the effectiveness of purposive social action. Why?

One way of answering this query is to say that in general purposive social action tends to lead to unanticipated consequences. In his classic analysis of this problem (7), Robert K. Mertion suggests that *inability to foresee* all consequences of social action may derive—apart from the obvious reason, namely, simple ignorance—from the intrinsic inadequacy of knowledge of human behavior which is available to us. Human behavior in any situation is not a constant but, rather, is represented by a *range* of possibilities. This range increases with any variation in the *conditions* of the situation. In very complex situations, determined by many conditions, the range of behavior resulting from the interplay of all conditions is so immense that for all practical purposes the probable outcome of social action cannot be predicted.

In addition, the effort at prediction is also contaminated by errors of judgment in appraising the conditions of the situation, by bias and by neglect, by an immediacy of interest in some one aspect of the problem, and by similar impedimenta.

For example, we recommended modifications in the policy of recreation centers and settlement houses, to one in which they would attempt to draw the anti-social gangs into some of the available activities. But how should they go about it? What approach, what steps are necessary to avoid a complete wreckage of the place?

In our wish to see this part of the program put into effect, we—in think-

---

[2] This summary, by necessity so very brief, does poor justice to the original argument—in fact, it reduces it to a cliche. A book containing both the findings of our studies and a proposal for preventive actions is in preparation.

ing out the techniques of approach—overlooked, as we were later told by
no less an expert than Fritz Redl, the low "deviation tolerance" of the regular members of the community house or playground. Just as the "cats" are
thrown into a turmoil of emotions at the prospect of civil contact with the
"squares," so the "squares" are likely to become anxious and disturbed by
the prospect of admitting the wild "cats" into their regulated world.

.   .   .

Besieged by these self-doubts concerning our ability to recommend the
best course, we felt impelled to turn for help to experts in the field, people
who have the actual "know-how." We felt that, even though so little of
their work had been carefully evaluated, much could be learned from them.
People who for many years continue in one type of work as a rule accumu-
late a wealth of intimate knowledge of the great variety of forces, pressures,
interests, conditions that play a role in the situation in which they work.
Every agency has an accumulation of past experience which could teach
others if not how to do things better, or how not to approach certain
problems, then at least what special conditions, usually overlooked, played
a role in the failure of a given venture. A survey of such experience was,
then, our next step. Through personal interviews with workers in the field,
we tried to learn what they have learned.

5. *The fifth step: learning from the experience of others.* The first difficulty in an experience survey is to dodge or get around the heads of the
various agencies, who often are far removed from the work experience of
field workers. The second difficulty is to get the field worker to feel free
and unconstrained, to talk openly about his experience. In some cases—
notably with the police, both obstacles are insurmountable in this type of
a survey. In all cases, the tapping of experience is a slow and painstaking
task. There are special reasons why this wisdom based on experience is not
easily made explicit and available to the public or even to qualified research
personnel.

One of these is the widespread reluctance to self-appraisal. This reluctance
springs from a variety of sources. One is the common fear of change—a
sense of security is derived from habitual routinized ways of doing things.
It would take us too far afield to pinpoint all the elements in our social
structure that contribute to this fear. But some of these contributors are
based on misconceptions and misunderstandings of the function of research
and those are of prime concern to us.

One such frequently encountered misconception is that only success is
worth mention and mistakes are to be shamefully glossed over or covered up.
Yet a careful analysis of how and why things have gone wrong can be extremely profitable. A good example is a survey of the accomplishments and
failures of the Neighborhood Center for Block Organization, which func-
tioned in Harlem in the mid-forties. (1) The survey spotlights the apathy
of the tenants which made it so difficult to mobilize them effectively for
self-help, and it provides some insight into the nature of this "apathy."

In fact, one might point out to those shy of their failures that these failures, if recorded and analyzed, are more rewarding for applied social science than successes. In terms of the logic of scientific method, interpretation of successes may easily lead to the "fallacy of affirming the consequent." If some theory of delinquency leads to some program of action, the success of the program does not confirm the theory—it merely demonstrates that it is not yet untenable.

Furthermore, an attempt to reproduce the conditions of success has at least two pitfalls: (a) it may include spurious or irrelevant factors or (b) it may easily overlook an important ingredient of it. But failures at least enable us to disprove a current hypothesis or focus the need to revise it. Specifically in the field of social action, failures point to the need for re-examining the premises of action more carefully and often pinpoint an important but overlooked condition in the situation. It is clearly our duty to explain these truths to heads of agencies and their financial backers and convince them that by keeping adequate records and periodically analyzing their mistakes and failures, they will provide a most enlightened and forward-looking attitude which will reflect most favorably on their management of their agencies.

Another reason why the learning value of failures receives so little publicity is related to our academic tradition of research. Our colleges and even graduate schools apparently fail to tell social science (and social work) students about this "royal road" to action-relevant knowledge and in general to scientific discovery. For while they carefully design laboratory experiments to disprove a hypothesis at great cost and effort, few students and few scholars are encouraged to avail themselves of the blunders, the mistakes, the failures in social action as a means for challenging and disproving commonly accepted premises on which this action was based. It may be true that such research, which evaluates retrospectively the causes of failure, can hardly be rigidly exact and lead to validated conclusions. Formal, traditional, academic research, very rigid, very exact, is oriented to neglecting the golden mine of hunches, hypotheses, insights. But, surely, these are as valuable and as scarce as carefully validated tests of specific hypotheses.

But not only heads of social agencies and not only the academicians neglect to exploit real-life experience for the knowledge it hides—much of our non-academic research on social problems fails in this respect. And here again it is the tradition, the established, sanctified routines that are to blame—not the individual researchers. To take an example, a large youth agency in one of our cities recently designed a research project to evaluate and improve one of their casework services. The design called for an analysis of some 150 case histories by a statistician, to be followed by a more intensive study of a sample of cases. There was no mention of exploiting the years of experience of some dozen social workers and obtaining their impressions, hunches, opinions concerning their current methods of work and ideas for improvements.

Industrial sociologists and psychologists long ago pointed out that it pays to lend an ear to the worker on the lot and to his straw boss. Their recommendations apparently became generally accepted in modern, up-to-date industrial establishments. And listening to the consumer is, of course, the essence of marketing research. Yet in both academic and applied research this principle of listening to the grass roots is less explicitly stressed and seldom followed. Whence the difference?

The difference, I propose, derives from the different accounting principles of industrial research on the one hand and academic and applied social research on the other. In the former type of research *the client pays* the researcher. In the latter, the client—the person in whose interests the research is conducted—is the passive subject of research; researchers get paid by academic institutions (in degrees more often than in money), by foundations, by the local and federal government agencies. The researcher naturally has the interest of his client at heart. But he also has at heart his own interests which have to do with professional standards, with the recognition that is accorded a methodologically "clean" job, a neat conceptual framework which is safely derived from standard, prestigeful conceptual frameworks currently in fashion. There is no one, outside the researcher's own conscience, to put pressure on his work for more "action-orientation." And in a peculiarly somnambulistic way, even the enlightened public often calls for "more research" (meaning more research on the causes of troublesome phenomena) than for more action. We have apparently succeeded in terrorizing this liberal public into the belief that much research has to be done before one may act safely. Yet in the slow progress from understanding to resolving social problems, action must precede full understanding, for much of the understanding comes from observing first attempts at remedial action fail.

It may be cogent to quote a conclusion of a committee of distinguished professional men after a survey of close to a thousand books and articles dealing with mental health activities and their evaluation:

> The frequency in which research and service agencies in the same community operate in "isolated cells" is impressive. A research center may operate in an "ivory tower" and fail to include for research validation valuable exploratory leads in an applied field because of lack of such information, and with efforts limited to the pursuit of preconceived hypotheses which preclude other experimental approaches. Conversely, in an operating agency, experimental leads are discovered and attempts made at scientific validation with faulty conclusions and interpretations, as a result of inappropriate or inadequate methodology and in the absence of technical research "know-how." (5)

What Must Be Done?

Further research into the origins of juvenile delinquency and of related symptoms of social and personal malfunctioning among our youth is not likely to produce much knowledge relevant to preventive and rehabilitative measures. What is needed now is a carefully recorded, analyzed, and evaluated trial-and-error method, using various approaches in various combinations in various conditions, learning all the while—unlearning and learning.

The need for such a "trial-and-error plus evaluation" approach is indicated not only by the uncertainty of our knowledge about prevention and by the difficulty of predicting in advance the effectiveness of any given program of action. This approach is also necessary to debunk the pessimism of those "experienced" workers who have become paralyzed by routine and have lost the daring for experimentation with new approaches.

Many types of services and methods of approach which appear to be vitally important as preventive measures for youths in deprived areas are now believed by many experts in the field to be either extremely difficult or totally impossible. Yet here and there an enterprising worker has tried and succeeded. In our own survey, we have learned that it *is* possible, though admittedly difficult, to draw anti-social gangs into a city recreation project. It *is* possible to teach many people who have work difficulties how to work in peace and productively. It *is* possible to establish good, friendly working relations with the police. Certain precautions must be taken, certain groundwork laid beforehand, certain resources made available for financial and spiritual sustenance and support. Not much cooperation should be expected initially from the largely apathetic, suspicious, frightened people in the deprived areas. Energy must be pumped into the area and this energy must be carefully sustained among the people who would become involved in preventive work, by tapping varieties of motivation, and by providing continuous rewards.

One source of motivation and of inner rewards that should be tapped and exploited to the full is the scientific interest in the principles of purposive social action. This interest should be stimulated both in our academic institutions and in operating agencies. This could be done in a variety of ways: encouraging more doctoral candidates to do their field work in social agencies; encouraging social workers to attend research seminars; publicizing among social agencies scholarly analyses of various experiences which stress the value of learning from failures; etc.

The responsibility for initiating such contact and stimulating scientific interest in social action rests with the social scientists.

REFERENCES

1. Bowens, Marx G., "The Neighborhood Center for Block Organization," in *Group Work in Community Life,* ed. by C. E. Murray, M. G. Bowens, and R. Hogrefe (New York: Association Press, 1954), pp. 13–60.
2. Burt, Cyril, *The Young Delinquent* (New York: Appleton, 1925).
3. Chein, Isidor, "Narcotics Use Among Juveniles," *Social Work,* 1 (April, 1956), 50–60.
4. Chein, Isidor, and Eva Rosenfeld, "Juvenile Heroin Users in New York City," *Law and Contemporary Problems,* 22 (Winter, 1957).
5. *Evaluation in Mental Health,* U. S. Dept. of Health, Education and Welfare, 1955.
6. Gerard, Donald L., and Conan Kornetsky, "Adolescent Opiate Addiction: A Study of Control and Addict Subjects," *The Psychiatric Quarterly,* 29 (July, 1955), 457–486.

7. MERTON, ROBERT K., "The Unanticipated Consequences of Purposive Social Action," *American Sociological Review*, 1 (December, 1936), 894–904.
8. WITMER, HELEN L., and EDITH TUFTS, *The Effectiveness of Delinquency Prevention Programs*, Children's Bureau Publication No. 350, 1954.

5   Evaluation of Delinquency Prevention Programs: Ideals and Compromises

JAMES C. HACKLER

Sociologists tend to write for other sociologists forgetting that much of their work could be utilized by nonacademicians. This article is not designed for academicians unless they are also concerned with "action programs."

Applied social science has recently become a more prestige worthy area of concern but authors still try to speak to people who share a similar professional orientation. I am interested in helping to bridge the gap between those who are attempting to develop explanations of human behavior and those who wish to utilize that understanding to modify the situation. This does not mean that sociologists necessarily want to change the world or that they should be the vanguard of any proposed changes; but it is clear that governments, organizations, and individuals will continue to tamper with the lives of those who live within their society. Most of us feel that this tampering is, if not desirable, at least inevitable. My feeling is that social scientists could help others tamper more effectively. This is the purpose of this article.[1]

Evaluation Is Part of the Game

A variety of programs is being established today "to do something about juvenile delinquency." Battles will be fought between agencies, communities will vie for federal funds, and optimistic predictions of success will be made. But one thing is certain: Almost all of the fund-givers will insist on some form of evaluation. The nature of the evaluation can vary consider-

Reprinted from *Federal Probation*, 31 (Mar. 1967), 22–26, with permission of *Federal Probation*.

[1] The author would like to thank the Ford Foundation, the Seattle Housing Authority, and Boeing Employees' United Good Neighbor for financing the Opportunities for Youth Project in Seattle. This paper is a response to some of the problems which arose in that program and probably plague others.
The results of the Opportunities for Youth Project are reported in James C. Hackler, "Boys, Blisters, and Behavior," *The Journal of Research in Crime and Delinquency*, July 1966.

ably, however, depending on who is doing the evaluating and his particular set of goals. Everyone will not agree on what approach is best. Moreover, some forms of evaluation will be seen as a threat, some can create chaos, others can endanger future programs; but without some form of assessment, systematic progress is impossible.

I should like to examine the various types of evaluation open to us and the problems inherent in each; the incompatible goals of researchers and action workers; the threats posed by evaluation; and, finally, some procedures which could alleviate the stress in each of these problem areas.

What Is Evaluation?

I shall mention five approaches. These approaches are by no means mutually exclusive. In fact, they could be considered five aspects of evaluation, each serving a separate function.

1. *Changes in official rates.* The most obvious way of evaluating a delinquency prevention program would be to see if the program led to lower arrest rates. These criteria are usually the ones best understood by the public. The Cambridge-Somerville program, carried out in Boston in the 1940's, used this type of evaluation. Approximately 300 boys were given rather intensive counseling for 8 years while another group of similar boys did not take part in the program. At the end of the program the two groups were compared in terms of the number of boys who were committed to institutions for delinquent acts or were arrested. There were no essential differences between the treated and the control groups.

When these criteria have been used as the basis for evaluation, prevention programs have almost universally been failures. However, these indices have several weaknesses. "Official statistics" may reflect public sentiment and could be influenced by the political climate and other factors quite unrelated to delinquent behavior itself. For example, when a police chief is threatened with the loss of his job if the crime rate does not decrease, policemen may arrest fewer persons. In a similar manner, the opening of a brand new prison may make it more feasible for judges to send a convicted offender away for rehabilitation. If conditions were badly overcrowded, the judge may have considered probation more carefully.

Another weakness of these publicly recognized criteria is that they may not be particularly relevant to the type of therapy or program being used. For example, the Cambridge-Somerville study was a counseling program designed to modify the personality, self-image, or some other aspect of the individual subject. The assumption is that if the individual does change in some way he will automatically be treated differently by the rest of society. However, becoming committed to an institution involves the way the court system operates, the manner in which individuals are processed by the police, etc. Even if the counseling program were successful in modifying the personality, self-image, and even the behavior of an individual, there is no guarantee that such changes would be reflected in commitment rates if external factors play a more important role. Under these conditions, it might be well to measure changes in personality directly to see if the counseling accomplished the first step.

2. *Subjective opinion.* One can simply take a poll of all those working with or under the influence of the program. If these people felt the program was successful, some persons might be satisfied. Unfortunately, one can hardly lose under such conditions. When you ask boys who have been given a job under an employment program if they think they have been helped, the answer is fairly obvious. A subjective evaluation, then, is really not an evaluation at all, but rather a statement of faith. Such an intuitive assessment of a program should not be overlooked, however, because many tools used by the social scientist are insensitive to some revealing information. In addition, many action workers can avoid the temptation to justify their work and look at their programs critically. The hardnosed researcher should not overlook the value of a subjective evaluation; the action worker, on the other hand, should not assume that such an assessment can be considered a true evaluation.

3. *Changes as predicted by the theoretical framework.* Although a clear theoretical framework is not always a part of every action program, there are usually implications inherent in most attempts to change behavior. One does not simply say, "Let's provide psychiatric counseling because it will stop delinquency." Rather a social worker might make the claim that psychiatric counseling would modify one's self-concept which, in turn, will modify the roles one seeks to play and hence modify behavior. A sophisticated plan for a social action program does not make a single prediction but rather a series of predictions. The evaluation of such a program requires not one test but many. For example, the Opportunities for Youth Project in Seattle was based on the assumption that the behavior of juveniles is affected by the way they perceive the people around them and how they feel these same people expect them to act. This project, then, attempted to modify the boys' perception of their surroundings. If the boys in the experimental program began to believe that their teachers expect conforming behavior instead of deviant behavior as the result of holding a job, the program, in one sense at least, would be considered successful. Similarly, if the boys came to think that their peers expected conforming behavior, we could say that a change had taken place. Too often, the hopes for many programs are unrealistically high. Attempts are made to modify official rates of arrest without taking into account the many other factors involved which are outside the control of most programs. A clear theoretical framework, however, directs our attention to specific, though subtle, results which might be more reasonable.

The Mobilization for Youth program in New York City is based on the assumption that deviant behavior results when the social structure is a barrier to the acquisition of desired goals. For example, Negroes often cannot get jobs which provide status and good income. An evaluation of such a program would look for measures of increased Negro employment, a lower dropout rate in schools with a large nonwhite attendance, and other indices which reflect *changes in the opportunity structure.* To expect a complete solution of all major problems is obviously ridiculous; it is reasonable, however, to see if intermediate goals have been achieved.

4. *A test of theoretical ideas.* There is no clear line between a test of theoretical ideas and the type of evaluation previously mentioned, but a community wide experiment to test a set of ideas does have different implications. The "pure" scientist may not be concerned with "helping" any-one. He simply wants to devise powerful explanatory theories. An excellent test of a particular theory might involve creating a situation which would lead to delinquency. One could argue that such a test might provide information that would clearly outweigh the harm done to a few individuals, but few communities could condone such an experiment.

Researchers may frustrate college sophomores when using them for guinea pigs, this is an occupational hazard of being a student, but such a viewpoint is not shared by many lay members of a board faced with the task of administering funds for an antipoverty program. Simply testing theoretical ideas is not enough for most community based experiments. A test of the "success" of the efforts is also necessary.

5. *The integrity of the program.* Should the action worker be evaluated according to the success or failure of a program? My answer would be a resounding NO! The social worker given the responsibility of carrying out an experimental task should be evaluated according to his integrity in carrying out the original plan. True, the action workers should join in any planning stage; but once a plan of action has been adopted, a modification of this plan as the result of personal wishes on the part of an individual action worker threatens the entire experiment. This does not mean that criticisms should not be voiced. On the contrary, these may be extremely useful. But eventual success of such experiments depends on the faithful execution of a prearranged plan. Unfortunately, action workers are sometimes considered to be responsible for the *results* of an experiment.

These five aspects of evaluation would suggest that the researcher must modify his idealized evaluation procedure in order to meet the demands of community programs.

The Incompatible Goals of Research and Community Action

What are the implications of these various approaches to evaluation for those who are responsible for a community action program?

1. *The researcher versus the action worker.* We can view the situation from at least two perspectives. Those who are responsible for the "action" portion of the program are naturally concerned with the effectiveness of their efforts. A colossal failure which yields a great deal of information about what should *not* be done is a small consolation to both professional and lay members of a community action team. On the other hand, social scientists who consider themselves "researchers" are primarily oriented toward a basic understanding of the phenomena involved.

The conflict between the two perspectives becomes more visible when the question of a control group arises. Let us assume that a project hopes to provide jobs for 200 boys and uses a control group of 200 other boys as a comparison. They expect 400 boys to apply for the 200 jobs and by drawing names from a hat, 200 of the boys will be assigned jobs in a random manner. On the day of the drawing only 200 boys arrive. The social worker argues that all of the boys should be given jobs. The researcher argues that only 100 boys should be given jobs and the remaining 100 should be used as a control group. One can empathize with both individuals here. The former is concerned with accomplishment; the latter is more concerned with an understanding of what might happen.

It is easy to ignore these conflicts by claiming that both the action worker and the applied social scientist have the same long-range goals. While this may be true, each is trained to approach that goal by a different route. It is unrealistic to expect the immediate goals and the steps to reach those goals to be compatible with both perspectives. The researcher will be concerned with comparison groups, extraneous factors that might cloud interpretation, methods of gathering data that do not bias the findings and the integrity of the research design. Such concerns could be a genuine restriction to the person who is trying to make a program effective.

The community action worker and members of the lay community may view the social scientist as living in an unreal world of esoteric theories that are fine for textbooks but have little meaning for solving "real" problems. The researcher may be considered as preoccupied with detail and statistical sophistication to the extent that he fails to see the larger problem. On the other hand, the social scientist may view the lay members of a community-wide committee as similar to amateurs trying to send a rocket to the moon using bubblegum for fuel. He sees the trial and error techniques of experimentation as ineffective compared to the application of basic scientific knowledge and feels that a heavy concentration on the accumulation of that knowledge is a necessary prerequisite to successful action programs, be it rockets or the modification of behavior. Both viewpoints contain elements of truth as well as unreasonableness.

Sociologists are perfectly aware of the irrational characteristics of human groups and the cumbersome operations of social systems. They cannot, on the other hand, comprehend how a group of community leaders can be so obstinate when it comes to guaranteeing the integrity of a research design. "Why," says the sociologist (who is now acting very emotional and completely human himself), "don't these people stop acting like normal individuals with their own self-interests, concerns, personality conflicts?"

Researchers have trouble visualizing the problems faced by civic boards which often have been created to initiate various aspects of brand new programs. Responsibilities are unclear, there are conflicting interests, and a host of internal problems are usually present. As civic leaders wrestle with these bewildering tasks they somehow fail to appreciate all the fine points which are so crucial to the researcher.

It should be clear that a plan of evaluation is going to be a compromise. The parties involved will lack the godlike qualities to establish the ideal design. You and I may have the clarity of vision necessary to resolve these conflicts, but those lesser mortals who must do the job get very preoccupied with trivialities which concern their own work. No single evaluation plan is going to satisfy the wide range of interest groups which have a stake in the success (or possibly the failure) of a community action program. But why be limited to one type of evaluation? Two levels of evaluation may be more appropriate.

2. *Two levels of evaluation.* The first level of evaluation would be primarily concerned with meeting community needs. Such information as the rate of participation, the way a program is received by the public, and the subjective opinion of those involved may not be considered very scientific data to many researchers; but without "nose counting" and other less rigorous approaches, it would be difficult to "feel the pulse" of a project. Those responsible for an action program may not find that a highly sophisticated statistical analysis provides interesting or meaningful information for the general public.

The second level of evaluation might be considered basic research. These activities may not strike a responsive cord from action workers. When working on the forefront of knowledge, a researcher may find that it is often impossible to convey just exactly what he is trying to accomplish to someone who is not also familiar with the field. In fact, he typically finds that many of his ideas lead to dead ends. Unfortunately, the admiration for the perseverance of Thomas Edison does not carry over to the social scientist who meets with failure after failure. The researcher, then, needs some insulation from the public gaze and from the policies of nonresearchers. It is unrealistic to expect a committee of community leaders to sit in judgment over such activities. Much scientific work is supported on faith—a faith which seems to be justified in terms of long range goals but which may pay very poor dividends for a given undertaking.

At the first level of evaluation, however, community leaders should not only understand what is being done but have a definite say in what should be done. The researcher should not judge this type of evaluation from the perspective of an editor of a journal. He must compromise his standards of research at times in order to establish communication. Mistaken and unsupported interpretations of some information will result, but even careful research leads to erroneous conclusions. It is important that action workers and those responsible for policy decisions are capable of understanding a major portion of this level of evaluation. This does not imply that a researcher should be careless in providing information. Rather he can assist others to deal with data in a more sophisticated manner. But when claims are made which seem unwarranted according to his rigorous standards, he should not sulk in a corner or refuse to provide other information. The researcher cannot afford to ignore the public relations need of any community-based activity.

In return for research at this level, action workers can provide access to populations hitherto unavailable to all but a few researchers. By supporting and protecting research activities, action programs make an investment in long range goals. In addition, capable researchers are more willing to work under conditions which provide them with flexibility and security to pursue tasks of their own choosing at least a part of the time.

The Threat of Evaluation

Evaluation can be a threatening word to institutions and agencies that come to have a vested interest in the success of a particular program. Pressures can be brought to bear on researchers to provide evidence that a project accomplished something and therefore deserves to receive funds for more efforts of a similar nature. Hence, this aspect of evaluation needs insulation from such pressures if a truthful picture is to be obtained.

However, the search for integrity in judging a program could have unforeseen consequences. In the light of the dismal record of most attempts to mitigate, let alone solve, our major social ills, it would be ill-advised to label any program a failure if it fails to make changes which can be measured by one of the crude yardsticks devised by social scientists. The funnelling of money into the hands of the poor without the loss of dignity and self-esteem, the feedback of information from recipients of various programs, the establishment of channels of communications between various agencies, the increased awareness on the part of professional workers who have previously been unexposed to certain aspects of our society are no mean accomplishments. Researchers rarely try to assess these achievements.

An objective, scientific evaluation that ignores such intangible and difficult-to-measure factors could do a great disservice. There is little reason to anticipate much success from most of the proposed plans at this stage of development. Those responsible for evaluation must naturally not create the impression of success where none exists, but researchers also are obligated to glean the rubble of the more courageous attempts for promising beginnings.

Problems of Identifying
Potential Delinquency

A variety of tactical approaches are available to those interested in preventing delinquency. One of the more significant approaches assumes that preventive efforts can and—given limited resources —must be restricted to those individuals who would otherwise engage in delinquency, rather than to entire populations of juveniles. If many juveniles never engage in delinquent behavior, preventive efforts directed toward them are unnecessary. Because resources tend to be relatively limited, attention devoted to this group detracts from that available for juveniles who are more likely to engage in delinquency.

This approach requires identification of potential delinquents and potential nondelinquents. If one can identify those juveniles who are likely to engage in delinquent behavior before they have actually done so, steps can then be taken to modify their orientations, thus preventing the predicted behavior from occurring. This assumes, of course, that one knows what kinds of preventive actions will be successful, an issue to be discussed in later sections. The issue here is whether or not instruments can be devised to accurately identify those who, if left alone, would engage in delinquency.

It is possible to devise predictive instruments at several different levels of analysis, although this has not been the main concern of research to date. Thus, although one could predict delinquency rates on an intercommunity basis, or on the basis of social areas within a particular community, and implement programs only in those areas or communities that possess a likelihood of high delinquency rates, identification research has instead tended to focus on the prediction of individual behavior and the identification of those individuals who are likely to deviate. The data used in building the predictive instruments therefore consist of various measures of individual characteristics, individual behavior, other people's perceptions of specific individuals' behavior and characteristics, and so on. This focus maximizes the possibility of utilizing available resources only for those most

likely to become delinquent, while minimizing the likelihood
that preventive efforts will be applied to those who are unlikely
to deviate.

Numerous difficulties have hindered the development of adequate delinquency prediction instruments. One difficulty is the
lack of a meaningful and measurable concept of *delinquency*.
Only when delinquency can be adequately defined and measured
can one evaluate the validity of prediction instruments. A second problem involves the selection of predictors. The items
available for use in instruments are limited by existing theoretical formulations which minimally provide hints as to what
might be useful in making accurate predictions. Items included
must consist of variables that can be assumed to have some degree of stability through time. To be useful the instrument
must have a high degree of reliability and be applicable to a
variety of populations. Finally, the selection of individuals for
participation in prevention programs might influence their behavior and prevent an accurate assessment of the instrument's
validity.

S. Kirson Weinberg summarizes the two basic theoretical approaches that have been used in devising prediction instruments. He argues that neither the individual nor the group
approaches considered separately can provide a complete understanding of delinquent and criminal behavior and offers a series
of integrative hypotheses that minimize the difficulties he sees in
each approach. He states that prediction is intrinsically interrelated with theories of crime and delinquency, indicating that
prediction studies may be assessed in terms of the implicit or
explicit theories utilized and that his "unified" approach suggests particular kinds of variables as potentially significant for
developing predictive instruments.

Assuming that personality variables are related to delinquency
and that a personality inventory is a convenient way to measure
personality patterns, Starke R. Hathaway and Elio D. Monachesi
summarize the results of a study in which they utilized the
Minnesota Multiphasic Personality Inventory in an attempt to
identify delinquency proneness among Minnesota grade-school
children. Simon Dinitz, Frank R. Scarpitti, and Walter C. Reckless use a combination of methods to differentiate between
"good" and "bad" boys in Columbus, Ohio, in an attempt to
discover what factors prevent some boys residing in high-delinquency areas from engaging in delinquent behavior. They conclude that *self concept* not only can be a useful predictor but
might account for the differential impact of delinquency-producing environmental circumstances. B. B. Khleif relies on school
records produced by teachers as a basis for identifying delin-

quency (appearance in the juvenile court) and psychiatric disturbance (referral to a child guidance clinic). Khleif concludes that teachers' judgments are useful sources of data for predicting problematic behavior. Finally, Jackson Toby presents a comprehensive critique of prediction programs. He summarizes and evaluates the two most famous prediction programs that have been implemented (the Cambridge-Somerville Youth Study and the New York City Youth Board Prediction Study), and also outlines the kinds of issues that must be resolved if prediction is to serve as a useful tool in the prevention of delinquent behavior.

6 Theories of Criminality and Problems of Prediction

S. KIRSON WEINBERG

The aims of this paper are (1) to appraise the group and individual approaches to criminal behavior, (2) to seek a tentative theory of criminal behavior which reconciles these differences and (3) to relate theories of criminal behavior to the prediction of criminal behavior.

Although sometimes overlooked in actuarial studies, theory and prediction have an integral relationship in a scientific endeavor. The function of theory is to explain the processes which contribute to or cause criminal behavior. The function of prediction is to test the theory by relating the processes to outcome for a series of cases. Since different theories emphasize diverse processes in the causation of crime, prediction studies should be able to test these theories. But many prediction studies have been so separated from theory that they have not been concerned with testing specific theories. In order to relate prediction to theory we shall first elaborate on the varying theories of criminal behavior, see to what extent these theories have been tested by prediction techniques and how these theories can aid in predicting criminal behavior.

Of the various theories of criminal behavior, we shall consider (1) the sociological version which deals with criminality as a product of learning

Reprinted from the *Journal of Criminal Law, Criminology and Police Science* Copyright © 1954 by the Northwestern University School of Law, Volume 45, Number 4, November–December, 1954, pp. 412–424, with permission of The Northwestern University School of Law and the author.

and acculturation, and (2) the individualistic versions which explain criminality in terms of distinct personality traits.

I

Modern sociological theories of criminal behavior arose during the decline of social Darwinism. Human behavior was explained by learning and acculturation, and explanations based upon instincts and innate characteristics were repudiated.[1] The person generally was defined as a subjective aspect of his culture and as a cultural type.[2] The criminal, from this perspective was viewed as a product of a deviant subculture within the urban community.[3] The criminal, was a deviant type who became acculturated to a special behavior system in a learning process by association with other criminals.

Sociologists drew these inferences primarily from delinquents in high rate delinquency areas, and from confirmed adult offenders. Later they extended these theories to upper-class and middle-class persons, specifically to white-collar criminals.[4] The delinquents who were studied were in urban areas where the criminal culture was dominant, and where a network of relations extended from adult criminals to predelinquent children.[5] The other subjects, who were usually confirmed criminals, were also characterized as having a minimal opportunity to select conventional orientations. Although these inquiries have demonstrated conclusively that criminality is learned instead of inborn behavior, sociologists left unanswered why the individual selected, accepted, and executed his criminal behavior, except for certain delinquents in very high rate areas where conventional alternatives of behavior are few. But this left open the well-known questions why non-delinquents exist in very high delinquency areas where alternatives for conventional behavior are few; or why in low-rate delinquency areas, where the middle class conventional peer group and culture predominate, the juvenile seeks and selects delinquent associates. These aspects of criminal development are integral aspects of a total learning process. Despite the voluminous literature on delinquency and crime, these questions have not been answered adequately, except for two studies. One study has shown that many non-delinquents are actually undetected delinquents; the other study has sifted out the pre-schizophrenics who were dominated by their mothers and who were too timid to participate in delinquent peer groups.[6]

---

[1] Karpf, Fay B.: *American Social Psychology*, 1932. Faris, Ellsworth: *The Nature of Human Nature*, 1937.

[2] See Thomas, William I., and Znaniecki, Florian: *The Polish Peasant in Europe and America*, 1927.

[3] Shaw, Clifford R., Editor: *The Natural History of a Delinquent Career*, 1931. Sutherland, Edwin H.: *Principles of Criminology*, 4th ed., 1947.

[4] Sutherland, Edwin H.: *White Collar Crime*, 1949. Elliott, Mabel A.: *Crime in Modern Society*, 1952.

[5] Shaw, Clifford R., et al., Editors: *Brothers in Crime*, 1938.

[6] Kobrin, Solomon, The Conflict of Values in Delinquency Areas, *Amer. Sociol. Rev.*, 16 (October, 1951), pp. 653–661. Dunham H. Warren, The Social Personality of the Catatonic Schizophrene, *Amer. Jour. of Sociol.* 12 (May, 1944), pp. 574–576.

Seemingly, this limitation in the sociological theory of crime resulted from a limiting theory of personality. First, since the individual reflected his culture or his role in the group, the dynamisms as to why he selected or did not select a singular organization of attitudes and meanings, were not explained adequately, and, in some instances, were not considered necessary for explanation. Hence singular motives, meanings, and aspirations of the criminal were muted in these descriptions in order to emphasize the shared behavior of the criminal as a cultural participant. Second, the process of selecting criminal or conventional norms of behavior was analyzed in terms of preferring one alternative from a series of alternatives as a means of renewing interrupted or disrupted action. This preference process, in turn, was explained by the theory of differential associations. Third, this theory of differential association was based upon a rational psychology, reminiscent of utilitarian psychology, and it conceived of preferred alternatives of behavior in terms of quantity and rational deliberation. From this approach, a given person would accept criminality because his contacts and definitions favoring violating the law exceeded his definitions and contacts favoring conforming to the law.[7]

But it is evident that the attachments and aversions, the diffuse and focused kinds of hostility, are acquired from past relations and experiences, and can affect contemporary decisions. In this respect, an individual may select criminal associates for reasons which he does not understand and of which he is unaware. This point is too frequently dismissed by claiming a fortuitous or advantitious theory of crime based upon chance association or upon chance combination of circumstances. The process of deciding upon, accepting, and incorporating criminal behavior means that an individual has internalized certain norms because of attachments to one or a series of persons who might be called reference points or reference groups.[8] These interpersonal attachments and the needs for social approval as bases for selecting and accepting motives and ideas, are not functions of frequency of association, and are not fortuituous, but are based upon emotional security, feelings of self-enhancement, or upon expressive behavior and conflict solution.

For example, one aspect of delinquent behavior during the 1920's concerned American born delinquents who rejected their parents' immigrant culture as inferior and who accepted their American peer culture as status-enhancing and superior.[9] This rejection of the parents' values by the children sometimes meant also rejecting the parents as role-models and hence accepting delinquents as role-models. Although the parents of many contemporary delinquents are natives, still the juveniles prefer the youth culture because of its prestige in our youth-oriented society. In the discontinuity of generations between parents and children, conformity to adults becomes

---

[7] Sutherland, Edwin H.: *Principles of Criminology*, 4th ed., 1947, pp. 6–9.

[8] Newcomb, Theodore M.: *Social Psychology*, 1950, pp. 240–243. Zucker, Herbert J.: Affectional Identification and Delinquency, *Archives of Psychology*, 286 (1943).

[9] See Sellin, Thorsten, *Culture Conflict and Crime*, 1938.

mitigated by the peer group. Schachtel found that defiance of adult authority was one crucial symptom of delinquent behavior. He stated: [10]

> The most important consideration in answering (whether a boy would or
> would not become delinquent) was whether or not the boy showed much de-
> pendence on or fear of authority. The more such fear and dependence has
> become part of the character structure and the prohibitions of the significant
> authoritative adults had been internalized, the more likely it seemed to me
> that the boy would not become delinquent.

It might also be pointed out the potential schizophrenics from high rate
delinquency.areas identify with the adult culture and tend to reject the
peer culture or are rejected by their peers. In fact, in the Glueck study
many indicators seem to point to some non-delinquents in their control
group as potential schizophrenics: they were extremely ectomorphic, dependent upon others, had vague feelings of anxiety and felt overwhelmed
and helpless.[11]

Clearly when youths are more attached to an adult conventional culture
than to a peer delinquent culture they will not necessarily resort to delinquent behavior even though they have learned delinquent techniques and
experienced some relationships with delinquents. Healy and Bronner have
specified that the criminal ideology is very pervasive and that the individual
should have slight difficulty in acquiring criminal techniques.[12] But sociologists have, for this very reason, emphasized that criminal influences stem
from direct association with other delinquents.[13] Hence they have stressed
that delinquency usually arises from this direct association and not from
indirect sources. Consistent with the reference group theory, however, association is necessary but is not sufficient as an explanation for accepting
delinquent behavior; for the individual internalizes the types of behavior
from persons with whom he has definite rapport and to whom he is attracted and frequently attached emotionally. The mode of relationships
with a given person in a total content of person's modes of relationships
will indicate the direction of his influences towards delinquent or towards
conventional behavior.

In this respect, parent-child conflict means not only displaced hostility
from a parent to another person but also the possible rejection of the parent
as a role-model and the search for other approving role models. Frequently,
these other role-models can be delinquents or criminals. Also, the individual
who has ambivalent attitudes towards his parents, may have certain guilt-
ridden reactions to crime which are residual from past attachments. Thus,
the selection of delinquent values is a resultant process of social relations.[14]

[10] Quoted in Glueck, Sheldon and Eleanor: *Unraveling Juvenile Delinquency*, 1950, p.
217.
[11] Glueck, Sheldon and Eleanor: *Unraveling Juvenile Delinquency*, 1950, pp. 193, 221,
222, 224, 225.
[12] Healy, William and Bronner, Augusta: *New Light on Delinquency and Its Treatment*,
1936, pp. 135, 136.
[13] Sutherland, Edwin H.: *Principles of Criminology*, 1947, pp. 6–9.
[14] Reckless, Walter: *The Etiology of Delinquent and Criminal Behavior*, 1943. Weinberg, S. Kirson: *Society and Personality Disorders*, 1952, pp. 290–295.

In short, the sociologists have isolated delinquents and criminals as cultural types. They have limited their explicit theories either to persistent juvenile offenders or to systematic adult property criminals. They have demonstrated that this behavior is learned in an acculturation process by association with other criminals. They have stressed the shared techniques and attitudes which the criminal expresses in the criminal culture. But they have not explicitly integrated the rise of criminal behavior of the singular person with the individualized meanings which go into the selection and acceptance of criminal behavior. Sometimes, the person has been analyzed as a passive rather than as a dynamic participant, by the contention of the fortuitious nature of his crime, and second, by the theory of culture conflict in which the individual is described as being pulled by two forces which create polar influences that he can not dispel or resolve.[15] But the active phase of individual selection emerges from accepting the attitudes of those persons to whom one becomes attracted and attached. The incomplete part in this learning process is that personal attachment was not acknowledged as affecting the acceptance of one set of attitudes and practices in preference to another set of attitudes and practices.[16] The cultural approach has explained one dimension of delinquency and adult crime. It has explained one type of delinquent or criminal who has experienced a minimal set of alternatives in selecting his criminal behavior. Thus the sociologists have formulated a framework for understanding the development of crime as learned behavior. They have made this causal formulation from subjects who were already delinquents and criminals. But these processes which lead to delinquent and criminal behavior, as we shall see, can also be used as predictors of potential criminals.

II

The gap which pertains to the development of criminal behavior has been supplemented by studies of the criminal as an individual. Nonetheless, these clinical studies have not answered these questions within a theoretical framework of learning and acculturation and inter-personal relations. Aichhorn recognized the gap of development in criminality when he stated: [17]

> When I ask parents how they account for the dissocial behavior of their children, I usually receive the answer that it is the result of bad company and running around on the streets. To a certain extent this is true, but thousands of other children grow up under the same unfavorable circumstances and still are not delinquent. There must be something in the child himself which the environment brings out in the form of delinquency.

The Gluecks have been more explicit when they said: [18]

> They (the Sociologists) do not explain why the deleterious influences of

[15] This "fortuitous process" would be very difficult to verify.
[16] For a discussion of role-taking and learning, see Mead, George H.: *Mind, Self and Society*, 1935, pp. 73–81.
[17] Aichhorn, August: *Wayward Youth*, 1939, pp. 39, 40.
[18] Glueck, Sheldon and Eleanor: *Unraveling Juvenile Delinquency*, 1950, p. 5.

even the most extreme delinquency area fail to turn the great majority of its boys into persistent delinquents. They do not disclose whether the children who do not succumb to the evil and disruptive neighborhood influences differ from those who become delinquents, and, if so, in what respects.

Healy and Bronner, among others, have recognized these facets of delinquent behavior as points of departure, although this does not necessarily mean that they have produced a conclusive answer.[19]

Since both personality maturation and character structure theories seek something physically, temperamentally, or emotionally distinctive in the delinquent's or criminal's personality make-up, then how does the person acquire these distinctive characteristics which lead to criminal activity?

The biopsychological maturation theorists, such as Sheldon, Seltzer, and Glueck, emphasized the constitution-temperament trait couplet as predisposing the youths to selecting and to accepting criminal behavior.[20] The individual with a tightly-knit muscular, predominantly mesomorphic constitution, has an aggressive, outgoing temperament, and will be attracted to activities that may defy or oppose conventional constraints. Hence he becomes delinquent because his mode of expression differs from that of the non-delinquent who, at the extreme, predominates as an ectomorphic body-type. Of course, physical anthropologists and constitutional biologists do not explain why so many conventional children with similar physiques and temperament do not become delinquent. This approach may impute to constitutional factors what also is a product of a particular peer culture. The constitution-temperament trait-couplet seems to imply a built-in kind of delinquent potential. It does not explain the manner in which selection of the delinquent or criminal norms of behavior occurs, although it does show that the majority of delinquents, fit this body type. In brief, does body-type and temperament have a bearing upon predicting criminal behavior.

The clinicians who advocate indirect learning and fixation in early life as the basis of a potential delinquent character structure, have tried to show that these roots of personality difficulties are the anti-social tendencies. The most pervasively distinct characteristic in these studies has been the outgoing aggressive behavior among delinquents in contrast to non-delinquents. They minimize the effects of learning from the delinquent peer-group in a tolerant neighborhood situation. When they preclude the probability of a stable person becoming delinquent, they make criminality coincide with character disorders, such as Abrahamsen or, Healy and Bronner who specifically assert that delinquency results from "thwarted wishes in early life" or the Gluecks who conclude that delinquency is a "character disease." They see in these early predispositions the bases for selecting and accepting de-

---

[19] Healy, William and Bronner, Augusta: *New Light on Delinquency and Its Treatment*, 1936, pp. 68, 69.

[20] Sheldon, William H.: *Varieties of Delinquent Youth*, 1949. Seltzer, C. C. Body Disproportions and Dominant Personality Traits, *Psychosomatic Medicine*, 8 (1946), pp. 75–97. Glueck, Sheldon and Eleanor: *Unraveling Juvenile Delinquency*, 1950, Chapters 15, 21, Appendix C.

linquent behavior.[21] While the Healy and Bronner study does not specify the given community areas, the Gluecks' study did identify the high rate delinquency areas.

But the clinicians have difficulty in differentiating between the anti-social person and the criminal. The characteristics of outgoing hostility, defiance, destructiveness, and impulsive aggression, are not the same as criminal behavior. An anti-social person may engage in random acting-out behavior, and still not violate the law—or he may engage in stealing. This view errs in dismissing the learning process in criminal behavior or in appraising it as of slight importance. Boys who are behavior problems in conventional middle-class areas do not necessarily become delinquents or criminals, but boys in lower-class areas frequently become delinquents. This approach somehow attributes an inevitability to the selection of delinquent associates and to the learning of crime when the early frustrations and subsequent hostility are present. But connecting the sequence between predisposition towards and acceptance of delinquent behavior remains to be demonstrated. On the other hand, it must be recognized too that the process of social definition is important. The lower-class juveniles may be defined and arrested as delinquent, whereas middle-class boys for somewhat similar activities, might be spared from arrest.[22]

The theory of character disorders as the crucial causal basis of behavior does not explain the different distribution of delinquents and criminals in different areas of the city by diverse childhood training techniques, or even by constitutional temperamental types. Seemingly, the most plausible explanation is the concentration of delinquent traditions in these areas of the urban community. Since lower-class juvenile and adolescent males participate in perhaps one of the most unrestrained and aggressive peer subcultures of any society in the world, if rated by unrestrained individual fighting as well as by unsupervised inter-group fighting, then an emotionally normal boy who associates with his peers would become aggressive by sheer participation in the peer group.[23] Hence a person's aggression can be explained by one of three levels. Some boys become very aggressive, defiant and destructive from the influence of their peers. Other boys become very aggressive as a defensive formation from the helplessness and guilt in anxiety neurosis. Still other boys become very aggressive from psychopathic tendencies and minimal guilt. Seemingly, there has been no satisfactory differentiation of these levels of aggression in terms of their relevance to criminal behavior.

Aggressive behavior which is so pervasive among lower class boys cannot

---

[21] Healy, William and Bronner, Augusta: *New Light on Delinquency and Its Treatment,* 1936, p. 133. Glueck, Sheldon and Eleanor: *Unraveling Juvenile Delinquency,* 1950, p. 289. Abrahamsen, David: *Who are the Guilty?* 1952, pp. 26–28. Eissler, K. R.: General Problems of Delinquency, *Searchlights on Delinquency,* Edited by Eissler, K. R., 1949, pp. 3–25.

[22] Porterfield, Austin L., and Clifton, C. Stanley: *Youth in Trouble,* 1946.

[23] Davis, Allison and Dollard, John, *Youth in Bondage:* 1940. Weinberg, S. Kirson, Occupational Culture of the Boxer, *Amer. Jour. of Sociol.,* 57 (March, 1952), pp. 460–469.

be explained satisfactorily by early child training except in a very general way. One difficulty in assessing the aggression as well as other traits of the delinquent boy results from the methods in the individualistic clinical inquiry. It does not see the boy as an integral part of his cultural context. Instead, it sees a series of actions which are abstracted away from the cultural context. Thus, it imputes certain rash actions as personality difficulties when these may possibly be expected reactions in the given cultural context. Frequently the clinician has a middle class bias in evaluating the behavior of the lower-class delinquent boy, particularly when his interpretations are based upon interviews. Furthermore, the boy's behavior acquired by participation in the peer group may resemble superficially behavior resulting from personality difficulties. As we shall see, these discrepant interpretations affect the kinds of predictors used in forecasting potential delinquent behavior.

A gang member may have the same lack of empathy for an out-group enemy that a psychopath has for another person. He may show the same lack of guilt by peer identification that the psychopath has. Many activities of delinquents which have been attributed to temperament or to early frustrations can be explained too by participation in and by learning from the peer group of lower-class boys in slum areas. What is considered early frustrated training may, in some instances, be the acquisition of the motivational emphases of a gang in a neighborhood milieu.

But from another vantage point, the individualistic clinical approach to criminal behavior has complemented the collective approach in the following ways: It has dealt with individualized meanings as distinct from shared attitudes. Hence criminal behavior has been viewed as symptomatic of, and as a defensive formation from, personality conflicts which are distinct from the shared norms and practices of a deviant group. Delinquents satisfied their individual needs and also responded to shared norms of behavior by their delinquent behavior. This means then that delinquency is a response not only to the social control of a deviant group but also is the activity stemming from private emotional needs.

Both sociologists and psychiatrists have recognized that delinquents become attracted to each other and cultivate socially intimate relations. Perhaps delinquents have certain predisposing attitudes which make for a certain inter-personal rapport among themselves and which non-delinquents do not share because they have different personal needs to satisfy in their social relationships. Still we cannot conceive of delinquents and non-delinquents as arrayed in two neat, separate rows as some of the matched studies of experimental and control samples implicitly and explicitly may lead one to believe. In some high rate delinquency areas, the two groups may mingle but their relationships do not become sustained. These subtle aspects of the communicative process in social interaction must be considered along with the cultural view as a medium for transmitting and imparting criminal norms and techniques.

For the sociologists have emphasized the conjunctive relations among delinquent associates as tutelage media in transmitting crime. They have seen delinquency as a positive and rewarding form of behavior either in terms of thrill, peer group approval, or status enhancement, which reinforced the learned delinquent patterns of behavior. The psychiatrists have emphasized the disjunctive relations in the family as instrumental to delinquency; have seen delinquency as a negative form of behavior either in terms of residual hostility acquired from inter-personal relations in the family, or as compensatory association for parental or familial rejection or indifference. Thus the two views emphasize diverse aspects of learning. The sociologists, from a cultural approach, regard the criminal as acquiring and sharing symbols and actions in a variant sub-culture. Clinicians have emphasized the individual manner in which the criminal learns to execute his actions, to confront his difficulties, to relate with people, and to solve his conflicts, either as private defenses against anxiety or as the forms of hostility and of other perverse traits persisting from childhood. For example, two individuals may learn to drive an automobile, which is a new technique. One person may never have an accident; the other may have repeated accidents. Two individuals may learn to steal. One may never get caught. The other may get caught repeatedly. The mere learning of new behavior on a shared, rational level does not tell us how the individual will execute his knowledge in terms of the private meanings it has for him as an individual. These individualized meanings have been the preoccupation of the psychiatrist and psychologists who approached the delinquent as a unique person rather than as a cultural participant or as a social type. And these individualized meanings which may be witting and unwitting affect the manner in which the individual will learn and use his skills and socialized values. Thus the delinquent or criminal who conforms to a given socially deviant value system on a group level also uses these values as symptoms or as defenses to solve his personal conflicts on an individual level.

III. Types of Theories

These diverse approaches to criminality describe different aspects of crime and place diverse emphases upon the factors which can predict criminal behavior. Since the first or cultural approach regards systematic crime as an acquisition by social participation, the criminal is viewed in a benign way in terms of his similarity to the conventional person: Both learn their behavior and abide by the norms peculiar to their respective groups. Both have similar goals—such as money, prestige, success. Although criminal and conventional norms differ, insofar as the criminal has acquired his behavior by social participation, he is basically not different in degree of stability or maturity than the conventional person. Hence the advocates of this approach stress the normality of the criminal, and disregard the personality differences as an explanation of crime. It is not surprising, then, that in one critical review of the studies of personality attributes among criminal and conventional persons, the authors concluded that personality traits are distributed in the criminal population in about the same way as in the general population.[24] They write: [25]

> When the (test) results are considered chronologically, there is nothing to indicate that the personality components of criminal behavior are being established by this method. On the contrary, as often as not the evidence favored the view that personality traits are distributed in the criminal population in about the same way as in the general population.

The advocates of the individual approach who regard crime as deviant and non-conforming, view the criminal as an anti-social individual who cannot be restrained by conventional norms and who has a distinctive personality. Hence they search for the combination of personality traits which cause his deviation, and depict the criminal negatively as one who cannot participate successfully in conventional society.

Seemingly, these two images of the criminal as it has been thus far depicted have resulted from different implicit questions. The sociologists have asked: "Why does systematic criminality exist?" And their answer is that it is a group and cultural process that cannot be explained by individual differences. Then, how does the individual become a criminal? They answer: By learning. The psychiatrists and psychologists, as clinicians, have asked: "Why do individuals become criminals and not remain law-abiding persons?" Their answer is that the criminal has distinct traits, stemming either from personality maturation or early conditioning which differ from the traits of the conventional person.

IV. Bases for an Integrated Hypothesis of Criminality

From the foregoing discussion, can we synthesize the group and individual versions of delinquent behavior—as limited to systematic property offenses—within an integrated frame of reference? This does not mean arriving at a coordinate eclecticism in which diverse variables are juxtaposed to each other, but rather seeking an analysis of behavior within an integrated theoretical scheme.

If we begin with social relations as a way of learning new behavior, we would have to investigate the function of social relations upon the group and individual aspects of behavior. First, social relations vary by meanings, form, and motives. Thus, the meaning of social relations as pertinent to delinquency would vary for children who become delinquents and for adults who become criminals. The boy who values the companionship of his delinquent associates may steal to retain the approval of his companions rather than to get the monetary gain. On the other hand, the adult may consider the gain as foremost in his relationship with other criminals. Thus the salience—that is, the peripheral or central importance—of the attitudes in forming and retaining the relationship, varies for the two age-groups.

[24] Schuessler, Karl F. and Cressey, Donald R.: Personality Characteristics of Criminals, *Amer. Jour. of Sociol.*, 55 (March, 1950), pp. 476–484.
[25] *Ibid.* p. 483.

Second, the positions of the interactants in their relationships must be considered. Although an individual learns to become a criminal by the influence of his social relations, the criminal also can learn to become a conventional person by his relations with conventional persons. Thus the role of the person in the association process must be explicitly defined. From the available evidence, it appears that the novitiate in crime tends to be emotionally dependent upon the criminal. Were the dependence upon a conventional person, such as a therapist, the influence would flow towards a conventional orientation.

Third, the individualized satisfactions in the inter-personal process lead to the attraction and rapport of persons whose needs are similar. These needs which may be verbalized and unverbalized, pertain to the selection of delinquent associates apparently by persons who seem to come from families and other groups that fail to provide these juveniles with definite feelings of personal security and that do not create the kinds of relationships by which the juvenile internalizes deep attitudes towards conventional behavior.

Fourth, when these juveniles encounter accessible delinquent associates, they seem to prefer them as companions to more conventional persons, because these delinquents satisfy verbalized and unverbalized emotional needs. In this association process, the individual becomes responsive to accepting and sharing delinquent techniques and practices. But the situations leading to acceptance of crime vary considerably. The 6 year old boy who is initiated into crime by his older brothers has an entirely different problem of selection than the 16 year old boy who leaves conventional friends in his neighborhood to associate with delinquents in another neighborhood.

Fifth, when the delinquent group is not accessible, or when delinquent companions do not gratify the juvenile's individualized needs, then he will seek conventional outlets in a process of dynamic selection.

In short, we might suggest that criminal behavior as manifested among juveniles, arises when, for individualized purposes of emotional security, self-enhancement, or conflict-resolution, they seek and select accessible associates from whom they learn, accept, and express criminal attitudes.

By assessing the varying theories of delinquent and criminal behavior and by presenting a unified theory of criminal behavior, we shall have some gauges for checking the implicit and explicit theories in the prediction studies. From the individualistic approach, the emphasis would be upon the body-type, temperament, family relations, early personality development and personality structure of the potential delinquent. From the group approach, the emphasis would be upon the type of neighborhood, the kinds of accessible peers and perhaps the family relations. The unified approach would combine personality organization with accessible peer relations in a given cultural context.

Seemingly, the psychiatric and sociological approaches intersect in the discontinuity between the family and the peer group. In a synthesis of these approaches, the predictors of potential delinquency would include (1) the independent variables of family relations, capacity for peer relations, and accessibility of delinquent or conventional peers, and (2) the intervening variables of satisfaction or dissatisfaction with conventional role-models and of the search for delinquent or conventional companions or outlets, while (3) the dependent variable would be the uniformly specified criterion of property offences. In this manner, perhaps the use of interdisciplinary theory of the behavioral dynamics of delinquency could be tested concertedly by prediction of outcome.

7   The Personalities of Predelinquent Boys

STARKE R. HATHAWAY and ELIO D. MONACHESI

Delinquents tend to be greatly similar in only one respect, namely the fact that they have committed an act which is regarded, legally, as delinquent. This statement or generalization concerning delinquents seems, on the basis of the present state of knowledge, to be the only uncontestable one that can be made. No variable or factor among the many social and personal ones that have been studied is selectively and closely associated with the delinquency variable.

Delinquency Proneness

Yet, there is reason to believe that personality variables or patterns are related to the occurrence of delinquency in the sense of delinquency proneness. Some boys are so resistant to delinquent behavior that they will conform to social requirements under extremely difficult circumstances. By contrast, other boys will find ways to misbehave in good environments. Such observations make appropriate the acceptance of the construct "delinquency-proneness" manifested in the various rates of delinquency observed among children with various personalities living in a constant environment. Of course, no study can completely control the effect of environment, and all observed rates change as both personalities and environments vary.

Reprinted from the *Journal of Criminal Law, Criminology and Police Science* Copyright © 1957 by The Northwestern University School of Law, Volume 48, Number 2, July-August, 1957, pp. 149–163, with permission of The Northwestern University School of Law and the authors.

Supported in part by a grant from the Graduate School of the University of Minnesota and by a grant from the National Institute of Mental Health, U. S. Public Health Service.

The environment can be manipulated to prevent the occurrence of delinquency in even the most delinquency-prone individuals. Such children could be institutionalized to insure that they would have no opportunity for delinquency. Under normal circumstances the rate of delinquency associated with any personality pattern will vary with cultural environments, and in any community delinquency rates will be the result of the average level of delinquency-proneness and the environmental situations which either suppress or facilitate the expression of proneness to delinquency.

Data presented by studies designed to provide a generalized description of the delinquent personality support this line of reasoning. Although such studies suggest that practically every hereditary or environmental factor is in some way positively or negatively related to the occurrence of delinquency among groups, no one pattern of factors, whether environmental, hereditary, or both, yields a basis for accurate individual prediction of delinquency or, for that matter, of any other form of behavior.

The construct, delinquency-proneness, is not presented to suggest the acceptance of an individual determinism. Nor is it intended that license is given to say that proneness determines delinquency and that children who differ in this way are not amenable to personal psychological treatment or that the environment of such children cannot be improved in order to reduce the rate of delinquency. In practice, we should use both approaches. It is often easier to improve the environmental conditions than to give group or individual psychological help to delinquency-prone children. But it must be remembered that the reverse is often true. It is, at times, much more feasible and profitable to help children to adjust in the existing environment until we improve it. Slums offer an environment congenial to delinquency-proneness and slums should be eliminated, but there may be ways to help children who must, in the meantime, live in slums. Even if individuals cannot be treated to correct delinquency-proneness, it does not follow that these tendencies must be expressed in antisocial ways. Individual and group psychological help appropriate to the psychology of the individuals should contribute to alternative expressions of the personality pressures that make them prone to delinquency in addition to diminishing the more general maladjustment. Such preventive efforts can be directed toward the development of socially acceptable psychological equivalents of delinquency. To make any of these approaches effective, it is important to identify and measure the personality correlates of delinquency-proneness.

It is not necessarily assumed in this argument that delinquency-proneness is either hereditary or acquired as a personality pattern. Early conditioning or congenital prepotency would lead to the same problem for the adolescent in his social world. It seems likely, however, that no society, however healthy, can avoid the occurrence of delinquency-proneness among a considerable proportion of its adolescents. These ideas are not novel. They have been expressed over and over again. Their implications, however, are rarely applied to the prevention of delinquency.

Prediction and Postdiction

Another common and difficult problem in the studies on delinquency is that of postdiction. The personality of a child who has transgressed, become delinquent, is changed by that fact. This is even more true if he is caught and identified. Not only will the child be different, but people around him will change their attitudes toward him. Neither the child nor the observers are free of bias after the acts have occurred. It is much easier to find psychological items that postdict the delinquency than it would have been to find personality factors predicting the delinquency. This is true not only of the personal factors but also of the environmental ones. It is easy to say of a delinquent boy that his trouble is due to a broken home or to some other adverse social factor, but it is not at all easy to say which boy among all those with adverse environment will be delinquent. Most of our delinquency scales and data on adverse environments are more or less directly based on postdiction. They merely depict the social or personal consequences of past acts of delinquency or near-delinquency. Such factors or items, when employed for the analysis of delinquency, are circular in character in that they reflect the fact that a child is delinquent if he has had difficulty with authority or has had a bad relationship with his father, mother, or other persons. The personalities described by such items are nearly identical with those suggested directly by the fact of delinquent behavior which is the phenomenon we are trying to understand. As a consequence, little new information is discovered about the less obvious antecedent psychological factors. For example, the stealing of automobiles is delinquent behavior, but boys who steal automobiles may go against society in other ways as well, and it does not necessarily reveal much new about the personality patterns preceding delinquent behavior to find that such boys are also rejected by their teachers, have trouble with their parents, and underachieve at school. Knowledge of those personality patterns that are associated with more general psychological symptoms and not with delinquency alone is the area that should be explored.

In calling attention to the inadequacies of postdiction data as precise information about personality, we do not mean to imply that items and scales derived from studies of delinquents or misbehaving children do not yield some knowledge of the nature of the disorder. If one wishes to make predictions of delinquency, he will be most often right if he bases his prediction upon postdiction. No one fact is more predictive of future delinquency as the fact of past misbehavior or rebellion against society. We want to emphasize that it is useful to make a distinction between the psychology of boys already showing misbehavior and the psychological patterns of thought and character that are precursors to the maladjustment. True prediction-information leads toward the study and control of human personality among a variety of psychological patterns of adjustment where delinquency is just one among symptoms. We advocate a change in the narrow approach to delinquency wherein the symptom is treated as an illness, to an approach in which delinquency is considered as an occasional symptom of any one of a number of causative patterns.

In the early days of medicine, fever was considered an illness, and specialized professional efforts were directed at its reduction and control. Modern medicine recognizes the many social and organic origins of illnesses of which a fever is only one symptom. It is time to view delinquency similarly. We should treat the social and personal disorders that lead with varying frequency to actual delinquency. These disorders should be of concern although delinquency never occurs in all of the affected cases. This reasoning is based on the assumption that delinquent or delinquent-like behavior follows premonitory psychological signs rather than appearing without warning undistinguishably in normal persons.

Research directed toward the elimination of postdiction contamination of data is relatively simple to design but difficult to execute. The problem suggests longitudinal studies, involving the collection of a mass of what is hoped to be pertinent data on a large number of children who are predelinquent. The investigator must patiently wait for delinquency to occur in part of the sample and then make tests concerning the relevancy of preformulated hypotheses while carefully assuring that the data are not contaminated by knowledge of which cases have become delinquent. Relatively adequate research designs often suffer from contamination of the initial observations even though the longitudinal approach is used.

In longitudinal studies of personality, it is simpler and experimentally safer to collect objective data derived from standard and objective personality tests or inventories in which the subjects themselves provide the information desired without recourse to an intermediator. At the present time it appears methodologically more efficient and practicable to correct for the biases of the subjects rather than of the numerous raters who collect the data in those designs that use data from sources other than the subjects themselves. Personality inventories contain items and scales each of which provides the hypothesis that the item is associated with the occurrence of delinquency. If such items and scales reflect a variety of behavioral and attitudinal areas and are not too directly based upon narrow preconceived notions of what should be related to delinquency, then conditions are favorable for the discovery of new and basic information.

The Present Project

The data in this report are drawn from a project in which the Minnesota Multiphasic Personality Inventory (MMPI) was administered to 88.5 percent of the ninth grade school children of Minneapolis (2, 3, 4). The general project was initiated to provide empirical evidence about the value and practicality of using objective personality tests in providing analytic and predictive data on personal and social adjustment among school children. In the present context the measure of maladjustment is delinquency, and only the records of the boys are used. Although the most common and dramatic of the symptoms of adolescent maladjustment is delinquency emphasis upon this symptom must not lead to ignoring the fact that other problems of adolescence exist.

The MMPI is widely known and used so that it provides a familiar terminology and item content to facilitate communication and application of findings. Originally devised and applied to the analysis and measurement of adult personality deviations, the MMPI items and scales are not directly related to the phenomenon of delinquency. It is, however, a not unreasonable hypothesis to suggest that adult maladjustment patterns appear in adolescents and that some of these may be variously related to varying delinquency rates.

Nineteen hundred and fifty-eight relatively unselected ninth grade boys from the public schools of Minneapolis, Minnesota, constitute the basic sample that completed the test. Certain phases of the careers of these boys were checked two years after the MMPI had been administered. This follow-up consisted primarily of a search of the records of various public and private agencies for the names of the boys in the sample. The great majority of the boys whose names were found were listed in the records of the police department and in the records of the juvenile court; very few had had contacts with other agencies. A delinquency rating was made on a scale of 0 to 4 as follows. (Some of these findings have already been published (3)).

Delinquency 0: No definite evidence of significantly deviant behavior.

Delinquency 1: In this classification the names were found in police records for at least one minor difficulty such as traffic contact (overtime parking) or for being picked up when involvement was poorly established or the individual was contributing in a minor way, not justifying a classification into one of the following groups.

Delinquency 2: The youngsters placed in this class had committed minor offenses such as destruction of property (especially when this was connected with play activities), drinking, one or more traffic offenses (escapades involving speeding, driving without a license, and/or going at high speed through a stop light or sign), curfew violation, and immoral conduct. The misbehavior was relatively nondelinquent in comparison to that of the following two categories. Nevertheless, these children as a group demonstrated clear evidence of undesirable conduct.

Delinquency 3: This involved the commission of one serious offense such as auto theft, grand larceny, or gross immorality, or more than one less serious offense such as petty larceny, immoral conduct, assault, disorderly conduct, malicious destruction of property, shoplifting, flagrant curfew violations, truancy, and incorrigibility. These youngsters were not clearly established as delinquent, but nevertheless they were showing behavior that needed more than casual explanation.

Delinquency 4: This level of misconduct denoted those who committed repeated offences such as auto theft, burglary, grand larceny, holdup with a gun, and gross immoral conduct (girls), accompanied by less serious offenses. In this category were placed all youngsters who were considered to have demonstrated an established delinquent pattern.

Four years after testing, a more extensive and intensive follow-up was completed. In addition to another check in the records of official and private agencies, information concerning the children was gathered by field workers through interviews with the child, his parents, or other persons acquainted with the boy. On the basis of the information available from this follow-up, another delinquency rating was made for the second two year period. The two delinquency ratings show the amount and kind of misconduct that each boy was alleged to have engaged in during each two year period.

The two ratings made in the first and second two year periods were added to produce a total scale from 0 to 8, suggestive of the severity and duration of delinquent conduct. This sum was the final rating when the group modal age of the boys was 19. It should be kept in mind that a rating over four means that subjects were in some difficulty during both follow-up periods, but a boy could be mildly delinquent in both periods and have a rating of 4 or less.

The Personality Patterns

Table I is nearly self-explanatory. It presents the percentage of delinquents within the various rating categories. If a rating of 4 is construed

Table I

Delinquency Rating	Frequency	Percentage	Cumulative Frequency	Cumulative Percentage	Cumulative Frequency	Cumulative Percentage
0	1158	59.1	1158	59.1	1958	100.1
1	193	9.9	1351	69.0	800	41.0
2	203	10.4	1554	79.4	607	31.1
3	259	13.2	1813	92.6	404	20.7
4	54	2.8	1867	95.4	145	7.5
5	42	2.1	1909	97.5	91	4.7
6	25	1.3	1934	98.8	49	2.6
7	15	.8	1949	99.6	24	1.3
8	9	.5	1958	100.1	9	.5
Total	1958	100.00				

This table shows the number, percent, cumulative frequencies and percentages of the 1,958 boys assigned at various levels of delinquency.

as definite evidence of delinquency, then our findings show a rate of 7.5 percent for these boys. In contrast, 59.1 percent had no public record. It is of interest to note that the home follow-up at the end of four years added very few names not discovered in police and court records.

Table II presents more of the general findings. The data show the frequencies of ratings over time. The first period is before testing and the

Table IIA

Delinquency Rating	First Period before Testing		Second Period First Two Years after Testing		Third Period Second Two Years after Testing	
	N	Rate Among All Boys	N	Rate Among All Boys	N	Rate Among All Boys
Delinquent 2	56	2.9%	88	4.5%	95	4.9%
Delinquent 3	150	7.7%	131	6.7%	76	3.9%
Delinquent 4	41	2.1%	33	1.7%	17	0.9%
Total 2, 3, and 4's	247	12.6%	252	12.9%	188	9.6%
Delinquent 1 (Contact Only)		125 (6.4%)			224	11.4%

boys in this group had acquired a record before testing. The second and third periods represent the first and second two year periods after testing. One or two items are of especial interest. The percentage of severe delinquents decreases for the third period when the group modal age is over 18 years. This decrease contrasts with the increase in non-severe delinquency which results from an increase in the number of traffic offenses committed after the boys had become legally old enough to drive automobiles. It is interesting to note (Table IIB) that nearly half (41 percent) of all the

Table IIB

Period	Modal Age	Delinquency 2, 3, or 4		Delinquency 1, 2, 3, 4	
		N	Rate	N	Rate
First	15	247	12.6	—	—
Second	17	461	23.5	586	29.9
Third	19	556	28.4	800	40.9

These tables show the occurrence of the delinquency levels among all delinquent boys of the sample as related to time of the acts. The rates are derived from the whole sample of 1,958 boys. Table IIB gives cumulative data showing the rates on reaching the indicated modal age levels.

boys had their names in some police record by the time the modal group age was 19 years. However, it cannot be too strongly emphasized that such records were most commonly minor in implication. Any meaning attached to this large number should be tempered by the fact (Table I) that only 7.5 percent of the boys had a record that was rated 4 or worse.

Let us turn now to a consideration of the main thesis of the study, namely the personalities of the predelinquents. In the analysis of personality characteristics, the data are based only upon the true prediction cases—those boys who were delinquent after testing. Boys who had acquired a delinquency record before testing are omitted (including those who were delinquent after testing but who were also delinquent before testing). The present sample also omits 244 boys whose ratings were at the Delinquency 1 level. These boys were rarely delinquent in any real sense. Even the boys with Delinquency 2 and 3 ratings that remain in the sample often were not characterized by any significant misbehavior. The sample size was the problem. On the one hand, severe cases were too infrequent to permit statistical reliability after breakdown into smaller groups; on the other hand, inclusion of mildly delinquent boys attenuates the findings because these boys have personalities very little different from the completely non-delinquent boys with whom the data contrast them. The purified sample contains 1,467 boys for this analysis.

The data presented in Table III were obtained by first coding (1, 2, 3) the personality profile for every child, then dividing the total group of delinquents into subgroups according to which one of the ten MMPI personality variables was the most deviant point on the profile.

The first line of Table III, 'No high point,' indicates that 35 boys had profiles that showed no abnormal deviation on any scale. Only four of these boys became delinquent. The second item in the table shows that Scale 0 was the highest point of the profile for a total of 91 boys. Scale 0, when elevated, indicates social introversion, nonparticipation in social groups. Ten of these boys became delinquent. Continuing, Scale 2 was the highest elevation for only 47 boys. This scale is a measure of depression and ninth grade boys are not often so characterized. The general average on this scale steadily rises with age. The remainder of the table reads in like manner.

Table III also shows the percentage of delinquents that contributed to the entire total of after-test delinquents by the various profile high point patterns. As will be noted, the 35 boys whose MMPI profiles showed no deviant scores contributed only 1.5 percent of the total boys who later became delinquent. This most normal group is not only least frequent among nondelinquents, but it also contributes an even smaller proportion of the delinquents. Scales 1, 3, and 6 are also infrequent among nondelinquents, but they make a relatively equal contribution to the delinquents. In general, if a scale measures a factor not related to delinquency, then the percentage of the delinquents will equal that of the nondelinquents. This is approximately true of Scales 1, 3, 6, and 7. By contrast, boys characterized by profiles with deviant Scales 0, 2, and 5 and those with no high point show relatively decreased delinquency rates. Finally, profiles with deviant Scales 4, 8, or 9 show disproportionately high rates.

These data are treated differently in Table IV where the three scales that predict a relatively low rate of delinquency are grouped together and called

Table III

	Non-Delinquents	Delinquent After-Test	Total	(Valid Tests Only) Percent Among 247 After-Test Delinquents	Percent Among 1096 Non-Delinquents
No high point	31	4	35	1.5 (−)	2.8
0 (Si)	81	10	91	3.6 (−)	7.4
1 (Hs)	37	10	47	3.6	3.4
2 (D)	58	9	67	3.3 (−)	5.3
First 3 (Hy)	32	7	39	2.6	2.9
Scale in 4 (Pd)	211	65	276	23.7 (+)	19.3
High 5 (Mf)	79	9	88	3.3 (−)	7.2
Point 6 (Pa)	30	8	38	2.9	2.7
7 (Pt)	72	17	89	6.2	6.6
8 (Sc)	154	48	202	17.5 (+)	14.1
9 (Ma)	249	68	317	24.8 (+)	22.7
Indeterminate	62	19	81	6.9	5.7
Total Valid	1096	274	1370	100.0	100.0
L > 9	26	7	33	2.3	2.2
F > 15	36	28	64	9.1 (+)	3.1
Total Invalid	62	35	97	11.4 (+)	5.3
Overall Total	1158	309	1467	—	—

MMPI scales with the frequencies of occurrence of each scale as most extreme among the scales of the profiles. After-test delinquents only, at delinquency levels 2 through 8 inclusive. The (+) and (−) indicate larger differences in rate between delinquent and non-delinquent boys.

inhibitory scales. The rate of delinquency for each subgroup is indicated, and the effect of greater deviation in the scale is indicated by the primed scale frequencies which means that the deviant scale was at least two standard deviations above the mean for adult norms. The data suggest that whatever personality factors are represented by these scales, they operate to lower the delinquency rate.

The middle of Table IV shows the four scales that have variable or no effect on the delinquency rate. This could be due either to the fact that these personality variables are not related to the occurrence of delinquency or that the effect is obscured by the method used to analyze their effect. The delinquency rate of this group is roughly the same as the over-all rate of 21.1 percent. The over-all rate used here is the observed rate of after-testing delinquency 2 through 8 inclusive for the 1,467 boys.

Finally, boys with profiles dominated by Scales 4, 8, and 9 show higher delinquency rates subsequent to testing. The factors tapped by these scales seem to foster the occurrence of delinquent behavior.

In evaluating the changes in rate, it is important to remember that in order to obtain large enough numbers we were forced to use the data for

Table IV

	All Profiles			Primed Profiles (70 T score and above at highest)		
Scales	Total N	After-Test Delinquents	Rate for the Class	Total N	After-Test Delinquents	Rate for the Class
Inhibitory Scales						
0 (Si)	91	10	11.0%	10	1	10.0%
2 (D)	67	9	13.4%	24	3	12.5%
5 (Mf)	88	10	11.4%	22	1	4.5%
No high points	35	4	11.4%	—	—	—
Total	280	33	11.8%	56	5	8.9%
Variable Scales						
1 (Hs)	48	10	20.8%	24	4	16.7%
3 (Hy)	39	7	17.9%	5	1	20.0%
6 (Pa)	38	7	18.4%	14	3	21.4%
7 (Pt)	89	17	19.1%	49	6	12.2%
Total	214	41	19.2%	92	14	15.2%
Excitatory Scales						
4 (Pd)	276	65	23.6%	116	37	31.9%
8 (Sc)	202	48	23.8%	119	31	26.1%
9 (Ma)	317	68	21.5%	166	48	28.9%
Invalid	97	35	36.1%	—	—	—
Indeterminate	81	19	23.5%	11	3	27.3%
Total	973	235	24.2%	412	119	28.9%
Total Valid Profiles	1370	274	20.0%	—	—	—
Overall Totals	1467	309	21.1%	560	138	24.6%

Delinquency rates among groupings of the profiles by most deviant single scale illustrating scale relations to delinquency rates.

boys as near normal as Delinquency 2 on the eight point scale. This means that a large percentage of the boys represented by the ratings are minimally delinquent, and all the differences are attenuated because so many boys were little different from the nondelinquents. Evidence that this attenuation does occur is supplied by the fact (not in the tables) that the effect of Scales 4, 8, and 9 on delinquency rate is markedly greater if one restricts the comparison to the severely delinquent boys who had a delinquency rating of 4 or greater. Parenthetically, with reference to the above discussion of postdiction, the boys who had been delinquent before testing showed still larger differences. These more positive findings could be due to younger delinquents having stronger proneness or to postdiction error in which the differences are magnified by the effects of the fact of delinquency.

As will be noted in Table IV, the three scales that seem to depress the rate of delinquency are called inhibitory, and the three that are likely to be associated with a high rate are called excitatory scales. To further demonstrate the effect of deviation on the inhibitory and excitatory scales, the data of Table V were compiled. These data show the effects of the combination of two scale deviations. For example, the top row of Table V shows that when a boy deviates on both of any combination of 4, 8, or 9, the delinquency rate will be still higher than it is when only one of the scales shows definite elevation or when averages are calculated for any one of them in combination with all other scales. Here again the more deviant the scale (primed code combinations), the higher the delinquency rate. As would be expected, a combination of two inhibitory scales also depresses the rate to a greater degree. It is interesting to observe the effect of combinations of the psychological factors represented in the excitatory and inhibitory scales. We feel that the data on these combinations support the statement that the effect of having, in a marked degree, the personality character of one of the inhibitory scales is more clear cut than is the effect of a similar deviation on one of the excitatory scales. There is a definite tendency for the rate to be low when an excitatory scale is combined with an inhibitory one even when the excitatory scale is the more deviant of the two.

Table V

	All Combinations			Primed Combinations (70 T score and above)		
	After-Test Delin-			After-Test Delin-		
	N	quents	Rate	N	quents	Rate
Combination of two among 4, 8, 9	391	111	28.4%	220	76	34.5%
Combination of two among 0, 2, 5	53	6	11.3%	12	2	16.7%
Combination with 4, 8, or 9 high and 0, 2, or 5 next lower	134	16	11.9%	58	10	17.2%
Combination with 0, 2, or 5 high and 4, 8, or 9 next lower	86	10	11.6%	24	3	12.5%

Some effects of combined deviation of two scales (first two scales of high point code). General base rate for comparison: 309/1467 or 21.1%.

Table IV also provides a somewhat different type of information. As will be noted, the delinquency rate among boys who obtained invalid MMPI profiles is the highest of all such rates. Thirty-six percent were delinquent, and 20.2 percent were severely so! The invalid profiles are mostly a result of a high F score which indicates that the boy was careless in answering or was a very poor reader or was very disturbed and psychologically ill. At this point we cannot say which of these factors contributed the most to rendering the profiles invalid. The reading level required for the MMPI is low. Other factors could be responsible for invalidity, but those mentioned are probably the most common ones. It is suggested that either the pre-delinquent boy is strongly characterized by a tendency to be careless in responding to such an inventory when it is administered in a routine school situation where other boys and girls are working carefully and consistently or that such boys read so poorly that they answer the items in a random fashion or, finally, that they are psychologically ill. More data on the psychologically ill boys will be reported later. A few cases that produced high F score profiles have already been studied in a hospital setting and have been found to show evidence of encephalitis or other brain damage.

Once again it is interesting to note that one of the lowest delinquency rates is observed among those boys who get a clearly valid profile (with no abnormal score). Future analysis will shed more light on all these data. For the present, however, it may be assumed that those personality characteristics which are associated with carelessness and uncooperativeness in boys are also closely related to delinquency. It is also likely that these boys would under-achieve on other tests, i.e., would make poor scores on reading tests, not because of a lack of reading ability but because of the lack of a need to conform and to achieve. It appears that all test data from such boys in group testing programs should be re-examined to give assurance that low scores really mean a low ranking in the same sense as would be the case among boys who are more docile and cooperative.

In summary, the scale data make tenable the conclusion that although the socially withdrawn, depressed, or feminine personality factors in a boy may indicate the presence of some sort of maladjustment with which we should be concerned, high scores on relevant scales suggest that his involvement in delinquent acts is unlikely. Most comforting of all, however, is the fact that boys with no high point profiles are least prone to get into any difficulty. At the other extreme, the data indicate that boys with rebellious, excitable, or schizoid traits are most prone to delinquency.

We also have data to show that many of these deviant boys come from less desirable social settings. When one selects cases from any one setting, however, the differences still hold. Boys from the best neighborhoods who have these delinquency-prone profiles still show a high delinquency rate, although both the number of such profiles and the number of delinquents are smaller.

These findings, relating juvenile forms of adult maladjustment to delinquency, will not greatly surprise educational and other professional workers; they seem to support clinical impressions. However, not all personal maladjustment patterns in boys are indicators of delinquency-proneness. This significant fact leads to the possibility that a boy with inhibitor traits could be psychologically harmed by exposure to a preventive program designed for boys who are characterized by excitatory traits. Such a boy may also impair the effectiveness of the preventive program. At any rate, the two groups are psychologically different and not likely to respond to the same appeals or controls.

The personality test data not only provided indications of delinquency-proneness or lack of it in some boys but also indicated that a large percentage of the abnormal profiles were achieved by nondelinquents, suggesting that a great many of these boys were maladjusted. These nondelinquency-prone forms of maladjustment are not as disturbing to adults as is delinquency and are of correspondingly less concern to the community.

We may finally turn to the MMPI items themselves. Each of these items provides an hypothesis to be tested in that each can be assumed to be related to the delinquency rate. Among the 550 items, 33 stood up in a double cross-validation both as against all delinquents and as predicting delinquency that occurred after the time of testing. The statistical significance requirements for these items were such that it is unlikely that more than one or two of them would be included as a result of random variance. The majority of those found significant seem related to the personality of the predelinquent child. These items with the delinquent response are listed in Table VI.

It is unreasonable to expect that relatively uncorrelated trait patterns contributing to delinquency will show up with clarity in item analyses. The main tendency in item analysis differentiating delinquents and nondelinquents is toward the emergence of items having postdictive meaning. In spite of the fact that prediction was emphasized in selecting items, in part this is what occurs. Trouble in school and in the home as well as a strong need for adventure and thrill are dominant factors. It may surprise some investigators that some of the MMPI items more obviously expressive of direct aggressive feelings toward people and society did not emerge. As examples one could select:

"I get a raw deal from life."
"I easily become impatient with people."
"At times I feel like smashing things."
"I am often said to be hotheaded."
"At times I feel like picking a fist fight with someone."

These and many more that did not stand up in this predelinquent personality analysis may teach us more than do the items that survive. If any interpretation of a general sort is possible relative to this list of items, it might be that they express a psychological state of youthful exuberance with a love of danger and resentment of restriction. These trends are clearly related to the scale findings for Scales 4 and 9.

It is of interest that several odd items are included. While one or two of these may be due to random variance, it should be recalled that Scale 8, which is related to adult schizophrenia, is one of the best examples of an excitatory factor; and it is therefore, not surprising to find items in the list that come from that scale.

Table VI

MMPI Delinquency Scale
33 Items

Booklet Number	Card Number	Item	Delinquent Response
21	C-6	At times I have very much wanted to leave home.	True
26	E-3	I feel that it is certainly best to keep my mouth shut when I'm in trouble.	True
33	H-12	I have had very peculiar and strange experiences.	True
37	E-17	I have never been in trouble because of my sex behavior.	False
38	D-32	During one period when I was a youngster I engaged in petty thievery.	True
56	D-29	As a youngster I was suspended from school one or more times for cutting up.	True
111	D-35	I have never done anything dangerous for the thrill of it.	False
116	D-36	I enjoy a race or game better when I bet on it.	True
118	D-30	In school I was sometimes sent to the principal for cutting up.	True
143	D-34	When I was a child, I belonged to a crowd or gang that tried to stick together through thick and thin.	True
146	G-33	I have the wanderlust and am never happy unless I am roaming or traveling about.	True
173	C-35	I liked school.	False
177	C-14	My mother was a good woman.	False
223	I-51	I very much like hunting.	True
224	B-52	My parents have often objected to the kind of people I went around with.	True
254	E-33	I like to be with a crowd who play jokes on one another.	True
260	C-36	I was a slow learner in school.	True
294	E-12	I have never been in trouble with the law.	False
298	E-1	If several people find themselves in trouble, the best thing for them to do is to agree upon a story and stick to it.	True
342	G-35	I forget right away what people say to me.	True
355	I-2	Sometimes I enjoy hurting persons I love.	True
419	D-27	I played hooky from school quite often as a youngster.	True
421	C-8	One or more members of my family is very nervous.	True
427	C-55	I am embarrassed by dirty stories.	False
434	J-2	I would like to be an auto racer.	True
458	J-39	The man who had most to do with me when I was a child (such as my father, stepfather, etc.) was very strict with me.	True

Table VI—Continued

Booklet Number	Card Number	Item	Delinquent Response
464	H-23	I have never seen a vision.	False
471	D-28	In school my marks in deportment were quite regularly bad.	True
477	E-5	If I were in trouble with several friends who were equally to blame, I would rather take the whole blame than to give them away.	True
485	D-4	When a man is with a woman he is usually thinking about things related to her sex.	True
537	I-52	I would like to hunt lions in Africa.	True
561	J-28	I very much like horseback riding.	True
565	I-55	I feel like jumping off when I am on a high place.	True

Conclusions

The data presented are not sufficient nor adequate to make any extensive discussion of the origin of delinquency-proneness and of other personality characteristics. It is possible that the personality traits indicated by the MMPI variables were acquired in the process of ontological development. It is also possible that some or part of the potential for exhibiting delinquent behavior came from genetic factors operating in an environment that permitted a development of such behavior.

This is not to deny the operation of social factors in the development of personality; but the data suggest that, for some delinquent boys at least, there are personality deviations familiar to clinicians that may be better treated and understood by an individual approach. Such an approach would be directed toward discovering broader and more analytically useful psychological groupings than are provided by classing boys by their socially delinquent acts which for many are an occasional symptom.

Deviant MMPI profiles were much more common among this group of boys than was delinquency. One must either assume that these deviant patterns have no validity as an indication of personality difficulty or that there is real and measurable stress in adolescence, part of which is related to delinquency. The MMPI provides some evidence that part of these stress patterns could be juvenile forms of adult maladjustment. The possibility is suggested that for such boys another attack on delinquency would be the provision of more freely available and skilled counseling and group activities. This does not mean the employment of clinical psychologists and psychiatrists, although these are needed, but rather a shift of emphasis on the part of community personnel from delinquency-centered efforts to adjustment-centered ones.

Of even greater importance, the collected data indicate that any community seriously interested in preventing delinquency should have several kinds of programs rather than concentrating upon a single program. Boys should, by guidance and inclination, be permitted to choose an appropriate program. Our data indicate the possibility that a program of controlled revolt and even danger might help some boys, but others need something very different. These are not new ideas; we hope, however, that the empirical data provided will give greater effectiveness to preventive programs.

REFERENCES

1. HATHAWAY, S. R. A coding system for MMPI profile classification. J. CONSULT. PSYCHOL., 11: 334–337, 1947.
2. HATHAWAY, S. R. AND MEEHL, P. E. An Atlas for the Clinical Use of the MMPI. Minneapolis: University of Minnesota Press, 1951.
3. HATHAWAY, S. R. AND MONACHESI, E. D. Analyzing and Predicting Juvenile Delinquency with the MMPI. Minneapolis: University of Minnesota Press, 1953.
4. McKINLEY, J. C. AND HATHAWAY, S. R. The Minnesota Multiphasic Personality Inventory. New York: The Psychological Corporation, 1943.

8 Delinquency Vulnerability: A Cross Group and Longitudinal Analysis

SIMON DINITZ, FRANK R. SCARPITTI,
WALTER C. RECKLESS

We report here the terminal part of a research project concerned with the attempt to discover what insulates early adolescent boys in high delinquency areas against delinquency. More particularly it deals with the assessments of a group of 70 white boys, currently 16 years of age, who were part of a cohort of 101 twelve-year old white boys, nominated four years previously by their sixth-grade teachers in elementary schools of Columbus (Ohio) high delinquency areas as headed for trouble with the law. Euphemistically, we have referred to them as the "bad" or the "vulnerable" boys. Four years after initial contact, 70 of the original 101 "bad" boys could be located in Columbus, so that re-assessment could be made.

The original group of 101 "bad" boys, of which 70 were located for re-

Reprinted from American Sociological Review, 27 (Aug. 1962), 515–517, with permission of the American Sociological Association and the authors.

This research and the three antecedent studies were made possible by grants from the Development Fund of The Ohio State University. The Development Fund receives yearly contributions from the alumni of the University.

assessment, constitutes the second of two complementary cohorts. The first cohort is made up of a group of 125 twelve-year old white boys who had been nominated by their sixth-grade teachers in the same elementary schools of Columbus, Ohio as likely to stay out of trouble with the law. We have referred to this cohort as the "good" boys or the boys insulated against delinquency. Four years after initial assessment, 103 of this cohort of 125 good boys were located and re-assessed.

Method

The methods utilized in this project have been described extensively in other papers and require only brief mention here.[1] In the Spring of 1955, all sixth-grade teachers in selected elementary schools in the high delinquency areas of Columbus, Ohio were asked to nominate the white boys in their classes, who were unlikely to experience contact with the law. A cohort of 125 twelve-year old white boys was thus constituted. Their cases were officially established as "good" by clearance through the files of the police juvenile bureau and the juvenile court. In other words, they as well as their siblings had not had contact with police and court. These 125 boys were then contacted at home. Our field worker administered a research schedule which assessed whether the boy was veering toward good or poor socialization and whether he had a good or poor image of himself and others. Four years later, 103 of these 125 good boys could be located in Columbus, Ohio and a re-assessment of them was made. In the Spring of 1956, the sixth-grade teachers in the same schools were asked to nominate the white boys in their rooms who were (in their judgment) headed for trouble with the law. A cohort of 101 was constituted. These boys were contacted in their homes and were administered a schedule getting at socialization and concept of self. Four years later, 70 of this cohort of 101 could be located in Columbus and were re-assessed.

The findings from the assessments of the two complementary cohorts can be separated into two parts: (1) a comparison of the 70 from the 101 bad boys cohort with the 103 from the 125 good boys cohort; (2) a comparison of the assessments of the 70 bad boys at 16 years of age with themselves four years earlier at 12 years of age as well as with the total of the original cohort of 101 bad boys. Number 1 is a cross group comparison; number 2, a longitudinal comparison.

[1] Walter C. Reckless, Simon Dinitz, and Ellen Murray, "Self Concept as an Insulator Against Delinquency," *American Sociological Review*, 21 (December, 1956), pp. 744–746; Walter C. Reckless, Simon Dinitz, and Barbara Kay, "The Self Component in Potential Delinquency and Potential Non-Delinquency," *American Sociological Review*, 22 (October, 1957), pp. 566–570; Simon Dinitz, Barbara Ann Kay, and Walter C. Reckless, "Group Gradients in Delinquency Potential and Achievement Scores of Sixth Graders," *American Journal of Orthopsychiatry*, 28 (July, 1958), pp. 588–605; Jon E. Simpson, Simon Dinitz, Barbara Kay, and Walter C. Reckless, "Delinquency Potential of Pre-Adolescents in High Delinquency Areas," *British Journal of Delinquency*, 10 (January, 1960), pp. 211–215; Frank R. Scarpitti, Ellen Murray, Simon Dinitz, and Walter C. Reckless, "The 'Good' Boy in a High Delinquency Area: Four Years Later," *American Sociological Review*, 25 (August, 1960), pp. 555–558.

Cross Group Comparison

At sixteen years of age, four years after original assessment, four of the 103 insulated ("good") boys in the slums had had one minor complaint for delinquency each. One of these was taken to court and placed on probation, while three were settled in the field by a warning from the juvenile bureau. On the other hand, 27 of the 70 vulnerable boys ("bad") from the same slum neighborhoods had had serious and frequent contact with the court, during the four-year interlude between initial assessment at 12 years of age and the assessment at 16 years of age. These 27 boys averaged three plus contacts with the court, involving separate complaints for delinquency.

On a seven item delinquency check list (taken from a larger list devised by James F. Short)[2] which specifies frequency of acts, the 103 insulated slum boys at 16 showed an average score of 1.3 admitted delinquencies during their lifetime, while the vulnerable group of 70 slum boys had a mean frequency score of 3.1. (Each delinquency item was scored 0 to 2; 0 equalling never; 1, once or twice; 2, several times. The maximum frequency score on all seven items would be 14.)

On a nine-item quasi-scale or inventory, which measures the boy's favorable or unfavorable projections of self in reference to getting into trouble with the law, the cohort of 103 sixteen-year old insulated slum boys showed an average score of 15.8. In this instance, the inventory was scored from 10 for the most favorable answers to 19 for the most unfavorable answers on all nine items. The 70 vulnerable 16-year old slum boys scored on an average of 18.9 on this quasi-scale.

The mean score of the insulated cohort on the De scale of the California Personality Inventory[3] was 13.6, while the mean score of the vulnerable cohort on the De scale was 23.4. The De scale (now called Socialization scale) measures a veering toward delinquency or poor socialization or a veering toward non-delinquency or good socialization. A score of 13 for the insulated cohort was in line with the average scores of criterion groups of "good citizens," according to the norms of the scale. The average score of 23 was up close to the mean scores for delinquent groups, court martial cases, and prisoners in the national norms.

Not only had the vulnerable cohort become involved in delinquency very much more than the insulated cohort, but also on the three mentioned

---

[2] F. Ivan Nye and James F. Short, Jr., "Scaling Delinquent Behavior," *American Sociological Review*, 22 (June, 1957), p. 328.

[3] Soc scale (formerly De) is part of the California Personality Inventory, devised by Harrison J. Gough, Department of Psychology, University of California (Berkeley). The CPI is conceived as a substitute for the Minnesota Multiphasic Personality Inventory. However, the scoring on the De is the reverse of what it is on the Soc. Low score on De, that is down around 14, corresponds to a high score on the Soc, up around 40, and vice versa. We are calling the Soc scale the De scale and scoring it reversely, because we started this way in 1955 before Gough re-named the De scale and reversed the scoring. We used 46 out of the total of 54 items on the De scale, eliminating 8 which were too adult oriented for 12 year old children, and we used a correction factor, approved by Gough, to equate the score on the 46 items with the score on the total of 54 items.

supplementary measures, the vulnerable cohort stood in marked, unfavorable contrast with the insulated cohort.

Longitudinal Comparisons

Here the interest is in comparing the assessments of the 103 "good" boys at 16 years of age with the assessments of the same boys at 12 years of age and the assessments of the 70 "bad" boys at 16 with the assessments of the same boys at 12 years of age. On the De scale, which measures veering toward or away from delinquency or toward poor or good socialization, the 103 good boys had, at 12, a mean score of 14.2; at 16, 13.6. The 70 bad boys at 12 had a mean score on the De scale of 23.6, while at 16 their mean score was 23.4. This is notable cohort stability in self orientation over time.

The individual scores of the 70 "bad" boys on the De scale at 16 correlated with their scores at 12 years of age to the extent of r = .78, which shows a high degree of individual stability in direction of poor socialization over time. However, the coefficient of correlation (r) of the De scores for the boys in the "good" cohort at 16 and at 12 years of age was only .15, which of course does not show individual stability longitudinally.[4]

Eighty-eight per cent of the cohort of good slum boys at 12 years of age professed that their close friends had not been in trouble with the law. Of the same 103 boys at 16 years of age, 91 per cent said that their close friends had not been in trouble with the law. In contrast, 35 per cent of the 70 boys from the vulnerable cohort claimed at 12 years of age that their close friends had been in trouble with the law; four years later the same 70 boys claimed 34 per cent.

Regarding favorable or unfavorable concepts of self as measured by responses to questions such as "up to now, do you think things have gone your way," "do you feel that grown ups are usually against you," "do you expect to get an even break from people in the future?" there was no major change in the percentage distribution of the responses of the two cohorts at 12 and at 16. The good cohort had a very high percentage of favorable responses and the bad cohort a low percentage of favorable responses. On all three questions listed above, the percentage of favorable responses for the 103 good boys at 16 was 90. For the 70 bad boys at 16 the percentage of favorable responses on the first of the above listed questions was 50; on the second, 29; and on the third, 30.

---

[4] Examination of the scores of 100 boys (the schedules of 3 of the 103 were incompletely filled in) of the good cohort at 12 and at 16 reveal a tendency of the boys at 16 to gravitate toward the mean. Fifty of the 100 scored on an average of 6.28 lower at 16 than at 12 which is in the direction of improvement; 44, an average of 5.64 higher at 16 than at 12; 6, no change. Hence, the best of the good cohort moved from scores of 6 to 14 up toward the mean and beyond the mean, while the poorest of the good cohort moved down toward the mean or slightly below the mean. The SD for the mean (14.2) of the 100 boys of the good at age 12 (on the De scale) was 6.2; the SD for the mean (13.6) at age 16 was 4.7, which shows less variation at 16 than at 12. The corresponding figures for the boys of the bad cohort were: at age 12, M = 23.6, SD = 6.9; at age 16, M = 23.4, SD = 6.1.

One is struck with the fact that there is a notable cohort stability of responses of the two groups of slum boys over a critical four year period, namely from 12 to 16 years of age. We feel that this cohort stability is not due to the memorization by the boys of the answers to the same questions administered four years apart.

Conclusion

In our quest to discover what insulates a boy against delinquency in a high delinquency area, we believe we have some tangible evidence that a good self concept, undoubtedly a product of favorable socialization, veers slum boys away from delinquency, while a poor self concept, a product of unfavorable socialization, gives the slum boy no resistance to deviancy, delinquent companions, or delinquent sub-culture. We feel that components of the self strength, such as a favorable concept of self, act as an inner buffer or inner containment against deviancy, distraction, lure, and pressures. Our operational assumptions are that a good self concept is indicative of a residual favorable socialization and a strong inner self, which in turn steers the person away from bad companions and street corner society, toward middle class values, and to awareness of possibility of upward movement in the opportunity structure. Conversely, the poor concept of self is indicative of a residual unfavorable socialization (by 12 years of age probably not the result of participation in delinquency subculture) and indicative of weak inner direction (self or ego), which in turn does not deflect the boy from bad companions and street corner society, does not enable him to embrace middle class values, and gives him an awareness of being cut off from upward movement in the legitimate opportunity system.

We feel that the selective operation of the self element is not specified in the response to the models of behavior presented to the person by his associates in differential association theory (Sutherland) [5] and is even less specified in delinquency sub-culture theory (Cohen, et al.) [6] as well as "opportunity structure" theory (limited access to legitimate means, alienation, neutralization, etc., according to Cloward, Sykes, et al.).[7] We feel that a self factor in these theories is missing; this self factor can explain selective resistance to deviant patterns or veering away from the street corner and delinquency. On the other hand, we think that the research findings of Albert Reiss [8] and F. Ivan Nye [9] definitely point to this overlooked self-contain-

[5] Edwin H. Sutherland, *Principles of Criminology*, 4th ed., Philadelphia: J. B. Lippincott Company, 1947, pp. 6–7.

[6] Albert K. Cohen, *Delinquent Boys: The Culture of the Gang*, Glencoe, Ill.: The Free Press, 1955.

[7] Richard A. Cloward and Lloyd E. Ohlin, *Delinquency and Opportunity*, Glencoe, Ill.: The Free Press, 1960, p. 150; Gresham M. Sykes and David Matza, "Techniques of Neutralization: A Theory of Delinquency," *American Sociological Review*, 22 (December, 1957), p. 665.

[8] Albert J. Reiss, Jr., "Delinquency as the Failure of Personal and Social Controls," *American Sociological Review*, 16 (April, 1951), pp. 196–206.

[9] F. Ivan Nye, *Family Relationships and Delinquent Behavior*, New York: John Wiley & Sons, Inc., 1958, pp. 3–4.

ment factor when they called attention to the operation of personal controls (Reiss) and internalized indirect controls (Nye), in accounting for the veering away from delinquency.

9   Teachers as Predictors of Juvenile Delinquency and Psychiatric Disturbance

B. B. KHLEIF

This paper reports the results of an attempt to identify children whose disturbed behavior eventually leads them into legal or psychiatric trouble. The data are taken from the school cumulative record of the pupil's first five years of school life.

A number of recent studies have shown that teachers can identify rather accurately children who are in need of psychological services as well as those who are likely to appear in juvenile courts. Mitchell, Thompson, Ullmann, Bower, et al., and Glidewell, et al., for example, report that teacher ratings of problem children correlate highly with those of psychologists, psychiatrists and psychiatric social workers.[1] FitzSimons has shown that teachers make accurate judgments in clinical referral of pupils—accurate in that they agree at statistically significant levels with long-range psychiatric

Reprinted from *Social Problems*, 11 (Winter 1964), 270–282, with permission of the Society for the Study of Social Problems and the author.

This paper is part of work done on the Kansas City, Missouri, Youth Development Project, a joint endeavor between the Kansas City, Missouri, Public Schools and the Greater Kansas City Mental Health Foundation. The project is concerned with research and action for dealing with behavioral disturbances of school children. Initially, the project was supported by a special grant from the Kansas City Association of Trusts and Foundations; it is now supported by a research grant from the National Institute of Mental Health (OM-535). The author is indebted to Dr. T. S. McPartland for provocative suggestions in the initial stage of the paper, to Dr. R. H. Barnes for helpful reading of an earlier draft, to Drs. Blanche Geer and H. S. Becker for critical remarks, and to two anonymous editorial readers of *Social Problems* for cogent remarks.

[1] Mitchell, Thompson, Ullmann, Bower, et al., and Glidewell, et al., report correlations ranging from 0.70 to 0.87 between teachers' ratings of problem children and those of mental hygienists. See:

(a) John C. Mitchell, "A Study of Teachers' and Mental Hygienists' Ratings of Children," *Journal of Educational Research*, 39 (1949), pp. 29–307.

(b) Charles E. Thompson, "Attitudes toward Behavior Problems," *Journal of Abnormal and Social Psychology*, 35 (1940), pp. 120–125.

(c) Charles A. Ullmann, *Identification of Maladjusted School Children: A Comparison of Three Methods of Screening*, Public Health Monograph No. 7, Washington, D. C.: U. S. Government Printing Office, 1952.

outcomes.[2] On the other hand, Ferin concludes that while teachers are able to identify boys who have behavioral problems and who become delinquents, they fail to identify their actual brothers who are not behavioral problems in school but who turn out to be equally delinquent.[3] Moreover, Havighurst and his co-workers report that on the basis of teacher ratings 66 per cent of boys who have pronounced aggressive behavior in school become delinquent, while only 14 per cent of girls do so.[4]

In most studies, however, teachers have been confronted with *a priori* items, such as those of check-lists on pupil maladjustment. These cover a wide range of behavior, much of which is irrelevant to the educational work situation, and ask the teacher to view the pupil in a psychological frame of reference—as a discrete individual, rather than as a part of the web of classroom interaction. It seems correct to say that by the nature of their work, teachers are group workers, not individual case workers; they meet their clientele all at once, rather than one at a time. When the teacher is asked to assess the individual child on the basis of predetermined items, she may be taken away from her working frame of reference and far beyond the observations she can make in the school situation.

Because of the above considerations, we have attempted to gather teachers' naturalistic assessments of behavioral problems in the classroom. The naturalistic assessments used in this study are comments which are an integral part of the school cumulative record in the Kansas City, Missouri, Public Schools. These comments are written at the end of every school year by every classroom teacher about each of her pupils. The comments are free and unstructured statements on the pupil's social and academic performance. Since they flow out of the teacher's work situation and are meant for her colleagues, they may provide strategic information for prediction. It is the hypothesis of this study that sets of comments written by different teachers on the behavior of the pupil during his first five years of school contain a common core of content that predicts whether or not the youngster will become a juvenile delinquent or a school-age psychiatric referral. (It is to be noted that this hypothesis deals with children's behavior and that it does not extend to adult performance.)

(d) Eli M. Bower, *et al.*, " A Process for Early Identification of Emotionally Disturbed Children," *Bulletin of the California State Department of Education*, 27, No. 6 (1958), pp. 1–111.

(e) John C. Glidewell, *et al.*, "Behavior Symptoms in Children and Adjustment in Public Schools," *Human Organization*, 18 (1959), pp. 123–130.

[2] FitzSimons reports a coefficient of contingency of 0.365 at the 0.025 probability level between the original rating of children when referred by teachers for psychological and psychiatric treatment and a final rating obtained fifteen years after referral. See:

Marian J. FitzSimons, "The Predictive Value of Teachers' Referrals," in Morris Krugman, editor, *Orthopsychiatry and the School*, New York: American Orthopsychiatric Association, 1958, pp. 149–153.

[3] Lotus Carlotta Ferin, "A Study of the Relationship between School Behavior Problems and Juvenile Delinquency in Males," unpublished M.A. thesis, Detroit, Michigan: Department of Sociology, Wayne University, 1951, p. 27.

[4] Robert J. Havighurst, *et al.*, working paper entitled "Chapter on Delinquency," Quincy, Illinois: Quincy Youth Development Project, 1960, ditto, 30 p.

To determine whether there was, in fact, a common core of content in the comments of teachers about pupils, the cumulative records of a large number of pupils were examined and the content of their teachers' comments was subjected to scalogram analysis.[5] To determine whether this common core of content, if it existed, was predictively related to subsequent behavioral difficulties, a design which depended on later pupil contacts with the Juvenile Court or the Child Guidance Clinic was used. Of 256 fourteen, fifteen, and sixteen year old juvenile delinquents who resided within the boundaries of the Kansas City, Missouri, school district and who had two or more court contacts in the year 1958, only 104 had complete school cumulative records without any gaps. Of 105 cases referred to a child guidance service in the school-year 1958–59, 94 had complete records and did not attend special ungraded classrooms.

The 104 delinquents and 94 psychiatric referrals were matched, case by case, with 198 controls who had complete records. Each delinquent child was matched with a child born in the same year, of the same race and sex, who was in the same classroom in the first grade. This matching by first-grade classroom was done in an effort to control social class factors. For psychiatric cases, matching was possible only for sex and for classroom attended in the year of referral. Controls for the sample of delinquents had had no contact with the Police Youth Bureau, the Juvenile Court or the Visiting Teachers Service; controls for the psychiatric cases had had no contact with any of these agencies and were considered by their teachers as "not maladjusted."

Analysis of Teachers' Comments

The comments that teachers write on the school cumulative record are annual judgments of the pupil's social and academic performance. For a given grade and a given pupil, teachers' comments may consist of favorable assessments, unfavorable ones, or a mixture of both. Actual examples are: "very dependable, works diligently, has made splendid growth in reading"; "does not work unless coerced, disobedient, impudent, undependable"; or "good number work, effort poor, irregular attendance." Each pupil in the study had a set of comments written about him by different teachers and containing statements that either approved or discredited certain aspects of his performance.

Comments varied in style and intensity. Some were matter-of-fact or neutral in tone, such as "satisfactory progress"; others employed a sparkling epithet, such as "sunny disposition," or were lyrical, such as "attention span of a humming bird." While some comments embodied euphemistic state-

[5] For a comprehensive discussion of scalogram analysis, see:

(a) Samuel A. Stouffer, et al., Measurement and Prediction, Princeton, New Jersey: Princeton University Press, 1950, Chs. 3–5.

(b) Matilda W. Riley, et al., Sociological Studies in Scale Analysis: Applications, Theory, Procedures, New Brunswick, New Jersey: Rutgers University Press, 1954, Ch. 12.

(c) Allen L. Edwards, Techniques of Attitude Scale Construction, New York: Appleton-Century-Crofts, 1957, Ch. 7.

ments, such as "cannot be depended upon for the truth" or "takes things that do not belong to him," others used direct statements such as "liar" or "thief." Some comments were frugal in their praise or blame, consisting of one statement, such as "excellent worker" or "isn't too interested in anything"; others abounded in details, synonyms and superlatives.

In the analysis of teacher comments, compliments were disregarded and derogations were taken into account: every statement that discredited the pupil's performance—regardless of the style, intensity or substance of the derogation—was taken into consideration. This choice was guided by the study's focus on deviant behavior. For each pupil, comments written by teachers of kindergarten and grades one through five were analyzed. It was hypothesized that delinquents and psychiatric cases would have more derogations of more aspects of their behavior in the first six years of their school life than their controls.

Unfavorable teacher comments were abstracted verbatim from the school cumulative records of subjects and controls. In the analysis, inferential interpretations were avoided. For example, a statement such as "improved in self-control" was not taken to mean "once lacked self-control" but instead was not counted. Similarly, ambiguous statements such as "not as sullen when corrected" and "improving in citizenship though still not trustworthy" were also excluded. Only direct, clear-cut derogations were considered.

It was discovered that teacher comments had a finite range of derogations —a range that was collected in eight content categories [6] which, together, included every derogation found. The categories were (1) misconduct, (2) objectionable personality traits, (3) withdrawn personality traits, (4) poor work habits, (5) poor attitude toward schooling, (6) poor attendance, (7) poor ability to do the grade's work and (8) poor academic achievement. To improve the precision of the last three categories, teacher comments were disregarded and numerical ratings and test scores from other data on the school cumulative record were adopted. The following is a description of each category:

1. *Misconduct:*
Statements indicating action emanating from pupil and having adverse effect on others, e.g., "bothers other children," "thief," "extremely destructive," "creates disturbances," "temper tantrums to acquire attention," "disciplinary problem."
2. *Objectionable Personality:*
Statements indicating pupil's disagreeable reaction, resistance, or unsteady state of emotions, e.g., "hard for him to accept correction," "sullen," "nervous," "confused," "resents criticism," "flighty," "stubborn."
3. *Withdrawn Personality:*
Statements indicating pupil's seclusiveness, lack of courage, confidence, or

---

[6] In addition to statements that discredited the pupil's social and academic performance, teachers had others that could be grouped under two residual categories: "physical ailments and defects"; and "broken or emotionally unresponsive home." However, in both samples these categories were about equally distributed between cases and controls and failed to discriminate between them.

self-assertion, e.g., "timid," "lacks faith in his own ability to do things," "lonely," "is not as aggressive as he should be," "retiring."

4. *Poor Work Habits:*

Statements dealing with pupil's work that refer to bad method in getting his work done—his lack of perseverance, planning or concentration to finish an assignment, his laziness, sloppiness, or carelessness—e.g., "cannot stay with lesson till completion," "works by spells," "procrastinator," "very messy with his work," "poor effort," "bad planning of work," "wastes time."

5. *Poor Attitude towards Schooling:*

Statements dealing with pupil's apathy, hostility or opposition to school as an institution, his lack of interest in his work or enjoyment of work, or that he requires coercion or push, e.g., "a 'don't care' attitude," "needs constant push to accomplish anything," "able to work—won't!!," "indifferent to school," "does not try at all to learn."

6. *Poor Attendance:*

Instead of statements such as "out of school most of the time" or "irregular attendance," poor attendance was defined as absences that total 25 or more days per school year.

7. *Poor Ability to do the Grade's Work:*

This category combines ability and achievement. For statements such as "immature for grade," "not prepared for 2nd grade work," "poor student," "lacks all fundamentals," "has poor foundation," the Revised Stanford-Binet form L I.Q. score was substituted. Poor I.Q. was defined as a score of 90 or less.

8. *Poor Academic Achievement:*

This category was treated in two different ways:

(a) Instead of statements indicating poor achievement in specific subjects such as reading or arithmetic, a mode of 2 or less—taken from the 1–5 numerical ratings that teachers apply to each grade's "learning experiences" or school subjects—was used. Later on, scores of two standardized achievement tests were also used for delinquents and controls and psychiatric cases and controls: those of the Metropolitan Achievement Elementary Form T and the California Achievement Elementary tests. A relative score of 2 or 1, designating zero to 30 percentiles, was considered poor achievement.

(b) Since it was thought that poor achievement in reading might help to differentiate cases from controls, a rating of 2 or less—taken from the 1–5 teacher entries for rating reading—was adopted. Also, reading scores on the aforementioned achievement tests were utilized. The cutoff point for poor readers was a relative score of 2 or 1.

The above categories define eight aspects of deviant pupil performance with which teachers are concerned. Since the last three categories have been centered around numerical ratings rather than teacher comments, the following table reports the number of derogations counted only for each of the first five categories. For delinquents and their controls, the number of counted derogations covers grades one through five; kindergarten is omitted because of infrequent attendance. For psychiatric cases and their controls, the number of derogations covers kindergarten and grades one through five for pupils who attended the fifth grade before the year of referral, and grades up to the year of referral for the younger age group. If in a given grade the pupil received more than one discrediting statement in a given category, such as "destroys materials; annoys pupils; a trouble maker on the play ground," only one derogation for that category (misconduct) was counted for that grade. Thus, figures in the table represent *instances of derogation* counted as one category per grade over a number of grades for all subjects and controls.

If the number of derogations made by teachers is an indication of their concern, it can be seen from ranks in Table 1 that teachers pay most attention to poor work habits of pupils and least attention to withdrawn personality traits. Since this table represents total derogations and not individual pupils, certain pupils within each sample may have had most of the derogations.

Table 1

Total Instances of Derogation for Each Category

	Misconduct	Objectionable Personality	Withdrawn Personality	Poor Work Habits	Poor Attitude toward School
Delinquents	92	88	43	154	74
Controls	43	45	37	85	35
Psychiatric Cases	135	146	46	89	73
Controls	41	22	39	40	22
Total	311	301	165	368	204
Ranks	(2)	(3)	(5)	(1)	(4)

Table 2 shows the number of pupils who had two or more derogations with regard to each category. This table, like the former one, deals with each category separately. However, the goal of the analysis is not to find out how many pupils in a given sample had only poor work habits or only withdrawn personality traits, but to focus attention on each individual in relation to all the categories. The ultimate goal of the analysis is to find a combination of categories that have a common core of content that can differentiate delinquents from non-delinquents, as well as another combination that can differentiate psychiatric cases from their controls.

The Guttman scalogram technique, known as scalogram analysis, was applied to the categories of derogations. This technique permits empirical decisions to be made regarding which categories fall along a single content dimension, i.e., permits us to combine categories and to discover by trial-and-error whether or not there is a natural order in the critical comments which teachers make about their pupils. In the analysis, only five categories of derogations proved to be cumulative and scalable. In one combination, these categories could distinguish delinquents from non-delinquents; in another, psychiatric cases from their controls. The five categories were "misconduct," "objectionable personality," "poor work habits," "poor attitude towards school," and "poor attendance." The combinations will be discussed separately for each sample.

Table 2

Pupils With Two or More Derogations on Each Category

	Misconduct	Objec- tionable Personality	With- drawn Personality	Poor Work Habits	Poor Attitude toward School
Delinquents	22	22	12	48	19
Controls	11	12	9	21	10
Total	33	34	21	69	29
Ranks	(3)	(2)	(5)	(1)	(4)
Psychiatric Cases	37	42	10	26	21
Controls	11	3	12	12	4
Total	48	45	22	38	25
Ranks	(1)	(2)	(5)	(3)	(4)
Grand Total	81	79	43	107	54
Ranks	(2)	(3)	(5)	(1)	(4)

With regard to the remaining categories that failed to discriminate between subjects and controls, the following can be said: "withdrawn personality" was about equally distributed between cases and controls in both samples. This may suggest that withdrawnness is not especially indicative of what teachers regard as bad classroom behavior. However, this category of criticism was too rare for both groups of subjects and controls to be usable in scaling. I.Q.'s and poor academic achievement—based on teachers' numerical ratings and also on scores on the Metropolitan and California Achievement tests—was distributed randomly in both groups. Poor reading—based on teachers' numerical ratings and on reading scores from the two aforementioned achievement tests—was not found to be associated with delinquency or with psychiatric disturbance. The specific findings for each sample are discussed below.

Juvenile Court Sample

The Juvenile Court Sample consists of delinquents born in 1942, 1943 and 1944. There are four distinct sub-groups in this sample: white boys (41), Negro boys (48), white girls (10), and Negro girls (5). Scalogram analysis was applied separately for each sub-group of boys and its controls; white and Negro girls were combined. Since some of the above-mentioned scalable categories were not distinctly independent in content, they were combined. For white boys (cases and controls), the combination resulted in three major categories or behavioral areas. In a descending order of prevalence, they were: (a) misconduct combined with objectionable personality traits (three or more derogations); (b) poor work habits (two or more derogations); and (c) poor attitude toward school together with poor attendance (three or more derogations).

Table 3 reports frequencies in relation to the school cumulative record's "delinquency scale" for white boys. (The last column is added as a visual aid in interpreting results.) It shows that if in grades one to five a white boy has three or more derogations of his conduct or personality, two or more reports of poor work habits, and criticism of his attitude towards school or a bad attendance record in three grades or more, then, in this sample he will be delinquent four times out of five. If he has a score of one or two, the chances of delinquency are about even. If he has no derogations, his chances of being delinquent are one out of five.

Table 3

Delinquency Scale for White Boys

Scale Score *	Cases	Controls	(Chances of being a Case)
3	21	5	4 in 5
2	9	8	about even
1	6	8	about even
0	5	20	1 in 5
	41	41	

$X^2 = 19.12$.   D.F. $= 3$.   P is less than 0.01.

* Scale score 3 represents major categories (a), (b), and (c); 2 represents (a) and (b); and 1, (a).
Coefficient of reproducibility is 0.92. Minimum marginal reproducibility is 0.65.

On the basis of the three major categories of teacher derogations that distinguish juvenile court cases from their controls and the order of these categories, the white delinquent boy may be designated as a "bad school citizen," who has been described by his teachers as follows:

(a) "Bad Boy," who creates disturbances, is sullen or resistant to correction (misconduct and objectionable personality traits).
(b) Lazy and careless (poor work habits).
(c) Indifferent to school, does not want to work, and is absent a good deal (poor attendance and poor attitude toward school).

The same major categories that proved to be cumulative and scalable for white boys proved to be so in the case of Negro boys. However, for Negro boys the categories turned up in a reverse order. In most common to least common prevalence, the major categories for Negro boys, with two or more derogations for each, were:

(a) Poor attitude toward school and poor attendance.
(b) Poor work habits.
(c) Objectionable personality and misconduct.

The following table reports frequencies in relation to the "delinquency scale" for Negro boys.

Table 4 shows that if, in grades one through five, a Negro boy has at least two or more derogations of his attitude towards school or his attendance, plus two or more derogations with regard to his work habits, or if in addition he receives two or more derogations regarding misconduct or objectionable personality, then two times out of three in this sample he will be a delinquent. If he has no derogations at all, or if he receives two or more derogations only with regard to his attitude toward school or his attendance, then his chances of being or not being a delinquent are about even.

Table 4

Delinquency Scale for Negro Boys

Scale Score	Cases	Controls	(Chances of being a Case)
2 and 3	21	11	2 in 3
zero and 1	27	37	about even
	48	48	

$X^2 = 4.688.$ D.F. = 1.   P is less than 0.05.

Coefficient of reproducibility is 0.92. Minimum marginal reproducibility is 0.71.

On the basis of the three major categories that were used in differentiating Negro juvenile court cases from their controls and the order of the categories, the Negro delinquent boy may be said to be described by his teachers as an "indifferent client" who is disinterested in school and has irregular attendance, who is lazy, and who may be already resentful and misbehaving in class.

The same three major categories that distinguished Negro delinquents from their controls did so, and in the same order, in the case of white and Negro girls. Table 5 shows that if in grades one through five a girl receives

Table 5

Delinquency Scale for White and Negro Girls

Scale Score	Delinquent Girls	Controls	(Chances of being a Case)
1, 2 and 3	13	5	7 in 10
zero	2	10	1 in 5
	15	15	

$X^2 = 8.90.$ D.F. = 1.   P is less than 0.01.

Coefficient of reproducibility is 0.91. Minimum marginal reproducibility is 0.68.

two or more derogations with regard to one or more of the major categories of (a) poor attendance and poor attitude toward school, (b) poor work habits and, (c) misconduct and objectionable personality, then in this sample she will be delinquent seven times out of ten. If on the other hand she receives no derogations at all, then her chances of being a delinquent are about one out of five.

On the basis of the major categories used in distinguishing between white and Negro delinquent girls and their controls, the delinquent girl can be said to be primarily described by her teachers as an "indifferent client" who is not interested in coming to school.

Psychiatric Sample

The psychiatric sample consists of (a) 32 boys over eleven years old who were referred after the fifth grade; (b) 20 boys between nine and eleven who were referred in the fourth or fifth grade; (c) 14 eight year old boys who were referred in the third grade; (d) 14 six and seven year old boys who were referred in the first or second grade; (e) 7 girls over eleven who were referred after the fifth grade; and (f) 7 nine and ten year old girls who were referred in the fourth or fifth grade. Among the 80 boys and 14 girls of the sample, there were 9 Negro boys and 5 Negro girls. Because there were very few of them in each sub-group, Negro boys and girls were not considered separately. Also, because of their small number, girls in sub-groups (e) and (f) were combined in the analysis.

Derogations were counted for each sub-group of boys and girls from kindergarten through the grade preceding that of referral. The same five categories that were used for the juvenile court subjects and controls proved to be cumulative and scalable in a different combination for psychiatric cases and controls. The three major categories, in a descending order of prevalence, were: (a) misconduct, poor attendance, and poor attitude toward school; (b) objectionable personality; and (c) poor work habits. For boys over eleven years old (KG through grade five), as well as for nine and ten year old boys (KG, 1–3; and KG, 1–4) the number of derogations for each major category was three or more, two or more, and three or more, respectively. For eight year old boys (Kindergarten through grade two) and for girls (KG, 1–3; KG, 1–4; and KG, 1–5), the number of derogations was two or more for each major category. For six and seven year old boys (KG; and KG–1), the number of derogations for each major category was one or more.

Table 6 reports frequencies in relation to the school cumulative record's "psychiatric disturbance scale." These frequencies are for psychiatric boys and their controls who are over eleven years old. If, in kindergarten through grade five, a boy receives three or more derogations with regard to his conduct, attendance, and attitude toward school, and two or more derogations with regard to objectionable personality—or if in addition he receives three derogations with reference to his work habits—then, in this sample his chances of being a psychiatric case are nine out of ten. If he receives three or more derogations with regard to the first major category, then his chances are about even. If he receives no derogations or less than two derogations with regard to the first category, then his chances of being a psychiatric case are only one in five.

Table 6

Psychiatric Disturbance Scale for Boys Over Eleven Years of Age

Scale Score	Cases	Controls	(Chances of being a Case)
2 and 3	21	2	9 in 10
1	5	6	about even
0	6	24	1 in 5
	—	—	
	32	32	

$X^2 = 26.59.$ D.F. = 2.   P is less than 0.01.

Coefficient of reproducibility is 0.90. Minimum marginal reproducibility is 0.73.

Table 7 reports frequencies with regard to nine and ten year old boys (KG, 1–3; and KG, 1–4). It indicates that with three or more derogations with reference to his conduct, attendance and attitude toward school and two or more derogations with regard to objectionable personality—as a sufficient minimum, or together with three or more derogations pertaining to his work habits—then, in this sample, the chances of a boy becoming a psychiatric case by the end of the third or fourth grade are nine in ten. With three or more derogations regarding the first major category, or with no derogations on any category, the boy will be a case three times out of ten.

Table 7

Psychiatric Disturbance Scale for Nine and Ten Year Old Boys

Scale Score	Cases	Controls	(Chances of being a Case)
2 and 3	14	1	9 in 10
1 and zero	6	19	3 in 10
	—	—	
	20	20	

$X^2 = 18.02.$ D.F. = 1.   P is less than 0.01.

Coefficient of reproducibility is 0.96. Minimum marginal reproducibility is 0.72.

Table 8 deals with eight year old boys (KG, 1–2) on the basis of two or more derogations per major category. Chi-square is not significant. No prediction is made for this sub-group of the sample.

Table 9 deals with six and seven year old boys (KG; KG–1) on the basis of one or more derogations per major category. It indicates that if, by the end of kindergarten or the first grade, a boy receives at least one derogation with regard to misconduct, poor attendance, and poor attitude toward school, and at least one derogation with regard to objectionable personality—as a minimum, or with one additional derogation with reference to poor work habits—then, in this sample, his chances of becoming a psychiatric case are four out of five. If he receives at least one derogation concerning misconduct, poor attendance, and poor attitude toward school, or

Table 8

Psychiatric Disturbance Scale
for Eight Year Old Boys

Scale Score	Cases	Controls
2 and 3	5	1
1 and zero	9	13
	14	14

$X^2 = 2.22.$ D.F. $= 1.$ P is over .10.

if he receives no derogations at all, then, his chances of becoming a psychiatric case are one in three.

Table 9

Psychiatric Disturbance Scale for Six and Seven Year Old Boys

Scale Score	Cases	Controls	(Chances of being a Case)
2 and 3	5	2	4 in 5
1 and zero	9	12	1 in 3
	14	14	

$X^2 = 7.34$ corrected.   D.F. $= 1.$ P is under 0.01.

Coefficient of reproducibility is 0.95. Minimum marginal reproducibility is 0.91.

Table 10 reports frequencies for girls who are nine, ten, and over eleven years of age (KG, 1–3; KG, 1–4; and KG, 1–5). It indicates that if the

Table 10

Psychiatric Disturbance Scale for Nine, Ten, and
Over Eleven Year Old Girls

Scale Score	Cases	Controls	(Chances of being a Case)
2 and 3	8	0	10 in 10
1 and zero	6	14	3 in 10
	14	14	

$X^2 = 9.32$ corrected.   D.F. $= 1.$ P is less than 0.01.

Coefficient of reproducibility is 0.90. Minimum marginal reproducibility is 0.73.

school cumulative record of a girl is examined at the end of the third, fourth, or fifth grade and is found to have two or more derogations with regard to misconduct, poor attendance, and poor attitude toward school, and two or more derogations with reference to objectionable personality—or if

in addition it has two or more derogations regarding poor work habits—
then, according to this sample, the girl will definitely become a psychiatric
case. If, on the other hand, her school cumulative record shows only two or
more derogations with regard to misconduct, poor attendance, and poor attitude toward school or shows no derogations at all, then the girl will be
a psychiatric case in about three times out of ten.

On the basis of the three major categories that were used to distinguish
subjects from controls in the psychiatric sample and the order of the categories, the psychiatrically disturbed boy or girl may be designated as a "negative person," who has been described by teachers as follows:

(a) One who annoys other children, is absent from school a good deal,
and when present has a "don't care" attitude for learning (misconduct, poor
attendance, and poor attitude toward school).
(b) Sullen, nervous, or resentful (objectionable personality).
(c) Works by spells, very messy with his work, and wastes time (poor work
habits).

Discussion

The teachers' comments that have been used in predicting juvenile delinquency and psychiatric disturbance are not objective measures of the
child's behavior but subjective teacher judgments about it. Nevertheless, such
judgments have been found to be indicative of those that are subsequently
made by four community agencies that deal with deviant behavior—the Juvenile Court, the Child Guidance Clinic, and, by extension, their two screening agencies: the Police Youth Bureau and the Visiting Teachers Service.
This suggests that teachers do make sensitive and reliable observations of
behavioral problems—observations that may be used in picking out children
for remedial action programs.

Scalogram analysis has revealed some rather interesting findings. Neither
low I.Q., poor academic achievement, nor poor reading are associated with
either delinquency or psychiatric disturbance. The categories of teacher
comments that could distinguish subjects from controls dealt with the child's
social, rather than academic, performance. This suggests that the teacher
can be regarded as a guardian of norms, and that the school is not merely
an academy but a social institution—an interactive setting in which the
child first comes in contact with authority outside the home. This is con-
sonant with frequent findings of sociology.

The finding that the withdrawn personality category was not only non-
discriminative, but also the least frequently mentioned, shows that withdrawnness is not associated with legal or psychiatric referral of the child,
and suggests that the withdrawn child may not be a serious problem to the
teacher because he neither encroaches upon her authority nor disrupts her
classroom equilibrium. That the categories of misconduct and resistant personality could discriminate between delinquents and non-delinquents and
psychiatric cases and their controls lends support to this conclusion. These
categories, together with the three other discriminating ones—poor work
habits, poor attendance, and poor attitude toward school—further imply

that the deviant child who will get into trouble, and with whom teachers have primarily to contend, is the one who creates classroom emergencies for them and thwarts their teaching efforts.

The findings of this study show that the universe of discourse about the behavior of children in school is different for the psychiatrically disturbed than it is for delinquents. That is to say, the content categories which were found to be scalable when dealing with a sample of juvenile court cases and their controls were not the same as those which were scalable for the psychiatric cases and their controls. For one thing, the psychiatric cases had more bad conduct, and the category of objectionable (sullen and resistant) personality—which was combined with misconduct for delinquents—stood out as a distinct one for psychiatric cases. Moreover, there are sex and color differences that distinguish the sub-groups of each sample. While the white delinquent boys can be described on the basis of teacher judgments as "bad school citizens," and the Negro delinquent boys as well as the white and Negro girls as "lazy and indifferent clients," the male and female psychiatric cases, who in this sample are predominantly white, can be termed "negative persons."

At this stage of the study, however, the use of different combinations of categories for prediction of juvenile delinquency and psychiatric disturbance calls for a word of caution. Through successive combinations of categories, scalogram analysis permits us to discover by trial-and-error whether or not there is a natural order in the critical comments which teachers make about their pupils. For example, misconduct and objectionable personality have been combined for the Juvenile Court sample; misconduct, poor attendance, and poor attitude toward school for the psychiatric sample. In the choice of categories to be combined, such a scaling procedure capitalizes on chance distributions; it is unlikely that these would be the optimum category combinations in new samples. In other words, we would expect different combinations to be optimum by chance alone in a single sample. This, obviously, is the difference between construction of a predictive instrument and its validation, and is why validation is a necessary step before any conclusions as to the predictability of the scales can be fairly drawn.

This study has employed naturalistic teacher comments about pupil behavior, rather than a priori check-list items. Although the delinquency and psychiatric disturbance scales which have been derived from the naturalistic data contain few categories, they are, nevertheless, significant predictors that "hit" more than 75 per cent of the cases in the two matched samples. Moreover, with the exception of the scale for Negro delinquent boys, the scales of this study, unlike measures of other studies that employ matched samples, seem to cut down on the number of "false positives," that is, on controls who appear as possible cases.

The question, however, is whether or not the scales would have the same predictive efficiency when applied to a natural population, a school-age population. It is assumed that in a natural population the rates of referral to the Juvenile Court and the Child Guidance Clinic are, among other things, different for different age groups, for boys than for girls, and for Negroes than for whites. In testing the predictability of the scales, such referral rates have to be taken into consideration. For example, in a school-age population perhaps one in twenty white boys would come in contact with the Juvenile Court over a two or three year period. Hence if this study's delinquency scale for white boys is to be applied to a cross-section of school children, the number of controls for each scale score should be multiplied by twenty or so. This would give us an idea about the actual chances of a pupil being a case in a normal population, rather than in a one-to-one matched sample.[7] It would also, realistically, give us more "false positives" than is suggested by a matched sample. The use of teachers' comments for prediction purposes may be useful, but at this stage of the study all that can be said is that teachers' comments only discriminate for matched samples.

One of the concerns of this study has been what types of conduct emerge as important to the teacher in the classroom. Consequently, it might be profitable to examine possible changes in the relative frequencies of the five categories of derogations as children move from kindergarten through the fifth-grade. It may be discovered that the predictive efficiency of the categories may be less related to their content than to the age of the child at which they are most likely to be recorded, i.e., more related to the teachers' expectations regarding not appropriate classroom behavior in general, but appropriate behavior for a given grade-level. One would perhaps expect that derogations noted closer to the time of the events to be predicted might be more predictive than those noted earlier. Further work on this study may show whether or not there are temporal shifts in the teachers' categorization of children's behavior, shifts that may point to the probability of improvement or deterioration in later behavior.

It is thought that if the school cumulative records of Negro delinquent boys and their controls are analyzed on the basis of teacher commendations, rather than derogations, the delinquency scale for this sub-group of the Juvenile Court sample might be more discriminative. Moreover, since the effort of this study can be considered as first approximation, it is thought that its gross scales can be refined by considering not only the frequency of teacher derogations but also their intensity.

The delinquency and psychiatric scales of this study will be tested in their present form. The school cumulative records of a sample of school children will be analyzed on the basis of these scales. The predictive ability of the scales will be determined by finding out what children have actually come in contact with the Juvenile Court and the Child Guidance Clinic.

---

[7] In multiplying the controls for each scale-score in Table Three by 20 for instance, we see that the actual chances of being a case in a normal population, rather than in a matched sample, would be roughly as follows: For scale-score 3, 1 in 5 rather than 4 in 5; for scale-score 2, 1 in 19 rather than about even; for scale-score 1, 1 in 27 rather than about even; and for scale-score zero, 1 in 81 rather than 1 in 5.

10   An Evaluation of Early
Identification and Intensive
Treatment Programs for
Predelinquents

JACKSON TOBY

The "early identification and intensive treatment" approach to delinquency control is breathtakingly plausible. A plausible argument is not necessarily correct, as Columbus showed those who believed that the world was
flat. "Early identification and intensive treatment," though probably not as
erroneous as the flat-world theory, is more a slogan or a rallying cry than a
realistic assessment of the difficulties that delinquency control programs must
overcome. This paper points out the need for sharper definition of the implicit assumptions of "early identification and intensive treatment" programs
and then examines two of the best-known early identification programs in
the light of this need.

Early identification programs are based on either of two logically distinct
principles: extrapolation or circumstantial vulnerability. The principle of
extrapolation assumes that predelinquents are youngsters in the early stages
of a delinquent way of life; the principle of circumstantial vulnerability
assumes that youngsters who have been exposed to circumstances believed
to cause delinquency are likely to become delinquent. The Cambridge-
Somerville Youth Study emphasized the extrapolative approach to prediction. "Difficult boys" and "average boys" were nominated by teachers and
policemen. The expectation of adolescent delinquency was based primarily
on quasi-delinquent behavior during preadolescence. Although the three raters
on the Cambridge-Somerville research team made a clinical assessment of
each case and made predictions on a variety of family and personal circumstances, the great majority of the predictions were that difficult boys would
remain difficult and average boys, average.[1] Early identification meant in

Reprinted from *Social Problems*, 13 (Fall 1965), 160–175, with permission of the Society
for the Study of Social Problems and the author.

A preliminary version of this paper was published in *Social Work*, 6 (July, 1961), pp.
3–13. The research on which it is based was financed by the Ford Foundation.
[1] Professor Robert Stanfield found in his re-analysis of the Cambridge-Somerville data
that 81 to 84 per cent of the "difficult" referrals were given a *delinquent* prognosis; 59 to
68 per cent of the "average" referrals were given a *nondelinquent* prognosis. (Personal

short that anti-social tendencies would persist and develop further—unless checked by outside intervention. This is quite different from identifying potential delinquents by a theory of delinquency which holds that youngsters exposed to certain sociocultural conditions will become delinquent. Yet the latter is also called "early identification." Criminologists Sheldon and Eleanor Glueck claim to be able to predict delinquency on the basis of factors distinct from the child's early behavior: (1) affection of mother for the boy; (2) affection of father for the boy; (3) discipline of boy by father; (4) supervision of boy by mother; and (5) family cohesiveness.[2] The New York City Youth Board has attempted to test this claim by applying the Glueck prediction table to a sample of 223 boys who in 1952 entered the first grade of two New York City schools in high delinquency neighborhoods. Note that the Cambridge-Somerville approach to prediction is less ambitious than the Youth Board-Glueck approach. One can extrapolate without knowing much about causes. One presumably ought to know a great deal about the causes of delinquency if one hopes to make accurate predictions on the basis of the sociocultural circumstances to which the child is exposed.

This distinction between an extrapolative prediction and a circumstantial prediction, though clear in theory, is often obscured in practice. Diagnostic interviews or self-rating scales (like the Minnesota Multiphasic Personality Inventory) combine the youngster's reports about his own antisocial behavior and/or attitudes with his reports about his family and neighborhood environment. Thus, in many attempts at early identification, the basis for the prediction of future delinquency is not clear.[3] Of course, it can be contended that a better prediction can be made if it is based *both* on the child's early be-

---

communication, March 24, 1965.) Nevertheless, the extent to which the raters were influenced by the source and nature of the referrals is not clear. The seeming extrapolations might be accounted for by systematic differences in the environmental circumstances of "difficult" and "average" boys. The three raters themselves claimed to give considerable weight to the nature of the neighborhood and the family situation. See Donald W. Taylor, "An analysis of Predictions of Delinquency Based on Case Studies," *Journal of Abnormal and Social Psychology*, 42 (January, 1947), pp. 45–46. Recall, however, that the design of the study was such that the raters started with a bimodal universe: boys identified by teachers and policemen as troublesome and boys identified as law-abiding. Although the ratings ranged from minus 5 (most delinquent) to plus 5 (most nondelinquent), comparatively few borderline ratings (zero) were made. In characterizing the predictions as extrapolative, I am assuming that a troublesome boy was predicted to be more or less delinquent depending on his family and neighborhood situation and a law-abiding boy was predicted to be more or less nondelinquent, but troublesome boys did not usually get into the nondelinquent prediction range nor law-abiding boys into the delinquent range by virtue of their family and neighborhood situations. In Tables 1 and 2, any prediction from minus five to minus one was considered a prediction of delinquency, and any prediction from plus five to plus one was considered a prediction of nondelinquency. Zero predictions were eliminated from the analysis. See also the discussion in Edwin Powers and Helen Witmer, *An Experiment in the Prevention of Delinquency: The Cambridge-Somerville Youth Study*, New York: Columbia University Press, 1951, pp. 29–36.

[2] Sheldon and Eleanor Glueck, *Unraveling Juvenile Delinquency*, New York: Commonwealth Fund, 1950; Sheldon and Eleanor Glueck, *Predicting Delinquency and Crime*, Cambridge, Massachusetts: Harvard University Press, 1959; Eleanor T. Glueck, "Efforts to Identify Delinquents," *Federal Probation*, 24 (June, 1960), pp. 49–56.

[3] D. H. Stott, "The Prediction of Delinquency from Non-Delinquent Behavior," *British Journal of Delinquency*, 10 (January, 1960), pp. 195–210.

havior and on his exposure to known deleterious influences. Possibly so. However, such predictions emerge like sausages from a sausage machine but without real insight into *why* they are correct. The drawback of predictions made without theory becomes all too evident when treatment is attempted. Since the prediction is mechanical and does not imply an understanding of the causes of delinquency, it provides no guidance for treatment. "Treatment" becomes an umbrella word meaning all things to all men. A therapeutic program based on family casework is not the same thing as one based on individual psychotherapy,. the improvement of reading skills, participation in organized sports, or vocational counseling.

Predictions made without a theory of delinquency causation can be matched with a treatment program that is similarly eclectic. Sometimes it is very difficult indeed to find out what "intensive treatment" consists of. The therapist may contend that each case is unique and that treatment is tailored to the individual case. One might well be suspicious of such vagueness. Vagueness can conceal two kinds of ignorance: ignorance as to what is causing the antisocial behavior and ignorance of the best strategy of intervention. In any case, most "individual treatment" programs and programs claiming to "co-ordinate" community resources are in practice not genuinely eclectic. They implicitly answer the question, "What kind of treatment?" by selecting resources ideologically congenial to the agency. For example, the same predelinquent child may be treated through casework techniques if he comes to the attention of one agency and through group work techniques if he comes to the attention of another. Presumably the type of treatment selected should be governed by the etiological factor involved in the youngster's predelinquency. The type of treatment selected by practitioners of "individual treatment" seems more closely related to the practitioners' preconceptions than to the child's problems. This is said, not to condemn efforts to treat predelinquency, but to point out that in the present state of knowledge the frequently invoked analogy between medical practice and delinquency control is misleading. Whereas medical practice aims at precise diagnosis and specific treatment, early identification and intensive treatment of delinquency usually address themselves to an unknown problem with an unproved technique. Is it any wonder that the few treatment programs that have been rigorously evaluated reveal disappointingly small effects? For instance, the Cambridge-Somerville Youth Study offers little support to proponents of "early identification and intensive treatment" as an approach to delinquency control. Whereas 41 per cent of the 253 boys in the treatment group subsequently were convicted of at least one major crime in a state or federal court, 37 per cent of the 253 boys in the control group were so convicted. Considering (a) that treatment began by age 10 for 121 boys and by age 13 for the remaining 132, and (b) that treatment lasted for four years or more for 171 boys, *more* criminality in the treatment group is rather surprising. The McCords point out that only 12 of the 253 boys had intensive therapy (according to their quite reasonable criteria of "intensive"), and they suggest that for this reason intensive treatment was not really tested. Perhaps so. On the other hand, hardly a probation or parole system in the United States gives as intense supervision as was given routinely in the course of the Cambridge-Somerville Youth Study. The case loads of Cambridge-Somerville workers were 34 youngsters per counselor at the beginning of the study and even fewer when the boys grew older.[4]

Tacit Assumptions of Early Identification and Intensive Treatment Programs

Presumably the rationale of early identification is to economize treatment efforts. Otherwise, society would expose all youth to whatever resources are available for delinquency control. But in order to achieve economy, the predictions must be accurate. If delinquency occurs in too many cases where nondelinquency was predicted or *fails* to occur in too many cases where it *was* predicted, economy may not be realized. Once the predictions are found to be sufficiently accurate, greater intensity of treatment efforts is possible because youngsters not in danger of becoming delinquent can be ignored.

The conditions under which accurate predictions may be anticipated are therefore important. For the occurrence of adolescent delinquency to be predicted accurately from either preadolescent behavior or preadolescent circumstances, no crucial etiological factors should make their appearance after the original predictions have been made. For instance, in the New York City Youth Board project, the ratings of the family backgrounds of the 223 boys were made when they were 6 years old. If family relations are the major factor in delinquency and if family relations change appreciably in the course of the study, the predictions ought not to be very accurate.[5] Peer group relations are even more prone to change than family relations. Since studies of adolescent street-corner groups reveal that youngsters who join such groups are more likely to commit delinquent acts than youngsters who do not join such groups and since delinquent groups rarely recruit members younger than 10, preadolescent ratings of school misbehavior or family background ought not to predict delinquency during adolescence very accurately. Of course, if we assume that early childhood experiences are so important that they establish a differential vulnerability for all subsequent experiences, early predictions might be accurate despite later changes in family and peer relations. Freudian psychiatrists subscribe to this assumption of the disproportion-

---

[4] See Powers and Witmer, *op. cit.*, pp. 85, 88; William and Joan McCord, *Origins of Crime: A New Evaluation of the Cambridge-Somerville Youth Study*, New York: Columbia University Press, 1959, pp. 20, 26, 29, 38–39.

[5] Professor Isidor Chein of New York University suggested that the Youth Board rate the family situations of the 223 boys *again* several years after the original ratings were made. How well would the two sets of ratings correlate with one another? If the later ratings were less closely related to outcome than the earlier ratings, this would tend to support the Glueck hypothesis that the early family situation is the major factor in delinquency. If the later ratings were more closely related to outcome than the earlier ratings, this would suggest that the contemporary situation—familial and extrafamilial—is more important in the genesis of delinquency than the Gluecks think.

ate importance of early socialization; sociologists, on the other hand, believe that socialization continues throughout life and that the course of a child's life can be radically changed by subsequent experiences.

Correct identification of youngsters who will ultimately become delinquent is the first step of "early identification and intensive treatment" programs. The second step is to upset these initially correct predictions by an effective treatment program. It is usually assumed by the proponents of "early identification and intensive treatment" that treatment is effective merely by being intensive. This is not necessarily so. The focusing of treatment efforts on youngsters most likely to become delinquent necessarily involves special handling for them. It is extremely difficult for a focused treatment program to avoid stigmatizing the recipients of the "benefits" of the program. Early identification does not necessarily imply early stigmatization, but early *discriminatory* treatment seems to. Thus, it is conceivable that a boomerang effect will occur and that greater intensity of exposure to treatment will be *less* effective than less intense but less discriminatory exposure. Suppose, for instance, that a community has an organized recreational program for *all* children up to the age of 16. Someone convinces the city fathers that organized recreation can prevent delinquency, and the program is changed to focus on identified predelinquents. Instead of 1,000 boys using the facilities occasionally, 200 boys use them frequently. Before leaping to the conclusion that these 200 boys are less likely to become delinquent, let us consider what the impact of their segregation is on "predelinquents." We know from experience with ability groupings in the schools that the evaluations of the adult world cannot be concealed from youngsters. Just as the children in the "dumb" classes know that they are not in the "smart" classes, these 200 boys are unlikely to think of themselves as the pride of the community. It is possible that less intensive recreational participation would have been more effective in arresting their delinquent tendencies than the more intensive—and incidentally more stigmatizing—exposure.[6]

The Cambridge-Somerville Youth Study and the New York City Youth Board Prediction Study did not assess the effect of neighborhood, ethnic background, or socio-economic status on the *accuracy* of their predictions. As a result, they missed an opportunity to clarify the conditions under which predisposing personal or family factors eventuate in delinquency. I propose to examine both studies in the light of these omissions in order to demonstrate that explicit consideration of the social context is necessary for further progress in delinquency *prediction* and ultimately control.

[6] Proponents of early identification and intensive treatment might argue that stigmatization occurs but that it is helpful in preventing delinquency (by nipping the deviant tendency in the bud). Law enforcement officials sometimes use this argument, but they usually talk in terms of "punishment" rather than "treatment." Social workers and psychiatrists seem unwilling to face the logical possibility that well-intentioned "treatment" can do more harm than good. For an analysis of the comparative consequences of punishment and treatment, see Jackson Toby, "Is Punishment Necessary?" *Journal of Criminal Law, Criminology and Police Science*, 55 (September, 1964), pp. 332–337.

The Cambridge-Somerville Youth Study

Table 1 shows a positive relationship between the original predictions of

Table 1

Comparison of Original Predictions and Final Outcomes of Boys
in the Cambridge-Somerville Youth Study

| | Outcomes | | |
Predictions	Delinquent	Nondelinquent	Total
Delinquent	114	191 *63%	305
Nondelinquent	18 * 12%	132	150
Total	132	323	455

* Errors of prediction.

delinquency or nondelinquency made in 1937–38 and the outcomes as of 1956.[7] Insofar as errors of prediction occurred, they were mainly overpredictions of delinquency. That is, of the 305 boys for whom delinquency was predicted, 191 turned into "good" boys (63 per cent); but only 18 of the 150 for whom *nondelinquency* was predicted subsequently committed offenses (12 per cent). Bear in mind that the Cambridge-Somerville Youth Study assumed that, unless the service program were successful, preadolescent boys who manifested antisocial behavior would continue such behavior in adolescence. In point of fact, the majority of identified predelinquents did *not* persist in their delinquent activities. The obvious question is: Why not?

It might be possible to find out why delinquency was overpredicted and, hopefully, the conditions making for more accurate predictions if the data in Table 1 were partitioned into meaningful subsamples. For example, various ethnic groups are represented in the study population: "Italian," "Other Latin," "Negro," "Eastern European," "Western European," and "Native American."[8] If predictions were more accurate for Italian boys than, say, for native American boys, this might throw light on the relationship between cultural values and delinquency.[9] Similarly, several socioeconomic

[7] The unpublished tabulations in Tables 1 and 2 were made available to me through the graciousness of Professor William McCord of Stanford University, Professor Gordon W. Allport of Harvard University, Dr. Stanton Wheeler of the Russell Sage Foundation, and Professor Robert Stanfield of the University of Massachusetts. Note that these tabulations include boys from both treatment and control groups. Since the treatment program proved ineffective, the exclusion of treatment cases from the analysis was unnecessary.

[8] The ethnic data relating to the study population do not appear in *Origins of Crime* but are found in a second volume, which explored the causes of alcoholism rather than crime. For information on ethnic groupings, see William and Joan McCord, *Origins of Alcoholism*, Stanford, California: Stanford University Press, 1960, p. 38.

[9] See Jackson Toby, "Hoodlum or Business Man: An American Dilemma," in Marshall Sklare, ed., *The Jews*, Glencoe, Ill.: The Free Press, 1958, pp. 542–550, for a discussion of the relationship between ethnic background and delinquency.

levels were represented in the study population. If predictions were more accurate for slum-dwelling youngsters than for boys living in better residential neighborhoods, this might throw light on the relationship between social class and delinquency. Table 2 explores the latter question by breaking down

Table 2

Partition of Cambridge-Somerville Youth Study Cases by Neighborhood of Residence

Predictions	Outcomes					
	In Slum Neighborhoods			In Better Neighborhoods		
	Delin-quent	Non-delinquent	Total	Delin-quent	Non-delinquent	Total
Delinquent	90	126 *	216	24	65 *	89
Nondelinquent	12 *	62	74	6 *	70	76
Total	102	188	290	30	135	165

* Errors of prediction.

the data of Table 1 into subsamples of neighborhoods. What does Table 2 reveal about the effect of the socioeconomic milieu?

Facts

1. Predictions of delinquency were more likely to be made in slum neighborhoods than in better residential neighborhoods. Seventy-five per cent of the 290 boys from slum neighborhoods were predicted by the raters to become delinquent as compared with 54 per cent of boys from better neighborhoods.

2. Predictions of delinquency were more likely to be correct in slum neighborhoods than in better neighborhoods. Forty-two per cent of the 216 boys predicted delinquent from slum neighborhoods actually became so as compared with 27 per cent of the 89 boys predicted delinquent in better neighborhoods.

3. Predictions of *nondelinquency* were more likely to be correct in better residential neighborhoods than in slum neighborhoods. Ninety-two per cent of the boys predicted nondelinquent from better neighborhoods remained law-abiding as compared with 84 per cent of the boys predicted nondelinquent in slum neighborhoods.

4. The differences between the later delinquency rates of troublesome and conforming preadolescents are striking. In slum neighborhoods, 42 per cent of the troublesome preadolescents, as contrasted with 16 per cent of the conformists, subsequently committed offenses. In the better residential neighborhoods, 27 per cent of the troublesome preadolescents, as contrasted with 8 per cent of the conformists, subsequently committed offenses.

Interpretation

1. Predictions of delinquency could have varied by neighborhood for either one of two reasons (or a combination of both):

   a. Because preadolescent misbehavior at school and in the community is more common in slum neighborhoods than in better residential neighborhoods.

   b. Because preadolescent misbehavior was likely to be discounted by the Cambridge-Somerville raters on the basis of favorable family situations, and such situations are more frequent in better residential neighborhoods. That is to say, the raters were more likely to predict nondelinquency or to assign an undecided (zero) rating if the troublesome preadolescent came from a "good" neighborhood.

2. The greater tendency of predictions of delinquency to come true and predictions of nondelinquency to be incorrect in slum neighborhoods may be explained by differing neighborhood traditions of delinquency. Precisely how these traditions originate and are sustained is not clear. One relevant factor is a concentration of disorganized families exercising ineffective control over children, especially over adolescent boys.[10] Another is the proliferation of highly visible street-corner groups that are frequently delinquent. Sociologists have suggested that the weakness of family control and the influence of the peer group are different sides of the same coin.[11]

3. The negligible tendency of *conforming* preadolescents to become delinquent in later years—in both slum neighborhoods and in better residential neighborhoods—may mean that boys controlled effectively by their parents in preadolescence continue to be controlled effectively in adolescence and young adulthood. External controls, however, may not be so crucial as the conforming preadolescent develops a nondelinquent self-conception that insulates him from involvement in delinquent peer groups.[12] Thus, the delinquent peer group is likely to have a quite different impact on troublesome and on conforming preadolescents. Not only were the differences between the delinquency records of the troublesome and the conforming preadolescents substantial in later years. The conforming preadolescents from slum neighborhoods had a less delinquent record than the troublesome preadolescents from the better neighborhoods.

4. The reason or reasons for the overprediction of delinquency are not clear. An obvious possibility is that a considerable amount of delinquency goes unrecorded.[13] If this "hidden delinquency" could somehow be put into

[10] Jackson Toby, "The Differential Impact of Family Disorganization," *American Sociological Review*, 22 (October, 1957), pp. 505–512.

[11] Frederick M. Thrasher, *The Gang*, Chicago: University of Chicago Press, 1927; William Foote Whyte, "Social Organization in the Slums," *American Sociological Review*, 8 (February, 1943), pp. 34–39.

[12] Walter C. Reckless, Simon Dinitz, and Ellen Murray, "Self-Concept as an Insulator Against Delinquency," *American Sociological Review*, 21 (December, 1956), pp. 744–747; Simon Dinitz, Frank R. Scarpitti, and Walter C. Reckless, "Delinquency Vulnerability: A Cross Group and Longitudinal Analysis," *American Sociological Review*, 27 (August, 1962), pp. 515–517.

[13] Fred J. Murphy, Mary M. Shirley, and Helen L. Witmer, "The Incidence of Hidden Delinquency," *American Journal of Orthopsychiatry*, 16 (October, 1946), pp. 286–296.

the record, the predictions might well seem more accurate. Another possibility is that delinquent tendencies were somehow "nipped in the bud." Troublesome preadolescents were salvaged. The difficulty with this interpretation is that the planned program of intervention did not result in a lower delinquency rate in the treatment group as compared with the control group. As a matter of fact, Table 3 suggests more strongly than the overall treat-

Table 3

Delinquency Among Treatment Boys and Control Boys in the Cambridge-Somerville Youth Study, by Type of Neighborhood

Type of Neighborhood	% of Convictions in Treatment Group. (N = 233)	% of Convictions in Control Group (N = 250)
Good	38	26
Fair	37	33
Poor	40	44
Worst	46	49

ment group-control group comparison that a boomerang effect might have occurred.[14] The difference between the treatment group and the control group in the "good" neighborhoods was greater than the difference in the "worst" neighborhoods. This difference can be explained by sampling peculiarities. On the other hand, it is clear that the program of intervention was not *more* successful in the better residential neighborhoods. Since delinquent peer group influences are relatively weak in better residential neighborhoods, one would expect a program of delinquency prevention to have a *better* chance in such neighborhoods. The planned treatment program of the Cambridge-Somerville Youth Study staff may have been ineffectual; yet there is still the possibility that unplanned circumstances intervened to arrest delinquent tendencies. For example, parents may have moved to more wholesome communities to escape the delinquent influences of the slum. (The neighborhood ratings in the Cambridge-Somerville files date from the start of the study; they do not take into account subsequent moves.) The possible benefits of movement into low-delinquency neighborhoods is, unfortunately, pure speculation.

New York City Youth Board Prediction Study

The New York City Youth Board Prediction Study differed from the Cambridge-Somerville Youth Study in important respects. In the first place, all the boys for whom delinquency predictions were made came from two high-delinquency neighborhoods. Second, the predictions were based on home visits by social workers when the youngsters entered the first grade. They gave negligible weight to a factor particularly stressed in the Cambridge-

14 William and Joan McCord, *Origins of Crime*, pp. 71, 204.

Somerville Youth Study, the boy's own behavior. The critical question, of course, is: By what mechanism do "bad" family situations lead to delinquency in high-delinquency neighborhoods? Consider two quite different mechanisms by which a bad family situation might lead to delinquency:

1. Parental rejection and neglect damage the personality of the developing child. Lack of impulse control results from pathological socialization.[15] The psychopathic or neurotic boy reacts with violence to trivial provocations, sets fires, and steals purposelessly.

2. Parental inadequacy and neglect, by reducing family control, thereby orient the boy toward his agemates in the neighborhood.[16] (The family and the peer group are in a sense competing for the allegiance of boys in high-delinquency neighborhoods.) If the peer group is delinquent, a boy's desire for acceptance by his peers attempts him to participate in delinquent activities.

The Youth Board researchers do not make clear which of these mechanisms they suspect has greater influence. Although both are probably at work, mutually reinforcing one another to produce delinquency, a delinquency control program cannot do all things at once; hence it would seem desirable to be explicit about suspected etiological mechanisms. In point of fact, the intensive treatment program undertaken by the Youth Board addressed psychiatric problems; a clinic was set up in one of the two schools, and treatment was offered by a team consisting of psychologists, psychiatrists, and social workers to all of the boys predicted delinquent by the original Glueck scale.[17] The boys who were likewise predicted delinquent in the other school were to serve as a control group. Although the experimental program lasted four years, it failed in its objective. As in the Cambridge-Somerville Youth Study, members of the treatment group were no less likely to become delinquent than members of the control group.[18] A possible explanation for the failure is that the treatment program was predicated on the first mechanism whereas the second mechanism may have been more relevant to the delinquency of these underprivileged boys. Let us examine the relationship between predictions and outcomes in the light of this hypothesis.

Table 4 reports the relationship between 1952 predictions and 1959 outcomes utilizing three different prediction techniques:

[15] Kate Friedlander, *The Psychoanalytic Approach to Juvenile Delinquency*, New York: International Universities Press, 1944.

[16] Thrasher, *op. cit.*

[17] New York City Youth Board, Research Department, *A Study in Variance from Predicted Delinquency: A Study of 20 Negro Boys Who Were Overpredicted*, mimeographed, 1962, ch. 4.

[18] Based on a personal conversation with Mrs. Maude Craig, research director of the Youth Board. To the best of my knowledge the New York City Youth Board has not published a full account of this experiment, apparently on the assumption that something went wrong in the execution of the experiment that did not reflect on its underlying assumptions. This attitude strikes me as dubious, particularly in view of the Youth Board's awareness of the similar results of a project in Washington, D.C., which also used the Glueck scale to identify predelinquents and which also attempted clinical treatment. *Ibid.*, p. 58.

Table 4

A Comparison Among the Youth Board Two- or Three-Factor Table,
The Glueck Five-Factor Table, and a Single Factor (Public
Assistance) in Predicting Delinquency

1952 Predictions	Outcomes, 7 Years Later		
	Delinquent	Nondelinquent	Total
Based on Five Factors			
Probably delinquent	17	50 *	67
Probably nondelinquent	4 *	152	156
Total	21	202	223
Based on Two or Three Factors			
Probably delinquent	13	24 *	37
Probably nondelinquent	8 *	178	186
Total	21	202	223
Based on Single Factor (Economic Status of Family When Boy Entered School in 1952)			
Public assistance	13	39 *	52
No public assistance	8 *	163	171
Total	21	202	223

* Errors of prediction.

(1) the five-factor scale designated by the Youth Board at the beginning of the research as the official prediction device; [19]

(2) a two- and three-factor scale developed late in the research to adapt the Glueck scale to the ethnic groups represented in the Youth Board population (especially Negroes); [20]

(3) a single-item predictive device (based on whether or not the family was receiving welfare assistance in 1952), the purpose of which is to provide a basis for comparing the predictive power of the Youth Board scales with predictions based on a readily available socioeconomic datum.

Note that the original five-factor prediction table made 54 errors, more

[19] Sheldon and Eleanor Glueck, *Unraveling Juvenile Delinquency*, New York: Commonwealth Fund, 1950.

[20] Further modifications of the Glueck scales occurred after eight years. Instead of getting rater agreement on total scores, the Youth Board researchers insisted now on rater agreement on each factor going into the score. Second, aware of the fact that the scales were overpredicting delinquency, the Youth Board researchers reviewed some cases and reclassified them from probably delinquent to probably nondelinquent. These changes were seemingly made for cogent research considerations. Unfortunately though, they were made long after the research began and could no longer be regarded as uncontaminated "prospective predictions." For a history of these changes, see New York City Youth Board, *An Experiment in the Use of the Glueck Social Prediction Table as a Prognosticator of Potential Delinquency*, mimeographed, October, 1961.

than the 47 errors made by the table based on the public assistance criterion alone. The two- and three-factor table did considerably better: only 32 errors. But *why* did the two- and three-factor table do better than the five? What factors were eliminated? The revised scale used "mother's supervision" and "cohesiveness of the family" supplemented by "father's discipline" in those cases "where a father or father substitute has been in the home a sufficient length of time to have had an influence in the boy's life." [21] From this improvement of prediction resulting from the elimination of "affection of mother for the boy" and of "affection of the father for the boy," it might be inferred that these factors are not important to the etiology of delinquency in this population. (Bear in mind that the universe consists of boys from *high-delinquency* neighborhoods.) Eleanor Glueck assures skeptics that "this is not the case." [22] She explains the greater accuracy of the two- and three-factor table as compared with the original five-factor table as due to inconsistency of ratings of parental affection by social workers of different intellectual persuasions and to the difficulty of making ratings for families where the father has long been out of the home. To me this argument is not convincing. Only 28 of 224 boys lacked fathers (or father substitutes) in the home for a major portion of their lives, and presumably the absence of mothers or mother substitutes was rarer.[23] Why was "affection of the *Mother*" not a useful predictive item? Mrs. Glueck's argument is essentially that parental affection is etiologically important but that the Youth Board researchers were unable to measure parental affection reliably. An alternative interpretation is that parental *affection* is less closely correlated with delinquency in high-delinquency neighborhoods than is parental *control*. The explanation of the greater accuracy of the shorter scale as compared with the five-factor scale may simply be that mother's supervision, family cohesiveness, and father's discipline are more closely related to parental control than are affection of the mother and affection of the father.

Is there any other evidence in favor of the hypothesis that parental control is the crucial variable affecting the accuracy of the Youth Board predictions? The Youth Board itself provided such evidence in a study of 20 Negro boys who were predicted delinquent by the five-factor Glueck prediction table and failed to become so in the subsequent eight years.[24] In a chapter entitled, "Mother's Supervision Counteracting Peer Group Environment," the author of the Youth Board monograph (Dr. Philip W. Furst) emphasizes the role of the mother or mother-substitute in preventing gang membership or defining it as undesirable (dangerous). "She uses various means: exhortation, reason, rewards, example, tongue-lashing, threats, discipline, manipulation of the environment, coaxing, cajoling. And this process

21 *Ibid.*, p. 10.
22 Eleanor T. Glueck, *op. cit.*, pp. 55–56.
23 New York City Youth Board, *op. cit.*, 1961, p. 13. Note that the total of 224 boys includes one Puerto Rican youngster not included in earlier reports I have examined and therefore not included in Tables 4 or 5.
24 New York City Youth Board, *op. cit.*, 1962.

goes on with ever broadening content into the middle teens and beyond." [25]
Seven of these 20 boys had been rated in 1952 as effectively supervised by
the mother—as contrasted with *two* of 14 Negro boys predicted delinquent
who confirmed the prediction.[26] Four additional boys "were saved in the
school years by mothers' supervision even though the mothers' original
supervision ratings were poor. . . ." [27] In another four cases, recognition
of the *grandmother's* part in supervision and in the cohesiveness of the family might have led to a more hopeful prediction. For instance, one of the
two boys out of the 20 considered to have the *highest* probability of becoming delinquent had little contact with his parents. "What the interviewer
did not grasp in 1952 . . . was the fact that the person who really counted
in those children's lives was the marvelous grandmother in whose home the
family was living." [28] Thus, 15 of the 20 incorrect predictions of delinquency
might have been avoided by emphasizing parental control more strongly.

Those mothers and mother-substitutes who were concerned about supervising the activities of their sons may have been distressed at the growing
crime problems of their neighborhoods. Although the schools were selected
by the Youth Board in 1952 because they lay in high-delinquency neighborhoods, the delinquency rates in the two neighborhoods increased over the ten-
year period of the study. Three families moved from the Bronx to rural areas,
at least one for the express purpose of providing better child supervision.[29]
Bear in mind that choice of neighborhoods was limited for these 20 Negro
families. Furthermore, half of them were receiving public assistance at some
time during the study, reflecting economic disabilities that must have also
reduced their opportunities to relocate. Nevertheless, eight of the twenty
families had moved by 1961 to better neighborhoods. Perhaps it is only a
coincidence, but four of the seven families where the mother's supervision
was rated effective in 1965 had relocated into neighborhoods with lower
delinquency rates—as compared with four of the 13 families where the
mother's supervision was poor.

Residential mobility was not confined to Negro families; 29 of the 53
white boys in the Youth Board study were Jewish, and other studies have
shown that Jewish families move readily to better neighborhoods when their
old communities deteriorate.[30] Mobility is not motivated exclusively by a
concern for the upbringing of children, important though this is; population
flow is to be expected in a large city. The Youth Board researchers have
complained about the difficulty of keeping track of 61 boys scattered by
1961 in out-of-town schools in 12 states, Puerto Rico, and Malta.[31] And

[25] *Ibid.*, pp. 28–29.
[26] *Ibid.*, p. S6.
[27] *Ibid.*, p. S15.
[28] *Ibid.*, p. 36. See also pp. 63–68.
[29] *Ibid.*, pp. S7–8.
[30] *Ibid.*, p. 4; Nathan Glazer and Daniel Patrick Moynihan, *Beyond the Melting Pot: The
Negroes, Puerto Ricans, Jews, Italians, and Irish of New York City*, Cambridge, Massachusetts, M.I.T. Press, 1963, pp. 53–67, 160–163.
[31] New York City Youth Board, *op. cit.*, 1961, p. 15.

of course moves occurred within New York City. Regardless of the motivation for residential moves, however, an important consequence is to provide a new environment for children. Of 14 boys predicted *nondelinquent* in 1952 whose families moved to a *better* neighborhood, none became delinquent; of 31 boys with exactly the same prediction score whose families moved to neighborhoods with the *same* or *worse* levels of delinquency, 7 became delinquent.[32] The Youth Board has not yet analyzed the moves of all the families in the study in relation to prediction scores and outcomes. Hence, it is not known whether boys predicted *delinquent* in 1952 were less likely to become so if their families moved to better neighborhoods. It sounds plausible.

If indeed weak family control predisposes a boy living in a high-delinquency neighborhood to become delinquent, it would be helpful to know the ethnic and socioeconomic circumstances that reinforce this tendency. The question is not *whether* the various prediction tables predict delinquency but *how* both successful and unsuccessful predictions provide clues to underlying causes and ultimately to programs of intervention. As an illustration of this approach Table 5 breaks down the relationship between the two- and three-factor prediction table and delinquent outcomes (shown in Table 4) for three ethnic groups and two socioeconomic statuses.[33] What does Table 5 reveal about the reinforcing effect of the social milieu?

Facts

1. Predictions of delinquency were more likely to be made for Negro boys than for Puerto Rican or white boys. Twenty-one per cent of the 131 Negro boys were given better than a 50–50 chance of becoming delinquent—as contrasted with 13 per cent of the 39 Puerto Rican boys and 8 per cent of the 53 white boys. To look at the data in another way, of the 37 boys predicted delinquent, 33 were Negro or Puerto Rican.

2. Although the number of cases in some categories were very small, e.g., only four *white* boys and five *Puerto Ricans* predicted delinquent, predictions of delinquency were more likely to be correct and predictions of nondelinquency to be wrong for Negroes and Puerto Ricans than for whites. Whereas one out of four of the white boys predicted delinquent became so, 36 per cent of the Negroes and Puerto Ricans predicted delinquent fulfilled the prediction. None of the 49 white boys predicted non-delinquent became delinquent but 8 per cent of the Negro and Puerto Rican boys did within seven years.

3. Predictions of delinquency were more likely to be made for boys from public assistance families than for boys from self-sufficient families. Thirty-eight per cent of the 52 public assistance boys were given better than a

---

[32] New York City Youth Board, Research Department, A *Study of Mobility and Delinquency in a Sample of Boys in Glueck Project*, mimeographed, February, 1963, p. 6.

[33] Mrs. Maude Craig, research director of the Youth Board, graciously provided unpublished data on the economic status and the ethnic backgrounds of the 223 boys in the study.

Table 5

Differential Impact of a "Bad" Family Situation on Economically Dependent and on Self-sufficient White, Negro, and Puerto Rican Families

| | | 1959 Outcomes | | | | | |
| | | For 1952 Public Assistance Families | | | For 1952 Self-sufficient Families | | |
Ethnic Background	1952 Predictions Two- and Three-Factor Table	Delinquent	Nondelinquent	Total	Delinquent	Nondelinquent	Total
White	Probably delinquent	1	2*	3	0*	1*	1
	Probably nondelinquent	0*	0	0	0	49	49
	Total	1	2	3	0	50	50
Negro	Probably delinquent	4*	9*	13	4	11*	15
	Probably nondelinquent	4*	19	23	3*	77	80
	Total	8	28	36	7	88	95
Puerto Rican	Probably delinquent	3	1*	4	1	0*	1
	Probably nondelinquent	1*	8	9	0*	25	25
	Total	4	9	13	1	25	26
All	Probably delinquent	8	12*	20	5	12*	17
	Probably nondelinquent	5*	27	32	3*	151	154
	Total	13	39	52	8	163	171

* Errors of prediction.

50-50 chance of becoming delinquent—as contrasted with 10 per cent of the 171 boys from self-sufficient families.

4. Predictions of delinquency were more likely to be correct and predictions of nondelinquency more likely to be wrong for public assistance families than for self-sufficient families. This tendency was characteristic of white, Negro, and Puerto Rican families looked at separately; the fact of public assistance had an adverse effect on outcomes regardless of ethnicity.

Interpretation

1. Since the predictions of delinquency were based on pathological family situations, the greater tendency for predictions of delinquency to be made in Negro and Puerto Rican families must be due mainly to the greater incidence of family disorganization in these ethnic groups. This disorganization is highly correlated with dependency and, very likely, with employment opportunities. Note, for example, that only 16 per cent of the boys from self-sufficient Negro families were predicted delinquent—as contrasted with 36 per cent from dependent Negro families.

2. Recall that in the Cambridge-Somerville Youth Study the greater tendency for predictions of delinquency to come true and predictions of nondelinquency to be wrong in slum neighborhoods was interpreted as due to differing neighborhood traditions of delinquency. In the Youth Board study we see again a greater tendency for predictions of delinquency to come true and predictions of nondelinquency to be incorrect in disadvantaged segments of the population, this time among Negroes and Puerto Ricans and among the children of welfare recipients rather than among boys from poorer neighborhoods. Part of the explanation here may be that ethnic traditions of delinquency are analogous to neighborhood traditions of delinquency. Obviously, however, differing ethnic traditions of delinquency cannot explain the fact that boys from public assistance families were more likely to become delinquent within the same ethnic group and the same Glueck prediction category. It is unlikely that public assistance families constitute a community within a community and that the children of such families have a distinct tradition of delinquency. Possibly boys from economically dependent families are more likely to be *recorded* as delinquents than boys from self-sufficient families who are behaving similarly; this assumes that the police know the welfare status of the family and discriminate against the most deprived. This seems to me far-fetched. More likely, economic disadvantage has adverse effects on the school adjustment and (ultimately) on the occupational opportunities of public assistance children.[34] Their greater proneness to delinquency may stem from their lesser hopes for and commitments to legitimate enterprises.[35]

3. Bear in mind that all of the preadolescent boys followed up in the Youth Board Prediction Study came from two high delinquency neighbor-

[34] Richard A. Cloward and Lloyd E. Ohlin, *Delinquency and Opportunity*, Glencoe, Ill.: The Free Press, 1960.

[35] Larry Karacki and Jackson Toby, "The Uncommitted Adolescent: Candidate for Gang Socialization," *Sociological Inquiry*, 32 (Spring, 1962), pp. 203–215.

hoods characterized by considerable gang activity. Yet those members of the Study population *predicted nondelinquent,* i.e., closely supervised by their parents, usually avoided delinquent associates and bore out the prediction. Exceptions to this generalization are Negro boys from public assistance families predicted nondelinquent; 17 per cent of them became delinquent within seven years. Perhaps the double disadvantage of race prejudice and poor economic prospects reduced their stake in conformity.[36]

4. One reason for the overprediction of delinquency is that Table 5 does not include *all* delinquencies committed by the boys in the study from 1952 to 1959; some delinquent acts were undetected or unrecorded. Another reason for the overprediction of delinquency in Table 5 is that some boys became delinquent for the first time *after* 1959. But there remains the possibility that many of the prophecies of delinquency were defeated because deliberate as well as unintentional interventions occurred in the lives of these boys. Families moved to neighborhoods with fewer delinquent gangs; boys joined boys' clubs or the Boy Scouts; social agencies helped the families to solve their problems and thereby improved parental supervision; the schools offered remedial education to slow learners.

Conclusion

The problem of delinquency control has long been the subject of jurisdictional disputes among sociologists, psychologists, social workers and psychiatrists—not to mention lawyers and the police. Recently, "early identification and intensive treatment of predelinquents" has attracted much interest, and it seemed at first that this approach offered a relatively uncontroversial technique of delinquency control.

Careful analysis of two notable experiments in early identification and intensive treatment of predelinquents shows that intellectual confusion lurks beneath the surface plausibility of early identification and intensive treatment. The following issues have not been resolved:

1. Does early identification depend on extrapolating antisocial tendencies already observable in the preadolescent boy or girl into adolescence? Or does early identification consist of locating youngsters who have been exposed to family or community experiences known to cause delinquency?

2. Can *early* identification be accurate? The issue of accuracy is essentially a theoretical problem. Accurate early identification is possible only (a) if no crucial etiological factors make their appearance *after* the predictions are made or (b) if early experiences establish a differential vulnerability for all subsequent experiences.

3. What *kind* of intensive treatment should be given? Does the type of treatment have to be individualized according to the problem of the

---

[36] Jackson Toby, "Social Disorganization and Stake in Conformity: Complementary Factors in the Predatory Behavior of Young Hoodlums," *Journal of Criminal Law, Criminology and Police Science,* 48 (May–June, 1957), pp. 12–17. Arthur L. Stinchcombe, *Rebellion in a High School,* Chicago: Quadrangle Books, 1964, chs. 3 and 4.

youngster? Or are all types of treatment equally effective with all types of delinquents providing treatment is "intensive"?

4. How intensive must "intensive treatment" be and how early must it start in order to satisfy the early identification and intensive treatment formula? (The McCords have dismissed the negative results of the Cambridge-Somerville Youth Study as irrelevant to the validity of the early identification and intensive treatment approach because the treatment program was not sufficiently intensive.)

5. How can early identification and intensive treatment programs avoid "self-fulfilling prophecies"? If the treatment program concentrates its efforts on youngsters who are especially vulnerable to delinquency, how can it justify its discriminatory policy except by stigmatizing predelinquents? And may not the delinquency-producing effects of the stigmatization equal or exceed the delinquency-preventing benefits of the treatment?

6. Finally, is it likely that an effective approach to delinquency control can emerge without clarification of the underlying intellectual issues in the etiology of delinquency? Although they approached early identification of predelinquents in theoretically distinct ways, both the Cambridge-Somerville Youth Study and the New York City Youth Board Prediction Study show that attention to the social context can improve the accuracy of predictions. The neighborhood of residence in the Cambridge-Somerville Youth Study and the dependency status of the family and its ethnicity in the New York City Youth Board Prediction Study were relevant to later outcomes. However, in neither study is it clear *why* predictions of delinquency were more likely to be correct and predictions of nondelinquency wrong for youngsters of disadvantaged social origins. The relationship among social origin, family functioning, individual self-conception, and peer group influence was ignored. Can a theoretically blind prediction technique provide the basis for effective intervention?

III   Problems of Implementing Prevention Programs

Successful prevention programs are predicated upon the existence of adequate theories of delinquent behavior as well as the knowledge and ability to translate these theories into effective programs. However, the existence of adequate theories alone does not guarantee success because of the difficulties of putting theories to effective use. Prevention programs are not implemented under controlled laboratory conditions where problems can always be anticipated and planned for, but are instead implemented in the complex and sometimes chaotic environment of the community where frustrating and disruptive contingencies are likely to arise.

A basic problem in effecting delinquency prevention seems to be that of organizing available resources in order to optimize the attainment of theoretically specified delinquency-reducing conditions. In order to achieve this end, two imperatives must be followed. First, attempts must be made to anticipate difficulties that may interfere with the implementation of the program. Second, the ability to cope with unanticipated problems must be developed.

The specific problems that may pose difficulties for prevention programs are so numerous and diverse that a complete listing is impossible, let alone the provision of precise formulae to serve as a basis for dealing with them. It is possible, however, to mention a number of general problem areas within which the majority of the more specific problems are contained.

First, prevention involves *political* issues, in the broad sense of the word. Obstacles are posed by the belief systems of various citizens who oppose attempts at manipulating human behavior on patriotic, religious, ethical, or other grounds. Individuals whose cooperation is necessary for success sometimes impede achievement of program goals by battling among themselves for positions of authority, resisting innovations in procedures and techniques, resisting surveillance by outside evaluators, and by refusing to coordinate their services and activities with other program. In addition, modification of existing practices or the individuals and agencies who may also be necessary parts of the introduction of new ones often disrupts established routines and evokes resistance from tradition-oriented personnel. If prevention efforts are to be successful, persons responsible for their administration must anticipate these kinds of problems and develop strategies for dealing with them. Otherwise, valuable resources (such as time, energy, and money) will be directed away from the basic goals of the program.

The *target population*—that is, those who are to be the focal point of the program—must also be considered as potential generators of problems. If a program necessitates their active participation, information must be presented to them in a manner that will elicit their cooperation. This is often a sensitive and complex problem because those to be served must be convinced of the benefits that will accrue to them as a direct result of their participation in the program, even though definitive evidence of positive results is frequently not available.

The introduction of a prevention program into a community can stimulate action on the part of other agencies, organizations, and groups, leading to *changes* that can impede as well as facilitate achievement of the goals of the original program. In some instances the changes emanating from the original program may be so extensive that the basic structure of the community or neighborhood is altered. At the very least, changes in orientations, opinions, and activities of individuals and organizations can be expected. Other change problems, such as those of staff turnover and extracommunity events and conditions, must also be anticipated.

Finally, difficulties may be anticipated regarding one of the most essential aspects of any prevention program: its *evaluation*. The evaluative dimension is especially problematical in that frequently strong resistances are encountered from those who work with juveniles regarding objective independent scrutiny of their methods and orientations. Traditionally, those in the helping disciplines have not generally encouraged outside assessment of their claims to producing successful results. The question of evaluation also poses difficulties for the administrator because if the program fails to accomplish its publically stated goals he must face the reactions of those who have been induced to give their time and effort. Shifting the blame to erroneous theories, faulty techniques, or lack of resources is not likely to be successful in alleviating their demands for positive results.

The articles selected for this section illustrate some of the difficulties that preventive efforts encounter. Although they deal to some extent with the issues mentioned above, they also show

that the resolution of problems is not easy and that the present
state of knowledge does not permit the accurate anticipation of
numerous difficulties.

Walter B. Miller discusses the experience of a community in
trying to initiate and carry out a prevention program, and reveals the great range of conflicts that arose between individuals,
agencies, committees, ethnic and religious groups, and others
over a period of several years. He maintains that conflict arises
on a number of issues, and that because institutional structures
vary in terms of these issues, conflict is the natural result. Successful prevention, then, seems to be in part dependent upon coping
with the relationships between these institutional structures.

Michael Schwartz similarly outlines a variety of issues that made
the failure of a prevention planning project a foregone conclusion. Specifying some of the problems that were confronted, he
indicates that some of them were insurmountable despite the
resources available. As Schwartz concludes, "It was always a case
of knowing what needed to be done and being continually unable to do it."

Seymour Halleck takes up the topic of the relationships between professionals and adolescents in clinical settings. He maintains that professionals consistently communicate attitudes and
information to adolescents that both know to be untrue. Such
"dishonesty" does not appear to be highly conducive to preventing misbehavior on the part of juveniles. It is possible to apply
Halleck's discussion to many instances of adult-adolescent contacts and to draw significant implications for the possibility of
successful prevention.

Henry McKay deals specifically with the application of the
theory of differential association to problems of prevention. He
argues that use of this theory implies that one will attempt to
modify value systems, socialization content, and/or opportunities
for misbehavior. He discusses various strategies for prevention and
also shows how several existing programs and practices deal with
issues directly related to the theory of differential association.
Similar kinds of analyses must be made when one selects a particular theoretical framework to use in formulating and implementing prevention programs.

11   Inter-Institutional Conflict as
a Major Impediment to
Delinquency Prevention

WALTER B. MILLER

Juvenile delinquency is a major area of concern in the United States today. Although there is evidence of some increase in the actual incidence of
juvenile crime, it is equally evident that the intensity of public concern
over this issue has increased far more rapidly than the demonstrated statistical increase. This paper will focus, not on juvenile crime as such, but on
the larger adult community, and, in particular, on that segment of the community which maintains explicit responsibility in this area.

It is the thesis of this paper that the nature of current concern over juvenile delinquency serves important latent functions for substantial segments
of the adult community. If this thesis is true, we would expect to find, as
in all areas where a significant discrepancy exists between the overt or recognized aspects of a phenomenon and its covert aspects or latent functions:
(1) Discrepancies and contraditions between officially stated policy and
actual operating procedure; (2) recurrent failure to follow through on plans
whose objectives conform to officially stated positions but whose execution
would in fact run counter to the latent function; (3) much conflict over
goals and methods both between concerned institutional systems and between sub-units within these systems. The net result of these forces would
be to produce action stalemates both through failure to take action and
through mutual blocking of efforts to the end that the latently functional
status quo is preserved.

That public concern over juvenile delinquency serves *psychological* functions for adults as individuals has been maintained by several investigators.
This paper will attempt to show that the nature of current institutional
practice regarding delinquency serves important *structural* functions as well;
that is, for the great majority of organized institutions which maintain
programs directed at juvenile delinquency, the adoption of operating procedures and philosophies which would be effective in reducing juvenile crime
would, in fact, pose severe threats to the viability of the institution. The
focus here will be on the area of delinquency *prevention* rather than on

Reprinted from *Human Organization*, 17 (Fall 1958), 20–23, with permission of the Society for Applied Anthropology and the author.

methods of dealing with the adjudicated delinquent. Since the area of prevention is far less structured and has developed fewer established operating procedures than the area of treatment or disposition, the dynamics of institutional functioning in this area are revealed in much sharper relief.

It has been established that there is far more law-violating behavior by adolescents than is officially acted on; according to one study, the actual number of potentially arrestable delinquents is three times that of those actually arrested. Once an individual is officially apprehended for the commission of a delinquent act or acts, a whole series of established procedures are set into motion; the individual may be released with a warning, put on probation, or sentenced to undergo a variety of corrective measures ranging from a citizenship course through psychiatric treatment to straight confinement. But in the area of "prevention" things are much less well established. There is growing sentiment to the effect that "prevention" of juvenile crime would be a much sounder procedure than attempting to deal with the individual once he has already committed a crime, and would be much more economical in the long run. But then the question becomes—how does one "prevent"? Once something has happened you can take steps as a consequence of that occurrence, but what steps should you take for something that has not happened yet, but which might? Thus, while there are many well-established institutions—courts, police, correctional institutions, psychiatric agencies—whose operating procedures and philosophies are geared to handling individuals who have committed delinquent acts and been apprehended, there are, with a few exceptions, *no* established institutional structures whose major responsibility is delinquency prevention, and whose institutional values and operating philosophies are geared to that objective. Existing organizations undertake prevention, if at all, as a relatively minor adjunct to major institutional responsibilities which lie elsewhere—a fact which has important bearing on the potential effectiveness of prevention programs.

Following sections will describe very briefly the experience of one large eastern city in attempting to institute and maintain a "preventive" program on the community level. In 1950, rising public apprehension over juvenile delinquency in general, and gang violence in particular, produced demands for action from many quarters. Since gang activity was a focus of concern, and much gang delinquency is undetectable or undetected, traditional approaches based on restriction or treatment were seen as unfeasible, and pressures to institute some sort of community-based preventive program were exerted on the major institutional structures with assumed or assigned responsibility in the area of juvenile crime.

I

The city contained scores of intricately interrelated organizations, both public and private, varying widely in size, scope and method of operations, and in assigned or claimed area of jurisdiction or concern with juvenile crime. Of these, about a dozen public and private organizational groupings maintained major responsibility in the area of juvenile crime. The principal public agencies were the municipal government, the recreation department, the police department, the courts, the public schools, and the state youth corrections division. Major private groupings were medical and psychiatric clinics, social work agencies, churches, universities, and various special cause groups, such as ethnic associations and crime prevention societies.

Initial pressures produced a variety of statements as to the desirability of a preventive program, but no action. A complex set of maneuvers was carried on for about three years, usually involving the appointment of special committees which then appointed a study group which turned in a set of recommendations strongly affirming the desirability of a preventive program, and at the same time explaining why such a program was not the responsibility of that particular organization. This continuing stalemate was finally broken early in 1953, primarily through combined pressures from two ethnic groups, the Jews and the Negroes, after a prominent Jewish clergyman had been murdered, allegedly by a Negro teenage gang. The Jews, acting through their organized representative groupings, inferentially charged the Negroes with anti-semitism; the Negroes, through their organized groupings, intimated that this charge indicated anti-Negro sentiment on the part of the Jews. Two other groups whose interests were being threatened by gang activity—the public schools and the settlement houses—added their pressures to those of the Jews and Negroes, and, in the spring of 1953, a central delinquency committee was created, comprising representatives of over one hundred youth-concerned groupings in the metropolitan area, including the major groups cited above. At the time this committee was formed, many statements were made by all groupings—police, courts, the municipal administration, churches, private agencies—pledging their fullest mutual cooperation in this enterprise aimed at coping with the city gang problem.

Despite the sense of urgency and crisis which attended the organization of the central committee, no concrete action was taken for more than a year. This year was filled with indecision, groping for direction, and constant mutual blocking and conflict, sometimes veiled, sometimes overt, among the agencies represented on the central committee. A great variety of proposals was forwarded and debated, reflecting many divergent conceptions of the causes and proper treatment of juvenile crime, and the group seemed unable to reach any agreement on a positive course of action. After six months, a sociology professor at a local university was persuaded to accept responsibility for formulating a plan of action, and in June of 1954—four and a half years after the initial moves, and a year and a half after the murder which had broken the stalemate—a special demonstration project in delinquency prevention was set up in one district of the city. By this time, several of the major organizations originally represented on the central committee had terminated active affiliation—principally, the police and the Jewish clergy. The Jews lost interest rapidly when it developed that anti-semitism had played a relatively small role in gang attacks on Jews.

The prevention project, which was to operate for three years, was staffed primarily by social workers, and included three service programs—a program of direct service to selected "delinquogenic" families, a community organization program, and, as a major effort, a program of direct work with delinquent corner gangs. Although it was the creation of the central committee, once project operations actually started, the committee became progressively disenchanted with its offspring. As the project took action in more definite and visible ways, it became clear that many of its methods and the operating philosophies behind them were in radical conflict with the institutional ideals of the various groups represented on the central committee. This was evidenced in responses ranging from passive non-participation, through withdrawal, to active opposition.

During the three years of the project's existence, the executive board of the central committee became a battleground for its component organizations, with the project and its methods serving as a pawn in these conflicts. After the first meeting, at which a project worker presented a report on his activities, the representative of the Catholic Archdiocese resigned in indignation from the executive board. Following this incident, a watchdog committee was set up to oversee the project; the chairman of this committee was a Protestant clergyman who was strongly opposed to major methods of the project. About a year later the project became involved in direct conflict with the state division of corrections, with enmity reaching sufficient intensity that the corrections division issued an order forbidding its parolees to participate in project activities, and, in fact, jailed one parolee who defied this order. The social agencies initially regarded the program with great suspicion, as did the schools. During the latter part of the program the city recreation department representative on the central committee, incensed by a report issued by the project, demanded that no further reports be issued unless approved by the central committee. During the second year, funds to support the project, which were raised by the central committee, became increasingly difficult to obtain, and about this time the committee's original chairman, who had been active in initiating and supporting the project, was replaced, without his prior knowledge, by another man who was far less assertive.

Shortly after the start of the project's third year, its director resigned, partly because of increasing difficulties in obtaining financing, and no attempt was made to replace him with a person of equivalent status. Before the director left, he formulated a detailed proposal for the establishment of a permanent delinquency prevention agency under state and municipal auspices, using the project's experience as the basis of recommendations. The three-man committee chosen to present this program to the mayor and governor consisted of an amiable but aged chairman and the two most outspoken opponents of the project on the central committee. The recommendations for a state-municipal program presented under these auspices were rejected both by the mayor and governor. Once the program was officially terminated, the central committee appeared eager to forget that it had ever existed. Although federal support for post-project research had been obtained, members of the central committee were most reluctant to permit such continuation and questioned the right of the project to have sought these funds, despite the fact that authorization had been officially voted.

During the period when the project was subject to increasing opposition by its parent organizations on the central committee, these agencies were also engaged in attacking one another both in the arena of central committee meetings and through other media. A judge accused the police of inefficiency in dealing with delinquents and in keeping adequate crime statistics; a police chief accused the social welfare agencies of coddling delinquents; the director of a medical group accused the corrections division of increasing the delinquency of those in their care; a Catholic prelate accused the social work agencies of neglecting religion in their dealings with delinquents; a psychiatric agency head accused the police of harmful advocacy of punitive measures; the Archbishop accused enforcement agencies of politically motivated laxness in prosecuting delinquents; a group of legislators attempted to oust major officials of the youth corrections department over the issue of personnel qualifications. In addition, sub-units within these larger organizations feuded with one another; a judge accused other judges of excessive leniency in dealing with juvenile offenders; a committee of the school department claimed that some teachers were fostering delinquency by being unable or unwilling to cope with school behavior problems; the Police Commissioner castigated and demoted a sizable group of patrolmen, charging them with inefficiency in dealing with juveniles in their area of jurisdiction; a Protestant clergyman claimed that some Protestant sects were failing in the fight against delinquency by remaining too aloof from community involvement.

II

We have, then, a situation which involves these elements: first, a social phenomenon—gang violence—which is universally condemned; a crisis incident which arouses deep feelings and provides a spur to direct action; the mobilization and pledged cooperation of all the major concerned institutional groupings of a major American city; and then—much delay and misdirected energy by these institutions in setting up a project to which they become progressively more hostile; constant inter-institutional conflict over a variety of issues; and finally a virtual stalemate in launching any sort of effective action to cope with the problem. This situation is by no means unique; it is found in many cities faced with similar problems; in particular, conflicts between the police, churches, courts, social agencies, and schools in the New York City gang situation have been widely publicized. This prevalent phenomenon—apparently universal agreement on a basic objective, gang control, coupled with mutual conflict leading to almost complete blocking of action, may be explained by focusing on the *means* proposed to secure the end—means which derive from the operating philosophies of the various concerned organizations. This paper suggests that operating philosophies may be *non*functional for the purpose of reducing juvenile crime, and that a consequence of differences in institutional philosophies is that a significant proportion of energy potentially directable to delinquency reduction is instead expended in conflict between institutions.

The nature of these differences may be illuminated by specifying six dimensions along which conflict takes place: these relate to differences in conceptions of the *etiology* of delinquency; of the *disposition* of the delinquent; of the *approach priority*; of the appropriate *organizational method,* and of the proper *status of personnel.*

Morality-Pathology: A major difference in assumptions as to the etiology of juvenile crime, as well as other forms of behavior, involves fundamental concepts of human nature. According to one school of thought, deviant or criminal behavior must be viewed in terms of morality and immorality; an individual is morally responsible for his own behavior, and failure to conform to norms and standards represents a triumph of evil forces over good in an inner struggle for which the individual is held personally responsible. The opposing school maintains that deviant or criminal behavior should be viewed in terms of sickness and health; that an individual who violates social and legal norms is, in fact, driven by inner forces over which he has relatively little control, and which have their origins in pathological conditions of the organism.

Individual Locus-Social Locus: A second important difference involving etiological concepts relates to the locus of deviant behavior. One school attributes criminal behavior to forces within the *individual*—moral or physical-psychological—which may be dealt with by corrective measures directed at the individual; the other school finds the significant factors in the nature of the *social milieu,* and sees basic alterations in social conditions as the necessary course of action.

Restriction-Rehabilitation: This dimension relates to the proper method of dealing with offenders. The restrictive school of thought advocates the separation or isolation of the individual from normal social intercourse on the assumption, first, that the *protection of society* is the paramount necessity, and second, that punishment both serves as a deterrent to future violation and is merited in consequence of transgression. This dispositional prescription is generally forwarded by those espousing the morality concept of etiology. The treatment or rehabilitative school, basing procedure on the "pathology" conception of etiology, postulates "cure" or directed efforts to modify behavior patterns of the offending individual as of prime importance, with his restoration to normal social interaction a desired objective.

Action-Research: This dimension relates to consideration of priority in approaching the problem. One school maintains that the urgency of the situation, or the intensity of need, demands immediate action, based on the best knowledge currently available; the other maintains that far too little reliable information exists as to the nature of the involved phenomena and methods of treatment, and that the most productive expenditure of energy can be made by undertaking systematic research to gain essential knowledge.

Localization-Centralization: This dimension concerns the issue of the most desirable method for organizing preventive programs; one school believes that programs should be undertaken within and by the local community, on the grounds that only local people are sufficiently familiar with the special conditions of the local situation for adequate understanding, and that local autonomy must be maintained; the centralization school maintains that the nature and magnitude of the problem demand mobilization of resources which local groups, operating independently, could not afford, and that, to be effective, resources must be pooled and efforts coordinated to avoid duplication and overlap.

Lay-Professional: This dimension relates to the qualifications and status of personnel who are to implement preventive programs. One school holds that only those who manifest characteristics similar to those of the subject population—either through similarities in class or locality status—can be effective, and that attributes essential to effectiveness, such as warmth and sympathy, are independent of training; the other school maintains that work in so difficult an area demands that practitioners be exposed to a course of professional training which both imparts knowledge as to specialized procedures and eliminates those whose personality characteristics would be detrimental to this kind of work.

The various institutional structures related to delinquency tend to maintain characteristic syndromes of these etiological and procedural positions. The described positions are seldom maintained in the "pure" form, since they are presented here as polar extremes which define variable dimensions —and "middle positions," such as equal stress on action and research, may be taken, but most institutions involved do maintain definitely identifiable positions of varying intensity along these dimensions. Conflicts along the varying dimensions take place, both *between* and within, concerned institutions, but intra-institutional differences are generally concealed from public notice. The most severe conflict occurs between institutions which take extreme opposing positions on all or most of these dimensions; conflict is less severe when there is disagreement on only one or two. For example, the major juvenile court of the city described above strongly supported the "morality" and "individual locus" concepts of etiology: the restrictive dispositional method, action priority, and localized organization. The major child psychiatry clinic supported the "pathology" etiological concept: rehabilitative treatment method, centralized organization, and use of professional implementary personnel. These positions put the two organizations in direct conflict in four of the six dimensions; in agreement over one—individual etiological locus—and in minor opposition over the action-research issues. Similar comparisons could be made between each set of involved institutions.

Summary

The argument of this paper may be summarized as follows: There is much conflict over the issue of proper procedure among the different groups which maintain varying orders of responsibility for delinquency prevention. This conflict results in a lack of coordination and mutual blocking of efforts leading to a stalemate in reference to a community-supported objective. But these conflicts over method derive from the basic institutional philosophies of the several institutions; although these philosophies may be effective in facilitating achievement of the stated objectives of the institution, their maintenance is vital to the institution's continued existence and this latent objective has greater priority than the achievement of the institution's explicit objectives, and much greater priority than achieving objectives only peripherally related to the institution's primary explicit aims.

This situation would appear to have important implications for delinquency prevention. It would imply that the major impediment to effectiveness in this field relates more to the nature of relations among the various concerned institutions than to a lack of knowledge as to effective procedure. Much is now known about the causes of delinquency and promising ameliorative techniques have been developed. The principal difficulty lies in the *application* of these techniques, and any realistic possibility of such application depends almost entirely on existing institutional structures. This would suggest a shift in emphasis in current research and action efforts, from a primary focus on the relations between implementing institutions and the subject population, to the relationships among the institutions themselves. Both research and action efforts involve severe difficulties since they will touch on areas intimately related to the visibility of the institution—areas all the more charged and sensitive, since they are frequently unconscious or implicit.

12   The Sociologist in an Unsuccessful Delinquency Prevention Planning Project

MICHAEL SCHWARTZ

A few years ago, the late president John F. Kennedy formed the President's Committee on Juvenile Delinquency and Youth Crime, a group that sought to encourage local communities to plan and implement antidelinquency programs. Seventeen cities eventually received planning grants, with the clear understanding that only about half were to receive further financial

Reprinted from *Sociology in Action: Case Studies in Social Problems and Directed Social Change*, ed. by Arthur B. Shostak, pp. 166–176, Homewood, Ill., Dorsey Press, 1966, with permission of the Dorsey Press.

aid in support of their project's action phase. Only one planning grant was made directly to a mayor; the others were made to existing or newly formed nonprofit youth agencies or to coalitions of agencies, both public and private. Under study in this paper is the unique situation wherein the planning grant was made directly to our city's mayor and where the planning project failed to materialize into action—or success.

In all of the nation's delinquency-control planning projects the most essential goal was proposed action aimed at alterations of existing social structure. There was sufficient evidence to indicate that the overwhelming majority of delinquents were not psychotic, neurotic, or feebleminded. Thoughts of saturating high-delinquency areas with therapists were discarded from the start, and the general emphasis was not on personality shifts but on social structural modifications. This attitude was firmly set by members of the President's Committee, and few quarreled with it.

The implications of planning in order to alter the social structure are enormous, and it is not important to this paper to review all of those details here. The most essential point is this: the function of local planning committees was to create a new social system out of the bits and pieces of older ones. Most projects took as their tasks: (1) the innovation of programs for youth and their parents; (2) coordination of the activities of the various agencies dealing with the same population; and (3) changing the ways in which services are "delivered" to people. Some examples of these three activities may clarify the point:

First, certain programs for youth had never been tried before in our community. The establishment of "halfway houses" for juvenile offenders or nursery schools for the "culturally deprived" child are examples of innovations in programming for youth that were considered.

Second, as elsewhere, the local web of social service agencies was very complex. One agency might deal exclusively with a mother, another with her sons, a third with an alcoholic father, while a fourth attempted to interest the parents in the local school. Frequently enough, each agency was unaware of the activities of other agencies with respect to the same family. Some agencies jealously guarded their records to such a degree that sharing privileged information, even with other agencies, was out of the question. Coordination, then, of the various public and private social agencies had the potential for vastly increasing the effectiveness and decreasing the costs of services to agency clients.

Third, changing the nature of delivery systems of social services was considered a critical issue. For example, an unknown number of local people refrained from taking advantage of the facilities of local employment service offices. The reasons were varied, but clearly some feared the endless filling out of forms (which, of course, requires one to be able to read and write); others simply lacked the skills for behaving effectively in bureaucratic settings. Storefront branches of employment offices, run on an informal basis with clerks to fill out the forms, were thought by some planners capable of delivering a service to a segment of the eligible population never before reached.

The aims of the project were simple enough but there were innumerable factors that quickly caused them to become very complex.[1] Major issues were agency autonomy, agency control, and the proper allocation of available funds. Drawing social service agencies together for purposes of central record-keeping, training, and information initially seemed like a good idea—except that the fear of loss of autonomy was an easily predictable one. Dealing with bureaucratic-type personalities was also a predictable problem as were problems associated with motivating certain heads of institutions to sponsor pilot programs of innovative designs. While these problems were foreseen, the failure of the planning project clearly indicates that they were not well handled.

The task was large, but it was not impossible. There was resistance of the bureaucratic variety, but resistance came from other sources as well. When the planning grant was made, there was both overt and covert hostility in the city. Open criticism came from some mass-media sources which argued that the city had been involved in a number of planning programs in the past but little action had ever come from them. They argued that the money was about to be wasted again, that we knew what to do (i.e., get more police action) and we ought to get on with it. Covertly, middle-class whites argued that we were about to spend more tax dollars on the Negroes and that it would not help, while some Negroes resented the city's apparently saying that juvenile crime was only a Negro problem. Furthermore, while the planning committee was established and appointed by the mayor, the City Council had to approve expenditures. At this time the mayor was confronted by a relatively unfriendly council, representing yet another source of resistance.

Local business and industry engaged in what might best be termed "passive resistance." Representatives of these institutions did not offer aid, even though the question of jobs and job training for youth was of major importance to the project. A brief anecdote may serve to illustrate this point: In my capacity as a project consultant, I was visited by two representatives of an advertising agency who handled a large auto manufacturing account. They wanted to know how their client could best help in the program. I believe at that moment I had approximately 20 different ideas and offered them all with some enthusiasm: job training, after-school jobs, work-study programs, visits to the schools to tell the kids about the facts of economic life and the skills they will need, and so on. "Well, we were thinking more in terms of something like a soap-box derby." I believe that I spent several hours trying to describe what the real needs were and trying to convince them there was a long-run payoff for the company (altruism was clearly a futile appeal). But for the most part my suggestions fell on deaf ears.

Interestingly, a very major source of support for the program came from religious institutions. Since the formal church atmospheres seemed to have little appeal to either lower class Negroes or whites, the churches had al-

---

[1] For an excellent description of research problems in action programs of this sort see Walter B. Miller, "The Impact of a 'Total Community' Delinquency Control Project," *Social Problems*, 10 (Fall, 1962), pp. 168–91.

ready been involved in trying to establish storefront Protestant churches. They had also been working on informal church-sponsored recreation programs and coffee shops, and were trying to find employment for some youths. While the ministers provided great support for project morale, their power to influence key decision makers in government, business, or social agencies was very limited.

One final note on early resistance to the project: Without elaborating or belaboring the issue, it is obvious that in any delinquency prevention program, the public schools will be very heavily involved. Some criminologists, like Cohen and others, view the school as the key institution in terms both of its meaning for lower-class life and its possible role as the source of more problems for children than it solves. The planning program necessarily had to deal with the schools, which were not controlled by city government officials. But the time was inauspicious. Two teacher factions were waging war over unionizing the teachers; both were pressing serious demands on the school board. A referendum to increase property taxes for school support had just been defeated; and the superintendent had just put the first, third, fifth and seventh grades in all schools on half-day shifts. Approaching him with issues of expanding certain services, initiating new programs, and changing to nongraded primary schools proved futile. If ever a single situation contributed to the demise of a project, this was it. It placed such structural constraints on the planners that they, in effect, had to plan *around* what was perhaps the single most important institution in the community. The superintendent of schools refused any and all commitment to the project from its very beginning. That fact in itself was enough to doom the project, but there were other factors which made modification of the school situation impossible.

The point of all of this discussion is to indicate two things. First, there existed serious structural constraints on the success of the project in the community before the planning program ever began. Second, my attention as a sociologist had been almost totally diverted from these constraints and was focused almost entirely upon the scope of the delinquency problem and its etiology. Though most of these constraints were not immediately apparent to me, within a month or two they became clear. They seemed, however, important problems for the planning committee to handle, and it was my assumption that this was precisely what the committee was to do. But the external constraints were not overcome, and there are several important reasons for this.

It is necessary to emphasize again that the planning was carried out by a mayor's committee. That fact was important for two reasons. First, the mayor was permitted under this arrangement to make all appointments to the committee without the consent of the city council. And second, the members of the committee were not to be civil-service employees, since their positions were viewed as temporary ones. That is, everyone who was to serve on the committee would be on leave of absence from some other position, such as a university professorship. The first issue is most critical, but the second point is of some concern also, because a hostile city council was now free to harass the mayor by harassing his committee.

The council had no control over the appointments, but it did control the committee's funds. It pressed hard to place the committee on civil-service status and consumed an enormous amount of the committee's time in council hearings and in civil-service commission investigations. One reason for attempting to place committee members on civil-service status may well have been an attempt to cut salaries, which were higher than those of members of the council in several cases. When this attempt failed, the council exercised its right to control the allocation of funds earmarked for the committee's use. If we wanted to shift some money from one planning project account to another, it had to be approved; there were several battles on that score.

That all of this occurred was no secret to administrators of social agencies who were beginning to believe that the committee was being "emasculated," or, at least, was becoming a political football. This belief did not relieve their feeling that the committee threatened their autonomy, but rather reinforced the feeling. The private agencies were now less likely to become involved with the committee if involvement meant similar political entanglements and a reduction in freedom of operation. The political nature of the situation made the situation with the community service agencies much more difficult than it had been originally.

The mayor's plan was to appoint an executive director who would make other committee appointments with the mayor's approval. The selection of the director was a key issue in determining the success or failure of the project. It was not enough that the director be knowledgeable with regard to the city and its problems, he also needed to be respected by social agency heads, school personnel, law enforcement officials and the like. He had to be free as well from local political ties to prevent city council members from involving him in irrelevant disputes.

Even with 20-20 hindsight, I cannot be sure of the reasons for the mayor's final selection of his director, since I was not appointed to the committee until nearly a year later. But it had been widely rumored that the appointment was clearly political in nature. The man finally selected as director was a probation officer; some social agency personnel believed he had worked hard in the mayor's campaign for election and assumed that the mayor was now simply repaying him. At the same time an office manager and a "community organization coordinator" were appointed. The latter was a political hanger-on, and his appointment reinforced the community-wide notion that the directorship itself was now a political position.

These appointments were ill-advised for several reasons. They provided the hostile council members with a new weapon; they antagonized—even infuriated—local social agencies; they were unacceptable to the few community leaders in the local area where action was to have been directed. From this point forward, whatever supported the project had developed was lost. There was city-wide consensus that it was a political boondoggle—

but the appointments stood. The director tried to hire other staff members: a research coordinator, a program coordinator, an agency service analyst, and a person to serve as a liaison officer with the schools. In nearly a year he failed to fill even one of these positions. Locally, the community had been so broadly antagonized by the appointments that no one would accept a position, and a broader national search proved ineffective also, largely because the positions were only temporary ones. Consequently, on a two-year planning grant, the first year was lost. This was, then, a massive self-fulfilling prophecy. Local people believed the project doomed to failure; they withheld needed support; the project failed.

At about this point, the President's Committee intervened, it being clear to them that little was being done. Local persons concerned about the situation informed them of it and they made every effort possible to alter it. The situation was taking place, after all, during an election year in a politically important city, one with a liberal mayor but which had supported a Republican governor.

After a considerable amount of cajoling, coercion, and persuasion, it was announced that the present director of the project would become the administrative director and that an executive director would be hired. The mayor backed away from his appointment, and asked a search committee to locate a new director. The man chosen appeared a good choice. The new director had no political ties; he was a professor of education, well respected in his field; he knew many local agency heads, at least casually; and while the first director was white, the new one was a Negro. He did not live in the city, but took a leave from the university and moved to town.

The new director seemed equal to the task. Resistance was higher than it had been in the past, but some of the personal hostility toward the directorship had abated. There was still a wait-and-see attitude everywhere. The new director immediately began to locate and appoint personnel. His program coordinator came from the Urban League and it was generally agreed that he was an excellent man; I agreed to leave the sociology department of the university for a year and became research coordinator; the juvenile court statistician was hired; an unexpectedly fine public school principal joined the staff as liaison with the schools. In addition, a female social worker joined the staff and a second woman with an M.A. in sociology was hired as a sort of Jack-of-all-trades. All of these appointments took place within 30 days of the new director's taking office, but it was another month or two before all staff members were on the job. What had been a two-year planning project was now left with about nine months. That meant working seven days a week and evenings. We believed that we were beginning to move and we knew that our progress was being observed carefully.

My job as a research coordinator was clear. It involved locating a "target area" of the city—an area with the highest rates of delinquency, adult crime, welfare cases, unemployment, etc. These data were readily available and a block of contiguous census tracts was defined as the target area. The next step was to assess the variety and extent of social services available to people in that area, to determine the manner in which those services were delivered, and to estimate the degree to which people were not being served and the reasons for that lack.

This task proved nearly impossible. In the first place, agency data were either inadequate or were not made available to us. Second, the social worker who was to aid me in this work at one point simply refused to do so, claiming that she was a casework specialist and found the legwork of such data gathering to be demeaning. Her orientation to psychoanalytic casework caused her to oppose practically every bit of research and planning to be done. Five months later, she was fired.

The "target area" research task was never adequately completed. Aside from internal conflict and unavailability of data, time was short, and a research staff of one man seemed to be ludicrous. The best I could do was analyze the vast complexity of the network of interrelated agencies, indicating, for example, the fact that clients often had to travel long distances by bus to reach agencies which then sent them back across town to other agencies. Even from such a simple analysis, some reasonably fruitful ideas for programs did emerge.[2] Nevertheless, this bit of work was extraordinarily frustrating. The most difficult problem was the obvious lack of access to data protected by the agencies. No amount of pleading with the project director was sufficient to get him to intervene. I assumed, at that point, that he was willing to sacrifice the adequacy of the research in order to preserve the good will of the agencies for later negotiations with them over new programs. But since those programs would depend heavily on research, his attitude seemed self-defeating.

Three more research tasks of major concern were undertaken. First, I decided extended interviews with adolescents in the target area were necessary to plan programs to meet the self-perceived needs of the adolescents. The research went very well, and the interview data were transcribed, coded, and analyzed in about five months time. The interviews provided some first-rate insights into the problems that adolescents perceived and gave us some clues to the kinds of programming most needed and most likely to succeed.[3] In a second way, this was very satisfying work. While our main research

---

[2] For example, we were able to propose a central service agency for the target area. That was to have been one building with at least one representative from every relevant agency located in it. It was to have included facilities for central record-keeping, training of new personnel, and most important, it was to be open 24 hours a day, 7 days a week. It was designed to untangle the web of services, make data on families immediately available to concerned agencies, and to make access to service more open.

[3] These data have been published: Michael Schwartz and George Henderson, "The Culture of Unemployment: Some Notes on Negro Children," in Arthur B. Shostak and William Gomberg (eds.), *Blue Collar World*, Englewood Cliffs, N.J.: Prentice-Hall, Inc., 1964, pp. 459–68; Michael Schwartz and William Burkhart, "Self Concept In Casework With Adaptive Delinquents," *Social Work*, July, 1964, pp. 86–90; Michael Schwartz, "Some Collected Notes on Negro Youth From the Low Socio-Economic Class," *Interracial Review*, February, 1965, pp. 38–46.

concern was with providing interview-based data useful for programming, I was additionally able to examine some of Cohen's propositions [4] on working-class delinquency, and some of Miller's as well.[5] While this may seem to be a trivial point, one of my major problems was my transition from academic preoccupation with theoretical and methodological issues to an atmosphere of practical, applied research demanded on schedule. Importantly, there was little conflict between research and planning personnel on this project, but that is not always the case. This bit of research experience was gratifying.

The third study that was conducted was also most rewarding. The goal here was to determine differences in family structure, mobility, and employment patterns between the Negroes and the Southern white migrants in the target area. Our purpose was to determine the extent to which different patterns of social organization and subcultural phenomena might require different program approaches. We learned, for example, that the position of the Southern whites in the labor market seemed to be a fair equivalent to that of the Negroes. We also found evidence that the Southern whites were underrepresented on welfare and relief rolls and that Negroes were overrepresented. We located two important and related pieces of data: First, the Southern whites returned to the South when they were "broke" as often or more often than when they had money, and second, they often developed patterns of exchanging interfamilial economic aid when some were unemployed. These factors kept them off the relief rolls and supported the impression that the Southern whites maintained an ethic of independence and did not easily become urbanized. These were most important observations for our planning.

Armed with such data, members of our committee met with several social agency heads. And here, I think, came one of the greatest frustrations of the entire experience. I argued that our observations indicated that delivering services to Southern whites in the same manner as to Negroes would likely prove unsuccessful, or, if "successful," could mean increasing the dependency of the people served where such dependency had not previously existed. There is the possibility that the presentation of our data was not very tactful. But I had resolved to make my point as strongly and as logically as possible. I concluded by asking the agencies to consider alternatives to their usual approaches; I wanted the agencies to become part of the planning process and to develop some commitment to the project on their own. Their response was unimpressive. Follow-up phone calls usually produced no results, and we began to find fewer and fewer people in their offices. I was sure that the response to the data was hostile and that I had finished the job of thoroughly alienating the agencies.

Much later, after the program had collapsed, some agency people explained to me that they had found the data significant, especially since the

---

[4] Albert K. Cohen, *Delinquent Boys: the Culture of the Gang*, New York: The Free Press of Glencoe, Inc., 1956.

[5] Walter B. Miller, "Lower Class Culture as a Generating Milieu of Gang Delinquency," *Journal of Social Issues* 14: April, 1959.

data backed up many of their own hunches. They had not been responding to the data in a hostile way at all, but to something quite different. For nearly 18 months the agencies had been fairly well ignored as a source of planning ideas. Their interpretation of the meeting was that we were in a bind and could not understand an issue that was a social work problem because we were not social workers. Now it was their turn to let us "sweat a bit." At this point the new project director should have mollified the agencies and persuaded them to participate, and he did not.

Any social psychologist would agree that the determining of a man's motives is at best a difficult business. But my impressions of the situation are clear. The director gave an average of three or four public speeches a week, and he had moved to a very high-status area of the city. His prestige in the middle-class Negro community was soaring and he seemed to enjoy it. The building and maintaining of that prestige consumed much of his time and ours, at a period when time was the one fixed variable in the situation. Negotiating with agencies also required much time and energy, but the planning project received less and less of the director's time each week. While he possessed the requisite skills for negotiation, he apparently perceived his position as that of a figurehead occupying an honorific position with few obligations attached. He seemed to think of himself as the "company Negro" on display; the innumerable invitations to speaking and social engagements reinforced that self-percept. Agency heads began to think of him in this way also, and he was consequently eliminated from the negotiation process. This combination of his definition of his role and his delight with newly acquired status helped lead to the ultimate collapse of the project.

Only two of us were left to carry out the crucial negotiations: the research coordinator and the program coordinator. As negotiators, we were both most unsatisfactory substitutes for the director: neither was a social worker, neither was over 30, and neither was widely known in the community. Moreover, both of us were clearly defined by the agencies as staff people, well down on the status hierarchy. Nevertheless, the two of us had to carry on the negotiations, and this was added to our already enormous work loads.

The more we attempted to carry on the negotiation process the worse became our relations with other agencies. Heads of agencies did not expect to be asked to discuss such critical issues with people in lower administrative positions, and they began to withdraw all support. Recognizing that it was futile to continue in this way, we halted our efforts in this respect very quickly, and the end of the road had been reached. Only a rapid shift in the behavior of the director could have salvaged the project and we were quite unable to bring it about. It is clear that the members of the President's committee were aware of these problems and, while they made efforts to alter the situation, the extent to which they felt able to intervene again in local affairs was restricted and the time was too short.

In any case, by this time the planning period was ending. Committee members were going through the motions of completing reports and compiling them in book form. As research coordinator I went through the motions of designing evaluation research projects for programs of action which clearly would never come into being. It became an intellectual challenge, but there was always a feeling of futility about that work. And somehow, sociologist or not, I kept hoping for an accident to occur—some unexpected, low-probability event that would get us to the action stage. It did not occur. Our staff flew to Washington for a review of our work. It was all very polite —and the project was finished.

There remains the real frustration of having seen the outcome in advance and having been powerless to alter it. I would like to believe that I had not defined the situation as a failure in advance and then aided in causing that failure to occur. I believe that the structural and social-psychological constraints on success were so strong that little could have happened to alter the events. The frustration is increased because I could have resigned when the realities became apparent but I elected to stay on, since leaving might have damaged the project still further. And the feeling of defeat is only strengthened by the fact that there are about 80,000 children and adolescents who are, after all, the victims of such a failure. Their lives might not have been made easier by the proposed action programs, but there would have been at least some chance for them.

It should be clear to most observers of the human scene that the death of such programs only rarely is accorded a full-fledged funeral. In this case, to permit public awareness of the defeat would have been gross political stupidity, and a most convenient "out" was at hand. City government was getting some planning under way for an antipoverty program. The newspapers carried a story indicating that the delinquency prevention planning program was to be absorbed by the antipoverty program. Many of the programs planned by our committee were most suitable for inclusion in a "war on poverty" program. But while the delinquency prevention program was dead, the community never understood what had happened. The project appeared to be involved in bureaucratic reorganization at the point at which it disappeared from public view.

Much of the above description is, in my judgment, accurate. Some may wish to argue with my interpretation of the events, and I must point out that to some extent I have written from limited information. But, in any case, it is a view of the scene from the position of one of the actors. The work of the planning committee may yet pay off in unexpected ways. Personally I found much frustration and little gratification. It was always a case of knowing what needed to be done and being continually unable to do it. Other projects in other cities failed also; some for similar reasons, some for different ones. The sociologist's task in reviewing these situations is to point out the causes of failure and suggest possible directions for their elimination. In some cases he will be able to act in terms of his observations, in other cases he will not. Regardless, the task needs to be done.

13   The Impact of Professional
Dishonesty on Behavior of
Disturbed Adolescents

SEYMOUR L. HALLECK

The role of dishonesty on the part of those who treat the emotionally disturbed has been inadequately examined. Thomas Szasz, a provocative psychiatric theoretician, has made a beginning effort in this direction by examining the issue of lying, both conscious and unconscious, as it relates to communication of the patient to the worker.[1] There has been no attention paid, however, to the problem of dishonesty in the other direction, namely, from the professional worker to the client or patient. Szasz touched on this issue when he discussed the need of persons in our society to maintain traditional cultural patterns by lying to their children. He postulates that much of adolescent rebellion may be related to the fact that it is during this time of life that the adolescent first becomes intellectually mature enough to perceive that significant adults in his life have lied to him repeatedly.

These concepts raise intriguing issues for those who are entrusted with the professional management of disturbed adolescents. Is it possible that they communicate information, values, and morals to adolescent clients that they themselves do not believe fully? Do professional workers contribute to the perpetuation of rebellious behavior or do they perhaps even precipitate it by a failure to present themselves and their world in an honest, straightforward manner? The answer to these questions may unfortunately be a qualified "yes."

Most adults, including child care workers, do fail at times to communicate an honest picture of the adult and adolescent world to their patients. They are often less than straightforward in presenting themselves as helping persons. In subtle ways they communicate a wish for the adolescent to develop values and moral codes that many adults would themselves have difficulty in accepting. The dishonesty described in this paper is frequently perpetu-

[1] *The Myth of Mental Illness, Foundations of a Theory of Personal Conduct*, New York: Paul B. Hoeber, 1961.

ated by parents and other adults who come into contact with adolescents. While such behavior is obviously deleterious when nonprofessionals are involved, it is especially harmful when employed by a professional youth worker.

In approaching an issue as emotion-laden as lying, the author is tempted to be provocative, cynical, or pessimistic. It is not his intention to communicate these attitudes. He contends, however, that adult workers in all the clinical behavioral sciences tend to lie to their adolescent patients. The lying may at times be on a fully conscious basis; at other times it may be more or less beyond awareness. The net effect of this behavior is to confuse and at times infuriate the adolescent, which in itself may produce greater rebellion, more symptoms, and more pain—or exactly the opposite of the original goals. As is true for most dynamic situations, whether one is dealing with individuals or with groups, positive growth must often follow a painful appraisal of less acceptable behavior and motivations. A realistic examination of dishonest behavior on the part of professional workers can then be considered a painful but necessary procedure that may encourage freedom to develop new and more effective techniques.

This discussion is focused primarily on the interaction of professionals with adolescents who are either institutionalized or who are involved with community agencies. This group certainly constitutes the great majority of adolescents who come into contact with psychiatrists, psychologists, sociologists, and social workers. In some instances, particularly in private practice, when the worker may function only as the patient's—or at most the family's—agent, some of the aspects of dishonest behavior may not apply, and these exceptions will be noted. There are at least seven areas in which adolescent clients are deceived either through conscious fabrication or through subtle and unconscious communication of attitudes to which professional workers do not adhere.

The Lie of Adult Morality

In confronting the chaotic sexuality and poorly controlled aggressiveness of the adolescent, most professional workers tend to communicate the possibility of a world in which such impulses are resolved easily. They imply that adults control their impulses and that success in the world is dependent upon such restraint. To a limited extent this is certainly true. Too often, however, they present a picture of the world that is far removed from reality and does not take cognizance of the social usefulness of certain kinds of aggressive and sexual behavior. The adolescent boy knows that aggressiveness, and sometimes unscrupulous aggressiveness, may be a prerequisite for success. He knows that the interviewer sitting behind the desk has probably struggled aggressively to gain the status of a professional position. The sexually promiscuous adolescent girl knows (even if she has not read the Kinsey report) that on a statistical basis the professional person with whom she interacts has probably at some time in his life been guilty of the same behavior for which she is being punished.

It may be unrealistic to communicate readily the worker's own deficiencies and therefore provide the adolescent rationalizations for disturbed behavior. There is a frequent tendency, however, to err in the other direction. Professionals communicate a picture of themselves and their world as one in which only the highest type of values and moral standards prevail. The adolescent cannot understand this. His personal experiences, his observational powers, and his intuitiveness tell him that something is wrong. He wants to like and to identify with adults, but he is painfully aware of an inconsistency or basic dishonesty in their approach. He may then come to believe that adults are incapable of being anything but "phony" and react by rebellious behavior or isolation from the adult world.

This type of dishonesty is seen with considerably less frequency in private psychotherapeutic interactions, especially with adults. Here the worker tries to produce a climate in which the universality of antisocial impulses is accepted and usually discussed freely. An unwillingness to extend this same honesty to a large portion of adolescent patients is a serious error. The adolescent is struggling to understand the adult world. He will learn the truth about it whether he is told or not.

The Lie of Professional Helpfulness

The professional worker who confronts adolescents in the courtroom, the community clinic, or the state institution serves a dual role, as an agent of the community and as a helping person. The community wants him to control, attenuate, or in some way modify the behavior of an individual who is causing it some distress. The worker is also interested in his client; he feels some wish to make the disturbed adolescent a more comfortable and effective person. It is important to understand, however, that in the majority of these situations (there are exceptions in private practice) the worker does not function as an agent of the adolescent patient. His salary is paid by the community. When the community's needs conflict with the adolescent's needs, it is the community that must be obeyed and decisions are not always made entirely in the patient's interest. It is still possible within the limitations of this role for the worker to maintain an honest identification as someone who wants to help the adolescent. If he does not communicate, however, that one of his most basic roles is other than help oriented, he is being dishonest.

Most adolescents do not seek help; they are sent. For example, take the case of an adolescent boy who has been a behavior problem in school and has been referred to the school psychologist. The boy is told that he must see a professional person and that the psychologist will try to help him. He knows, however, that the school is somewhat provoked with him and that its officials are going to act to prevent him from being an annoyance. He does not know what will be done. He does know that the school psychologist, functioning as the agent of the community, may exert a tremendous amount of power over him. As a result of his interaction with this professional worker he may be removed from school, forced to attend special classes, or even removed from his home and sent to an institution. No matter how benign a person the school psychologist then turns out to be, it is very difficult for the adolescent to perceive him as a helping person.

As long as the worker and the adolescent are aware of the fact that the professional may be participating in mutually antagonistic roles, effective communication is possible. The situation is complicated, however, when the worker pretends that his only motivation in seeing the adolescent is to help him. The adolescent realizes that this is obviously untrue. He then perceives the adult worker as dishonest, which only makes him want to be dishonest in return. Experienced workers have learned that the word "help" rarely evinces a positive response from the adolescent. He experiences it as a kind of "Kafka"-like double-talk. In many settings, then, the word "help" is perceived by the adolescent as an unreliable and perhaps dangerous word.

The Lie of Confidentiality

The issue of confidentiality is closely related to the problem of helpfulness. Most caseworkers, psychologists, and psychiatrists have been taught that the model for a professional helping relationship is derived from the psychotherapeutic situation. In traditional forms of psychotherapy the communications of the patient or client to the worker are considered private material to be shared with no one outside the treatment situation. Many of the techniques professional workers use in interviewing, evaluating, diagnosing, or counseling the adolescent are derived from what they were taught about psychotherapy. Often the worker behaves as though the adolescent is entitled to expect confidentiality and as though it were going to be provided. It is extremely rare for the adolescent to be told directly who is going to see the report the worker writes, who is going to read it, and with whom the case is going to be discussed.

The issue here, as with helpfulness, is that the worker cannot guarantee confidentiality to the patient since he is not the agent of the patient. The worker has obligations to the child's family, his clinic, his agency, or his institution. Even if after submitting an initial diagnostic report he begins to see the adolescent in a more traditional psychotherapeutic relationship, complete confidentiality can rarely be promised. While it is true that useful communication can take place between the worker and the adolescent without the guarantee of confidentiality, it is also true that to imply that this guarantee is extended, or to extend it with the full knowledge that it is not meant to be kept, can result in development of situations that inhibit communication. It does not take a very clever adolescent to understand that the worker has primary responsibilities to his agency and to the community. He may fully understand that whatever information he gives will be shared with others and can be used in making important decisions about him. If professionals do not let him know this, he will perceive their behavior as dishonest, and his communications to the adult world will be effectively diminished.

The Lie of Rewards for Conformity

The necessity of conforming to adult standards is most often communicated to adolescents whose behavior deviates from the norms of the community. To this sizable proportion of disturbed adolescents, professional workers seem to be saying, "Your behavior is unacceptable, it produces more difficulty and leads you to experience more pain. It is to your own infinite advantage to be passive, to conform, to obey." There is ample evidence, however, that in attacking the behavioral defenses of the adolescent, workers remove character armor, leaving him more susceptible to anxiety. There is really little in the way of pleasure that can be promised to the adolescent if he risks giving up characterological defenses. This has been discussed previously in terms of the problems imposed on the criminal when he is viewed as a "patient."

> Society and the psychiatrist in particular may be imposing an almost intolerable burden on the delinquent in asking him to exchange the "bad" role for the sick role. It is not surprising that the criminal looks upon the usual rehabilitation program with cynicism and distrust. Only when those in charge of treatment searchingly ask themselves what they are trying to do to the delinquent when they try to make him into a conforming citizen and are able to appreciate what he is giving up in accepting the sick role can therapy be successful.[2]

It is always a moving, sometimes an overwhelming, experience to see an adolescent abandon behavioral expressions of conflict for a more introspective way of life. This is never accomplished without considerable pain and sometimes despair. If the adolescent is told that the simple expedient of conforming to adult standards produces pleasure, he is told a lie. Conformity on the part of the adolescent certainly meets the immediate needs of the community; whether it meets the needs of the individual adolescent is questionable. When workers pretend to him that it does, they encounter only confusion and anger, especially when he experiences the inevitable anxieties that come when he attempts to control his behavior.

Denial of Limitations

The majority of adolescents who come to the attention of community agencies are from troubled homes and lower socio-economic groups. Many of them have been subjected to severe psychological and economic deprivations. Their educational experiences have been limited. Psychiatric studies have produced data which indicate that the effects of early emotional deprivation are to a certain extent unmodifiable.[3] Deficiencies in early educa-

[2] Seymour L. Halleck, "The Criminal's Problem with Psychiatry," *Psychiatry*, 23, No. 4 (November 1960).

[3] J. Bowlby, "A Note on Mother-Child Separation as a Mental Health Hazard," *British Journal of Medical Psychology*, 31, No. 3–4 (1958), pp. 247–248; G. Engel, F. Reichsman, and H. Segal, "A Study of an Infant with Gastric Fistula in Behavior and the Rate of Total Hydrochloric Acid Secretion," *Psychosomatic Medicine*, 18, No. 5 (October 1956), pp. 374–398; H. Harlow, "The Nature of Love," *The American Psychologist*, 13 (1958), pp. 673–685.

tional experiences may also seriously limit potentialities for achievement in the world.

The average professional worker comes from a middle-class background, which in our culture implies a far greater potentiality than that seen in most adolescent clients. (Here we must, of course, exclude selected disturbed adolescents of superior intelligence, of middle-class background, or from reasonably well-integrated homes.) Many workers fail to see that with a few exceptions they are dealing with people of limited potential who will never be like them. Failing to realize this fact, the worker may then encourage identifications, ambitions, and achievements that are not possible for his client and which leave the adolescent with a feeling of frustration.

Few workers are guilty of consciously pushing their clients to achieve beyond their limits. Many of them, however, repeatedly deny the impressive limitations of some of their patients and assure them that the development of certain identifications and goals is entirely possible. This is a type of unconscious dishonesty that may produce considerable harm. The adolescent may righteously say to himself, "Who is this guy kidding? Is he trying to reassure me or reassure himself? Maybe he's trying to humiliate me by throwing my inadequacies in my face. He'll never understand me."

"Open Up; Trust Me; All Will Go Well"

A close relationship is a foundation of any successful therapeutic interaction. Experiencing closeness to another person leads to the possibility of examining one's behavior in such a way that unfavorable personality defenses can be modified or exchanged for more useful ones. Most professional workers leave school with the feeling that they will be successful with clients if they can persuade them to be open and close. The adolescent, however, especially the disturbed adolescent, frequently is struggling with some of the negative aspects of closeness that he experiences as stultifying or smothering. He has begun to find certain types of relationships among his peers that provide him with a feeling of considerably more safety. To abandon movement in this direction and again attempt to develop a close relationship with an adult involves grave risk-taking for him. He is well aware that the little freedom he has gained may have to be surrendered if too much closeness develops.

If the worker realizes this, he can gently, tactfully, and with some humility gradually allow a meaningful, nonsymbiotic relationship to develop between him and the child. In a healthy close relationship between adolescent and adult, the adolescent is allowed certain kinds of independence, dignity, and, of course, distance when he wants it. The social structure in which most professional workers function makes it extremely difficult to provide this kind of relationship. They usually begin in settings in which they have tremendous power over the adolescent, who is thrown into a forced dependency. The adolescent is often forced into a relationship that he, at least on a conscious level, has not sought. The possibility of prolonged relationships is often limited by the fact that both professionals and their clients are extremely mobile, frequently changing responsibilities, jobs, and geographical locations. A sustained, intensive relationship is not a common occurrence in most situations developed in community agencies.

Professional workers are guilty, nevertheless, of continuously exhorting the adolescent to "open up; trust me; if you rely on me and share things with me, all will go well." But the disturbed adolescent knows that this is not true! He knows that the person who is pleading with him to expose himself may be a person with whom he will have only limited future contacts and whom he can see few reasons for trusting. He is further aware of the possibility that he can lose much in such a relationship and that the worker may not really be offering a true intimacy between equals. To the adolescent it seems like a poor bargain. He feels that the worker is dishonest in offering this type of bargain and he reacts with fear, distrust, and cynicism.

"We Like You But Not Your Behavior"

Anyone who has spent much time with adolescents knows that their behavior can be provocative, frustrating, and at times infuriating. It is distressing to see how few professional workers are willing to admit honestly how angry they get with their adolescent clients. This anger frequently is rationalized with statements to the effect that "I like you but not your behavior." Sometimes the worker's anger is totally denied but comes out only through his behavior toward the adolescent. In these types of situations workers sometimes tell the adolescent that they are not really angry with him but they feel that he must be disciplined for his own good, and that by depriving him of privileges or changing his situation, they are really trying to help him. Frequently this anger is displaced onto the parents or onto other professional workers. Anyone who works with adolescents in a community or institutional setting is painfully aware of the extreme rivalry and sometimes open animosity between individual professionals and their groups. The fact is that it is almost impossible to work with adolescents for any period of time without becoming periodically angered.

It is dishonest and unfair both to the worker and to the adolescent to deny, rationalize, or displace this anger. It belongs in the therapeutic situation and should be communicated with as much restraint, tact, and honesty as the worker is capable of providing. To do less than this establishes a basically dishonest pattern of interaction and precludes the possibility of the adolescent experiencing positive emotional growth. He knows that adults at times find him intolerable and cannot be expected to co-operate or communicate with people who are unwilling to admit this fact.

Prerequisites to an Honest Approach

By the time the professional worker comes to his first meeting with the adolescent he is encountering a child who has probably been lied to repeatedly by his parents and relatives. If the adolescent has also had experiences with welfare agencies this situation may have been compounded through dishonest behavior on the part of professional workers. The child may by this time have learned a variety of techniques of resistance to cope with what he perceives to be the "phoniness" of adults. This situation is one of the most important contributing factors to the sullen inertia and negativism so often found with adolescent clients. A good portion of the malignant effects of this factor can be ameliorated through a change in techniques and attitudes on the part of the worker directed toward a more honest interaction. When efforts are made toward more scrupulous honesty with adolescent patients it is almost invariably gratifying to discover a child who is more open, talkative, and willing to discuss areas of life that are not ordinarily communicated. The child seems almost delightfully surprised to discover that he can talk to an adult in a free and easy manner.

The methods of developing an honest approach to an adolescent patient or client are uncomplicated and straightforward. They are based on a conviction on the part of the worker that he is going to be scrupulously honest with himself and the child when he discusses or implies attitudes toward the seven areas considered earlier. It is only necessary for the worker to be aware of any tendency to convey untrue attitudes and ideas and to make a constant effort to avoid doing so. A useful illustration can be obtained through outlining the behavior and attitudes of a professional who is trying to avoid the pitfalls previously discussed. The techniques and attitudes employed by this hypothetical worker in his interactions with adolescent patients will be described. These techniques, whether utilized by youth workers, teachers, or parents, can effectively increase communication between adults and adolescents.

With respect to the "lie of adult morality" no effort is ever made by the worker to criticize, disparage, or in any way condemn the adolescent's antisocial behavior. Rather, it is considered as something the community (rightly or wrongly) will not tolerate if done openly and, most important, as something that *has not served the social or personal needs* of the adolescent. A routine and essential part of an initial interaction with any adolescent consists of a careful assessment of the net gains and losses caused by his behavior. The social usefulness of certain kinds of aggressive behavior is never disparaged. No attempt is made to discuss behavior in terms of right or wrong, neurotic or normal, or good or bad. The worker will attempt at times to communicate his own moral standards, which may or may not be more stringent than those of the patient. These are always clearly labeled as the worker's personal beliefs and it is made clear that they may not be relevant for the patient.

The lies of professional helpfulness and confidentiality are handled directly by explaining the evaluator's own position as precisely as possible during the initial interview. The child is told who is employing the examiner, what the examiner's responsibilities to his employer are, what kind of report will be written, and exactly who will see and discuss it. Contrary to what might immediately be expected most adolescents respond favorably to such an approach. When the rules of the "game" of interviewing are wholly apparent to them, there is little need for defensiveness or negativism. The sheer surprising impact of having an adult be so direct with them often in itself produces a favorable effect that encourages them to be more open.

To avoid taking the stand that conformity or adjustment to adult standards breeds comfort and contentment the worker must have a deep and thorough understanding of the role of antisocial behavior in maintaining the adolescent's equilibrium. He must be thoroughly able to empathize with the "fun" and at times pleasure associated with behavior that flaunts rules. He must also realize that such behavior may be all that stands between feelings of hopelessness and despair. Adjustment to the adult world is not presented as something that necessarily brings pleasure but rather as a necessary and sometimes unpleasant requisite to survival. At times the worker might even openly discuss conformity as a burden and warn the patient as to some of the dangers of such behavior. Such an approach provides leverage when the issue of the adolescent's rigid conformity to his own peer group inevitably arises during a prolonged relationship.

Avoiding the communication that most adolescent clients have the same potential as the professional worker involves a careful attention to not confusing the worker's own needs with those of the child. Our hypothetical worker freely discusses with adolescents the problems of moving from one social class to another and makes no effort to pretend that class distinctions do not exist. The barriers to advancement which minority group adolescents profess are more often accepted as realities than interpreted as projections. The adolescent boy who has a long police record and who has missed out on many educational opportunities is not deluded into believing he can "be anything he wants." The girl who may have had one or more illegitimate children is not assured of her potential for making a favorable marriage. The worker's general attitude is that this can be a "tough world" in which only a determined few manage to overcome the deprivations of their early background.

While the worker may firmly believe that a relationship with an understanding and skilled adult promulgates favorable personality change all efforts are made to let the adolescent develop the relationship at his own pace and without extravagant, implied promise of its value. The patient is told exactly when and for how long the worker will be available. Full attention is paid to the risks the client takes in developing a relationship; sometimes these risks are actually spelled out. Strenuous efforts are made to deal with the adolescent's fear of being swallowed up in his dependency needs. "Openness" is encouraged as a necessary prerequisite to gaining understanding but it is not held out as a "cure-all" or as a goal in itself. Exhortations to trust the worker are avoided rigorously. Rather, the adolescent is told that he will have to decide himself about the worker's trustworthiness on the basis of his own experience.

Perhaps the most outrageous dishonesty perpetrated against adolescents by professionals involves their tendency to cover up their own angry feelings, which invariably develop toward the patient. It is surprisingly easy to tell an adolescent when he is annoying and such communications, when presented in a restrained but straightforward manner, rarely have a negative effect upon the relationship. A communication such as "I find your behavior during this interview extremely difficult and I'm having trouble keeping from getting annoyed myself" may in many instances be preferable to "What's bothering you?" or "How can I help?" or even to passive acceptance of provocative behavior. The adolescent appreciates this kind of straightforwardness. It tells him where he stands and enables him to look at his behavior without having to deceive either himself or the adult.

Conclusions

Anyone who has reared children knows that occasional dishonesty is essential if the child is to grow up with a reasonable degree of security. The truth to children, if understood, may be unbearable. If an orderly, sane, and relatively nonchaotic way of life is to be maintained, it is essential that children at times be deceived or at the very least kept in the dark as to issues they are not yet ready to master. In the treatment of adults there are clear landmarks for the worker to follow. Adults who enter psychotherapy are greeted with an atmosphere that not only condones but puts a premium on truthfulness on the part of all participants. Exceptions are made only when it is felt that the patient is too seriously ill to comprehend or tolerate the impact of truth. In these cases various deceptive practices may be used for the patient's benefit.

If one could argue convincingly that the great majority of disturbed adolescents were similar to children or to the severely disturbed adult, there would be considerable justification for withholding truth and practicing deception for the adolescent's own gain. Anyone who works with adolescents, even seriously disturbed ones, however, is quickly aware that such a comparison is invalid. Adolescents are extremely open to learning. They are in the process of discovering new aspects of the world around them, and are also increasingly preoccupied with their own inner world. Even the most disturbed adolescent has rarely developed a fixed pattern of rigid personality defenses that preclude being able to look at the truth in a reasonably open way.

The professional worker knows that the adolescent is capable of serious volatile impulsive behavior and does not have available to himself the controls that most adults have learned. Perhaps much of the explanation for an unwillingness to be honest with adolescents is related to a fear that they will not be able to tolerate the truth and that it will be used in a destructive, unhelpful way. One can also speculate that dishonest behavior might be related to the frightening impact of aggressive and sexually provocative adolescent behavior that touches upon areas of our own problems which have not been completely understood or worked through. When we present a dishonest picture of the world to our clients, we may really be trying to avoid the despair of facing the frightening world in which we live and thereby to reassure ourselves.

To interact honestly with an adolescent, all interested adults must believe that the growth of useful personality traits is more likely to take place in an atmosphere of truth than of dishonesty. This involves a willingness to take the risk of presenting communications that temporarily disturb the adolescent and a tolerance of the possibility that many of these disturbances will be directed against the adult. Any adult who wishes to communicate effectively in this manner must of course come to terms with self-deceptions in his own life so that they do not interfere with his ability to face reality with others.

14 Differential Association and
Crime Prevention:
Problems of Utilization

HENRY D. McKAY

Introduction

This paper is concerned with Sutherland's theory of differential association as it relates to the prevention of crime and delinquency and the treatment of offenders after they have been officially identified. For the purpose of this discussion it will not be necessary to evaluate differential association as a theory, or to appraise the concept in relation to alternative terminology used to express approximately the same idea. In most instances, it seems to me, the terms are used to draw attention to the fact that children reflect, rather accurately, the range of experience in the social world in which they grow up.

Conventional values dominate the social life of most communities, but in varying degrees, alternative value systems, which challenge conventional values, are present. And when conflicting value systems are present both will be transmitted to children. Variation in conduct among persons is accounted for by the fact that kinds of values are transmitted differentially, both because all persons do not have the same experiences, and because what appears to be the same experience has different meaning to each individual. In other words, the proportion of law violators and non-violators in different types of areas will tend to vary with the extent to which conventional values dominate social life.

Implicit in attempts to intervene in this process is the assumption that the ratio of values in communities is modifiable in favor of conventionality,

Reprinted from *Social Problems*, 8 (Summer 1960), 25–37, with permission of the Society for the Study of Social Problems and the author.

and the assumption that trends in the conduct of persons are not irrevocable. More specifically, from the perspective of the concept of differential association, this means that programs of prevention and treatment must change either the value ratio of the moral order in which the child lives, the heritage which is transmitted to him, the patterns of participation as between conventional groups and institutions, or the range of opportunities for newer forms of participation in conventional activities. Theoretically this can be accomplished either by changing the person so that he participates differentially in conventional situations, or by changing the situation to increase the ratio of conventional contacts. In this paper, therefore, programs of prevention and treatment designed to change either the person or the situation, and some natural processes which operate in favor of conventionality, will be discussed in terms of the extent to which they bring about such modifications.

.   .   .

The Problem of Intervention

. . . Prevention and treatment as related to differential association will be discussed under three headings: (1) intervention in the life of the person; (2) intervention in the situation; (3) unplanned intervention. The first two represent the basic theoretical orientations used in prevention and treatment. The third category includes some forms of spontaneous intervention which do not fit into either of the others. The specific prevention or treatment programs will be allocated in this scheme by taking into consideration both their basic presuppositions and their current institutional forms. If the presuppositions have not been articulated they will be assumed from the activities. Only the dominant postulations will be considered. Activities included in programs from time to time which are not consistent with these postulations will be ignored.

From a legal point of view, prevention and treatment are quite different. In treatment, it is assumed that the person already has been defined as an offender. In prevention, it is assumed that acts which could be defined as offenses must be prevented from happening. But, if, as assumed here, violative behavior represents a continuum in the population, then the differences between prevention and treatment are only differences of degree. It follows that programs may be needed for many who are not official offenders. The additional elements in treatment programs for those already defined as delinquent arise from the fact that the violations committed by this group of offenders may have been more serious or more persistent than the acts of others in the population, plus the possible negative consequences of being defined as offenders.

Probably any discussion of prevention and treatment should be prefaced by acknowledgement of the fact that programs designed for these purposes have had very limited success.[1] This applies both to the programs designed

---

[1] For an evaluation of delinquency prevention programs see (4; 5; 7).

to influence persons so that they will not get into trouble, and the programs designed to keep persons who have been in serious trouble out of additional trouble. In either instance it must be recognized that the processes involved are so complicated and pervasive that their control or manipulation by rational means is not easy to achieve.

In the face of this fact a very elaborate array of institutional arrangements has been created to influence the person or the situation. Some of these institutions were created on the basis of assumptions which may or may not be supported by the evidence, some because they were considered to be good things to do, some because of the feeling that something ought to be done, and some to serve other purposes not necessarily related to the basic problems. Many of these institutions are strong, well supported, and well directed, but for the most part they have not been tested empirically.

From a rational point of view the effectiveness of these prevention and treatment institutions should be tested, even though this task is not without its difficulties. Some of these difficulties are methodological. Some, however, stem from the fact that institutions seek to avoid critical examination through the use of protective devices, which might be called institutional rationalizations. These protect the institution by implying that the idea is sound, but that it has not been adequately or expertly applied. Implicit is the assumption that more of the same would solve the problem.

Intervention in the Life of the Person

Attempts to intervene in the life of the person are directed both toward prevention and toward treatment. Several different assumptions underlie these programs. When the legal system is involved some threat of punishment or censure for future action is implicit. If it is assumed, as it often is, that the crime problem developed in the family early in the life of the person, then some program for improving family life would be a preventive program. The alternative would be preventive psychotherapy to negate the effects of unfavorable family life. Psychotherapy also is the basic device for treatment. From the point of view of differential association, this might be presented as an effort to help the person to associate with others differentially.

The court system which deals with young offenders is oriented essentially toward the individual. The court defines the limits of tolerance of the community at any given moment, and deals with the offender within the limit of its facilities in terms of that definition. Of course, the policeman, or better, the juvenile officer, makes the first definition and, institutionally speaking, probably is in the most advantageous position for preventive work. He can deal with the alleged offender severely or gently, officially or personally, and for certain types of cases make use of whatever facilities are available outside of his own system. It seems probable that the significance of the role of the juvenile officer in the whole treatment and preventive program has been underestimated.

At this time in our country there is a lively debate over the value of the official defining process. Some take the point of view that a clear statement of the position of the community toward the offender is a necessary step in treatment. Others take the point of view that association with other young offenders in the detention home and in the court, plus the fact that a court record interferes with participation in conventional groups, makes appearance in court an experience which stimulates delinquent conduct. Since one of these positions accents the legal and the other the behavioral point of view, they represent different axes and cannot easily be reconciled.

Probation by the court as a treatment procedure could be an attempt to intervene in the situation for the purpose of helping the offender establish new contacts in conventional groups, and at times the program has been so defined. In practice, however, probation tends to take two other directions. The first is a police function. The officer checks on the probationer to see that he obeys the rules and outlines the consequences of violation. The other, favored by highly professionalized staffs, is relationship therapy. Here it is assumed that the person is to be redirected in the therapeutic process.

Commitment to a training school by the court introduces differential association in its simplest form. In fairness to the court it should be said that in many instances there may be no alternative. But it can hardly be denied that the training school provides an opportunity for offenders to associate only with other offenders in their own age group, and to organize to limit the influence of conventional staff controls. Thus it is that the standard institution created to make conventional persons out of offenders often tends to do exactly the opposite.

One popular type of preventive program directed toward the individual is the program sometimes identified as early identification. In this program it is assumed that children who are secretive, inhibited, aggressive, rebellious, troublesome, or who in any other way challenge conventional values, either in the school, the playground or in the home, are likely to grow up to be delinquent and should therefore be treated to prevent such a development. Probably children with such difficulties are more likely to become delinquents than are children without them. But this only states the problem. In answering it there are some real difficulties.

Psychotherapy usually has been considered to be the appropriate form of treatment for children identified early as potential offenders, and few would challenge the idea that children with serious personality problems should be treated to the full extent of our technique and knowledge. But a clear evaluation of the relation of this procedure to delinquency has been prevented by the uncritical assumption that the terms "personality problems" and "conduct problems" are two ways of saying the same thing. Actually, these are two types of problems representing separate axes. While some children with personality problems may be delinquent, and some delinquents may have personality problems, it does not follow even in these cases that one problem is causally related to the other.

Even without intervention the problems of some children are solved as they pass into other age grades, some keep their problems to adulthood without being more delinquent than their neighbors, and some do become delinquent. But this number represents a very small part of the delinquency problem. In fact, the proportion of distorted personalities in delinquent groups does not appear to differ much from the proportion of disturbed personalities in other groups.

But the most serious question about the early identification program arises out of the fact that it may increase delinquency. If the fact that a child has been defined as a troublemaker or a potential delinquent becomes known to his peers and defined by them negatively, his participation in social groups could be greatly affected. The negative results arising directly from this preventive program might be role problems, isolation, or definition of self as an offender.

In treatment programs for delinquents psychotherapy seldom is used unless the offender has personality problems as well as being an offender. There are many reasons for this fact. One is that most group delinquents will not submit to treatment; another is the fact that delinquents may be well adjusted but not in the conventional world; and another is that there aren't enough therapists to treat even a small percentage of the total number of offenders. In spite of the limited use of therapy as a treatment program, it is very popular and the suggestion that psychiatric treatment is included in a program evokes a very favorable general reaction. In recent years this fact has been somewhat exploited. Institutions and agencies without psychiatric service even for seriously disturbed persons make use of the terms "treatment" and "treatment program" in the hope that the word "treatment" will evoke the image of psychiatric treatment for all offenders. Others seek the same responses by providing psychiatric services on a token basis.

The popularity of psychotherapy or other psychologically oriented programs in contrast with the sociologically oriented programs is an interesting phenomenon. Since the effectiveness of neither of these types of programs has been established, other elements must be involved. While space does not permit an adequate analysis, it is suggested that the popularity of the psychological approach rests on the fact that it offers a direct and simple method of dealing with the person who is a problem. It offers an opportunity for parents to take children with problems to a specialist, just as a television set is taken to another kind of specialist for repair. In contrast, the sociological point of view, with its emphasis on the social process, offers no comparable simple course of action. Its programs are not so neat or so readily applied.

Intervention in the Social Situation

Differential association enters into programs directed toward the person somewhat indirectly. On the other hand, in programs involving intervention in the social situation it is a central concept. It may take two forms: In the first place, it may represent an effort to change the situation in which the child participates, to change the moral order of his community, or, as Plant says, "to change the street" (3). In the second place, it may represent an effort to control or manipulate the areas of participation of the child without changing the whole moral order. While these differences are real, it is possible that prevention and treatment programs might be designed to do either or both.

As related to intervention in the social situation, there is not much difference between prevention and treatment. In terms of association, prevention might be defined as an attempt to increase the areas of participation in conventional groups, and decrease participation in non-conventional groups. Assuming that the process of being defined as an offender tends to destroy contacts with conventional groups, if any existed, treatment involves efforts to re-establish these contacts. Clearly, if this does not happen the offender will establish contact with non-conventional companions.

No attempt will be made to discuss each program designed to change the situation or participation in it. Instead programs will be grouped by type. The first group is the whole cluster of agencies designated as recreation, character building, and group work agencies. Essentially, these are non-indigenous institutions because most of the control and support comes from outside of the area in which they are located. In fact, their presence in the areas of high rates suggests that traditional institutions have been disrupted and that these special institutions have been created by outsiders to help deal with certain types of problems.

These institutions represent a variety of ideologies. Unquestionably some of the early social settlements hoped to modify significantly the moral tone of the community where they were established, but there is little evidence to show that this has been achieved. Some of these institutions have put high value on recreation, others have emphasized contacts with group leaders, others favored arts and crafts and still others, athletics. No doubt these activities and others like them can be justified as ends in themselves. But the problem here is the relationship between these activities and conduct, and none has been established. From the vantage point of differential association the positive values would be those arising from bringing non-conventional persons into association with more conventional elements in the community, and from the presence of conventional staff members.

While some children in agency programs are insulated from delinquency it could be argued that others are inadvertently pushed in the opposite direction. Every agency tends unwittingly to pick its clientele. Conventional agencies favor conforming children and less conforming children tend to stay away. This results in a real separation on the basis of values. Thus, children in the agency have more contact with conforming children and fewer contacts with those engaged in violative behavior, while the children not in the agency lose the contact with conforming children and associate more with other violators. Whether the resulting differential participation is meaningful enough to be important in the total life experience of the child cannot be ascertained, but the nature of the process is clear.

Another type of intervention in the situation is the attempt to give leadership to groups of boys outside of the traditional institutional agency framework. This program will be identified as corner group work. About ten years ago, in a volume called *Reaching the Unreached*, the New York Board revealed to the public what had been known to workers for a long time, namely, that conventional agencies cannot reach serious offenders through regular programs. Since that time detached worker programs, outside of the regular conventional programs, have been established in many large cities. The forms of these programs have varied widely among cities and among agencies in the same city. Some of these programs have had modest success, but it is still too early to make a final appraisal.

The reason for the variation in corner group programs lies in the fact that there is no standard assumption about what is being done or why it is being done. On one axis the assumptions vary from the belief that the goal of the work is to protect the group because of its value to its members, to the other extreme, which has as its aim the destruction of the group. And there are many other axes along which assumptions vary in the same way. In spite of these differences there is one very positive assertion which can be made about the corner group programs: workers representing conventional values do reach and participate in the groups to which they have been assigned.

Only three other points will be mentioned briefly about this program. The first is that the worker has difficulty finding any substitute conventional activity which is as entertaining and as meaningful to corner boys as their own activity. The second is that workers report a tendency on the part of the more delinquent members of groups to split off into separate groups. The worker is likely to stay with the more conventional segment because there his prospects of success are greater. But lacking the influences of the more conventional members the prospects of serious crime are increased among those in the "splinter" groups. Finally, the role of the corner group worker is an extremely difficult one. Probably in few other occupations is a worker so completely without institutional support and dependent upon his own skill and resourcefulness. In this setting it is not surprising that some of the workers literally join their groups.

In addition to his own influence, it would seem that about the best chance the corner group worker has to increase the ratio of conventional contacts for the members of his group is to develop for them meaningful contact with powerful conventional local persons or organizations. The nature of the difficulties associated with such a plan suggests why the problem of leadership is crucial in this program.

Several types of intervention in the social situation fall under the general heading, "community organization programs." As the terms imply these programs represent attempts to change, through social action, the milieu in which children grow up. Some of the characteristics of three of these types of programs will be discussed.

First to be considered are the somewhat new programs of coordination which are expected to involve private agencies, official agencies and local institutions. Coordination programs are service-oriented and the theoretical assumption is the notion that if all kinds of services are provided for children there will be no serious conduct problems. Included with the usual welfare services are health, dental care, employment, and protective agencies. Underlying this type of program is the hope that all of the facilities in the local community can be used more advantageously.

Such a program for coordination has several strong points. It affords a possibility for better integration on the local scene of public and private agencies. This could be especially meaningful to police officers, particularly juvenile officers. But even more important, it offers a framework within which leadership and resources from outside the areas of high rates of delinquents can be combined with leadership and resources from the local area. This is the crucial problem. If the program is to succeed some opportunity for meaningful participation in it must be made available both to the people in the area and those outside. Both also must share in the control and the credit. Until such a division of power and responsibility is worked out there can be no real coordination of non-indigenous agencies and local institutions.

There are several difficulties with a coordination program. One is that institutions are not easily coordinated. Basically, social agencies are competitively oriented and jealous of their autonomy. Similarly, coordination of agencies adds little to what is being done. If an agency is totally unsuccessful in reaching the delinquent, coordination will not change this situation. Finally, there is little evidence to support the notion that services, as such, are preventive or therapeutic. Health services, a better chance to play, and good schools are justifiable ends in themselves. But there is little to suggest that improved facilities for such activities will influence the content of the social life of an area, or influence differentially the participation of children in delinquent or conforming groups.

Another type of community organization is called a community council. In many ways councils and coordination programs are alike. Both attempt to profit by unified effort. In practice, however, participants in council programs have been very largely the representatives of the social agencies in the area. Some local people have participated but the problems of power and credit between local institutions and agencies have not been satisfactorily resolved.

A third type of community organization is represented by the Area Project program which was developed under the leadership of the late Clifford R. Shaw. This program represents a shift of power from outside to inside the areas of high incidence of problems. Under their own name and without controls from outside the neighborhood, these autonomous groups, called community committees, make their own decisions and control their own affairs. To some extent at least this program has combined local resources with those from the outside. Several of the community committees receive grants from the Community Fund and the Board of Directors of the Chicago Area Project and several advisory committees from outside the local communities have given support to these programs over a fairly extended period of time.

The Area Project program represents, to some extent, efforts to change the community, efforts to control participation, and a type of group treatment. Since the processes which underlie the development of a community are general and not local, it is hardly to be expected that the social life of an area could be completely changed by a small indigenous group. But several activities aim in that direction. First, on the adult level the activities of the committee represent an increase in participation in conventional activities. Then the continuous discussion of the problems of the community and the problems of children tends to define the issues, create opinion, and open the way for action. What the committees do for children probably is not nearly so important as the fact that they are doing something. At least it is assumed that these activities represent an additional positive element in the milieu.

The committees, which are the heart of the Area Project program, seek to intervene in patterns of participation in several different ways. One is by using as much as possible the control afforded by local influential young men and adults; another by helping young people to stay in school or to get employment; and the third is through leadership furnished for corner groups. This corner group work, which has been part of the program for nearly thirty years, has been operated under the assumption that local workers might redirect groups of offenders or groups with some offenders in them, into conventional activities. More recently, through service-study projects, the Institute for Juvenile Research is studying the life cycle of groups, the effectiveness of different kinds of leaders, and the subsequent history of corner group boys. It is worth noting here that a local community committee office affords an ideal operating base for corner group workers.

One of the unplanned but probably most significant of the treatment programs growing out of the Area Project program has been the group effort of the committees in re-establishing offenders in the community. This has involved visiting offenders in institutions, welcoming them into participation in the committee's activities upon their return, and helping to establish contacts with employers and other local groups. These legitimate activities furnish the framework within which the offender can become accepted and also come to think of himself as a conventional person. In this program the entire community committee represents a differential influence toward conventionality.

This discussion of intervention in the life of the person and intervention in the situation has not been an attempt to participate in what Glaser has called "The Great Debates" over the relative merits of the two perspectives (1). Instead, programs representing the two points of view have been appraised within the framework of the concept, differential association. From this perspective most attempts to intervene in the life of the person, including legal and psychologically oriented programs, represent attempts to change the characteristics of the person and in this way to change differentially the pattern of participation. On the other hand, programs designed to change the situation represent attempts either to modify the conventional—non-conventional value ratio in the community, or to manipulate differentially the groups in which the child participates.

Most of the programs for prevention and treatment have been attempts to change the situation. In areas of conflicting values even modest success involves raising the ratio of conventional influences, because if this is not done, manipulation of participation will result only in an increase in the conventional contacts of some children and a proportionate decrease in the conventional contacts of others. Conventional non-indigenous institutions have had very modest success in changing this ratio. In an effort to increase their effectiveness some programs are seeking to combine resources from outside the area with local strengths and leadership.

Unplanned Programs

Finally, three "natural" or unplanned processes which fall outside the area of deliberate intervention should be mentioned. In the attainment of broad goals these processes seem to operate somewhat more effectively than our more rationally formulated plans. It is appropriate that their functioning should be recognized.

The first is the tendency of young men to get out of crime as they reach the age when they take on adult roles and obligations. Responsibilities which develop with marriage, parenthood, and the support of a family relieve somewhat the detachment from basic institutions which characterizes the late adolescent years by furnishing devices through which contact with conventional activities can be established. Participation in the conventional institutional arrangements automatically changes proportionately the pattern of association as between conventional and non-conventional activities.

The second natural process is the development of new institutional forms. Such a development can be assumed as a corollary to the loss in effectiveness in old institutional forms which comes with rapid social change. The tendency can be noted in corner groups which become much more conventional as social athletic clubs; in adult crime organizations which move toward more conventional businesses; and in non-professional offenders who seek conventional affiliations. It can be seen even more clearly in the numberless organizations and voluntary associations which are found in socially disrupted areas. Most of these social forms will not survive but some, if they meet real human needs, will develop in the direction of basic social institutions. Couple this with the tendency of disrupted institutions to develop new forms and you have the basis for a structure which might alter the pattern of association. Of course this will not happen in areas where mobility is very high, but given a little less change, stabilizing social forms tend to appear. Apparently we do not know how to stimulate such developments. It would seem that neither non-indigenous agencies nor present community organizations represent social forms which will develop into basic institutions.

The last of these processes is the movement of groups from inner city areas outward in space and upward in the social structure, and the decrease in delinquency and crime as they move. In a sense this parallels the population movement in earlier American history when the rejected and devalued members of communities moved westward to become leading citizens in new communities in one generation. Our data indicate that the rates of delinquents in the outer areas do not increase relatively with this outward movement. This suggests that the stronger, more integrated conventional institutions in these communities not only incorporate the newcomers and furnish them with new roles and opportunities, but also counteract the unconventional patterns brought from the inner city areas. In this way the odds in the differential association process are modified.

Social problems such as delinquency are not solved by services because services are not directed at the basic social processes. But it does not follow that the regenerative tendencies just described furnish a solution. They work slowly and sometimes are not permitted to work naturally. For example, some of the ethnic groups now occupying the inner city areas of large cities are encountering serious barriers in their outward movement. It follows that rates of delinquents in the inner city areas will continue to be high, and that the need for the development of more effective programs will continue to be urgent.

Summary

Programs for the prevention of delinquency and the treatment of delinquents in inner city areas characterized by value conflict are divided into three types. First are the programs aimed at intervention in the life of the person such as psychotherapy; second are the wide varieties of programs designed to change the situation either by modifying the moral order, with such activities as community organizations, or by altering the pattern of participation with programs such as corner group guidance; and third are the natural processes which tend to decrease delinquency without planned programs as seen when groups move out of inner city areas. All of these activities alter, or seek to alter, human experiences differentially. At the present time the combined influences of those rational programs and natural processes furnish only fair prospects for the control of delinquency in the inner city areas of large cities.

REFERENCES

1. GLASER, DANIEL, "The Sociological Approach to Crime and Correction" *Law and Contemporary Problems,* 4 (Autumn, 1958).
2. KOBRIN, SOLOMON, "The Conflict of Values in Delinquency Areas," *American Sociological Review,* 16 (October, 1951), 653–661.

3. PLANT, JAMES S., M.D., *Personality and the Cultural Pattern* (New York: Commonwealth Fund, 1937), 18.

4. PORTERFIELD, AUSTIN L., *Youth in Trouble* (Fort Worth: Leo Potishman Foundation, 1946).

5. POWERS, EDWIN and HELEN L. WITMER, *An Experiment in the Prevention of Delinquency* (New York: Columbia University Press, 1951).

6. SHORT, JAMES F., JR., and F. IVAN NYE, "Extent of Unrecorded Delinquency," *The Journal of Criminal Law, Criminology, and Police Science*, 49, No. 4.

7. WITMER, HELEN L. and EDITH TUFTS, *The Effectiveness of Delinquency Prevention Programs* (U. S. Department of Health, Education, and Welfare, 1954); and *The Annals of the American Academy of Political and Social Science*, 322 (March, 1959).

IV The Role of Existing Community Agencies and Institutions

Discussions of delinquency prevention are frequently limited to programs that involve primary and explicit commitments to the reduction of delinquency. However, the impact of *general* activities carried out by existing community agencies and institutions should not be ignored. The regular activities of the police, the courts, schools, families, welfare agencies, character-building organizations, churches, economic institutions, and so on, all have significance for both reducing and producing delinquent behavior. These organizations are largely responsible for the socialization of youth, social control, and many other essential social functions. It is generally accepted that when they are operating effectively rates of deviance tend to be relatively low. A rise in delinquency rates suggests that one or more are not functioning adequately, or that they may be working at cross purposes to one another.

Although it is often difficult to locate specifically the factors responsible for increases in deviance, such increases frequently lead to a critical evaluation of select community organizations and subsequent efforts to modify their activities or structures. When the problem is perceived as particularly severe, special programs such as those discussed in Section V may be developed to supplement the activities of existing agencies and institutions. We have limited our selections in this section to articles focusing on the police, juvenile court, family, and school. Limitations of space and the absence of adequate materials prevent a more comprehensive presentation of literature dealing with existing community agencies and institutions.

The role of the police in delinquency prevention is not always clear. Some of their activities may be clearly labeled as preventive, such as the sponsorship and operation of playgrounds and athletic leagues, while most other activities are less directly relevant. The routine patrol procedures of the police are significant for prevention in that they tend to reduce opportunities for the commission of delinquent acts. Effective apprehension of offenders also has some relevance for prevention in that it may serve to deter others from misbehavior. On the other hand, some police activities can be regarded as having "anti-preventive" consequences. For example, community members may perceive police investigations and the removal of juveniles from their homes as detrimental to the adjustment and well-being of the youths. Finally, other police procedures may be construed as either preventive or anti-preventive, depending upon how the police implement them. The way in which the police handle juveniles coming into contact with them for the first time is believed by some to significantly influence the juvenile's likelihood of further misbehavior.

The study reported by William W. Wattenberg and Noel Bufe suggests that the relatively brief contact between a boy and a police officer has great significance for the boy's future behavior, and that some officers are more successful than others in handling offenders. The characteristics of the more successful officers are described, and it is noted that police supervisors are able to identify those who are effective with a high degree of accuracy. This report implies that the careful selection and training of juvenile officers can be useful in preventing and reducing delinquency.

The juvenile court, with its special procedures and orientation, was developed as a means of protecting juveniles from the ostensibly harmful publicity, severity, and labeling that was thought to accompany trials in criminal courts. It was assumed that the early termination of delinquent careers was made feasible as a result of the juvenile court's emphasis on understanding and treating the problem child rather than punishing him. However, it is evident from the discussion by Albert W. Silver that many juvenile courts have been unable to achieve this goal in any substantial way. In presenting an analysis of the deficiencies of the juvenile court, Silver lists nine conditions that he thinks impede the court's effectiveness in preventing delinquency and in rehabilitating delinquents. Staff inadequacies, insufficient financing, professional conflicts, and faulty orientation are among the problems that he discusses.

The importance of family influences upon child behavior has long been recognized. It is commonly believed that when particular families fail to perform their expected functions or perform them inappropriately from the perspective of the dominant community, delinquency often results. Remedial efforts vary considerably. Sometimes programs are developed to modify the conditions of all families in a specific social category or geographical location by upgrading income or improving living conditions. At other times specific families will be selected to receive special services or aid.

In still other situations predelinquent children may be removed from their homes on the grounds that any changes made within their families would not be sufficient to prevent delinquent behavior from occurring. Joan McCord, William McCord, and Emily Thurber evaluate the long-range effectiveness of a foster home placement program as a method of preventing socially deviant behavior. Comparing a group of juveniles placed in foster homes with a group of controls, they found that a significantly greater proportion of those who had been placed in foster homes had criminal records in adulthood. They conclude that foster home placement may actually do more harm than good, particularly if the juveniles so placed interpret the placement as representing rejection by their family.

Ruth S. Tefferteller describes an attempt to control the gang activity of young children by working to restore parental influence and authority. A basic assumption of the program is that even a weak parent-child relationship has some value in controlling deviant behavior. The author concludes that the program, coupled with other settlement house activities, has a positive effect on the behavior of the children exposed to it.

School experiences also have tremendous relevance for the behavior of children. In the course of educating a child, the school exerts a variety of planned and unplanned influences that have important consequences that contribute to whether or not he engages in nonconforming behavior. The negative impact of the school is obviously not planned and is frequently unrecognized. It is generally things that the school fails to do that are labeled as delinquency producing, such as failure to motivate the child, failure to provide adequate facilities and teachers, limited programs, and inappropriate curriculum. Sometimes, however, certain activities that are designed to have positive effects actually result in pressures for deviance, such as the use of middle-class evaluative standards, compulsory attendance for unmotivated youth, and raising expectations regarding occupational achievement.

One aspect of the notion that educational practices might have results opposite to those intended is dealt with by Delbert S. Elliott. His study is designed to test the hypothesis that delinquency is a response to the frustration and insecurity developed in the school situation. Comparing the in- and out-of-school delinquency rates of high school dropouts, he finds that participation in officially known delinquency was higher when the boys were in school than after they had dropped out. Surprisingly, the delinquency rate of the dropouts after leaving school was in fact lower than that of individuals who graduated from high school. The differences are particularly striking for boys from lower socio-economic status backgrounds. The findings are consistent with a number of theories regarding delinquency causation and suggest that some re-evaluation of educational policies and procedures may be necessary.

A further question concerns the primacy and extent of the school's role in delinquency prevention. There are those who argue that the school, with its overtaxed facilities and resources, has a large enough task in simply trying to educate the young and should therefore limit its activities to those directly connected to formal education. Others argue that the school is the logical agency in the community to bear the major responsibility for this problem, especially in view of the fact that it is a public agency subject to public surveillance and control, it has a staff trained to work with children, and it has a stable financial base. The school's unique relationship to the child places it in a strategic position to identify potential deviance and to provide preventive services and programs.

The material reported by the Office of Education of the U.S. Department of Health, Education, and Welfare attempts to put the role of the school into a societal perspective. The article takes a definite position, arguing that the school has a major responsibility to actively and comprehensively participate in delinquency prevention. The report includes a variety of recommendations for programs that constitute both direct and indirect attacks on delinquency.

The last article in this section involves a discussion by William Reid of the role of interagency coordination in delinquency prevention and control. Using an analytical approach, Reid focuses attention on the prerequisites for coordination as well as the barriers to it. He points out that coordination that is functional from the perspective of the community can often be dysfunctional from the perspective of the agencies involved. Thus, agencies often resist coordination. He concludes that in many instances the greater coordination of services is not worth the efforts required to achieve it, and that consequently community resources might be more effectively allocated towards other goals.

15   The Effectiveness of Police Youth Bureau Officers

WILLIAM W. WATTENBERG and NOEL BUFE

The study reported in this article concerns a problem with not only immediate practical significance, but also with strong implications both for theory as to juvenile delinquency and for the design of programs to reduce delinquency. The study had its origin in the desire of officials of the Detroit Police Department to develop a more scientific basis for the selection of officers to be assigned to the Youth Bureau.

The theoretical significance of the research derives from the fact that the major viewpoints as to cause of delinquency seem to call for remedies which require relatively intensive individual treatment or far-reaching changes in the social structure of communities.

It is no secret that in the study of delinquency there tends to be emphasis as to cause which implicates either powerful social forces on the one hand or deep-seated personality difficulties on the other. In this article we shall not reopen the perennial debate between the sociologists and the psychiatrists. In passing it may be noted that as of the early 1960's a renewed interest is manifest in attempts to deal with social structure, possibly as a result of disenchantment with the effectiveness of various individual therapeutic techniques.

Without discussing or forecasting future swings of the theory pendulum, it should be stressed that the essential significance of both streams of thought is that delinquency being the result of very powerful forces must be attacked by equally powerful weapons. If one accepts what might be called loosely either a psychiatric or social work approach, as these would be found in the works of such pioneers as Alexander and Healy [1] or such present-day workers who use the insights of psychoanalysis as Redl and Wineman,[2] the

Reprinted from the *Journal of Criminal Law, Criminology and Police Science* Copyright © 1963 by the Northwestern University School of Law, Volume 54, Number 4, December, 1963, pp. 470–475, with permission of The Northwestern University School of Law and the authors.

The authors wish to express their appreciation to Inspector Francis Davey, of the Youth Bureau, Detroit Police Department, for his role in requesting and supporting this study; to Patrolman Christ Kotsopodis for his invaluable assistance with the statistical work; and to the Ford Foundation for the grant which made the study possible. For the conclusions drawn and the opinions expressed, the authors are solely responsible.

[1] Alexander and Healy, *Roots of Crime*, 1935.
[2] Redl and Wineman, *Controls From Within*, 1952.

implication is that the correction of the pathology involved calls for application of psychotherapeutic skills of a high order over a long enough period of time to permit genuine personality change.

The practical implications of sociological theories call for very different attacks, but these may involve equally high levels of skill. It certainly would be no simple matter to carry out the type of reversal of ecological forces which drew the groundbreaking attention of Clifford Shaw[3] and his co-workers, or to remake the social structure of a community in the fashion called for by Cloward and Ohlin.[4]

Seen from the perspective of any of these theories as to profound causation, many measures used day-to-day by many individuals who work with delinquents in recreation programs or in the functioning of law enforcement agencies or courts would appear to be very superficial. Compared with the possible need of a youth for psychotherapy, how effective can be the solemn little sermon with which a judge or referee in court embellishes his announcement of the disposition of a case? As contrasted with the need to reverse sub-cultural attitudes fostering delinquency, of what value can be the two or three hours of interviewing and possible advice-giving by a police officer?

Despite the apparent superficiality of such devices, court workers and police officers will continue to do what they see as within their power. Even if found to be ineffectual, they still would be strongly inclined to continue to do these things. *note*

Yet, in the overall design of delinquency prevention programs by communities it may be significant to know what real contribution to delinquency reduction can be achieved by the relatively "superficial" means. If it is a major contribution then these should be viewed more seriously as components in a community's efforts. If they are useless, there is no point in encouraging well-meaning individuals to fritter away badly needed time and energy going through meaningless motions.

It was against this background that the authors welcomed an opportunity to do a study designed to compare effective with less effective police officers. For, in order to make such a comparison one would have to be able to get some measure of relative effectiveness.

A survey of the literature unearthed a number of statements showing some faith that police officers could make an important contribution, although none of the statements had the type of documentation or research evidence that would be convincing to a tough-minded sceptic. For example, Kuharich after asserting, "The method used by police officers in handling these children during initial contacts may have a lasting effect on their lives, and may well determine whether they will respect community authority and the law," becomes quite specific as to how the officers should conduct themselves without citing any evidence as to the effects of the

[3] Shaw and McKay, *Juvenile Delinquency and Urban Areas*, 1942.
[4] Cloward and Ohlin, *Delinquency and Opportunity*, 1960.

recommended behavior.[5] Similar warnings were voiced by Votaw in reporting on observations made by the National Advisory Police Commission.[6]

That there was need for an evaluative study of the methods and techniques used by special police services for dealing with juveniles was recognized by the First United Nations Congress on the Prevention of Crime and the Treatment of Offenders as reported in this *Journal*.[7]

In the well-worn expression, "Easier said than done!" the closest thing to an evaluation was Weber's report on personnel in institutions based on clinical data.[8] For what interest they may have for comparison with the findings later to be reported in the present article, here is the essence of his findings:

> These determinants indicate that irrespective of technical or professional training, rehabilitative work with delinquents in institutions requires people who have genuine interest in children, who are emotionally mature and stable, and will react to problems with a high degree of adaptability and versatility; who will make a sincere attempt to understand human maladjustments and will react with personal warmth when dealing with personality problems of children; who can work agreeably with associates, and who can act with initiative, perseverance and leadership; who are sufficiently intelligent to learn quickly and deal constructively with the difficult problems arising in institutional rehabilitative work; who have the ability for critical abstract thinking yet can apply themselves to concrete problems; and who are free from social and religious prejudices.[9]

For use in the present study the Youth Bureau of the Detroit Police Department made available all files involving contacts by its officers with boys in the period 1952 through 1959. These files and the IBM cards incorporating their data included information on all contacts with each boy between the ages of 10 and 17 and recorded the badge number of the Youth Bureau officer who interviewed each boy and made the decision as to police disposition for each contact.

On the basis of these records it was possible to determine whether or not each boy became a repeater, that is, whether he had a second police contact prior to his 17th birthday. The follow-up period after the first police contact was not the same for all boys, because the age of first contact was variable. For most of the boys, the first contact was at age 14 or 15.

These data enabled us to determine for each officer what proportion of the boys for whom he was the first Youth Bureau contact became repeaters on the one hand or remained non-repeaters on the other. If we can consider it a sign of effectiveness for an officer to have a high proportion of

[5] Kuharich, "What Can We Do About Delinquency?," *Police,* 58–59 (Nov.–Dec. 1958).

[6] Votaw, "Programs for Delinquency," 31, *State Government*, 110 (1958).

[7] Lopez-Rey, "The First U.N. Congress on the Prevention of Crime and the Treatment of Offenders," 47, *J. Crim. L., C. & P.S.*, 526 (1957).

[8] Weber, "Clinical Approach to Selecting and Training Personnel for Institutions Serving Delinquents," 47, *J. Crim. L., C. & P.S.*, 33 (1956).

[9] *Id.* at 38.

non-repeaters among boys for whom he was the initial police contact, then we have a measure of the relative effectiveness of each officer. The size of any difference in this index would provide a clue to the over-all importance of the police work. If differences were large this would indicate roughly what reduction in the delinquency represented by repeating could be attained if the least effective officers could be upgraded so they achieved the records of the most effective officers.

Because the differences in delinquency rates vary widely in any large city it was necessary to take this into account. To eliminate as far as possible the influence of neighborhood factors it was decided to confine comparisons to officers within each precinct. For this purpose each officer was assigned to the precinct in which he had spent the largest proportion of this time. In Table I the reader will find the intra-precinct percentage comparisons. All data have been reported in such a way as to safeguard the identities of the men who made this study possible. The letters reported in the designation of the precincts were assigned randomly and bear no relation to either the number or name of the precinct. The number assigned to each officer is unrelated to his name or his badge number.

Comparisons were limited to officers for whom the records showed 30 or more first contacts during the 1952–1959 period. Table I should be read as follows: During the period, in the precinct we have given the fictitious designation, "A," there had been six officers who have served the preponderance of their Youth Bureau time in that precinct and had been the first Youth Bureau contact for 30 or more boys. Among them the officer to whom we gave the fictitious badge number 1 had 54 percent of "his boys" become non-repeaters, for Officer 6 only 28 percent remained non-repeaters.

The reader will note that the differences are quite large in some cases. For some of the "worst" precincts the best officer had been twice as effective as the one with the lowest non-repeater rate. The fact that the non-repeating rate in the "worst" precincts was so low for all officers attests to the power of social causation; the size of the repeating rate in the "best" precinct probably reveals the importance of individual psychological factors. In any case, the size of the differences indicates that had all Youth Bureau officers in every precinct been as effective as the most effective in that precinct there would have been a sufficient reduction in total delinquency in the city to have been worth the effort expended in either a selection program, a training program, or both, if such a program or programs could have so improved officers' effectiveness. This portion of the study, if it can be taken at face value, indicates that development of a good police youth set-up will pay off in delinquency reduction in a manner which compares quite favorably to effects thus far objectively measured for any of the presumably more profound efforts. This is not to say that a good police organization can be an adequate substitute for programs geared to deal with fundamental causes, but it cannot be ignored as a major ingredient in a community program.

Statistically sophisticated readers may well raise the question as to the possibility that the differences might have been due to chance. To get at

Table I

Intra-Precinct Comparisons of Non-Repeater Percentages Among
First Contacts by Officers

Precinct	Number of Officers	Percentages for Officers Having Thirty or More First Contacts		
A	6	(1)–54%	(2)–47%	(3)–43%
		(4)–42%	(5)–36%	(6)–28%
B	8	(7)–59%	(8)–54%	(9)–54%
		(10)–53%	(11)–53%	(12)–52%
		(13)–48%	(14)–46%	
C	10	(15)–61%	(16)–61%	(17)–56%
		(18)–54%	(19)–54%	(20)–51%
		(21)–48%	(22)–46%	(23)–46%
		(24)–45%		
D	10	(25)–57%	(26)–50%	(27)–46%
		(28)–44%	(29)–43%	(30)–43%
		(31)–42%	(32)–35%	(33)–31%
		(34)–29%		
E	3	(35)–46%	(36)–46%	(37)–41%
F	5	(38)–55%	(39)–53%	(40)–47%
		(41)–46%	(42)–44%	
G	2	(43)–46%	(44)–39%	
H	5	(45)–49%	(46)–47%	(47)–46%
		(48)–45%	(49)–44%	
I	7	(50)–54%	(51)–49%	(52)–46%
		(53)–43%	(54)–42%	(55)–39%
		(56)–37%		
J	12	(57)–47%	(58)–46%	(59)–42%
		(60)–42%	(61)–41%	(62)–40%
		(63)–40%	(64)–37%	(65)–36%
		(66)–32%	(67)–31%	(68)–31%
K	6	(69)–59%	(70)–57%	(71)–57%
		(72)–56%	(73)–50%	(74)–46%
L	12	(75)–54%	(76)–51%	(77)–50%
		(78)–47%	(79)–47%	(80)–46%
		(81)–45%	(82)–45%	(83)–43%
		(84)–41%	(85)–40%	(86)–36%
M	8	(87)–75%	(88)–71%	(89)–65%
		(90)–63%	(91)–61%	(92)–59%
		(93)–59%	(94)–55%	
N	6	(95)–61%	(96)–60%	(97)–59%
		(98)–54%	(99)–49%	(100)–41%
O	8	(101)–62%	(102)–53%	(103)–53%
		(104)–50%	(105)–45%	(106)–44%
		(107)–43%	(108)–38%	
P	9	(109)–56%	(110)–56%	(111)–53%
		(112)–46%	(113)–46%	(114)–45%
		(115)–45%	(116)–45%	(117)–41%

this question and prepare the ground for comparisons between officers, the following procedure was employed:

For each precinct, each officer was paired with every other officer. In Precinct E, for example, Officer 35 was paired with Officer 36 and, then, with Officer 37. Officer 36 was also paired with Officer 37. The standard statistical formula to determine the statistical significance of differences in percentages was used to determine the probability that the difference could have arisen by chance, in view of the number of cases for each officer upon which his percentage was based. In all, there were 445 pairings. Table II indicates for

Table II

Levels of Confidence, Chance and Actual

Statistical Level of Confidence	Number of Pairings Expected by Chance	Number of Pairings Actually Found
.0001	0	3
.001	1	11
.01	4	13
.02	4	12
.05	13	27

how many of these pairings the statistical level of confidence shown in the first column should have occurred by chance and for how many it appeared in reality.

The import of Table II is that the number and size of the differences found are very unlikely to be due to chance. For example, there were three pairings in the several precincts for which the differences were so great that they would have occurred by chance only once in 10,000 times; and 11 more, once in 1,000 times. Since there were fewer than 1,000 pairings, this should have happened "by accident" or "coincidence" only once. Thus, the number of these differences was 14 times (or 1400%) chance expectation.

The next step in the procedure was to interview all the supervising officers of the Youth Bureau in an effort to determine from their viewpoint what qualities appeared to be responsible for the relative success of the more effective officers. All the sergeants, lieutenants, and inspectors who had served with the Youth Bureau were presented with the names of all those pairs of officers for whom the difference in percentage of non-repeaters had proved statistically significant at the .02 level. Each supervisor was asked to give his judgment as to which man in each pair would have been the more successful in working with youth. Regardless of their judgment they were then asked to describe the salient characteristics of both men in each pair.

As shown in Table III, the supervisors were quite successful in their judgments. In this table, as in the previous ones, the men have been assigned fictional designations in no way related to their names, badge numbers, or

Table III

Accuracy of Supervisors in Selecting More Effective Officers

Supervisor	Accurate Judgments	Incorrect Judgments	Unable to Give Opinion
A	29	6	4
B	18	6	15
C	4	2	23
D	8	0	31
E	14	2	23
F	19	8	12
G	19	5	15
H	23	4	12
I	23	10	6
J	32	2	5
K	5	3	31
L	6	1	32
M	5	0	34
N	2	0	37
O	7	1	31
P	3	4	32
Total	217	54	343

other true identification. This table should be read to say that Supervisor A judged correctly who was the more effective officer in 29 pairs; picked the wrong man in six pairs; and was unable to give an opinion on four pairs. It will be noted that the over-all efficiency of the supervisors is indicated by the fact that they made correct judgments in better than 80 percent of the pairs. This can be considered confirming evidence that the statistics were pointing to a very real phenomenon.

The qualities or characteristics mentioned by the supervisors are tabulated in Table IV. To prepare that table, a record was kept for each man of all

Table IV

Items Mentioned by Supervisors as Characteristic of the More Successful and Less Successful Youth Bureau Officers

	More Successful Officers	Less Successful Officers
I. Attitude Toward Boys		
a. Genuine interest in children	75	23
b. Expended extra effort to help boys	14	4
c. Got jobs for boys	15	3
d. No outstanding interest in boys	3	19
II. Effectiveness as Police Officer		
a. "Time meant nothing"	46	9
b. Complained about overtime	9	25

Table IV (Continued)

	More Successful Officers	Less Successful Officers
c. "Successful policeman"	34	11
d. Thorough as an investigator; digger for facts	42	10
e. Cooperative with fellow-officers	12	0
f. Couldn't get along with fellow-officers	3	11
g. Receptive to new ideas	9	1
h. Knew "all the kids" in the neighborhood	21	0
III. Attitude While Dealing with Boys		
a. Manliness	24	4
b. Quiet and calm	22	5
c. Firm	45	10
d. Tough or scolding	9	24
e. Patient	12	4
f. Empathic or objective understanding	28	3
g. Ability to "get to" kids	30	6
h. "Salesmanship"	27	2
i. Sincere	27	2
j. Pleasing personality	22	5
k. Phoney personality	18	10
l. Aggressive	8	12
IV. Record-Keeping		
a. Good, accurate, complete records	54	14
b. Below average records	13	4
V. Appearance		
a. Neat, clean, sharp, above average	84	30
b. Below average, a little sloppy	3	14
c. Made a good impression by his appearance and deportment	18	3
d. Big	15	2
e. Small	2	2
VI. Outside Activities		
a. Boy Scouts	19	28
b. Active in neighborhood and business men's clubs	30	12
c. Church	10	4
d. "Fanatical" about extracurricular activities	0	10
e. Not too active in community activities	34	10
VII. Leadership		
a. Leader, organizer, "take charge" type	47	10
b. Not too strong as a leader type	27	6
c. Follower	12	20
d. Promotional material	8	3
VIII. Dealings with Parents		
a. Worked hard with parents	47	13
b. Visited homes	12	2
c. Contacted parents only as required by departmental regulations	14	12
IX. Communication Ability		

Table IV (*Continued*)

	More Successful Officers	Less Successful Officers
a. Good speaking or talking ability	41	18
b. Couldn't express self orally	2	7
c. Good report writer	29	8
d. Couldn't express self in writing	2	9
e. Could "con" information from a kid	15	2
f. Lowered his intellectual level when talking to a boy	13	0
X. Filing		
a. Considered cases on individual merits	52	6
b. Quick to file	8	18
c. Slow to file	9	17

the comments about him made by all of the supervisors who knew him. For each item mentioned a cumulation was prepared for all officers who in fact had been the more effective in their pairings, and for those who had been the less effective. The totals presented in Table IV, then, represent the total number of times a characteristic was mentioned by any supervisor for any man. This gives a rough picture of the qualities which were noted by supervisors.

If the items which most strongly differentiate the more successful officers were to be combined into a word description, the picture would be somewhat different from that of Weber earlier reported for institutional workers. In summary, the effective Youth Bureau officer can be described as follows:

As might be expected he has a genuine interest in young people, which shows itself in extra effort on their behalf. He is a good police officer, tending to give each task the time it requires to do a thorough job; he works well with his fellow-officers. In his dealings with juveniles he is calm, manly, firm, and patient. He talks well to them, wording his remarks to their level. He keeps his promises to young people and exerts "salesmanship" in support of a law-abiding course of action. He presents a good appearance and keeps his records well. Outside activities, surprisingly, did not loom as important. In fact, so strong an allegiance to an outside organization as to unduly influence dispositions appeared on the negative side. Leadership ability did not appear to be critically essential. However, competence in speaking and writing were highly important. So was willingness to work hard with parents. As to disposition, the key attribute was a tendency to judge cases on their merits as contrasted with a policy of either quickly filing charges with the juvenile court or being reluctant to do so.

Of these attributes, the ones which might appear at the time of selection would be attitude towards young people, general effectiveness as a police officer, appearance, record-keeping, and ability to speak and write.

Summary

This was a study of Youth Bureau police officers in Detroit in which effectiveness was measured by comparing officers serving in the same precincts as to the percentage of non-repeaters among boys for whom they were the first police contact. Highly significant differences were found among officers. The characteristics which supervisors considered salient in the more effective officers could be described.

The most significant result of the study was to produce evidence which would appear to indicate that the relatively brief contact between a boy or his family and a police officer may be highly influential on a future "career" in delinquency. Although such contact may tend to be regarded as relatively "superficial" by theorists impressed with the profound nature of the demonstrated causes of juvenile delinquency, its influence would seem to justify considerable attention being given to it as one element in any community effort designed to bring about substantial reduction in delinquency.

If this is the case for Youth Bureau contacts we need to examine with objectivity the effects of other presumably "superficial" elements which could be incorporated in a community program. These could include the manner in which juvenile judges or referees conduct hearings, discussions of moral issues in schools, chaplain interviews, church preaching, and public rallies. We cannot afford to neglect these without a detailed effort to appraise their worth.

In conclusion, it must be recognized that this study was based on one group of police officers in one city using one source of statistics. It is essential that its fundamental conclusion be submitted to a variety of tests in other situations using other techniques and different types of evaluation. Only after such modified replication can we speak with the conviction required for the multitude of practical decisions which would follow from the results.

16   Retooling for Delinquency Prevention and Rehabilitation in Juvenile Courts

ALBERT W. SILVER

America seems to have taken giant strides in recent years in recognizing that, as long as gross scarcities, injustices, and inequalities in employment,

Reprinted from *Federal Probation*, 30 (Mar. 1966), 29–32, with permission of Federal Probation.

housing, and educational opportunities exist, the breeding grounds for delinquency and crime will persist. For the child, adolescent, or adult who turns to crime is generally protesting against a social order in which he cannot achieve self-respect and recognition by fair and honest means. From an early age he has failed, therefore, to conform and identify with socially approved values and patterns of behavior such as honesty, industry, respect for person and property because the rewards forthcoming for abiding by them are not apparent or available to him.[1] To this extent, society assumes responsibility for supporting and maintaining a way of life fraught with gross injustices. These injustices represent the community's long-term, inherited ailments for which it has begun to seek revolutionary and controversial solutions.[2]

At the immediate and local level, the institution most clearly identified with waging the battle against juvenile crime, the juvenile court has, in the writer's opinion, failed to exert leadership in this struggle. The following conditions seem to hamper the effectiveness of juvenile courts in two of the Nation's five largest cities:

1. Low Level of Morale

One of the most consistent and striking impressions of juvenile court workers is their low level of morale. The feeling seems to be shared to a man that the juvenile court is a place of last and generally futile recourse for dealing with the alienated and the unreachable. This pessimism which to the writer's knowledge should have been documented but has not, serves as a destructive self-fulfilling prophesy—anticipating failure helps to bring it about through apathy and futility. Detention homes, for example, are employed as custodial domiciles rather than as rehabilitation centers; attention is heaped on flagrant recidivists rather than on first offenders or potential delinquents; psychiatric clinics are geared to diagnostic-dispositional functions instead of treatment functions. The dissatisfaction of court workers with the quality of service they render is then channeled into preoccupation with salaries and other secondary working conditions since only these appear to be amenable to modification through personal initiative.

2. Diagnosis in Place of Treatment

In juvenile courts of two of the Nation's largest cities, psychiatric clinics are devoted almost completely to diagnostic services although treatment facilities for delinquents elsewhere in the community, such as in residential treatment centers, at mental health clinics, and in child guidance clinics, are chronically overcrowded and for all practical purposes are virtually nonexistent, especially for typically delinquent cases. Consequently the majority of delinquents are evaluated and placed on probation with minimal advantage being obtained from costly, time-consuming diagnostic procedures. Completely new approaches to treating and preventing delinquency, such as

---

[1] Albert W. Silver, "Delinquency and Socially and Economically Deprived Youth," *Federal Probation*, December 1963, pp. 3–7.
[2] Paul Goodman, *Growing Up Absurd*. New York: Random House, 1960.

cooperative ventures with social agencies, the schools, settlement houses, and service organizations, should be initiated by court. For example, aggressive casework methods might be applied to identify and treat the predelinquent child in the lower grades while he is still amenable to remedial education and family therapy. Research has shown, for example, that teachers are quite accurate in identifying troubled, predelinquent children by means of brief, inexpensive questionnaire methods. Detached gang work programs should be utilized for making referrals and by cooperative staffing with court personnel. Court workers recognize the intense suspicion and resistance which their attachment to a physical symbol of authority, the court building, breeds. Now they must be given the freedom to operate outside of its restraining influence.

3. Inappropriate Treatment

Social workers, psychologists, and psychiatrists are most skilled and therefore most comfortable with traditional techniques of psychotherapy (derived primarily from the psychoanalytic model). Those techniques have very limited application with poorly motivated participants from marginal educational and socioeconomic backgrounds. Totally new techniques are called for in the juvenile court setting, techniques which emphasize habilitation (socialization) rather than rehabilitation (resolution of unconscious conflicts). Approaches such as those suggested by Schwitzgebel [3] and significant educational and vocational training orientations, such as those which Paul Goodman in *Growing Up Absurd* [4] advocates, seem to offer the most hopeful leads for the future.

4. Rehabilitation Instead of Prevention

The Protective Service Program of the Oakland County Juvenile Court [5] comes nearer than any other juvenile court program, in the writer's experience, in expressing its major thrust against delinquency by prevention (by community organization in this case) rather than rehabilitation. While it functions as a department of the court, it operates from decentralized offices situated in the various municipalities of the largest and second-most populous county in Michigan. A staff of 10 social workers whose salaries are paid by the court, while the schools and municipalities provide office and clerical expenses, provide casework services to more than 600 predelinquent children and their families annually on a voluntary basis. Of greater significance, however, are the citizens' committees organized by the Protective Service workers in 27 of the county's 30 school districts. These committees each consist of approximately 25 key people, such as police officers, school personnel, pediatricians, agency workers, lawyers, and so forth, and have

[3] Ralph Schwitzgebel, "A New Approach To Understanding Delinquency," *Federal Probation*, March 1960, pp. 31–35.
[4] *Op. cit.*
[5] Personal communication with Edgar W. Flood, Supervisor, Oakland County Protective Service, Oakland County Service Center, Pontiac, Michigan 48053.

become effective organs for providing services and for exerting pressure on municipalities to: (1) provide adequate recreation facilities, (2) take steps to deal effectively with the problem of school dropouts, (3) identify and contact delinquency-conducive hangouts, (4) provide parent education classes in cooperation with the local university, (5) offer camping programs for children and parents, and (6) arrange for free psychological and psychiatric evaluations by voluntary professionals. Less than 8 percent of cases referred require further official court service. Although the county population continues to grow and referrals to Protective Service keep pace with this increase, the number of referrals to the Juvenile Court remain constant. Beyond its emphasis on prevention this program places responsibility for the problem of juvenile delinquency at the level of the local community while providing the community with an effective tool for combating it.

5. Staff Vacancies

There are at present approximately 30 probation officer vacancies in one of these juvenile courts. In part, this is a question of establishing competitive salaries for which the Board of Auditors and the taxpayers assume some responsibility. There are, however, some imaginative solutions to this problem which have not been attempted.

One such solution would be to increase the supervisory staff of the Juvenile Court so that more graduate students-in-training from all three mental health disciplines could occupy these positions (at present only a small number of social work students fill probation officer positions).

Another solution is to work with carefully screened and supervised volunteer probation officers based on the pattern of the Big Brother Organization, provided adequate provisions are made for intensive professional supervision. Many universities have voluntary and prestudent-teaching programs which probably would welcome undergraduate student placements of this sort, particularly for teachers of the exceptional and emotionally disturbed. Lastly, new training programs for preprofessional mental health workers could be developed and coordinated with the cooperation of universities and juvenile courts.

The position of director of casework services of one juvenile court whose job it is to direct, organize, and energize the probation officers' work was also vacant for more than a year. This left a vacuum in the chain of responsibility in the court creating a condition analogous to that of a ship without a rudder.

6. Ongoing Staff Training

Staff seminars oriented to the legal, economic, sociological, anthropological as well as the psychological and psychiatric aspects of delinquency should be a continuing experience for all court workers. In one court clinic no consulting seminars are offered while in another they are conducted by a psychoanalyst whose practice deals primarily with neurotic middle- and upper-class children.

Although the juvenile court clinic may be staffed by trained social workers, psychologists, and psychiatrists, they generally play a negligible role in the ongoing training and development of the juvenile court staff. For professional workers to grow and derive satisfaction from their work they must have continuing opportunities for strengthening their skills, for supporting one another in their daily frustrations, and for keeping abreast of new developments in their field. This is another area in which a director of casework services should play a vital role.

7. Research and Evaluation Programs

The pressure of work in juvenile courts is frequently used as an expedient for continuing time-worn placement, treatment, or probation methods of questionable value. For example, one followup study of delinquents returned from the Boys' Vocational School in Lansing indicated that approximately 80 percent got into further trouble.[6] New approaches and objective attempts to evaluate both old and new methods by concurrent research projects are urgently needed. Graduate students could be encouraged to evaluate these treatment methods as part of their dissertation work toward the master's degree and as research essays in sociology and psychology at the undergraduate level.

At present few or no research or experimental service plans are in progress at juvenile courts. This surely is not an indication that everything is going as well as possible, that there are some things that could not be improved upon.[7] It is a well-known fact that the National Institutes of Health are searching for worthwhile delinquency research projects which also bring jobs and money into the city. It is suggested that all juvenile courts employ full-time research psychologists and/or sociologists whose function it would be to objectively evaluate the court's efforts at rehabilitation and to introduce new training and rehabilitation methods. Well-designed research proposals of this kind can attract foundation support and improved services which would more than offset the investment represented by the salary of the researcher.

8. Communication With the Community

At present the community at large has no direct contact with the juvenile court. Hospitals, child guidance clinics, and community centers, which are engaged in technical work comparable to that of a juvenile court, enjoy the guidance and support of a board of directors composed of concerned professional and lay people representing the community-at-large. A comparable plan would benefit the juvenile court greatly. In this way, for example, citizens could gain more knowledge about the work of the juvenile court

[6] H. Wilde, "A Follow-Up Study of Boys Conveyed by the Wayne County Juvenile Court to Boys' Vocational School, Lansing, Michigan in 1947" (unpublished master's thesis). Detroit: Wayne State University, 1961.

[7] One research project supported by federal funds which was of direct relevance to a juvenile court was removed from that court when it ran into repeated administrative snags.

and might consequently support it far more actively in such matters as tax issues and in providing it with volunteer workers while serving as a channel of communication with the community and inseminating it with dynamic ideas and challenges.

9. Conflict Between the Legal and Psychological Orientation

The lines of administrative and functional responsibility between legally and psychologically trained personnel in juvenile courts call for continuing, frank, and self-searching scrutiny. If the juvenile court is to live up to its promise as the "court of the future," where those who stray from society's paths are returned by prevention and rehabilitation rather than retribution, then these two groups of professions must learn to work together in a harmonious, democratic relationship. A common source for frictions between these two groups is that each does not seem to understand and respect the contributions, fundamental assumptions, and operating methods of the other.

In a previous article in this journal,[8] the writer contended that the following assumptions and operating methods seem to differentiate the legal from the psychiatric (mental health) professions:

> The legal profession evaluates and renders judgments. It deals primarily with concrete tangibles such as persons, facts, and events. It operates on the principle of narrowing by excluding details it considers irrelevant. It concerns itself mainly with objective data rather than subjective phenomena such as feelings and motives. It leans toward the concept of individual responsibility, conscious intent, and the analogous notion of single determinism according to which one individual and a single motive are responsible for a given act.
>
> The psychiatric professions, on the other hand, tend to assume that in order to understand one should avoid judging; that the significance attributed to facts and the relationships which obtain between them, or their context, rather than facts in isolation are significant for understanding the individual and his actions; that understanding is an infinite process gradually attained by ever-expanding areas of comprehension and awareness, that subjective phenomena such as perceptions, feelings and motives rather than objective data such as acts or events are important for understanding the individual; that in the family related, overlapping areas of responsibility are the rule.

Ongoing inservice seminars could be devoted to mutual discussions of this kind.

Experience as a consultant in a study of one juvenile court and more than 5 years as psychologist and chief psychologist in another, leads the writer to assert with some confidence that these problems are not unique to one court. If the question is whether juvenile courts are to assume a more dynamic task than mediators of proscriptions for youth, then a soul-searching analysis of their roles, functions, and effectiveness seems to be in imminent order.

[8] Albert W. Silver, "Operating a Psychiatric Clinic in a Juvenile Court," *Federal Probation*, September 1962, pp. 24–28.

17   The Effects of Foster-Home Placement in the Prevention of Adult Antisocial Behavior

JOAN McCORD, WILLIAM McCORD, EMILY THURBER

In the search for some effective solution to the problem of delinquency, a variety of experiments have been conducted. Many observers, impressed by the evidence linking familial experience with the causation of crime, have argued that placement of potential delinquents in foster homes might prove to be one of society's most useful instruments. While there is wide recognition that foster-home placement must be done in a careful, controlled fashion and that it should be used only when other means have failed, there seems to be general optimism concerning the potential effectiveness of foster-home placement. And yet, to our knowledge, there have been no studies which have systematically traced the adult behavior of children who have been reared in foster homes and compared them to a matched control group. This article reports one attempt to evaluate the long-range effectiveness of foster-home placement as a technique for the prevention of socially deviant behavior.

The Cambridge-Somerville Youth Study provided the subjects for this analysis. As various other publications have described,[1] this experiment produced detailed records based on extensive observations of the behavior, child-rearing practices, and attitudes of the families of 255 relatively lower-class, urban boys during childhood. These records were gathered between 1937 and 1945, when the children were 9–17 years old. In 1956 and 1957, records were secured from the courts, mental hospitals, and various private agencies in order to identify those individuals who had become alcoholic, psychotic, or criminal in adulthood. On the basis of direct observations made during child-

Reprinted from *Social Service Review*, 34 (Dec. 1960), 415–20, copyright 1960, The University of Chicago Press.

This research has been generously supported by the Ella Lyman Cabot Foundation, the Harvard Laboratory of Social Relations, and the National Institute of Mental Health (Grant M-2647 B.S.).

[1] See Edwin Powers and Helen Witmer, *An Experiment in the Prevention of Delinquency* (New York: Columbia University Press, 1950), for a detailed discussion of the original selection and the treatment of the subjects. See William McCord, Joan McCord, and Irving Zola, *Origins of Crime* (New York: Columbia University Press, 1959), and William McCord and Joan McCord, *Origins of Alcoholism* (Stanford: Stanford University Press, 1960), for detailed descriptions of the nature of the records.

hood and these records of adult deviance, various longitudinal analyses of the origins of crime [2] and of alcoholism [3] have been made. Both forms of deviance, we have found, were closely related to child-rearing practices and to the relationships between the parents and their sons.

The original goal of the Cambridge-Somerville Youth Study was the prevention of delinquency; the staff utilized a variety of techniques—individual counseling of the child, family guidance, educational tutoring, and various other forms of social assistance—in an attempt to achieve this goal. Foster-home placement was called upon only as a "last resort" when all other measures had failed. Consequently, only twenty-four boys were removed from their homes at the initiative of the Cambridge-Somerville staff. In every case, their placement occurred early in the child's adolescent years. Three of these boys were in foster homes during the major part of the Youth Study (and we therefore had little information about their natural families). Two boys later placed in foster homes were living with stepmothers before placement in foster homes. Thus, we had quite extensive information about the natural families of nineteen boys who had been placed in foster homes during early adolescence.

The Matching Process

Our problem was to attempt to estimate the impact of foster-home placement as an independent variable affecting the deviant behavior of these subjects in adulthood. In order to accomplish this goal, it was necessary to eliminate as far as possible all other influences that might have obscured the effect of foster-home placement upon the child. Consequently, from the remaining sample of 236 boys, we selected 19 boys whose early environments closely resembled the "natural families" of the boys who were later placed in foster homes. Each of these control subjects was individually matched to one of the foster-home boys on the basis of the following factors: presence or absence of the natural father in the home, deviance or non-deviance of the father, emotional attitude of the father toward the son, disciplinary techniques of the father, deviance or non-deviance of the mother, emotional attitude of the mother toward the son, and disciplinary techniques of the mother.

These seven factors have been demonstrated to be strongly correlated with adult deviance. Previous studies conducted on the Cambridge-Somerville sample have indicated the primary importance of these elements as causative influences.[4] Information on these variables was gathered during the subjects' childhood by trained counselors who visited the families on an average of once a week over a five-year period; previous studies have indicated that each variable could be categorized with high interrater reliability, that the factors were not contaminated by a halo effect, and that

---

[2] See *Origins of Crime, op. cit.*
[3] See *Origins of Alcoholism, op. cit.*
[4] *Origins of Crime* and *Origins of Alcoholism, op. cit.*

they had high predictive validity.[5] The matched variables were defined in the following fashion:

Presence of father in the home. A father was considered as "absent" from the home if he had been *permanently* separated from the natural family. (Eight of the pairs came from homes in which the natural parents were living together. One pair consisted of children of unwed mothers who had later married. The remaining ten pairs were from homes in which the father was absent.)

Parental deviance. A parent was considered as deviant if he was known to be an alcoholic (i.e., if excessive drinking had been the primary cause of financial or familial difficulties), a criminal (i.e., if he had been convicted by the courts for a major non-traffic offense), or a blatantly promiscuous person.

Parental attitudes toward the son. The father's attitude toward his son was considered affectionate if he showed actual concern for the boy's welfare and never evinced directly rejecting comments about the child; he was considered rejecting if he either neglected his son or showed open hostility toward the boy.

The mother's attitude toward her son was considered warm if she expressed her affection openly in the presence of the boy; she was considered passive if she seemed concerned for his welfare but showed little open affection for him; she was considered rejecting if she either neglected the boy or showed overt hostility toward him; and she was considered overtly ambivalent if she alternated between affection and rejection.

Parental discipline. In our ratings of discipline, we considered a parent as punitive if he depended upon beatings and severe spankings for control; we considered discipline as non-punitive if control was exerted through such techniques as showing disapproval, withdrawal of privileges, scolding, or reasoning; we considered it as lax if the parent exerted no direct control over the child.

The specific backgrounds of the boys placed in foster homes and their matched controls are presented at the end of the article. At the conclusion of the matching process, we had nineteen pairs of boys who, in terms of significant characteristics of their natural families, closely resembled each other. Because other important influences had been held constant, we assumed that any differences in the rate of adult deviance could reasonably (although not necessarily) be attributed to foster-home placement.

The Measures of Adult Deviance

After the boys had been matched in terms of familial background, each case was followed up through a variety of community agencies in Massachusetts. At the time of this investigation, the subjects were entering their early thirties. Three types of adult deviance were examined:

Criminality. A subject was considered as a criminal if he had been con-

---

[5] *Ibid.*

victed by the courts for assault (murder, manslaughter, robbery with a weapon, etc.), larceny (theft, burglary, etc.), a sexual crime (rape, sodomy, exposure), or public drunkenness.

Alcoholism. A subject was considered as an alcoholic if he had been arrested two or more times for public drunkenness but not convicted by the courts, had been committed to a mental hospital with a diagnosis of alcoholism, had joined Alcoholics Anonymous, or had sought aid from a private agency concerned with the treatment of alcoholism.

Psychosis. An individual was considered as psychotic if he had been committed to a state mental hospital with a diagnosis of schizophrenia, paranoia, or manic-depressive tendencies.

Although each of these measures of adult deviance is subject to a number of biases, we believe (and have argued elsewhere[6]) that they constitute the best operational standards available to contemporary social scientists.

The Results

We had hypothesized that the foster-home boys would have a lower rate of adult deviance than would the matched controls. As will be seen in Table 1, this expectation was not fulfilled. A *significantly higher proportion*

Table 1 *

Deviance in Adulthood of Boys Placed in Foster Homes and of Matched Controls

Type	Placed	Controls
Total	19	19
Deviants †	15	8
No deviance reported	4	11

* $X^2 = 3.96$; $P < .05$. Corrected for continuity.
† All were criminals. Five were also alcoholics. None had become psychotic.

of those who had been placed in foster homes had criminal records in adulthood.

There seem to be several reasonable explanations for the negative result. One might argue that the foster-home boys really had more pathological backgrounds than their controls. There are, of course, many elements in the environment which might contribute to adult deviance. We had, however, matched those conditions which were most strongly related to adult deviance in the Cambridge-Somerville sample. Yet the possibility remains that the foster-home boys may, in certain subtle ways, have had more "pathological" early environments.

6 *Ibid.*

A second reasonable explanation for these negative findings is that perhaps the foster homes into which these boys were placed were inadequate. Although we have no direct reports on the nature of these foster homes, they were, in the judgment of the staff, superior to homes provided by the natural parents. Since the staff [7] had training and experience in working with people, there is some reason to assume that the foster homes were at least superior to the natural homes.

A third possibility—and the one to which the authors would subscribe—is that foster-home placement may actually be harmful during adolescence.[8] Retrospectively, it seems reasonable to suppose that boys removed from their families would interpret this separation as an ultimate "rejection" by their families. From previous studies on the sample, we know that parental rejection was strongly associated with adult criminality. Some support for this interpretation can be seen in the fact that foster-home boys whose natural fathers lived at home had a significantly higher rate of adult deviance than did their matched pairs, as shown in Table 2.

Table 2 *

Deviance in Adulthood of Boys Whose Fathers were Still in Family Home

Later Behavior	Placed	Controls
Criminal	7	2
Not criminal	1	6

* Fisher exact test for a 2×2 table, two-tailed; $P < .05$.

This trend remained regardless of the father's deviance or affectional regard for his son and regardless of the mother's attitude toward the boy. Presumably, those boys who were removed from their natural fathers would be more likely to perceive the separation as rejection.

Summary

This paper reports the findings of a longitudinal analysis of the effects of foster-home placement during early adolescence on adult deviance. These boys were placed in foster homes as a last resort in the attempt to prevent delinquency. For the present study, the natural families of nineteen of these boys were matched to those of nineteen boys not removed from their homes. The pairs were individually matched on the affection of the parents for the child, the father's presence or absence, the deviance or non-deviance of the

---

[7] Eight counselors were professional social workers, six were students in social work, two were "boys' workers," one was a nurse, and two were psychologists.

[8] Ivan L. Russell, in "Behavior Problems of Children from Broken and Intact Homes" (*Journal of Educational Sociology*, XXXI [1957], 124–29), reported finding greater difficulties among children aged 5–15 from broken homes who had been placed in foster homes.

parental models, and the disciplinary techniques of the parents. Comparison of the two sets of boys indicates that foster-home placement was ineffective in preventing adult deviance. In fact, some evidence suggests that removal of the child from his natural home (at least, if his father is living there) may actually promote criminal tendencies.

18   Delinquency Prevention Through Revitalizing Parent-Child Relations

RUTH S. TEFFERTELLER

. . .

Juvenile delinquency can in large measure be prevented and controlled if it is identified and treated in its incipient stages. Symptoms can be detected long before blatant delinquency erupts in a dramatic way. The breakdown of respect for law and authority by 8 to 13-year-olds in gangs is one of the most obvious indicators of trouble ahead. Cohesiveness and exclusiveness are characteristic of children's groups in the 8 to 13 age range. This is the active period for gravitation into friendship peer groups, where a system of vigorous socialization through childhood society begins to grind and chip away at personality formation. In predelinquent gangs, the group pattern they have chosen to follow is a negative one.

From our recent experience at the Henry Street Settlement, we are convinced one of the ways to check juvenile delinquency in pregang stages is through programs which help these groups achieve status in socially acceptable ways and which reinstate parental and adult control by re-awakening parents' interest in what their children are doing. For two and a half years now we have been engaged in a special juvenile delinquency prevention project with several predelinquent groups. Our greatest emphasis has been placed upon dealing with preadolescent children who, with their companions, are experimenting with predelinquent behavior. Often the parents have no knowledge of their children's actions until the police officer knocks at the door, a neighbor complains, or a Settlement worker visits them. The Pre-Delinquent Gang Project was designed to prevent the development of new gangs in our neighborhood by first detecting the early symptoms of gang behavior in younger groups and then working intensively with them and

Reprinted from *The Annals of the American Academy of Political and Social Science,* 322 (Mar. 1959), 69–78, with permission of the Academy and the author.

their parents as groups in order to wean them away from the older gangs' influence. With teen-age gangs steadily on the increase in our neighborhood, it is inevitable that we also have a greater number of younger groups admiring and emulating them.

A settlement house, of course, is in a unique position to detect predelinquent group behavior in its early stages, because its staff see at first hand what goes on in the neighborhood. At Henry Street we have learned much about the evolution of gangs and have seen how well they can perpetuate themselves. Always, as one group grew up, going on into jobs, marriage, or jail, there was a younger one ready to step into their shoes, their reputation, their pattern of behavior, and even assuming the same name.

If the teen gang professes to be defending the block from Puerto Ricans, you can be sure the younger followers will say the same; if the teen gang sees fit to fight "dirty" by having the whole group jump a single opponent, the system of ganging up becomes wholly acceptable to the young admirers. The dynamics of growing up and identifying with heroes, who fire the imagination as well as any television thriller can, are rapidly at work here. Our challenge is to find ways of winning these children back to friendlier ties with adults who can control and redirect them. Young as they are, the group encasement can be a tough thing to break through. Because they are young, we feel we should be able to do this before antisocial patterns become hard and fixed and before familiar adult figures, such as parents, teachers, group workers, in fact the adult community as a whole, lose contact and the chance for wholesome influence.

All of the five predelinquent groups with whom we are presently working came to our attention through their disorganized and defiant behavior in the Settlement House. After voluntarily joining our after school program, they were disrupting the regular recreation groups, resisting all ordinary attempts to bring them into club activities on the same terms as the other children. They did not reject the Settlement; they attempted to participate in the program. But their group behavior was so disturbed they could not tolerate the mild discipline of having to share facilities with others; of meeting in accordance with a schedule; of listening to adults in charge; of respecting property, supplies, and equipment. They were tightly knit, inseparable, defiant, adventuresome, often destructive, yet always at loose ends, seeking and creating trouble, never able to concentrate on any interests.

In all five groups, despite their great variety, the parents, and the family problems, we are seeing a gradual lessening of predelinquent activity following the assertion and insinuation of parental authority. Calling the parents together at the earliest signs of trouble and as frequently as possible has brought about marked changes in the groups worked with so far. Ganging up on other children, stealing, breaking windows, defying adult authority outside the home, helping teen gangs in street warfare have been noticeably reduced through our efforts to team up with the parents.

Group Solidarity

What these groups continually ask and clamor for is the privilege of having a club of their own, a chance to be a club in an official way, under Settlement auspices. Traditionally, as we all know, we have looked favorably upon such requests and acted accordingly. With these children, however, the approach we use and find successful is to hold up their application until we have a chance to let the parents know more about the group and until we enlist parent action in determining whether or not to sustain them as a group. What we try to make very plain to the children is that their group behavior thus far has been unacceptable and that steps must be taken to be sure the official recognition of them as a club will not contribute towards strengthening them as a gang. Needless to say, they want the club very much, and this waiting period produces a greater desire and an incentive to talk and negotiate with us about what they hope to do when they get their club.

This approach provides us with endless opportunities for stimulating discussion with the children about their predelinquent behavior and how this could impair the success of a club. Children of this age have a capacity for insight into their own behavior and can be helped to recognize the seriousness of what they are doing if approached in a nonthreatening manner. They understand the seriousness of the deprecations of teen-age gangs and, in more confidential moments, will tell us how wrong they know it is, but that they are afraid to withstand the pressures of the older ones upon them. Our approach has been to speak openly and frankly against gang behavior, and, unorthodox as it may sound, we go so far as to even set limits on their choice of club names. If, during the planning, they choose one of the local gang names, we say this will not be acceptable if they intend to be a Settlement Club. If they ask what is wrong in calling themselves "Midget Cyclops" or "Junior Cyclops" (Cyclops being the name of one of our local gangs) we say firmly it is a gang name, it stands for trouble, aggression, fighting, vandalism, stealing, and so on throughout the neighborhood, and this immediately labels them, too, as being identified with delinquency. This, we explain, cannot be tolerated, and the children seem to understand what we mean.

Therefore, as a first step we try to work with the group informally to help them aspire towards a more constructive type of club with an adult leader, even though we do not allow them the privilege of functioning as a recognized club under Settlement auspices until we get acquainted with their parents. Then, simultaneously, we work to bring the parents into group meetings to help them understand the phenomenon of a natural, self-formed, juvenile antisocial group, and to what kinds of activities this leads. We feel that bringing all the parents together on a group basis affords the beginning of a home and Settlement approach to correct a problem which is basically group centered. We use a great deal of initiative in our meetings with the parents to introduce this problem of predelinquent group behavior and to explain how this differs from the problem of normal mischievous play.

Parental Interest and Authority

Parents need help in understanding the difference between a constructive boys' club of the useful variety and one which is fast developing into a young gang. They need sympathy and time to grasp the many subtle symptoms which we describe as indicative of gang development. So often they say their children are well behaved at home and the trouble outside is due to the company they keep. One of the clues for trying the group technique with the parents actually arose from the failure we were experiencing in seeing them one at a time.

From experience we know many of these parents do not join traditional mothers' and fathers' clubs or other social groups on their own, nor do they respond to poster appeals to enroll in parent education courses. But with persistence, friendship and an outgoing approach on our part, we find most will respond to special attention and will team up with other parents on matters concerning their children.

Even the least adequate of the parents whose children are heading for trouble are usually grateful for aid in putting them in touch with other parents who have the same problems. Many are not aware of all that is going on in the street. It is almost inevitable that the majority of the children in these groups come from homes where there is a high preponderance of inadequate parent guidance or broken homes combined with other social and economic pressures. The proportion of problems and weaknesses in family life may differ in each case, but the combination of their circumstances has made the parents unable to deal successfully with their children.

Bringing parents together in groups this way mobilizes adult opinion against juvenile misbehavior. It helps many who are individually timid or defensive to subscribe to a standard and take a more forceful stand in the eyes of their children. Often these are adults who heretofore have not had the strength or interest to be very vocal about juvenile aggression.

One boy's mother admitted she had been tacitly rooting for the local teen gang during a series of gang fights. But since her new and lively association with the Settlement and since the parents' meetings and discussions, she gained more courage to criticize publicly the behavior of several teen-age gang members whom she observed causing disruption in the Settlement building. Out in the street she went after those boys and gave them a sound tongue lashing.

Such expression against bad behavior has not been forthcoming from many of our neighbors. This mother said that when her own boy, aged 12, and several of his companions overheard her, it made a marked impression on them. She could plainly see, she has said on numerous occasions, that when parents take an open stand against gang tactics, it can do much to bring the younger ones into line.

Setting Limits and Standards

Our emphasis has not only been on helping the parents understand the phenomenon of negative group control over their individual children, but in encouraging them to work with us in planning the kinds of programs and activities best suited for their children's needs. Parents are first asked whether they want their children to have a club at all or whether they might prefer to break it up. Invariably they answer that it is impossible to do the latter, because the children "cannot be locked in the house. They find each other in the street and it's hard to separate them. Better let them have the club, and we all try to keep an eye on them."

Once a club program is launched with the help of parents, there is a commitment—deeper from some parents than from others, that is a source of strength. Subsequent difficulties or new plans for activity receive attention far more quickly and effectively because the parents, either as a group or individually, are consulted promptly. Control and discipline seem to work much better when the parents themselves, in cooperation with the Settlement, decide on the best plan to follow. Similarly, joint planning and approval of new programs lend importance and prestige to the event at hand. With this age group, parent participation seems wholly acceptable, even in cases where this may be the first time the child has seen his parent come out for a meeting. As one parent expressed it at a joint meeting attended by parents, children, and the Settlement staff:

> We are going to do our best to help you have your club so you won't have to act so tough and show yourselves to be such wise guys. But you kids have to co-operate to show us you can stay out of trouble. If this doesn't work, none of you will be allowed to play with each other any more, because as far as this rough stuff is concerned, that has to stop, no matter what. So here is your chance.

This parent is stronger and more effective than some of the others, but in the group situation the weaker ones interact with the stronger, and learning and reinforcement take place.

The parent group meetings, therefore, are crucial to launching the club program properly, for through these a number of goals are achieved.

Individual parents seem less defensive when discussing the children's behavior on a group basis in concert with other parents. They involve themselves more freely both in acknowledging the existence of a predelinquent group problem and in making concrete suggestings for dealing with it.

The parents' group demonstrates immediately to the children an expression of parental authority and awareness of their wish to have a club. Parents united in the presence of their children establish their authority vividly, and this makes an impression on the children.

It provides an opportunity for parents to meet other parents of the children with whom their youngsters play.

It stimulates parents to think about the necessity of close supervision for

8 to 13 year old children's groups (despite their apparent readiness to do many things on their own) and to plan supervised programs with us.

It places direct responsibility upon the parent for giving permission to the children to have a club with an acceptable club name and the conditions under which it must operate. In other words, it helps to set an expectation level for behavior prescribed by the parents themselves.

It involves the parents in setting time limits upon attendance in the club and the hour the children are expected home.

Interest develops in having us keep in touch with them on a regular basis to give them progress reports on the children and the group.

New opportunities open up for giving social services to the parents themselves, apart from the children. We are having more and more experience with this, as we gain their confidence and as they feel our support in helping them control their children.

It conveys to the parents our interest in working with them, both as parents and as adults, and leads to much more sociability between them and the Settlement.

Lastly, the meetings provide splendid opportunity for expressing not only concern for the children but an acceptance on our part of the parents themselves.

The Settlement Worker:
A Generic Practitioner

News that they may have their club is passed along to the children by the parents and is usually received with much cheering and delight. A special worker who is available almost daily is assigned to the group, and the formal club program is launched. Club meetings, trips, athletics, dramatics, camping, fishing, pet collections, and all sorts of special projects become the modus operandi for gaining a foothold with the group. Wider opportunities open up for studying the individuals involved and for learning more about their predelinquent activities. As relationships with children and families deepen through the steady contacts, our influence becomes stronger and more acceptable. All sorts of opportunities develop where social, ethical, and moral values of the group can be affected. It would be too soon to evaluate what basic changes, if any, are taking place with the adults, but we know that at least by gaining parent co-operation the effects of our own investment of leadership work are far greater. Indeed, we have come to feel that without this added dimension of parental involvement, the total result of our professional work would be infinitely less effective.

The active programs with the children, individually and as a group, take up most of the leader's time; but, in addition, he is in and out of the homes constantly—to leave messages concerning the time and place for a trip, to visit a sick boy, to clear up a misunderstanding with a child, to explain a new program or schedule. Often these visits have to do with difficulties arising from poor adjustment to school, settlement, home, or neighborhood and may already involve probation officers and Children's Court. Nothing can go ignored and with children nothing can wait. Individual problems must be followed through with child and parent and anyone else involved, hopefully to the understanding of everybody. These services are in addition to the individual services given by psychiatric case workers in our Mental Hygiene Clinic. As with hardened gangs, a fairly small percentage of these younger children are emotionally disturbed and require psychiatric or other treatment. But the steady, "on-the-spot" guidance to children and parents is given continuously by the Settlement worker.

It is important to mention we are conducting this special group work program within the heart of the regular and normal Settlement House program, which is located within the very community in which these children live. This means trying to effect change within the context of the children's everyday milieu and among other groups where they are known and will continue to live. This, we know, is not easy and is a slow process, but in the long run whatever improvement occurs should be more lasting.

.   .   .

Relationships with the Parents

The success of our work to date has depended upon employing intensive leadership for the children, combined with the mobilization of the parents of each group concerning their children's behavior. However, another important result of our close association with the parents is that it puts us in the position of trying to help them with many other family and individual problems.

Parents as well as children become the beneficiaries of this group work approach. For out of the joint experiences created by working firsthand on common problems, they derive not only fresh guidance for better understanding their children, but gain new strength and courage to proceed more confidently on their own, or feel easier about asking for help.

Mrs. Lanos, mother of one of the "Sabres," sought advice freely when she was worried about her status in the Housing Development. She described vividly the anxiety and the tension this produces in family life and what it feels like to live under the constant threat of being uprooted if there is the slightest increase in income over the maximum allowed. She did not know the new housing manager and hesitated to take her particular problem to her.

We interceded to explain this tenant's special problem to the new and socially minded manager. The manager found there had been an error somewhere along the line in that Mrs. Lanos had not even been notified she was officially reinstated and had nothing to worry over at present. When Mrs. Lanos ran into the Settlement that evening, she said she was so happy, she was going to put up new kitchen curtains!

When Mr. Bellio lost his job recently, his boy, a member of the "Hawks," urged him to go to the Settlement to see his leader. The boy took his father's lay-off hard, and that same evening Mr. Bellio came to see us. He had been clerking in a grocery on Madison Street. After four years he was told they could not keep him on. Mr. Bellio considered returning to his old job as a cab driver, but had difficulty in obtaining a permit due to a foot injury. Several steps were taken to help Mr. Bellio get clearance on this so he could have his permit if he wanted it. In addition we phoned for an appointment with an employment placement agency. We also made personal contacts with individual sources where we thought there might be job possibilities. Letters of recommendation were written. Though no jobs were found immediately, this parent got a great deal of comfort in knowing he could count on the Settlement. His boy's behavior had been improving right along; but this recent series of contacts between the father and the Settlement has created new thrusts of progress for us all.

Opportunities such as these for getting closer to the families of these children have been numerous and most fruitful. Each time we work through another problem with the parents, it adds depth and dimension to our work with the children. Certainly it becomes the clearest evidence to the children that the whole family is identified with the Settlement and the specific work with the individual child and the group gets carried further along.

Need for Love and Discipline

As close relationships develop between families and the Settlement, and often between families themselves, the erratic, confused behavior of their children becomes more stabilized and settled. The children seem to thrive on the attention given them as the immediate adult community attempts to prescribe regularity and order. It would seem that when adults, particularly the parents, close ranks and stand together, the very ground these children travel from home to various parts of the neighborhood becomes more solid. Over and over again as we deal with these particular predelinquent groups, we find them increasingly more relaxed, more co-operative, and more accepting of adult authority. There is evidence of more purpose in the groups, new values in their thinking, and boasts about putting things over on adults begin to be replaced with plans for activities which will give them a good reputation and recognition from their families.

Here, we say, the key to checking predelinquency in preadolescent groups lies in helping to reinstate parental influence where it rightfully belongs and in building stronger bridges between children and their parents and between families and community before it is too late.

. . . It was a strange thing that up to the age of seven children were noticeable in Catford Street: the babies in their well-kept perambulators and the little boys and girls in coat-and-legging sets were prominent, but after the age of seven the children seemed to disappear into anonymity, to be camouflaged by the stones and bricks they played in; as if they were really the sparrows the Miss Chesneys called them, they led a different life and scarcely anyone noticed them. At fourteen or fifteen they appeared again, the boys as big boys that had become somehow dangerous—or was it that there was too much about them in the papers?—the dirty little girls as smart young women with waved hair, bright coats, the same red nails and lipstick as the dancer in the bus queue; they wore slopping sling-back shoes and had shrill, ostentatious voices. The street prickled with the doings of these boys and girls, as it admired and petted the babies, but the children were unnoticed. . . .[2]

[2] Rumer Godden, *Episode of Sparrows* (New York: Viking Press, 1955), p. 23.

19 Delinquency, School Attendance and Dropout

DELBERT S. ELLIOTT

Theoretical explanations of delinquent behavior have come to place in-creasing emphasis upon some form of "status deprivation" as the motiva-tional source of lower-class delinquency.[1] According to these views, the socialization of lower-class boys does not adequately prepare them to com-pete effectively for status rewards in middle-class-dominated institutions. The intense frustration experienced by these boys consequently motivates them toward delinquent patterns of behavior in an attempt to recoup their loss of self esteem.

Albert Cohen in *Delinquent Boys* suggests that the school in particular awards status upon the basis of middle-class standards. Here, lower- and middle-class youths compete for status in terms of the same set of middle-class criteria, with the result that lower-class youths are relegated to the lowest status positions. As a result of the unequal competition, lower-class youths develop feelings of insecurity, become frustrated, and begin to search for some solution to their status problem.[2]

Delinquency is thus viewed as a by-product of the unequal competition at school. Youth who are denied opportunities to achieve higher status po-sitions because of their lower-class socialization are consequently "provoked" to engage in delinquent behavior in an attempt to avail themselves of

Reprinted from *Social Problems*, 13 (Winter 1966), 307–314, with permission of the Society for the Study of Social Problems and the author.

This study was supported in part by a faculty research grant from the San Diego State College Foundation. Grateful acknowledgment is made to Harwin L. Voss, University of Kentucky, and David L. Dodge, San Diego State College, for their critical reading of the manuscript.

[1] See David J. Bordua, "Sociological Theories and Their Implications for Juvenile Delinquency: A Report of a Children's Bureau Conference," U.S. Department of Health, Education, and Welfare, 1960; Albert K. Cohen, *Delinquent Boys*, Glencoe, Ill.: The Free Press, 1955; and Richard Cloward and Lloyd Ohlin, *Delinquency and Opportunity*, Glencoe, Ill.: The Free Press, 1960.

[2] Cohen, *op. cit.*, pp. 112–119.

illegitimate means to reach legitimate goals [3] or to express their rejection and disdain for middle-class goals which are not available to them.[4]

Delinquency is not the only alternative open to youth who experienced status deprivation in school. Dropping out of school also offers a solution to this problem and is not confined to those lacking intellectual ability. Studies of school dropouts suggest that capable youth are leaving school prior to graduation to escape a condition similar to that described by Cohen and Cloward and Ohlin. For example, Lichter and his associates concluded that the capable dropout leaves school because of his desire to escape frustrations encountered in the school milieu:

> The dropouts left school because they were motivated to *run away* from a disagreeable situation; they did not feel impelled to run toward a definite and positive goal. Although they discussed employment, their talk was vague, aimless, or unrealistic. . . . The decision to drop out was the outcome of an accumulation of school problems and the belief that it was too late to correct the difficulties. Dropping out was not only the easiest course to take, but a passive, not an active resolution of the educational problem.[5]

One significant point regarding the decision to drop out of school as an alternative to the status frustration experienced in school is that it should reduce the motivational stimulus to engage in delinquent behavior. The individual who drops out is no longer involved in the competition with middle-class youth at school and the adjustment problem described by Cohen as the motivational source of delinquency is at least partially resolved.[6] If status deprivation experienced at school is causally related to delinquency, it follows that the probability of engaging in delinquent behavior is less for out-of-school youth than for in-school youth.[7] This proposition is examined in this study in the form of two specific hypotheses:

[3] Cloward and Ohlin maintain that some communities have both conventional and criminal opportunity structures. Boys in these communities who experience aspirational blockage in the legitimate opportunity system turn to the illegitimate opportunity system in an effort to achieve their aspirations. This solution is essentially that described by Merton as an innovating mode of adaptation. Robert K. Merton, *Social Theory and Social Structure*, Glencoe, Ill.: The Free Press, 1957, pp. 141–149.

[4] Cohen, on the other hand, maintains that the delinquent subculture engages in behavior which expresses rejection and derogation of middle-class norms and goals. Vandalism, for example, is seen as an expression of the delinquent's disdain of the middle-class norm regarding private property.

[5] Solomin Lichter et al., *The Dropouts*, New York: The Free Press of Glencoe, 1962, pp. 247–248.

[6] It is possible, however, that the individual has merely traded the status frustrations encountered at school for those encountered in our economic institutions. The availability of satisfactory employment may well be a necessary condition for the effective resolution of the status deprivation problem.

[7] The hypothesis that delinquency is related to frustrations encountered in the school milieu and that leaving this milieu reduces the motivation for delinquent behavior appears consistent with the fact that offense rates in the U.S. drop significantly after 17, when most lower-class American youth leave school and enter the labor force. Walter Lunden, *Statistics on Delinquents and Delinquency*, Iowa: The Art Press, 1961, p. 28; Jessie Bernard, *Social Problems at Midcentury*, New York: Dryden, 1957, pp. 421–444; William McCord et al., *Origins of Crime*, New York: Columbia University Press, 1959, p. 21; W. H. Dun-

1. The rate of delinquency is greater for boys while in than while out of school.[8]
2. Delinquents who drop out have a higher delinquency rate while in than while out of school.

The Study Design

The study population is composed of 743 tenth grade boys who entered the two largest high schools in a large western city in September, 1959.[9] In this *ex post facto* design, data were gathered on this group of boys for a three year period beginning with their entrance into high school in September, 1959 and ending with their class graduation in June of 1962.[10] The research design specified a comparison of the delinquency rates of these boys while in and out of school. The "in-school" and "out-of-school" distinction requires that each boy be classified as a graduate or dropout. Boys who graduated in June, 1962 or were in school throughout the entire study period were classified as graduates. All those who left school (during the three years) were classified as dropouts. The dropout category thus includes those who were "pushed" out of school for disciplinary problems as well as those who left voluntarily. Those who left to move to another geographical area were excluded from the analysis.[11] All boys classified as graduates were in school during the entire study period and consequently contributed *only* to the in-school delinquency rate. Boys classified as dropouts were in-school for some part of the study period and out of school for the remainder of the period, contributing to *both* the in-school and out-of-school delinquency

---

ham and M. E. Knaver, "The Juvenile Court and Its Relationship to Adult Criminality," *Social Forces* (March, 1954), pp. 290–296. In England, the rate of delinquency drops much earlier, at the age of 14 or 15; again, this is when most English youth *leave school* and enter the labor force. John Barron Mays, *Growing Up in the City*, Liverpool: University Press, 1954.

[8] It is recognized that leaving school may not reduce the likelihood of a boy who is already delinquent committing another delinquent act. The delinquent's identification and involvement with an existing delinquent group may lead him to continue his delinquent activities, as a requirement of group membership, even though the original motivation stimulus for this kind of behavior has been eliminated. However, if the dropout is not a member of a delinquent group prior to leaving school, the probability of his joining this kind of group or committing another delinquent act should be reduced.

[9] The total number of males entering these two schools in 1959 was 821. Seventy-eight of this original group transferred out of the area during the three year study period and were dropped from the analysis, leaving 743 subjects.

[10] Police contacts during the summer months of 1960 and 1961 were not considered in this analysis. Almost all of the subjects were out of school during this period of time and there was no practical way of determining how many subjects left the area and for what periods of time. During the school year, all graduates were in school and only dropouts had to be contacted to determine their whereabouts. The official referral rate declines during the summer months. [San Diego Police Department—Juvenile Division Monthly Reports, 1960, 1961, and 1962.] Had contacts reported during the summer months been included, the most probable effect would have been a decrease in the out-of-school referral rate. Since this works in favor of the hypothesis, it was decided to exclude summer time contacts from the analysis.

[11] This was determined by a "request for transcript" received by the school of origin. In several cases boys indicated they were moving but no request for transcript was received. In this event, they were classified as dropouts and an attempt was made to locate them in the local area.

rates.[12] Of the 743 boys in the study, 182 were classified as dropouts and 561 were classified as graduates.

The comparison of in- and out-of-school delinquency rates also required that these rates be calculated upon a common base. Consequently, it was necessary to determine the actual number of days graduates and dropouts were attending school and the number of days the dropouts were out of school. The number of in-school days for graduates was constant. The number of in-school days for dropouts varied, depending upon the date they left school. School records were examined to determine this date, and an attempt was made to contact each dropout during September and October of 1962 to determine the number of days he was out of school and in the study area. This information was secured for 132 or 73 per cent of the 182 dropouts. For the remainder, an estimate of their out-of-school time in the area was made after examining all available records. The latest date the subject was *known* to be in the area was used to calculate the length of time this subject was out-of-school and in the study area. The estimate of the number of out-of-school days is therefore a conservative one.[13]

Official contact reports by police, sheriff, and other law enforcement agencies constitute the measure of delinquency. The date and nature of each offense, as stated on the contact report (referral), were recorded.[14] The use of official statistics as a measure of delinquent behavior has been questioned by many.[15] Certainly a direct measure of actual behavior which violates legal statutes would provide a more adequate test of the hypothesis. Short and Nye have suggested the use of a self-reported measure of delinquency to more closely approximate a direct measure of delinquent behavior, but the nature of this study precluded the use of such a measure of delinquency.[16] However, an indirect assessment of delinquent behavior can be

[12] There were two boys who dropped out of school for a period of time and then re-entered school. The number of days they were out of school contributed to the calculation of the out-of-school rate and *both* their in-school periods contributed to the in-school rate. Neither boy had an official contact.

[13] A conservative estimate works against the hypothesis in this case, since it maximized the out-of-school delinquency rate.

[14] Kobrin asserts that police "complaint records" or contact reports are probably the most inclusive measure of delinquency obtainable though he recognizes that they are not an accurate measure of delinquent behavior. Solomon Kobrin, "The Conflict of Values in Delinquency Areas," *The American Sociological Review*, 16, 1951, pp. 652–661. Since a comparison of in- and out-of-school delinquent offense rates is made, truancy offenses were excluded. The calculation of the total number of in- and out-of-school days does not include any days after an individual's eighteenth birthday since an individual is generally not treated as a juvenile after his eighteenth birthday and only juvenile records were consulted.

[15] Thorsten Sellin, "The Significance of Records of Crime," *The Law Quarterly Review*, 67, 1951, pp. 489–504; and "Culture Conflict and Crime," *Social Science Research Council*, Bulletin 41, 1938, pp. 17–32; James F. Short, Jr. and F. Ivan Nye, "Reported Behavior as a Criterion of Deviant Behavior," *Social Problems*, 5, 1957, pp. 207–213; Sophia Robison, *Can Delinquency Be Measured?*, New York: Columbia University Press, 1936; John I. Kitsuse and Aaron V. Cicourel, "A Note on the Use of Statistics," *Social Problems*, 11, 1963, pp. 131–139.

[16] Short and Nye, *op. cit.* While these authors are aware of the limitations of official statistics when used in etiological research they do not suggest that this type of data is

obtained from official referrals of law enforcement agencies. The definition of a delinquent act in terms of official referrals is comprised of two essential elements: 1) it involves behavior which violates legal statutes and 2) it involves the initiation of official proceedings by law enforcement agencies.[17] While the legal definition includes an illegal behavior component, official records are an inaccurate measure of this behavior since the second component requires that the illegal act be known officially and that some action be initiated against the offender. When an official definition of delinquency is used, therefore, any differences in rates of delinquency noted may be attributed to 1) differences in actual behavior, 2) differences in the knowledge or reaction of official agencies to the offender, or 3) both of these elements. If the design of the study permits the investigator to rule out the second possibility, then tests of theoretically derived hypotheses will not be biased by the use of an official definition of delinquency. The crucial question, therefore, is what determines the behavior of official agents and how will these factors affect the tests of these hypotheses.

Since the comparison is between dropouts and graduates there are some logical grounds for assuming that, to the extent differences in knowledge or reaction of official agencies are operating, they would work *against* the hypothesis being tested, i.e., the effect of these biases would be to increase the magnitude of the *out-of-school* delinquency rate. On the basis of available research evidence, it would appear that a major factor influencing the action of official agents is the social class of the offender. Not only is the surveillance likely to be greater in lower-class neighborhoods, but the risk of formal action after detection appears to be greater for those living in these neighborhoods.[18] Since the research evidence also indicates that dropouts come disproportionately from lower-class neighborhoods, the effect of this type of official bias on a comparison of in- and out-of-school delinquency rates would be to accentuate the out-of-school rate and increase the likelihood of rejecting the hypothesis.[19]

---

inappropriate for etiological studies. "No other system of data collection seems practicable on a continuing basis. Much etiological research must remain in the manipulation of officially defined problems and statistics. . . . We are inclined to accept Tappan's point regarding the validity of legal norms as a unit of study in preference to nebulous extra-legal concepts." (p. 48)

[17] Cloward and Ohlin, *op. cit.*, p. 3; Kitsuse & Cicourel, *op. cit.*, pp. 131–137.

[18] Clifford R. Shaw and Henry D. McKay, *Juvenile Delinquency and Urban Areas*, Chicago: The University of Chicago Press, 1942; William C. Kvaraceus, "Juvenile Delinquency and Social Class," *Journal of Educational Sociology*, 18, 1944, pp. 51–54; Ernest W. Burgess, "The Economic Factor in Juvenile Delinquency," *Journal of Criminal Law, Criminology and Police Science*, 43, 1952, pp. 29–42; Ivan F. Nye, *Family Relationships and Delinquent Behavior*, New York: John Wiley and Sons, 1958; Short and Nye, *op. cit.*; Martin Gold, *Status Forces in Delinquent Boys*, Ann Arbor: The University of Michigan, 1963, ch. 1; Edwin Sutherland and Donald Cressey, *Principles of Criminology* (6th ed.), New York: J. B. Lippincott & Co., 1960, ch. 15.

[19] R. A. Tesseneer and L. M. Tesseneer, "Review of the Literature on School Dropouts," *Bulletin of the National Association of Secondary School Principals* (May, 1958), pp. 141–153; August B. Hollingshead, *Elmtown's Youth*, New York: John Wiley and Sons, 1949; Edith G. Neisser, *School Failures and Dropouts*, Public Affairs Pamphlet No. 346, July, 1963, pp. 4–6; Division for Youth, *The School Dropout Problem: Rochester,*

It might be argued that those in school are more "visible" to law enforcement agents than are those out-of-school. One way the police may learn about delinquent behavior is through reports from school officials. To the extent schools make such reports to law enforcement agencies, the delinquent acts of those in school are more visible than are those of out-of-school youth. In connection with another study, contact reports filed in the county during 1963 and 1964 were reviewed to determine the source of each referral.[20] After excluding truancy offenses, it was found that less than one half of one per cent of the referrals identified the school as the source of the referral. Clearly the school is not a significant source for delinquency referrals in this community.

One other factor which might account for a different response on the part of law enforcement agents is the offense. If offenses committed while in school are characteristically different from those committed while out-of-school, this could account for a differential response on the part of law enforcement agents and a higher in-school delinquency rate. The relatively small number of offenses involved in this study precluded the use of a detailed offense breakdown, but the in- and out-of-school offense patterns were compared with respect to (1) property offenses, (2) offenses against persons, and (3) control offenses.[21] The proportions of in- and out-of-school offenses falling into these three categories were as follows: property offenses, 48 per cent compared to 50 per cent; offenses against persons, 4 per cent and 0 per cent; control offenses, 36 per cent and 25 per cent. The major difference noted was in the control offenses where the greater in-school proportion was due to a relatively greater number of curfew offenses. In terms of seriousness of offense, a greater proportion of out-of-school than in-school offenses would be classified as felonies. If there are differences in reactions of officials based on the seriousness of the offense, this would tend to operate against

Part I, State of New York, May, 1962, pp. 9–10; Daniel Schreiber, "The Dropout and the Delinquent: Promising Practices Gleaned From a Year of Study," Phi Delta Kappan, 44 (February, 1963), pp. 215–221; Bernard A. Kaplan, "Issues in Educating the Culturally Disadvantaged," Phi Delta Kappan, 45 (November, 1963), pp. 70–76; and Starke R. Hathaway and Elio D. Monachesi, Adolescent Personality and Behavior: MMPI Patterns of Normal, Delinquent, Dropout, and Other Outcomes, Minneapolis: University of Minnesota Press, 1963, pp. 92–98. This class differential was in fact observed in this study with 85 per cent of the dropouts compared to 69 per cent of the graduates residing in areas classified as lower SES areas. The measure of socioeconomic status (SES) is a social area measure based upon U.S. Census block data. Four block characteristics were considered: 1) average house value, 2) average contract rent, 3) per cent homes owner occupied, and 4) per cent deterioration and dilapidation. Blocks where two or more of these housing characteristics were below the city average were classified as lower SES areas. All remaining blocks were classified as higher SES areas.

[20] These data were gathered in connection with a five year longitudinal study on delinquency and dropout supported by a Public Health Service Research Grant No. MH 07173 from the National Institute of Mental Health.

[21] The offenses as listed on the police contact report were classified as follows: 1) Property Offenses—Auto Theft, Burglary, Petty Theft, Other Theft, Vandalism; 2) Offenses against Persons—Sex Offenses, Assault and Battery; and 3) Control Offenses—Runaway, Dangerous Drugs, Drunkenness and Possession of Alcohol, Incorrigible, Beyond Control, & Curfew. Other offenses were classified as miscellaneous. Twelve per cent of the in-school and 25 per cent of the out-of-school offenses were classified as miscellaneous.

the hypotheses in this study. In general, the observed differences in offense patterns do not appear great enough to evoke a systematic difference in response on the part of law enforcement agents.

In the light of the above discussion, it is argued that the use of official referrals as a measure of delinquency should result in a conservative test of the hypotheses since the kinds of distortions or biases introduced by the knowledge and reaction of official agents would tend to work against the hypotheses. If the rates of actual delinquent behavior among boys in and out of school were in fact equal, the most probable effect of using official police contacts to measure these rates would be to over-estimate the out-of-school delinquency rate among the dropouts who are more likely to be drawn from a lower-class background.

Findings

The comparison of the in- and out-of-school delinquency referral rates is presented in Table I. The overall in-school referral rate is 4.95 compared

Table I

Delinquent Referral Rate * Among Boys in and out of School

SES Areas	In School			Out of School ** Dropouts
	Graduates	** Dropouts	Sub-total	
Lower	4.13	8.70	4.96	2.42
Higher	4.92	4.95	4.92	4.63
Total	4.34	8.03	4.95	2.75

* Number of referrals per 10,000 in- or out-of-school days.
** These are the same individuals during two different time periods.

to an out-of-school rate of 2.75. This difference is substantial and in the direction hypothesized. Table I also presents the in-school delinquency rates for both graduates and future dropouts and for those residing in lower and higher socioeconomic (SES) neighborhoods. The highest delinquency rate was observed among lower SES dropouts prior to their leaving school. It is quite possible that their involvement in this kind of activity was responsible for some of them being pushed out of school. What is surprising is that this same group of boys had the lowest referral rate after dropping out of school. Their out-of-school rate is less than one-third their in-school rate. These data clearly support the hypothesis.

Cohen's explanation of delinquency applies specifically to working class boys and the status deprivation variable automatically incorporated the class variable. Since there was no attempt to obtain a measure of this independent variable in this study, it seemed important to calculate separate rates for those from lower and higher SES areas. While the in-school rate for boys from higher SES areas is greater than their out-of-school rate, the difference is quite small and may be of little substantive significance. In fact, there appears to be little difference in any of the rates shown for boys from higher SES areas. The in-school rates for dropouts and graduates are almost identical and are only slightly greater than the out-of-school rates. It would appear that leaving school does not have the same impact on boys from higher SES areas as it does on those from lower SES areas. One might expect that leaving school would affect boys from these two SES areas differently. While leaving school should help to eliminate the status frustration of boys from lower-class areas, it would not necessarily solve the adjustment problem of those from middle- and upper-class areas. Boys from lower-class areas can retreat into the lower-class community where they may seek employment in the unskilled or semi-skilled occupations which are available to them. Their parents and other adult members of their community are willing to accept these occupations as legitimate endeavors for young men.

Boys from middle-class areas who leave school subsequently find themselves limited to lower-class occupations while their parents and other adult members of their community continue to hold middle-class expectations for them. They are unable or unwilling to meet the formal expectations of school and are equally unable to meet the expectations of their parents if they drop out of school.

A separate but related issue involves the effect of leaving school on the referral rate of boys who were known officially as delinquents while in school. Although the rate of delinquent referral is less for boys while out of school than while in school, it does not necessarily follow that those who have official referrals while in school will have fewer referrals after leaving school. To test the hypothesis that delinquents who drop out have a higher referral rate while in school, in- and out-of-school referral rates were calculated for this group (Table II).

Table II

Offense Rates * for Delinquent Dropouts Before and After Leaving School

SES Areas	Before	After
Lower	64.96	34.52
Higher	40.12	23.75
Total	60.78	31.01

* Number of delinquent referrals per 10,000 student-days.

The data in Table II supports this hypothesis. The in-school referral rate for delinquents is almost twice their out-of-school referral rate. This relationship holds for delinquents from both lower and higher SES areas. The rates in Table II also suggest that delinquents from lower SES neighborhoods have a higher referral rate than do delinquents from higher SES neighborhoods. This is particularly interesting since there is little difference in the proportions (.112 and .118) of boys from each of these two areas who are delinquent, i.e., who had one or more official referrals on file. It appears that delinquents from lower SES neighborhoods are more frequent offenders than are those from higher SES areas.

Conclusion

Cohen suggests that delinquency on the part of lower-class boys is a response to the unequal competition encountered at school. Delinquency is thus associated with frustration and failure particularly experienced in school, for it is in this milieu that youth from disparate cultural backgrounds are forced to compete for middle-class success goals.

There are several alternatives available to those who experience frustration at school. They may remain in school and attempt to deal with their frustration by attacking the system of norms and values which they believe to be the source of their difficulties. Delinquent behavior may thus be viewed as an expression of their resentment toward this system and those who attempt to enforce its norms. On the other hand, those experiencing failure may leave school making a "retreatist" adaptation in an effort to escape from the situation which produces the frustrations. No longer frustrated by the unequal competition at school, there is little or no need to attack the school or the normative system it represents.

It was hypothesized, therefore, that (1) the rate of delinquency referral is greater for boys while in school than while out of school; and (2) delinquents who drop out have a higher referral rate while in school than while out of school. The data supported both hypotheses. The small difference between in- and out-of-school offense rates for boys from higher SES neighborhoods suggests that dropping out of school may not constitute a solution to problems of status deprivation for boys from higher SES areas. One might infer that dropout is a satisfactory solution for those from lower SES areas for the delinquency rate of such youth is lower after leaving school than it was while they were in school.

20   Delinquency and the Schools

OFFICE OF EDUCATION, U.S. DEPARTMENT OF
HEALTH, EDUCATION, AND WELFARE

Introduction

(The school is the major public socializing institution affecting the lives of today's youth. Extra-school forces are acting upon youth concurrently

Reprinted from *Task Force Report: Juvenile Delinquency and Youth Crime*, The President's Commission on Law Enforcement and Administration of Justice, Washington, D.C., U.S. Govt. Printing Office, 1967, pp. 278–304.

with their schooling. However, something happens in the school setting which tends to confirm in some youth anti-social behavior patterns.

Three deficiencies of schools probably contribute to delinquent behavior in youth: (1) The educational enterprise is not meaningfully related to the real world outside—the world of employment, changing social conditions, etc. (2) The school does not present itself as a model of the pluralistic society. Groups are kept apart by ability, race, by economic class. The school isolates. It excludes. (3) The school often does not prepare youth for mature life; it infantalizes them. Kids learn largely through imitation. Therefore, they have to be presented with a model of future expectations. The school must allow the exercise of self-responsibility and opportunity for decision-making to prepare youth for adulthood.

How do these deficiencies in the school contribute to delinquency? (1) School experience, irrelevant to life experience and to employment opportunities, contributes heavily to dropout rates. An unemployed dropout stands a good chance of becoming delinquent. (2) School organization, which isolates and excludes according to ability, race, or economic class, denies to youth the opportunity to meaningfully interact with diverse segments of society. Delinquency can be defined in part as the inability to generalize the effects of one's own behavior on others. This inability is sustained by the organizational arrangements of schools. (3) A school which denies opportunity for youth—all youth, 'bad' as well as 'good'—to actively participate in meaningful decision-making does not assist the development of mature behavior. Delinquency can be described as a dramatic manifestation of immature behavior.

What can be done? (1) School offerings can be made relevant to experience in the real world outside the school and can be coordinated with opportunities which exist there. (2) Schools can be arranged so that meaningful group interaction is possible within an inclusive school setting. (3) Opportunities can be provided by the school, and in the school, for youth to assume real responsibility.

The school should prepare youth for the stated ideals of the society, i.e., for being responsible citizens in a democratic pluralistic society where individuals can be upwardly mobile by their own efforts; where individuals can operate as individuals, where they can be cooperative, and need not be conformist. Moreover, the school must actively seek ways to constructively involve the total community in providing opportunities for youth development.

The school must build a bridge to employers, community action programs, colleges, universities, community service and other groups. This linkage is necessary to enhance the relevance of educational offerings to employment opportunities and to other training and educational programs. Each child should be assured adequate access to health, legal, welfare, employment and other services which will enable him to remain and function adequately in school.

The school is made up of a physical plant, teachers, students, and materials. The quality of their interaction, and of the interaction between the school and the world outside, can lead to, or impede, an educational experience which may prevent, or contribute to, delinquent behavior in youth.)

. . .

We recognize that extra-school forces are acting upon youth concurrently with their schooling; however, it is the purpose of this paper *not* to pass the buck back to the family, or on to the courts. Rather we shall attempt to thoughtfully examine the school as a socializing institution, and to suggest some possibilities for re-creating the school as a positive, constructive socializing force in American society.

Such an examination leads directly into an exploration of basic assumptions about the nature of American society, and the relationship of educational goals to that society. A question basic to this exploration is the capacity of American society as a whole to tolerate diversity.[1] This question comes into sharper focus when we consider the labels which are used to describe behavior of those who are called delinquent or delinquency prone; words such as 'acceptable'/'unacceptable'; 'normal'/'deviant'; 'non-conformist'/'conformist'; 'constructive'/'destructive'; etc. In attempting to deal with the problems of which delinquency is a symptom, are we proceeding with the end in mind of eventually producing behavior which is acceptable to that which is traditionally 'white middle-class'? If this is our end, then we should attempt to intervene in existing patterns of behavior which deviate from this 'norm', and develop a strategy to alter deviancy through education and training for 'normative behavior'.

On the other hand, if our goal is to encourage and provide for a diversity of cultural and economic styles of life within our society, then our means of intervention and our strategy for changing 'deviant' behavior will be governed by very different assumptions about behavior itself.[2]

Another basic and related assumption which bears examination is reflected in the growing use of the term 'disadvantaged' to indicate specific racial or economic groups. Such limited use of the term disguises the fact that the basic disadvantage—social disadvantage—affects all racial and economic groups. Social disadvantage lies "in the fact that one who is born into poverty cannot have social relationships with those who transmit to him what will enable him to leave a poverty environment and still survive." [3] It is the disadvantage of the non-poor as revealed by their attempts to administer programs for the poor:

> In its role of educator of the poor, the public school is one obvious example of institutionalized disadvantage in reverse. The faculty and administrative personnel of almost all public schools are disadvantaged when it comes to

[1] This question is basic to all efforts to bring about 'the Great Society', and we suggest that its implications for program design and allocation of resources are vastly greater than the attention it has thus far received.

[2] This latter goal is obviously that which we are attempting to look toward in this investigation. However, we are aware that many of our suggestions require further analysis to determine whether they are truly consistent in furthering its attainment.

[3] Daniel Jordan, "Social Disadvantage—The Real Enemy in the War on Poverty," *World Order*, Fall 1966.

understanding and educating the poor, and it has caused them to fail in that job.[4]

It is the limitation in understanding and experience of members of all economic and racial groups—affluent as well as poor—produced by their continued isolation from each other.

Public education which isolates segments of the total population along economic or racial lines fosters and perpetuates social disadvantagement. The devices of isolation—*de facto* segregation, rules and regulations which prescribe behavior patterns uncharacteristic of and unnecessary to certain life styles, removal of disturbed children to special environments, curricular materials portraying accomplishments only of a particular ethnic group, grouping and grading practices (the 'labeling syndrome') etc.—these devices are manifold and are often unrecognized by educators. They are, however, quickly perceived by youth. The transition from isolation to inclusion, necessary to overcome social disadvantagement, is a problem of overwhelming importance affecting every school in America today.

We are not suggesting that the following report presents comprehensive solutions to these and other complex problems with which we are concerned. Rather we see this as an attempt to relate a manifestation of deep societal unrest—delinquency—to a major institution of American life—the schools— and as a means to explore the capacity and promise of the latter to deal meaningfully and realistically with the former.[5]

I. Educational Programs Sufficient to Meet Community Needs

Unless there is a 'pay-off' for kids who stay in school, dropout and delinquency problems will not be solved. This 'pay-off' must be either opportunity for further education, training, or experience leading to jobs, or immediate placement in jobs in the community—a placement which offers opportunity for training and advancement.

Peace Corps and Vista are two types of experiences available for youth. However these are 'volunteer' activities, and they will provide opportunities only to those who can afford one or two years of 'financial irresponsibility' and will consequently attract mainly those youth who are economically secure. Job Corps will meet the needs of a very small number of those with whom we are concerned. Neighborhood Youth Corps offers larger-scale possibilities, but its eligibility requirements are too often high, and many of its

---

[4] Ibid.

[5] Note: We have spent considerable time in the course of this effort in observing programs and practices (educational, community action, legal aid, court) at the local level and in discussions with troubled kids and with persons who are planning and administering programs. We have tried to shape our response to meet the actual needs as we have perceived them.

Our recommendations are, we believe, based on workable program models. In no case have we recommended a practice or a program design which is not being carried out somewhere across the country. Unfortunately we have not been able to insert the illustrative material which we have compiled, but given time it would be possible to do so.

job offerings have been largely 'make-work' with no future. Both these programs, however, have offered models which may well help to provide answers to the problems of locked-out youth. The combination of work-for-pay, skill development, and education *if* it can lead to job placement with career-ladder possibilities, seems to offer the most promising solution to the needs of this growing number of youth for which the traditional system offers small promise.

Jobs, however, are hard come by for youth from ghetto areas, areas which are producing the greatest numbers of dropouts and delinquents. *This existing and projected lack of meaningful employment opportunities for large numbers of youth growing into adulthood is perhaps the major domestic problem in America today.*

The school must share the responsibility not only for training for jobs, but also for job development and job placement. Local educational agencies can and must participate in cooperative and comprehensive job development efforts. Particularly promising are possibilities for 'new careers' in educational and other service-related occupations.[6] These and other job development possibilities should be thoroughly explored and cooperatively developed with industry, labor, community action, employment services, and other community groups.

. . . Some Indicators of the School's Responsiveness to the Needs of Youth and the Community

1. Acceptance of the responsibility for providing educational opportunity to *all* children up to the age of eighteen. (*ALL* includes dropouts, suspensions, expulsions, delinquents, young parents, unwed mothers, etc.)

2. The provision of each student with the opportunity to engage actively in planning and carrying through his individual educational goals and objectives.

3. The structuring of its teaching methods, curricular offerings, services, rules, regulations, use of school and other facilities, groupings of students, etc. so that each student may receive preparation for employment and/or further education or experience geared to his specific interests and skills.

4. The establishment of appropriate linkages with employers, community action programs, colleges and universities, community service and other groups to: a) assure the relevance of its educational offerings to immediate and projected employment opportunities and to other training and educational programs within the local community and State; b) help assure the adequate provision to each child of health, legal, welfare, employment and other services which will enable him to remain and function adequately in school.

5. The assisting of each student to find placement either in work or in further education at the termination of his school career, and the engage-

---

[6] See Arthur Pearl and Frank Reissman, *New Careers for the Poor*, New York, Free Press, 1965.

ment in cooperative job development efforts with other community groups to make such placement possible and meaningful.

6. The extension of school services into the community to meet the immediate, specific, and demonstrable needs of the residents of that community who may be alienated from the existing school setting or whose access to it may be difficult.

7. The cooperative utilization of resources and facilities in the community for the development and location of educational programs and activities, thereby assuring the fullest possible provision of educational opportunities for youth.

8. The development by the school of means for continuous assessment of its overall goals, immediate objectives, and on-going activities and practices whereby it can determine progress and identify impediments in meeting the needs and interests of all of its students and staff, and the continuous interpretation of these goals and this assessment to students, to staff, to parents, and to the community at large; a joining with the community in developing and maintaining an overall assessment and planning process to enable the effective utilization of total community resources to meet total community needs.

.   .   .

II. Curricular Designs and Materials
Relevant to the Needs of Youth
in a Changing Society

It has become increasingly obvious to many youth that much of what is taught in the school bears little relevance to life outside the school building, that it does not prepare them to hold jobs or to continue with their education beyond high school.

Schools are all too often viewed as a 'holding operation' by both students and teachers. It is time that not only educators, but other concerned segments of our society, demand of our schools a curriculum which frees teachers to teach, and students to learn about that society, about getting and holding a job, about legal rights and responsibilities, about the characteristics and implications of the technological revolution, about exciting developments in the arts.

It is manifestly clear that what is needed is not just a major revision in curricular offerings but a massive effort to provide a new and different kind of educational experience for youth. The following trends are worth noting:

1. An increase in numbers of schools and instructional personnel willing to engage in curriculum design specifically geared to the individual student's interests, talents, and needs.

2. Experimentation with approaches to the learning process which utilize the 'clinical' or real life experience as a basis for development of conceptual skills, and which imaginatively utilize the juncture of the clinical and con-

ceptual experience for stimulation of students' interests and development of analytical skills.

3. Increasing willingness on the part of instructional personnel to depart from traditional distinctions between subject areas and to develop inter-disciplinary approaches to broad areas of knowledge which will increase the relevance of the educational experience to the inter-related nature of knowl-edge characteristic of other experience.

4. Adoption by many schools of work-orientation and work-experience curricular offerings into an integrated comprehensive curricular design for *all* students, thus overcoming the distinction between 'academic' and 'vo-cational' curriculum which has served to label and stigmatize students and to pre-determine their educational and occupational future.

5. Pilot programs which are developing and utilizing curriculum which view citizenship responsibilities, work experience, cultural enrichment and family responsibilities as inter-related and necessary educational offerings for all children.

6. Development of curricular offerings which involve and rely upon the particular resources of the surrounding community—both in terms of phys-ical facilities and equipment and instructional capabilities for supplement-ing and increasing the relevance of courses provided by and in the school. In several places the surrounding community is being used as a 'living lab-oratory for learning,' with the city itself providing the 'clinical environment' leading to the development of communications, computational, conceptual and analytical skills as described (see 2).

7. Participation in curriculum design by representatives of various seg-ments of the community—labor, industry, professional and public service groups, university personnel, civil rights and community groups, who have joined with teachers and administrators to develop educational materials and courses relevant to immediate and projected employment opportunities, current issues, and social needs. Such efforts have in some instances been greatly strengthened by the additional expertise provided by parents and by the students themselves.

8. Major efforts in development of curricular materials (programmed in-structional materials and equipment, books, films, classroom supplies, lab equipment, etc.), integrally related to the total educational experience, which are designed in such a way as to provoke investigation by the student, to cause him to ask questions, and to become actively involved in discovering answers. "These materials assist in the interpretation of observed events, and act as vehicles by which the student obtains a broad, fundamental understanding of a part of the world in which he lives as well as a personal sense of his ability to control and manipulate this 'world.'" [7]

9. Increasing cooperative activity on the part of educators and publishers to develop curricular materials which provide an honest portrayal of the di-

[7] "Final Report of the Summer Study on Occupational Vocational and Technical Edu-cation," Massachusetts Institute of Technology, July 6–Aug. 13, 1965, p. 61.

versity of ethnic, national, and racial contributions to and characteristics of American life.

10. A growing recognition of compensatory educational programs as a short-term urgent necessity in disadvantaged areas, and a designing of the curriculum for these programs to serve as transitional or 'bridge' until more comprehensive programs begin to emerge. This 'transitional' design involves a shift in emphasis in compensatory programs from a concentration on 'what is wrong' with kids and designed attempts to 'repair' them, to a focus on 'what is right' with kids, utilizing strengths to stimulate interest and self-reliance. In other words a shift from helping students to helping students help themselves. "These bridging curricula should aim at providing a size-able body of articulated work-study courses with heavy community involvement, reflecting the apparent present urgent and relatively early need of these students for gainful employment." [8] Such short-term compensatory educational programs are being carried out, in increasing numbers, in the summer months. Free from normal administrative regulations, they enable teachers, administrators and youth to focus more clearly on their true educational objectives.

"Our Nation is the product of our people. And our people are the product of our schools." [9] The unrest in urban areas today, the 'white backlash,' the growing crime rate—these are strong evidence that our schools have failed to convince generations of students of the viability of democracy and of individual opportunities and responsibilities in that democracy. Major revisions in the 'basic curriculum,' the school experience itself, must take place if present and future generations of Americans are to be convinced that human beings do in fact have dignity as human beings, and that the worth of individuals must be fostered and respected if the democratic system is to survive.

Such a total re-structuring of the educational enterprise requires the re-examination by every teacher and administrator of his own attitudes and practices in the classroom and in the school, of his basic beliefs about the educability of all children, of his respect for himself as an educator and for his students as human beings. This type of 'total curricular revision' further demands a reappraisal of rules, regulations, disciplinary procedures, and ways of grouping children, to ascertain the underlying assumptions about human dignity, human rights, and human opportunity which they evidence. . . .

. . . . .

III. Strengthened Educational Manpower

The critical existing and projected shortage of educational personnel cannot be measured solely in terms of numerical insufficiency. The persons we wish to attract must exhibit particular skills in combination with certain personality characteristics—drive, imaginativeness, and a kind of 'gutsy' op-

[8] Summary Report of the Summer Study on Occupational, Vocational and Technical Education, Massachusetts Institute of Technology, July 6–Aug. 13, 1965, p. 10.
[9] Harold Howe II, U.S. Commissioner of Education.

timism. They must be committed to the educability of all children. They must be willing to engage in experimentation and innovation. They must be sufficiently confident of their own abilities and sufficiently familiar with the life styles of their students to be able to function freely in the classroom. A large portion must be men. It is obvious that our present educational system is attracting far too few persons of this type.

The following conditions have been identified as those which must be met by school systems if the vicious cycle of educational failure, leading to dropouts, leading to delinquency, is to be broken—as it can only be by the attraction to educational professions of able personnel.

1. *Increased pay*—sufficient to allow education to compete with other occupations which attract personnel with the characteristics described. The Federal government has no mechanism for providing funds to States or to localities which can be used to subsidize salaries for teachers. It is to the States that we must look for the commitment to education which will provide the financial resources necessary to attract and retain able and qualified personnel in the educational professions. The cost of quality education is high. The States must weigh the relative costs and benefits of welfare payments, delinquency and crime, unemployment and urban unrest against teachers' salaries in their allocation of resources. The role of the Federal government as junior partner to the States is nowhere more clearly described than in this area—perhaps the most critical in education today.

2. *Improvement in working conditions*—including reasonable teacher-pupil ratio, reduction of administrative and clerical responsibilities, increased opportunities for meaningful decision-making re the total educational process;

3. *Opportunity for development of interests and skills*—provided through such mechanisms as released time for participation in community, cultural, or educational activities relevant to occupational goals; improved matching of personnel with subject area interest; improved matching of personnel with individual students whom they believe they can 'reach';

4. *Opportunity for professional advancement*—such as the institution of career ladders which would reward experience (and demonstrated educational achievement of students) with increased responsibility, status, and pay; provision of broad opportunities for continuous training, study, and research;

5. *Efficient utilization of personnel*—through training and utilization of para-professional staff, team teaching, provision of courses in locations other than the school, utilization of part-time instructional staff with particular expertise through released-time arrangements with their employers, utilization of volunteers, offering regular staff twelve-month employment with paid vacations.

·   ·   ·

IV. Structural Flexibility Within the School and Within the School System

In recent years the problem of bureaucratic rigidity within the school and within the school system has received considerable attention from concerned educational commentators. The description of the school as a closed self-perpetuating system which locks in middle-class mediocrity and locks out diversity, innovation, and imagination, has become a commonplace cry of alarm. There is sufficient evidence of rigidity as witnessed by those the school does not serve—dropouts, truants, expulsions, suspensions—as well as by those the school purports to serve—large subgroups of our population whose achievement levels decline as they go through the schools and do indeed graduate—to warrant a serious consideration of these charges, and a concentrated effort to effect change.

It is our contention that the purposes of public education are best served by an organization of educational functions which exhibits the characteristics of the ideal society for which the youth is being prepared. In our society, therefore, the organization of the school should duplicate the conditions necessary for the democratic process. In this type of organization, responsibility for decision-making resides ultimately with the people (students—parents—community) who select representatives to voice their needs, determine goals, and develop methods for achieving those goals. A democratic process is inclusive—that is, it is representative of *all* the people, weighs their needs and aspirations equally, and allocates resources in ways which will provide opportunities equally to all.

We believe that there is significant correlation between educational achievement and an educational process which exhibits the characteristics of the democratic process. An increase in active participation by students in educational decision-making itself results in increased learning achievement; increased participation by teachers in curriculum design and other areas of educational development results in lower teacher-turnover and in attraction to the teaching profession of a higher quality of personnel. Increased participation by community groups, industry and labor, assures educational programs which meet the broad needs of the community, and which provide to the individual student an increased likelihood for employment.

How can structural flexibility within the school and the school system be created and maintained?

Major factors determining the relative rigidity or flexibility of the system are on the one hand, the strength and willingness of the administration to share responsibility and to allow diversity and change within the system, and on the other, the capacity and the willingness of the instructional and service staff, students, and community to assume such responsibility, to tolerate such diversity and to foster change. These factors are determined in part by the recruitment and selection procedure affecting administrators and staff and by the degree of community interest and support for quality education.

Assuming that such strength and willingness exists, there are actions which schools can take to increase and to maintain the flexibility of the educational organization. These actions might include the institution of flexible ability groupings, and individualized curriculum design; expanded use of school facilities and of community facilities for educational purposes; an on-going assessment of rules and regulations to determine their usefulness and relevance in assisting the educational process; an on-going examination of the roles and relationships of students and educational personnel with particular attention given to creating and maintaining a democratic decision-making process within the school and within the school system.

Flexible Activity Groupings and Individualized Curriculum Design. While more and more "have" schools are reaping the educational and motivational benefits of flexible grouping and individualized instruction, the "have nots" are stuck with the rigidity of the standard classroom. The application of computer capability to instructional scheduling and the development of more sophisticated evaluation and diagnostic tests have increased the feasibility of flexible.grouping—but they require money, talent, and an innovative spirit. Likewise, individual instruction has been made possible by the rapid proliferation of educational technologies, new devices with infinite patience for individual drill, remediation, and tutoring. Here again, mounting a comprehensive program tailored to individual needs requires money, relevant knowledge, and the willingness to look at each individual with an understanding eye.

Expanded Use of School and Community Facilities for Educational Purposes. Industry has long ago discovered the economic efficiency to be gained from round-the-clock operation of its steel mills, oil refineries, and computer centers. Yet our educational plant lays idle much of the time, even though the educational needs of the community are growing by leaps and bounds. The current trend toward evening classes for adults is a healthy one but it would be even healthier to have adults moving in and out of our schools all day. Too many kids feel like outcasts from "adult society"; their feelings of usefulness are often assuaged only by dropping out and getting a job, thus reasserting their usefulness in a production oriented society. Opening the school to part-time "community" teachers would not only rejoin it to the mainstream of society but it would also provide students with more varied models of behavior and furnish them with a greater diversity of learning experiences. Conversely, the community itself is a rich educational environment and should be exploited by getting the kids out of the narrow confines of the classroom and into the offices, libraries, courts, factories, shops, and studios of the community. While work-study programs fulfill this function in part, a great deal more ingenuity should go into the creation of richer educational experiences.

Useful Rules and Regulations. The rules, regulations, laws, and standards of a more static age served us well by providing guidelines to successive generations. We are certainly not ready to give up such aids; however, it is clear that to provide a useful and necessary guide to behavior, rules must be responsive to ever changing conditions; they must be open to continuous review, discussion, and criticism. While this is true for society as a whole, it is especially true of our school system; for youth are exquisitely sensitive to the dynamic world about them and within them. To keep pace the system must develop both formal and informal channels of communication with them; it must be sensitive to their needs and to their suggestions; it should use its maturity and wisdom to guide and counsel, not to repress and sub-due.

Creating a Democratic Structure.   Our present educational system is a far cry from the democratic model outlined in this paper. To change this system will require nothing less than a revolution in our present thinking, for students and parents as well as teachers and administrators. The application of Carl Rogers' nondirective or client-centered approach to education, as exemplified by the use of basic encounter methods, offers some hope. The evidence is still sketchy but it appears that when used with teachers they become more open and creative; when used with students they become more independent, self-motivated and responsible; and when used with a whole school system it becomes more dynamic and innovative.

Role of the Student.   There is very little that the student *cannot* do in the educational process if his participation is solicited, welcomed, and rewarded. Youth must experience some sense of control over their present experiences if they are to believe that they have any control over their future. A sense of control is necessary to any meaningful understanding of personal or social responsibility—an understanding basic to the prevention of delinquent behavior. The learning situation provides endless opportunities for student participation. For example, a student can assist in the design of a course of study which interests him and which meets his needs; he can share the responsibility for drawing up and enforcing rules and regulations for behavior in the school and the classroom; he can be trained to participate in surveys of community-school needs and attitudes; he can be utilized as a tutor for younger children, or for students whose achievement in a particular area lags behind his; he can work part time for pay as an aide in the classroom, playground, or other education-related function. The student can also participate in the planning process.

·   ·   ·

V. Expanded and Coordinated Services to Youth

There is a growing public awareness that the responsibility of the school today extends beyond formal instruction. Homes which offer little intellectual stimulation or encouragement, families ignorant of social services which can help to meet their health and welfare needs, and neighborhoods comprised of persons too uneducated and unskilled to feel themselves a meaningful part of this competitive society, strongly influence a child's aspirations and motivations. Schools must counteract these influences at the same time as they reinforce and emphasize the strengths which the children bring with them from their home and community experiences.

Curricula geared to needs and aspirations of youth, empathetic faculty and administrators, instructional techniques which better ensure the experience of success, and the establishment of a climate of acceptance for all individuals are the earmarks of any good school. But to these must be added the ancillary services, provided by the school or through referral to community agencies and institutions, which may determine whether the hostile child, the withdrawn child, the socially deviant child can make the necessary adjustments so that he can continue his education, obtain a job, and become a self-respecting and productive member of society.

As of October 1964, 5.1 million young people between the ages of 16 and 24 had left school without graduating. Between October 1963 and October 1964, 604,000 persons dropped out of school. Their unemployment rate during this period was 31.7 percent. Although the dropout rate has decreased somewhat, the actual number of dropouts has increased. This large and growing group of young people enter adulthood with a severe disability, for the increasingly technological nature of our society is demanding a higher level of skills for job entry and for job progression. Those who are poorly prepared or who do not have a high school diploma are ten times more likely to become involved in delinquent acts than their peers who graduated from high school. If they can find jobs, their prospects for advancement are dim. When they can't find jobs, the resulting frustration and resentment may lead to antisocial behavior. At the same time, there are many young people whose criminal behavior is often forced on them by society—poorly educated, poorly trained, unemployable in today's job market, they turn to crime to obtain the money they need to support themselves and their families.

Guidance and Counseling Services. The importance of guidance and counseling services in the elementary schools, as well as in the secondary schools, is being increasingly recognized. The provision of these services has been much slower: in terms of manpower alone we would need an additional 80,000 secondary counselors to provide one counselor for each 300 to 400 students. But the problem of providing effective guidance service is more basic and complex than mere numbers. It involves restructuring the functions of the counselor to include not only testing and student evaluation, college-oriented guidance and curriculum planning, but also the establishment of relationships with the student which will enable the counselor to help him with his emotional, psychological, family, and even financial problems. For the counselor this means a revised preparatory pre-service curricula, a knowledge of community agencies and services, close coordination between the teachers and himself, a familiarity with the homes and neighborhoods from which the students come. It means that the counselor is available when the student needs him and where the parents can meet with him.

Social Work Services. The school social worker can provide an invaluable link between the school and the family. Like counselors, school social workers are in short supply: at present there are less than 5,000 such persons employed in the schools. Thirty-three thousand more are needed to provide one social worker for each 150 students in present poverty target areas alone.

Social work services are needed for both the in-school and the out-of-school students. Social workers responsible to the school but working primarily outside its walls, could identify the problem children among the in-school population and attempt to identify the factors in the home environment which hinder the child's progress. Working in coordination with the counselor to stimulate parents' understanding of ways to encourage the educational and occupational aspirations of their children, school social workers can also help these parents to become aware of community services which might be able to assist them.

"Reach-Out" Services.   A school social worker, or an aide responsible to the professionally trained person, should be utilized to reach out to the child who has dropped out of school and attempt to return that youngster to an educational program—either inside or outside of the formal school structure. An aide familiar to the neighborhood may be particularly successful in establishing rapport with the former student and in discerning the academic and social difficulties which forced or pushed that student out of school. Both the trained school social worker and the social work aide should be knowledgeable about the community resources to which a pupil or his family could be referred when additional help is necessary to alleviate family and personal difficulties.

Remedial Reading Specialists.   Perhaps one of the most difficult things for the slow learner or underachiever to accomplish is to be able to read. Often the parents cannot read and cannot help their children. Sometimes the teachers set a pace which the children are unable to keep. Many children don't have reading material at home and must wait until they are in school before they can practice their reading. If a child is unable to read in his early years of school, he will be unsuccessful in most of his school work. Obviously, this is one of the primary points from which to start an educational program. Whether the need exists for one child or a school of children, remedial reading must be instituted.

A remedial reading specialist should be used in at least two ways: to work directly with the students either individually or in classes; and to assist the regular faculty so that they can teach reading more effectively whatever the subject matter. Every school at all levels should have such a person available on a regular basis.

Health Services Within the School.   The American Dental Association estimates that about 50 percent of the American children have never been to a dentist. Public health officials often express their concern that too many families visit a doctor only when a health problem becomes critical. For low income or minority culture groups, this is often a matter of not having enough money budgeted to cover medical expenses and/or unfamiliarity with symptoms and how to treat them.

The school lunch program has dramatically shown the great need for more adequate meals for many school children of low income. Title I funds under ESEA are being expended in some cases for breakfasts for school children, and it is recognized that without these meals many children would have little or no food at all on a regular basis.

The recent attention to the needs of low income school children has revealed that some who have been under-achieving are actually suffering from eye defects which have never been corrected because the eyes have never been examined. Some children who have been considered dumb and slow are actually hard-of-hearing.

One of the most tragic and frequent situations is parental cruelty. Physical abuse of children by their parents occurs in all socioeconomic groups. And these children lack medical treatment because of the parents' fear of disclosure.

The problem of the emotionally disturbed children is even more serious. In some communities psychologists and psychiatrists are working with the teachers to help them identify these students and refer them to proper help. It is often precisely these children who need very personal attention, who without it become the hostile, violent, or withdrawn children who are the major concern of those wanting to prevent juvenile delinquency.

Every school should provide a wide range of health services for its student population, or make such services easily accessible. Every child should be given a thorough medical examination at the beginning of each school year by a competent physician. Any difficulties should be referred to the proper specialist or agency, and the school should follow up to see that the physical or mental health defect is corrected or alleviated. Whatever is done or recommended must be discussed with the parents so that they understand the necessity for the service being recommended. This is particularly true for the parents of an emotionally disturbed child, because it is often the parents themselves who are mainly responsible for the distress of their children, and need some attention themselves.

A psychologist or psychiatrist must be constantly available to each school to consult with the counselors and faculty about particular students who seem to have problems. Psychologists should either be on the regular staff of the school, in full-time attendance, or off-campus but accessible when needed.

Job Placement and Job Development Services. A job placement specialist should be included on the staff of every secondary school—with priority given to areas where the dropout rate is high, juvenile delinquency and misbehavior are prevalent, and where occupational orientation and guidance are particularly needed by a student body whose knowledge of careers is sometimes as limited as their neighborhood boundaries. The job placement specialist should be familiar with the current labor market in the community and within the State, the qualifications for job levels, and have good contacts with the employer groups in the community, including business, trade unions, and government. Such a specialist would exchange information with the counselor about job training as well as immediate and potential job opportunities. He should also work in conjunction with the school staff to develop and revise curricula to meet better the needs of the job market, with an appropriate mix of occupational preparation and general academic subject matter. Particular attention should be given to the student who appears to be a potential dropout by offering him a curriculum which will prepare him for a job or for advanced training outside the school structure.

The job placement officer and the guidance counselor must also work closely together in the implementation of work-study programs instituted by schools to help students who need financial assistance or work experience. They should make the employer and the community aware of their stake in joining with the school to provide jobs for these youth. Employers could respond by setting aside certain trainee positions to be filled by young people from the schools and by assigning qualified personnel to supervise their work.

Guidance·and Placement Center.   A guidance and placement center, if such a structure were formalized, could serve all who leave school, be they drop-outs or graduates. The center could continue its relationship with the student until he no longer required its support. Such service would include continuous evaluation of the student on the job and in his relations with his supervisor and fellow employees. It would also involve continuing the relationships established between the student, and the counsel or teacher. Working closely with the local employment service, the job placement officer would let the student know that every effort was being made to help him find, keep, and progress in a job, but that the fundamental responsibility was his own. The student who was forced to leave school for financial reasons or to terminate his education temporarily, would be encouraged by the understanding and accepting climate of the school to return as soon as he was able.

The School, the Child, and the Police.   Three community agencies have direct concern for the delinquent child: the police, the juvenile court, and the correctional institution. It is incumbent upon the school to establish a working relationship with each of these agencies.

The police and the school can work together to: (1) enable the child to stay in school if at all possible; and (2) prevent repetition of delinquent acts which come to the attention of the police. Many police departments have established Juvenile Aid units manned by officers trained in the problems which confront children. The school should assist the work of the police by inviting youth officers to the school to acquaint the students with police functions. Simultaneously, the students should be informed of their rights and obligations. Channels of communication between the schools and the police should be kept open so that the school is kept constantly and immediately informed of any police contacts incurred by its student population. If possible, the counselor and school social worker should attend the hearings to gain a better appreciation of the child's behavior. Efforts should be made to draw police into school-related recreation programs during their off-duty hours so that positive relationships between police and youth may develop.

University or other sponsored training programs should be set up for all police officers to instruct them in the rights of children, methods for assisting juveniles, and the psychology of the "streets" and the "suburbs." Police officers could be included in in-service training programs for school staff when areas of mutual interest are being discussed.

The School, the Child, and the Court. In too many cases, the juvenile court is forced to assume jurisdiction over problem children which might be more beneficially handled by another institution—particularly the schools, if proper facilities were available. The creation of channels of communication between these two institutions would facilitate the work of both. Representatives of the schools and the courts should be in constant contact to work toward solutions to problems of common interest, to discuss the relevance of certain types of behavior peculiar to juveniles in relation to the court, and to develop alternatives to adjudication and commitment of delinquent youth.

The School, the Child, and the Correctional Institution. The correctional institution has an extremely important stake in our educational institutions. For those youth not yet beyond compulsory school age, the correctional institution is only a temporary interruption of their regular school experience. Since most institutions for delinquent youth have educational programs, there is much to be gained by pooling the knowledge about educating troubled youth. It is a part of the responsibility of the correctional institution to assist its children to develop more positive attitudes toward school. At the same time, the attitude of the school toward the youth who has been committed is an important factor in the rehabilitation efforts begun by the delinquent facility. The probation officer and the school counselor or social worker should work together in helping the child adjust. Both should visit the families and work with them to instill confidence in their children and to assist them in encouraging the child's educational aspirations.

. . .

VI. Quality Control Within the School and Within the School System

Monitoring of the on-going activities of the school to determine their adequacy and effectiveness is necessary to the efficient operations of that school, the determination of needs, and the allocation of staff, physical and financial resources. Unfortunately, determining educational goals relevant to the characteristics of the attendance area, the setting of short and long-range objectives, and the measurement of progress toward accomplishing these objectives is only too rarely an on-going function in the schools. The collection and analysis of data, both demographic data and records of student achievement, transfer, dropouts, etc., are a necessary base for both planning and evaluation functions. Such collection and analysis, goal-setting, program planning and evaluation require trained staff with time to devote to these functions.

Ideally a quality-control unit should exist within each school or group of schools with a full-time trained person responsible for collection and analysis of data. This 'program evaluator' or 'program specialist' would work with a team consisting of teachers, administrators, service personnel and students to interpret this data and to utilize it for planning and evaluation purposes. The quality-control unit in the school would function as a liaison mechanism with a larger unit in the local educational agency, a unit which would be more fully staffed, which would have similar responsibilities for the larger area of its jurisdiction, and which would provide information vitally necessary to other community groups and agencies serving similar target populations. (See Recommendation A: Cooperative Self-Assessment, Planning and Evaluation by Local Educational Agencies, Section I—Provision of Educational Programs Sufficient To Meet the Needs of the Entire Community.)

Sufficient numbers of trained evaluators are not presently available. Arrangements can, however, be made for sharing of available personnel by local schools, school districts, and universities. Such cooperative arrangements can assure at least minimal capability at the local school level, and university personnel can assist in providing on-the-job training for such local school staff as are available. "In turn, the local schools can receive expert assistance in conducting the evaluations that are required now and can have increased evaluation expertise on their own staffs after the projects are completed. Also such collaboration will afford the universities an opportunity to study the evaluation process in the context of ordinary circumstances. This should facilitate the production of generalized evaluation designs which meet the requirements of school situations." [10]

.   .   .

VII. Research and Dissemination of Results

Research undoubtedly exists which deals directly with the relationship between educational practices and juvenile delinquency; more will be generated in the future. However, the results of such research are inadequately disseminated to potential users and often are not in a form suitable for translation into educational practice. We suggest a study be undertaken to determine the most effective and efficient method for disseminating such research.

Statistical Data Needs. A major part of the problem of conducting and evaluating delinquency research is the lack of adequate statistical data. We suggest a comprehensive study be undertaken which focuses on the following: (1) the kinds of data currently available to researchers and planners; (2) the kinds of data needed to conduct research and plan and evaluate programs; (3) the most suitable forms in which to present such data; and (4) the value of certain kinds of statistical data subject to variables which distort its meaning.

Educational Program Effectiveness. There appears to be limited knowledge available on the effectiveness of any particular educational program component in producing positive changes in the attitudes and behavior patterns of the delinquent and delinquency-prone child. We believe that the highest priority should be given to initiating longitudinal studies which

[10] Daniel L. Stufflebeam, "Evaluation Under I of the Elementary and Secondary Educational Act of 1965," an address at the Conference on Evaluation sponsored by the Michigan State University Department of Education, East Lansing, January 24, 1966.

attempt to evaluate the effectiveness of existing and proposed educational projects directed at this target group.

Attitudinal Research. Systematic studies of social interaction in educational settings should be undertaken. This should include an examination of the attitudes of student and teacher toward self, each other, race, class, education and society.

Self-Identification. Research should be undertaken to analyze the social-psychological process whereby certain children identify themselves as troublemakers and/or educational failures and become delinquency-prone, while other children acquire positive self-identifications.

Behavioral Controls. We suggest that research be undertaken which examines the disciplinary practices, behavioral codes sanctioned by faculty, student peer-group codes, etc., within the secondary and elementary school as they converge on students. In addition, and with particular relevance to the delinquency-prone child, there should be studies mounted which specifically examine the suspension, expulsion, and re-admission practices of our schools.

Social Mobility. Studies need to be made of the effect of the school setting on youth peer group organization. How do school groupings influence choices of friends and other associations? What is the relationship of associations by youth within the school to associations outside the school setting? How do these associations influence behavior norms, affect career choices, and determine other goals? To what extent do they enhance or impede social mobility among youth, and what is the relationship of this mobility to family background?

Pre-School Programs. Longitudinal research projects are needed to determine the value of day care programs and combinations of these with Head Start, nursery school, kindergarten programs etc., as means of preparing children for entry into formal school programs. Such studies might evaluate the educational components of these programs in relation to their potential for increasing the young child's readiness for schooling.

Federal Coordination. On the Federal level many agencies are involved in the problem of delinquency prevention and control. Some programs directly attack specific aspects of the problem; some touch it tangentially; some have only an indirect bearing upon it. The poor articulation between these programs results in much duplication and overlap while large gaps go untended. There is an absence of clearly defined, overall policy and planning.

The multiplicity of programs indicates that a major effort for management analysis and research must deal directly with the problem of adequate coordination and communication among Federal agencies. Given the results of such efforts it would then be possible to implement and expand demonstration programs on a statewide or, in some cases, a nationwide basis, in addition to creating a coherent policy base for future planning.

There are many broad issues bearing upon delinquency prevention and control which are in need of research if progress is to be made in the amelioration of the problem. We suggest only a few:

a. Research is needed to determine how much emphasis must be given to preventive measures; how much to treatment once the juvenile has become delinquent; how much to insure complete rehabilitation.

b. There has been much discussion on the effect of such preventive actions as quality education, racial integration, adequate school buildings and sites, electronic teaching aides, effective housing and health assistance. Research is needed to determine the type and degree of correlation which does in fact, exist, and to identify the variables.

c. More research is needed on the influence and extent of direct community involvement in any overall effort; the role of family, church and school; and the character and scope of coordination necessary for effective results among all the agencies involved in dealing with juvenile delinquents.

d. More research is also needed to determine the relationship between the rate of juvenile delinquency and immigration, inner-city decay and related problems of large cities.

e. Research is needed to determine the effects of police intervention and disposition practices in relation to youthful offenders.

.   .   .

Educational Testing.   There is need for extensive research directed toward the development of more valid and reliable testing techniques to measure a child's "real" achievement level, with particular emphasis on such development for sub-groups of children within our population.

.   .   .

21   Interagency Co-ordination in Delinquency Prevention and Control

WILLIAM REID

The low level of co-ordination among social welfare agencies has long been considered a major problem for community organization. The terms "duplicating," "overlapping," and "fragmentary" have become, in fact, pejorative cliché to describe the state of the social services. Despite efforts

Reprinted from *Social Service Review*, 38 (Dec. 1964), 418–428, copyright 1964, The University of Chicago Press.

by community organizers and others, the "co-ordination gap" has persisted and, in the eyes of some, has worsened. Kahn, for example, states that "co-ordination of services and programs [in child welfare] is urgent because the United States is experiencing an urban child care crisis of very considerable size."[1] In a report to Congress, the Children's Bureau observed: "Existing services which could contribute to treatment, control, and prevention are poorly co-ordinated, so that an integrated attack on the problem [juvenile delinquency] is not possible."[2] Such statements exist for most areas of social welfare organization.

This chronic problem raises some acute questions: What is really involved in co-ordination? What accounts for its relative absence? Why does it occur under some circumstances but not under others? Answers to these and other questions are necessary if there is to be a knowledge base for effective action. Ideally, such knowledge should be organized into a systematic body of concepts and hypotheses—that is, into a theory of co-ordination.

This paper presents a set of formulations that may contribute to theory development. These formulations will be limited to one type of interagency co-ordination, which may be called "unmediated" co-ordination, that is, co-ordination between two or more agencies through their own devices without mediation of another agency, such as a welfare council. Agencies of their own accord can develop referral agreements, sponsor joint programs, and so on. A theory of how and why such interaction occurs is perhaps a preliminary step toward understanding the role of the co-ordinating agency.

The current analysis will be further restricted to social welfare organizations offering direct services to individuals and families with the goal of juvenile delinquency prevention and control. As this broad field of activity includes most major types of social agencies, whatever theory is developed here may have relevance for the general social agency system. Specifically, however, analysis is focused on the direct-service agencies in corrections, family service, public welfare, child welfare, mental health, and youth services. To these are added the schools and youth divisions of police departments. As both the police and the schools assume "service" roles in relation to delinquency control, for purposes of this paper they will be considered as social agencies. The terms "agency" and "organization," as used generically in the paper, refer for the most part to the fore-going group of community agencies.

Co-ordination as a System of Interagency Exchange

The first task in developing a theory of interagency co-ordination is to specify the essential dimensions of this type of agency interaction. How can

---

[1] Alfred Kahn, " 'A Co-ordinated Pattern of Service'—Shibboleth or Feasible Goal?" In *Basic Issues in Co-ordinating Family and Child Welfare Programs*, ed. Charles P. Cella, Jr., and Rodney P. Lane (Philadelphia: University of Pennsylvania Press, 1964), p. 7.

[2] National Institute of Mental Health and Children's Bureau, U.S. Department of Health, Education, and Welfare, *Report to the Congress on Juvenile Delinquency* (Washington, D.C.: Government Printing Office, 1957), p. 9.

co-ordination be most fruitfully defined and described? What are its key components?

A particularly useful framework for viewing co-ordination has been developed by Levine and White.[3] These writers suggest that co-operative arrangements among agencies may be viewed as a system of exchanges. In order to achieve their objectives, organizations must possess or control certain resources—personnel, services, funds, etc. Since most agencies do not possess all the resources needed to achieve their goals, they frequently turn to one another to obtain them. In more general terms Levine and White define organizational exchange as "any voluntary activity between two organizations which has consequences, actual or anticipated, for the realization of their respective goals or objectives."[4]

It is legitimate to ask in relation to any new concept: How is it useful? What does it contribute? Any new addition to already overcrowded conceptual highways should facilitate the flow of traffic and not block it further.

First, the exchange formulation draws attention to the importance of agency goals. Organizational activity, including co-ordination, may be seen as directed toward achieving goals of concern to the organization, however the organization defines them. Viewing co-ordination as an exchange through which agencies attempt to achieve their goals forces consideration of what these goals actually are. In this type of analysis one need not assume that the most important agency goals lie in furthering the welfare of the community or that agencies in a community are bound together in a closely knit system in which each seeks similar goals through different means. Much of the prescriptive writing on co-ordination assumes that agencies have or should have common goals. It is another matter, however, to examine agency goals for what they are, without prior assumptions or illusions. Only in this way can the subject of interagency co-ordination be dealt with analytically.

Second, the concept of exchange calls attention to the fact that any co-ordinating activity involves agency resources—defined here as any elements the agency needs to achieve its goals. It then becomes possible to describe any co-ordinating activity in terms of the kinds of resources included in the transaction. Funds, facilities, personnel, services, information, clients (or other recipients of service) comprise the major resources most agencies need to achieve their goals. Lacking such needed resources, agencies may seek exchanges. Thus, agencies earlier in our history found themselves in need of information about clients' contacts with other agencies. Their solution was to develop a system of exchanging one resource—information about clients—through an organization appropriately called the Social Service Exchange. Other types of co-ordinating activities can be specified in similar terms. Contracted service arrangements are exchanges of funds for personnel and services. Referrals involve exchanges of clients. Joint programs may in-

[3] Sol Levine and Paul E. White, "Exchange as a Conceptual Framework for the Study of Interorganizational Relationships," *Administrative Science Quarterly*, V (March, 1961), 583–601.
[4] *Ibid.*, p. 588.

volve exchanges of facilities. Agencies may also exchange services. For example, a family service agency provides counseling services to clients referred by a welfare department. In exchange, the welfare department adjusts its concrete services to these clients in line with recommendations of the family agency. An exchange need not involve a transfer of resources from one agency to another. As in the above example, it may be carried out by using resources in special ways for the benefit of one another. In effect, however, agencies still derive from each other resources needed to further their own objectives.

By considering the extensiveness of the exchange in terms of the quantity and value of resources one can distinguish various types and levels of co-ordination.

The first or lowest level may be called "*ad hoc* case co-ordination." At this level co-ordinated activity is generated by individual practitioners to meet the needs of particular clients. Decisions about what and when to co-ordinate are left to the practitioner. Formal interagency agreements are not usually involved. Specific exchanges include chiefly information, referral, and, to a lesser degree, service. Perhaps the bulk of co-ordination takes place at this level.

A second level is "systematic case co-ordination" or, to use Kahn's terminology, "service integration." [5] Here co-ordinated activity is still on the case level, with the goal of meshing services from different agencies in relation to the particular case. This level of co-ordination, however, is carried on in accordance with specific rules and procedures developed by the agencies. Interagency agreements may cover referrals or allocations of responsibility relating to types of cases. Special interagency co-ordinating devices, such as case-conference committees, may be set up. At this level interagency exchanges are systematic and extensive. Exchanges of information and referrals are routine. There is emphasis on planned exchanges of services. For example, agencies may be accorded major service and co-ordinating responsibility for all cases in which they have made first contact, or agencies may be given responsibility for providing specific types of service.

A third level may be described as "program co-ordination." [6] Here co-ordination is centered not on individual cases but on agency programs. This level of co-ordination includes development of joint agency programs, mutual assistance in development or extension of programs, or mutual modification of programs to bring about more rational alignment of agency functions. Two agencies may develop a joint street-club program; an agency may send detached personnel to another to perform specialized counseling services; two child-care agencies with duplicating functions may decide to divide responsibilities, with one concentrating on homemaker service and the other on foster placement. Interagency exchanges at this level may be extensive and complex.

---

[5] Alfred J. Kahn, *Planning Community Services for Children in Trouble* (New York: Columbia University Press, 1963), p. 110.

[6] *Ibid.*, p. 112.

Within these three types and levels of co-ordination there is then a rough progression in terms of the extent and value of agency resources exchanged. *Ad hoc* case co-ordination draws minimally upon these resources, whereas program co-ordination may encompass a much larger portion of the agency's resources. With increasingly greater agency investment there may be progressive increase in agency caution about engaging in co-ordinating ventures. This may account particularly for the relative scarcity of co-ordination at the second and third levels.

Determinants of Co-ordination

A second major task in creating a theory of co-ordination involves specification of the conditions that determine whether co-ordination will take place. It may be generally hypothesized that at least three conditions must be present before co-ordination can occur in any substance. Agencies must have (1) shared goals, (2) complementary resources, and (3) efficient mechanisms for controlling whatever exchanges are involved. These three conditions will be discussed in some detail.

Shared goals. When agencies are seeking similar or identical goals, a major force for co-ordination is brought into play. Each agency has a stake in the goal attainment of the other, and both therefore may become willing to enter into exchanges to further mutual objectives. Moreover, sharing of goals leads to logical divisions of responsibility and labor which can reduce the burdens of each. The importance of this condition has been stressed by at least two studies of interagency relationships.[7]

Agencies, of course, have multiple goals that vary in degrees in explicitness, breadth, and vitality. General goals stated in official declarations of purpose often bear little relation to the operational goals that guide agency activities.

The operational goals of the agency determine decisions and actions. Though often difficult to locate and define, these goals are crucial in co-ordination. Two organizations may nominally share a broad, formal goal of "reducing juvenile delinquency." One organization—a police department—may view this goal primarily in terms of vigorous law enforcement. The other organization—a family agency—may interpret it as alleviating psychological problems of disturbed youngsters. The operational goals of the organizations may then be quite divergent and may offer little basis for co-ordination.

Most of the agencies of concern here acknowledge and, in a sense, share, broad, formal goals relating to delinquency control and prevention. At the level of operational goals, much of this apparent concensus seems to dissolve. If not working at cross-purposes, agencies seem often to be working at different purposes. Somehow the objectives shared on paper become reduced in practice to goals that are limited and discrepant. An examination of how

[7] M. M. Ahla Annikki, *Referred by Visiting Nurse* (Cleveland: The Press of Western Reserve University, 1950); Sol Levine, Paul E. White, and Benjamin D. Paul, "Community Interorganizational Problems in Providing Medical Care and Social Services," *American Journal of Public Health*, LIII (August, 1963), 1183–95.

this process of goal reduction operates will add to our understanding of why operational goals so often are not shared and why co-ordination so often fails to occur.

First, the operational goals of an agency may be determined by the resources at its disposal. Etzioni has remarked that "one of the most important observations of students of organizations is that the 'tools' in part determine the goals to which they are applied." [8] For example, an agency may select from a range of permissible goals those goals that can be most effectively achieved through the services it has to offer. Family agencies and mental health clinics, for example, have such general objectives as promoting family welfare or mental health. Such objectives would nominally cover the population and problems of interest in delinquency control. These agencies are free, however, to define within this goal framework the specific clientele and problems to be treated.

It is notoriously difficult to treat delinquent adolescents through the conventional casework and psychotherapeutic methods these agencies regard as their prime resources. Such treatment normally requires considerable professional time, not only with the youngster, but with family members and community agencies. The success rate is low. These agencies may therefore decide to expend their limited resources on clients who will yield maximal goal achievement with minimum strain. The goals of such agencies then become concentrated upon a selected clientele—individuals or families with problems, capacity, and motivation that fit the agency's definition of service. Delinquent youth may be regarded by these agencies as a marginal, second-best clientele. To a considerable extent they may be "defined out" of the agency's actual goals relating to kind of clients served or kind of problems treated.

In other cases, a scarcity of resources may force agencies to cut back goals to their essentials, as the agencies define them. An understaffed youth center in a congested urban area, seeing its actual goals in terms of "keeping the kids off the streets," may forego any serious aspirations to a program of delinquency prevention. An underbudgeted and overcrowded school may give up its concerns for the "whole" child and settle for imparting whatever classroom learning it can. In a social welfare system in which demands for service far exceed resources, agencies may be forced to settle for minimum objectives.

Organizational goals may also be tied to various procedural and administrative concerns—the well-known bureaucratic dysfunction of "goal displacement." Meeting deadlines, getting reports out, processing cases may assume the status of major agency goals. In emphasizing administrative routines the agency often loses sight of its larger objectives. One observer, for example, remarked that a certain parole department was "procedure-bound." Though charged with the objective of rehabilitating youthful offenders, its energies

[8] Amitai Etzioni, *Complex Organizations* (New York: Holt, Rinehart & Winston, 1961), p. 143.

actually were directed at completion of social studies. Rather than serving as a tool in the rehabilitation process, studies became ends in themselves. It was difficult for staff members to raise their sights above the immediate task and to see how their own organization related to others.

Limited agency goals must finally be seen in the context of the historical development of the social service system. Social agencies were created to meet specific social needs as they become manifest in the community. Limited goals relating to these original conceptions of function have usually continued. In some cases broader goals have been added as a way of rationalizing the agency's existence in relation to prevailing social welfare values rather than as serious aims. Thus, public welfare departments in many cases operate in terms of such hoary and circumscribed objectives as maintaining the sanctity of the means test, despite official goals of rehabilitation and the like. As Mencher writes, "the organization of social services frequently suggests that of an automobile plant in which a number of specialized centers manufacture parts according to their own unique specifications; then, after the processing of the parts has been completed, a group of experts is called in to see whether or not the parts can be assembled into a car." [9]

The more limited agency goals become, the less chance there is for sharing of goals to occur. Areas of common purpose are reduced as each agency seeks to discharge highly specific and narrowly defined functions. Often agencies formally concerned with delinquency control operate in terms of very limited objectives. The police department seeks to investigate criminal activities and arrest offenders; the probation department endeavors to gather information to enable the court to make a disposition; the parole department attempts to keep youngsters from being reinstitutionalized; individual treatment agencies see their function with delinquent youngsters as one of diagnosis and referral; youth-serving agencies have limited recreational goals; schools define their functions in terms of achieving specific learning objectives. These organizations may have "on their books" or acknowledge in one way or another common goals relating to a community-wide program of delinquency prevention or total rehabilitation of disturbed adolescents. Such goals may not be translated, however, into operational goals that guide day-to-day activities. If they are not, a base for exchange is lacking.

The "shared-goal" formulation can be used to examine a well-known precipitant of co-ordinated activity—the community crisis. It is fairly well-established that community crises may promote solidarity, cohesion, and co-ordinated effort.[10] Groups within the community react by pulling together and taking joint action to ward off the common threat. Most large communities have experienced juvenile delinquency crises of one sort or another. These usually consist of a widely publicized wave of youthful violence or criminal activity—gang fights, stabbings, murders. Important citizens, com-

[9] Samuel Mencher, "Principles of Social Work Organization," *Social Casework*, XLIV (May, 1963), 265.
[10] William H. Form and Sigmund Nosow, *Community in Disaster* (New York: Harper & Bros., 1958), p. 236.

munity groups, and social agencies become alarmed. Pressure for remedial action mounts. Meetings of agency representatives are held. Decisions are made about who can do what. Joint programs of action are developed. Many, if not most, demonstration projects involving co-ordinated agency efforts in this field have their origins in this kind of community crisis.

In terms of the current formulation the crisis can be seen as first expanding and activating individual agency goals relating to reduction of delinquency. Temporarily, at least, serving the delinquent population is accorded high priority in the agency's array of goals. Since the same phenomenon is occurring simultaneously in a number of agencies, shared goals emerge. Agencies then become willing to exchange resources as a means of achieving these superordinate goals.

This crisis-provoked co-ordination may prove quite evanescent. When the crisis dies down, so does the co-ordinated activity. In some instances patterns of co-ordination built up in crisis situations are preserved through specific structures and programs. Without such developments, however, co-ordinative arrangements tend to dissipate as agencies return to their precrisis modes of operation. Many crisis-based demonstration projects have met this fate. One carefully planned and well-executed project, for example, succeeded in developing an unusual degree of co-ordination among previously unrelated neighborhood agencies. With the project and crisis over, co-ordination quickly receded to its previous levels.

When the crisis serves to expand and activate goals relating to delinquency reduction, diminution of the crisis produces the opposite effect. As delinquency problems become of less concern, or at least less visible, agencies withdraw priorities attached to antidelinquency goals and return them to other objectives. The shared goal of delinquency prevention and control becomes dissolved in the process, or at least loses force.

Complementary resources. A sharing of goals may be a necessary condition for interagency exchange. It is not, however, a sufficient condition. For exchange to occur, each agency must be able to provide the other with resources it needs to achieve its goals. In other words, there must be complementary resources. For example, a police department and a youth-serving agency share the common goal of prevention of gang-fighting. Neither organization is able to achieve its goals without assistance from the other. The police need the on-the-spot intervention that skilled gang workers from the youth-serving agency are able to provide. That agency in turn needs help from police in spotting incipient flare-ups or in applying legal sanctions. Exchanges of information, clients, personnel, and services logically take place.

Complementary resources may be lacking for various reasons. The fact that agencies may have goals uniquely shaped to their resources, as noted above, may lead to insular self-sufficiency. To some extent this state of affairs characterizes many agencies specializing in psychological treatment. The goals of two agencies may be to provide the particular kind of casework that the agencies are in fact able to provide. Though goals may be similar, each agency has the resources to achieve these goals as it defines them, and significant exchanges are not likely to occur. An agency ready to co-ordinate is perhaps one whose goals exceed its resources.

Another form of agency self-sufficiency merits examination. This may occur in large organizations in which specialized personnel or departments provide the needed spectrum of resources. A school system in a large city is a common example. The school system may share with various agencies the goal of better adjustment of children. Because of its size, the school system may find it more efficient to develop its own resources to cope with the adjustment problems of its children. Adjustment teachers, counselors, school psychologists, social workers, guidance departments, or special schools may be brought into the system for this purpose. Referrals within the system may reduce exchanges with outside organizations that might also be able to supply similar resources. In a study of voluntary health organizations Levine and White found large corporate agencies engaging in fewer exchanges than small agencies organized in a federated structure.[11]

Such developments often lead to duplication of services within the community. The school system may develop its own child-guidance facilities despite the existence of community child-guidance agencies serving the school population. Nevertheless, the school may decide that it would be more efficient to have its own child-guidance resources and may not necessarily be concerned with problems of duplication.

Agencies may share goals but may have insufficient resources to achieve them. Attempts at exchange may prove futile as agencies become disillusioned with one another's ineffectiveness. Thus, a public employment service and a parole department share the objective of developing an effective job-location program for delinquent youth. An exchange involving personnel or facilities is worked out. An employment counselor is attached to the parole department. His mission is to work closely with parole officers toward setting up such a program. The obstacles, however—such as finding employers who will hire referred parolees—prove too great and the program fails to develop.

Such instances of resource inadequacy are often used to support the thesis that agencies need more resources and not more co-ordination. It is certainly true that co-ordination cannot take place in a resource vacuum; on the other hand, an increase in agency resources may stimulate co-ordination, as the agency then has more of value to exchange.

Co-ordination control and costs. It has been suggested that shared goals and complementary resources are essential prerequisites for interagency co-ordination. These in fact are often sufficient conditions for simple types of co-ordination—such as the *ad hoc* case variety. For more elaborate forms, however, some means of control must be established. For systematic case co-ordination such control mechanisms may take the form of interagency agreements, of regularly scheduled case conferences between staff members of different agencies, or of interagency committees. Program co-ordination may require such mechanisms as formal agreements, accountability procedures,

---

[11] Levine and White, "Exchange as a Conceptual Framework . . . ," *op. cit.*, p. 592.

interagency conferences, and allocations of co-ordinating responsibilities to specific staff members.

These control devices require an investment of agency resources apart from resources involved in the actual exchange. Staff time is the resource most heavily drawn upon to insure adequate regulation. This resource, however, is perhaps the most precious and costly for most agencies.

In a study of interagency relationships, Johns and Demarche found that agency staff members ranked "lack of time" first in a series of possible obstacles to co-ordination.[12] Time is often dismissed as a trivial factor in such considerations, particularly by those who do not have to expend it. Community organizers in the above study rated "lack of time" extremely low as a reason for lack of co-ordination. Time, however, becomes important when it is seen as an expenditure of resources—a cost. "Lack of time" may then be a way of saying that the values received from co-ordinating activities do not merit the costs of maintaining them.

These costs tend to increase as exchanges become more complex. Litwak and Hylton have made the point that activities that can be standardized can be co-ordinated most easily.[13] Interagency exchanges of information about cases can often be standardized on forms and handled by clerical personnel. Systematic co-ordination of the efforts of a number of practitioners in relation to a particular case, however, involves activities that are diffuse, complicated, and impossible to standardize. Consequently, the costs in staff time to engineer such co-ordinated efforts may be large.

Regulation of practitioner activities is difficult, not only because of their inherently diffuse nature, but also because of the differing basic policies of the participating agencies. Often policies run counter to the goals of whatever co-ordinated efforts are being attempted. If co-ordination control is at the practitioner or even supervisory level, policy issues cannot be resolved. The control operation must then be expanded to include agency administrators at various levels. Much the same may be said about program co-ordination. Not only are the activities likely to be highly complex and difficult to routinize, but control devices must often be expanded to involve total staff. Executives, for example, may make certain agreements about a co-ordinated program, but these may remain only on paper unless there is careful regulation of activities at the practitioner level—a time-consuming and costly business.

Such problems may be compounded when the agencies are large and heavily bureaucratic. Here co-ordination control must deal not only with an imposing agency array of department heads and specialists but also with the agency's own internal organizational problems.

Difficulties in co-ordination between a family service agency and a large school system offer a case in point. The family agency and the school system

[12] Ray Johns and David F. Demarche, *Community Organization and Agency Responsibility* (New York: Association Press, 1951).
[13] Eugene Litwak and Lydia Hylton, "Interorganizational Analysis: A Hypothesis on Co-ordinating Agencies," *Administrative Science Quarterly*, VI (March, 1962), 412.

had worked out a number of apparently simple arrangements for referrals of children and families and case conferences after referrals had been completed. Agency contacts with the school were complicated, however, in each case, because it was necessary to deal with so many of the school personnel— teachers, assistant principals, guidance counselors, psychologists, nurses, and so on. Usually no one of these school personnel possessed either sufficient information about the child or sufficient responsibility for him to serve as the sole contact point with the family agency. Moreover, the school specialists often did not act in concert. A referral might be made to the family agency by the assistant principal before receipt of psychological test results necessary for the agency to make a case decision. To obtain case data or to engage in case planning, family agency staff often found themselves in the position of co-ordinating activities of the school staff. Under the weight of these bureaucratic complexities, the arrangements frequently broke down. Repair and maintenance, needless to say, proved costly for both school and agency.

In sum, control of complex interagency co-ordination is both costly and difficult to achieve. The difficulty and the cost are directly related. Agencies may be unwilling to pay dearly for a questionable product. Thus they are often reluctant to devote expensive staff time and other resources to less-than-adequate regulation of complex exchanges. Unless commitment to shared goals and need of complementary resources provide sufficient force, agencies may decide that co-ordination is not worth the price.

Summary and Implications

Co-ordination in the field of delinquency prevention and control has been viewed as an exchange of resources among organizations. Different types of co-ordination have been distinguished and related to different levels of exchange. Three conditions for co-ordination have been set forth. For substantial interagency co-ordination to occur there must at least be sharing of goals, a complementarity of resources, and an efficient system of control whose cost is commensurate with values received. Various reasons for the scarcity of co-ordination have been examined in the light of these conditions.

The emphasis placed upon obstacles may leave the reader with the impression that unmediated co-ordination is very difficult to achieve and may even be an enterprise of dubious value. That is quite the impression we wished to convey.

The idea that co-ordination is difficult to achieve is, of course, not new. It has been repeated in endless ways throughout fifty years of community organization literature. What may be new—at least to some—is the notion that co-ordination may not necessarily be advantageous to the agencies involved, as they define their goals and functions. We have often tended to view co-ordination in terms of what is desirable or functional for the community. From the community's point of view, co-ordination of services is a cherished objective. Agencies may also desire this objective in the abstract, or for other agencies, but may not be committed to improving their own levels of co-ordination. What may be functional for the community may not be functional for the agency.

The view of the welfare community as a tight system of interdependent agencies may confuse wish with reality. In the ecology of the community, agencies perhaps may be viewed more realistically as relatively autonomous units, each seeking to achieve its own rather than common goals through use of resources that are difficult and costly to co-ordinate. In such an ecology, unmediated co-ordination of any substance and duration may be a relatively rare event. This at least seems to be the fact.

The view that co-ordination may be disadvantageous to individual agencies does not necessarily mean that it is undesirable from the community's point of view. This could mean, however, that means of achieving desired co-ordination may have to be altered. To accomplish co-ordination, much more may be needed than bringing agencies together, developing channels of communication between them, or providing mediation. These facilitative approaches are always useful but are sufficient only when agencies really want to co-operate and are waiting for the community organizer to help them to do this. If we do not make this assumption, then we may need stronger medicine—for example, the deployment of economic and political resources as a means of bringing about fundamental changes in agency goals. This view also means that greater co-ordination of services may not in many instances be worth the efforts to achieve it and that community organization resources may often be better allocated to other objectives.

V Special Programs and Approaches

The variety of approaches available to those concerned with the prevention of delinquency includes the development of organizations and programs that are designed specifically and primarily for that purpose. Instead of relying on existing agencies or institutions as the bases for orientation and support, this approach frequently leads to the development of independent organizations that allow the implementation of techniques and strategies not otherwise possible.

These special programs and approaches have had a rather turbulent history. Frequently, oversimplified views of the causes of delinquency and the means necessary for its prevention have been proposed. In some instances they have bordered on absurdity, such as claims that comic books are responsible for delinquency and that their elimination would lead to drastic reductions in the amount of delinquency. This kind of orientation has led in the past, and will probably lead in the future, to haphazard efforts to remove this and other kinds of "evil."

Fortunately, in recent years special programs and approaches have become generally more sophisticated in their fundamental premises and more limited in their assumed definitiveness. It has become increasingly evident that there are no panaceas for delinquency, but at the same time it is recognized that particular programs and approaches may serve as useful tools for at least partially forestalling delinquent behavior.

Two fundamental notions provide the bases for special programs and approaches. First, certain kinds of experiences and conditions are believed to be in and of themselves conducive to delinquency. It is argued that if they can be modified or eliminated delinquency will be prevented. An example of this is poverty and its accompanying sociocultural attributes. Many assume that these conditions increase the risk of delinquency and that such risks can be reduced considerably by eliminating the conditions.

Second, certain kinds of positive experiences are believed to be of crucial importance in altering adolescent behavior. The benefits that accrue from these experiences are generalized to include their effects on the child's behavior in other contexts and/or to the child's character structure, thereby lessening the likelihood of delinquent behavior should the contingencies conducive to that type of behavior arise. Employment programs are an example of such "positive" experiences. It is assumed that work training not only provides the skills necessary for steady and profitable employment, but also provides one who undergoes the training with skills, values, behaviors, and habits that he can apply to other non-work contexts and relationships. Work training thereby both directly and indirectly is assumed to reduce the likelihood of delinquency.

It is obvious that the possible variation in the kinds of special programs and approaches is nearly limitless. However, the number that have been instituted is quite small, partly because of the lack of resources for their implementation, although a general lack of creative and imaginative thinking also seems partially responsible. Carefully controlled and evaluated research focusing on these kinds of programs has been even more noticeably absent as compared with other prevention programs and approaches. Only very recently have increased government attention and renewed interest by behavioral scientists indicated that this situation may be only temporary.

The first article in this section provides a comprehensive view of employment programs and delinquency. Judith G. Benjamin, Seymour Lesh, and Marcia K. Freedman outline several recent governmental efforts in the area of employment and give examples of specific programs now or recently in effect in a variety of communities. Special attention is devoted to in-school and out-of-school youth and the unique problems presented by each.

James C. Hackler presents the results of a work program based upon a sociologically oriented theoretical framework. Using a series of experimental and control groups in several Seattle housing projects, Hackler varied work situations and degrees of supervision while also differentially attempting to modify community attitudes toward youth and differentially using a teaching-machine testing program. His study illustrates the coordination of a theoretical framework with a research design, techniques of analyzing data, and, especially, the necessity for evaluation.

David M. Austin discusses the role of gang workers and the problems that confront them in dealing with urban street-corner groups. He not only specifies the objectives that are involved in this type of approach, but also spells out the techniques whereby successful delinquency prevention can be achieved.

Roscoe C. Brown, Jr. and Dan W. Dodson compare delinquency rates in an area of Louisville where a Boys' Club existed with two similar areas where youth-serving agencies were absent. Although they found that the Boys' Club seemed to be influential in reducing delinquency rates, the authors indicate that other factors were also probably important. The study shows the uses and limitations of *ex post facto* research designs in the study of delinquency prevention, while at the same time providing relevant information on the efficacy of Boys' Clubs in preventing delinquency.

In a brief article, Bertram M. Beck and Deborah B. Beck assess the knowledge presently available on the role of recreation in the prevention of delinquency. They show how this topic is fraught with more speculation than research, and definitive answers are not now available.

The role of urban planning is among the issues dealt with by Jane Jacobs. She vividly questions attempts to get children off the streets and into parks and playgrounds via redesigning the physical environment. Arguing that delinquency is closely related to the amount of adult social control that exists within areas, she maintains that current planning practices actually help to decrease the amount of control available. As a result, delinquency rates may increase, and at the same time public areas actually may be less safe for children than they had been prior to implementation of the planning program. Jacobs shows the value of creative and imaginative thinking in this chapter from her book, *The Death and Life of Great American Cities*, by raising stimulating questions about the role of the physical environment in the prevention of delinquency.

22   Youth Employment Programs in Perspective

JUDITH G. BENJAMIN, SEYMOUR LESH,
MARCIA K. FREEDMAN

Recognition of the problems faced by unemployed youth is becoming widespread as various public and private groups and agencies undertake

Reprinted from *Youth Employment Programs in Perspective*, Washington, D.C., Office of Juvenile Delinquency and Youth Development, U.S. Dept. of Health, Educ. and Welfare, 1965.

the task of informing people and mobilizing them for action through the use of mass media, conferences, educational campaigns, and special youth employment programs. Nationwide meetings, such as the 1960 White House Conference on Children and Youth, and the Conference on Unemployed, Out-of-School Youth in Urban Areas (1961), where Dr. James B. Conant made his famous "social dynamite" speech, have focused interest on the problem of youth unemployment.

In November 1961, President Kennedy appointed a Committee on Youth Employment composed of 33 leaders from industry, labor, education, government, and social agencies, including six cabinet members. Its purpose was to analyze the problem and draw up a list of recommendations for action. This Committee's report, *The Challenge of Jobless Youth*, April 1963, stressed the urgency and need for a coordinated approach, with public and private groups at the local, State, and Federal levels participating on a broad scale in every community.

A number of Federal programs have been initiated which will have an effect on youth employment. The Area Redevelopment Act of 1961 introduced the concept of federally supported retraining for unemployed workers in distressed areas in order to equip them with new skills.

Retraining programs were started under the Manpower Development and Training Act of 1962 to prepare and train workers for unfilled jobs. Special projects specifically designed for unemployed youth also are being supported by the Act. Using either institutional or on-the-job training, these projects are concentrating on school dropouts, functional illiterates, delinquents, and handicapped youth between the ages of 16 and 22. Many of the youth being trained are members of minority groups.

The United States Department of Labor has expanded its programs and services through the Office of Manpower, Automation and Training; the Bureaus of Labor Standards and Labor Statistics; and the United States Employment Service. Other programs, such as the Public Works Acceleration Act of 1962, increased public welfare aid to long-term unemployed, and the raising of minimum wages, are also having an effect on the youth employment problem.

A major stimulus to programing has come from the Office of Juvenile Delinquency and Youth Development, in the Department of Health, Education, and Welfare. This agency, in cooperation with the President's Committee on Juvenile Delinquency and Youth Crime, provided special training and planning grants to a number of cities to establish demonstration programs for the community treatment of juvenile delinquency. A key goal of these programs has been to make "unemployable" youth employable.

The 1964 Economic Opportunity Act has extended these efforts still further. As part of its diverse attack on the causes of poverty, further community action programs are being developed. Youth employment is a central target in the legislation as a whole, whose provisions include the establishment of residential centers (Job Corps), neighborhood youth corps, and work-study programs.

On the State and local level, there have been scattered attempts for many years to create youth employment programs. Some of these have emanated from Federal legislation; but many more arose independently, from Mayors' and Governors' Conferences and Committees, local offices of the public employment service, agencies such as New York State's Division for Youth, voluntary groups working on a neighborhood basis, and school programs designed for different groups of youth.

The schools have felt the first and strongest pressure to act, because they constitute the only institution that has responsibility for all youth. The expectation that they will fulfill this responsibility has led them most often, not to thoroughgoing revisions of approaches to education, but rather to an attempt to program for "special groups"—the retarded, superior students, "slow learners," "potential dropouts." With the growing difficulty in finding employment, high school graduates who have taken a general course (that is, neither college preparatory nor vocational) are at a disadvantage in the labor market, a fact which has added new pressures for the schools to expand vocational preparation.

Other institutions and agencies have also responded to these pressures and to other current issues involving rising welfare costs, civil rights, and inmigration to urban areas, by sponsoring youth employment programs.

Whatever the reasons for bringing local attention to the problem—lack of entry jobs, unfilled demand for skilled workers, rising statistics on youth crime, a desire to compete in the scientific race with Russia—attempted solutions generally take the form of specific programs operated by specific agencies. The type of action taken in a particular community or program depends upon the nature and extent of the local problem, the availability of resources, and the concepts which lie in the minds of the makers of the program. Only very recently have there been attempts to implement a community plan with adequate resources for tackling the problem in a comprehensive fashion.

Youth Employment Programs

Youth employment programs have, in general, focused on those who are in the process of making the transition from school to work, or who, having failed to make it, are unattached, disaffiliated from the major institutions of the society. The major thrust is rehabilitation and improvement of habits, attitudes, or skills presumed to be necessary for becoming employed. Programs may offer one or a combination of such elements as guidance, remedial education, work experience, training, and in some cases, placement, to achieve this objective.

In the broadest sense, these programs may be described as attempts to make "unemployable" youth employable, even though this is not generally the articulated goal. Who are the "unemployable"? The definition is never fixed, because different levels of employment and demand for workers are at the heart of any designation of employability. He who is unemployable today may become employable under new conditions. In this respect, the unemployable differ from the mentally and severely physically handicapped whose disabilities always put them in a special position.

Under present conditions, the youth least likely to be employed is the unskilled high school graduate, the dropout, minority youth, rural youth, and the delinquent. But not every youth in these groups is unemployable. If, for example, someone in his family or among his friends or relatives can find him a job (no matter how marginal), he thereby becomes employable, even though he may differ in no important respect from any number of other youth.

In the face of this looseness of definition, the concepts developed by program makers have even greater importance. Criteria of selection for a program subtly become definitions, and the target group may come to be characterized on the basis of what the agency decides to offer in the way of program elements, rather than through assessment of individual needs. If it is difficult to characterize the "unemployable" by looking at programs that have been created for them, it is nevertheless apparent from the figures on unemployment and dropouts that there does exist a large number of young people who are unemployable under present conditions. Program makers are free to draw from this pool on any basis they choose.

. . .

Distinguishing by Approaches

Programs that attempt to make youth employable through educational-vocational adjustment can be distinguished by two broad approaches: the majority take the approach that youth need primarily *general preparation for employment*; a few take the approach that youth's biggest need is *occupational training*.

"General preparation for employment" describes an approach that seems to rest on the assumption that unemployability inheres in the youth themselves. They are viewed as being unable to perform well on a job—any job—because of poor work habits and attitudes, limited ability, and unrealistic notions about themselves and their vocational goals. They need help, according to this view, to improve their attitudes, give them greater self-awareness, and acquire some of the fundamentals for getting a job. Programs of this type may be called by various names; they are, however, more alike than different since they all offer general, rather than specific, job preparation.

In contrast, when a program reflects the occupational training approach, the chief assumption is that the problem of unemployable youth stems more from external economic conditions, particularly changing employment patterns, than from the nature of the youth themselves. There is little or no demand for unskilled youth, and, in fact, there are only certain occupations untrained youth can expect to enter; this is largely what makes them unemployable. A youth employment program especially designed for the least employable, according to this view, must consider the employment out-look and train youth specifically for those occupations where employment is possible.

Youth in these two types of programs may be the same in ability, but there seem to be different assumptions about what rung of the occupational ladder they will occupy, once they have made the adjustment to employment. In the first case (general preparation for employment), the program planners seem to picture these youth largely as low-skilled workers employed in the service trades. If some have more ability, they will rise to the top. In the second case (occupational training), the majority of these youth are seen as semiskilled workers employed in manufacturing as well as in the service trades. The assumption here is that they are manually inclined, that training for work with their hands appeals to them, as opposed to the academic emphasis that accounted for their failure in school. Training can, therefore, serve two useful purposes—it can provide them with skills for employment, and at the same time be the instrument for rehabilitation.

Some programs classified as "general preparation for employment" do include training for youth who want immediate employment, to give them the minimal skills that their prospective entry jobs may require. Some classi-fied as occupational training programs start with guidance and an orientation course in job fundamentals to determine whether a youth can profit from training and, if so, from what type. Yet even here, the approaches remain fairly distinct.

In the first instance, the primary need still is seen as providing the un-employable with better vocational understanding, so that he will know what the world of work is all about and where he fits into the picture. Skills are an afterthought, something added later on that he can acquire in a short time, something tangible he can sell to an employer. It is assumed that he needs only the most elementary type of skills, just enough to get a foothold; further skills can be acquired later through experience or through a formal training program.

In contrast, in the second instance, it is guidance and general job orien-tation that are tacked on to the basic element of training, but at the be-ginning of the program, rather than at the end. Guidance and basic job orientation are considered preparatory to the needed training; they can enhance it, but they cannot replace it. Training for specific occupations where these youth can expect employment is still seen as the primary need, under the assumption that these occupations require skills before entry is possible, skills that take considerable training to acquire, and without which a youth can gain no foothold in the labor market.

These opposing viewpoints reflect the conflict of two main streams in the thought of the educational community: between the merits of "basic," "fundamental," "general," "comprehensive" education, and the merits of vocational education.

.   .   .

Models of the Approach in Practice

Obviously, there can be many variations on the theme of work experience, as indicated by the examples already cited. No two programs are exactly the same. Many combinations exist, depending on the type of work experience offered, the supplementary elements added, the criteria for selecting the target population, the background and training of staff, and the choice of operating procedures. It would be impossible to show every variation without describing each program.

It is possible, however, to group programs under three models—those that accent work experience alone; those that accept guidance, with work used only as a guidance tool; and those that combine work experience and guidance with equal emphasis—because it is the degree of emphasis given to work that seems to determine the basic composition of the program.

. . .

Accent on Work—In-school Youth

The *Kansas City, Missouri, Work-Study Program.* This program, jointly sponsored by the Kansas City Public Schools, the Kansas City Association of Trusts and Foundations, and the Ford Foundation, is based upon Robert J. Havighurst's notion of work as a delinquency-prevention measure. It is a six-year controlled experiment begun in September 1961 to test the hypothesis ". . . that boys vulnerable to delinquency will become less delinquent if they are given a systematic work experience . . . ."[1]

The program has three work stages, beginning in the eighth grade. "Predelinquent" boys were identified in the seventh grade through a "Behavior Description Chart," a teacher-rated instrument; "Who Are They?" a sociometric instrument; and the cumulative records of the boys. An attempt was made to select an experimental and control group, matched as nearly as possible in age, IQ, social maladjustment, school record, color, and socioeconomic status. Two pairings were made, one in 1961 and the other in 1962, with each group to be followed for five years.

Work Stage I. The first stage begins in the eighth grade for boys 13 to 15 years old. A half day is spent in school where the basic subjects are taught by regular teachers in special classes and with subject matter adapted to learning level. An attempt is made to integrate the boys with regular students by allowing them to take one nonsolid subject in whatever area they wish. Counseling is provided on the same basis as for regular students, by the school counselors, teachers, and the work supervisors.

The other half of the day is spent in "socially useful work" in the school or in city agencies and facilities. The boys operate in work-teams of various sizes (usually 10 to 24) doing landscaping, trenching, planting, painting, furniture repair, etc., under the direction of a work supervisor and a work assistant. All of this work is unpaid during the school year. Two small groups (22 boys) were paid 50 cents an hour during the summer of 1962,

[1] Burchill, George W., *Work-Study Programs for Alienated Youth.* Chicago: Science Research Associates, 1962, p. 135.

one group doing gardening work for the city and the other group refinishing cafeteria tables for the School District. The boys are graded on their work as well as on their school subjects. Such qualities as cooperation, punctuality, and efficiency are stressed.

Work Stage II. Those youth who successfully complete Stage I (after approximately a year and depending on individual progress) and who are between 15 and 17 years of age, enter Stage II. This phase of the program includes a half day of school alternated with a half day in an individual work situation. The academic program continues with the basic subjects started in Stage I (social studies, English, math and science) for about three hours a day. The youth work for about three hours a day (possibly some work on weekends as well) doing such jobs as order billers, stock boys, service station helpers, attendants in small animal hospitals and helpers' jobs in various fields. They are generally paid a subminimum wage during the learning period with the exception of jobs that are classified under interstate commerce. The work supervisor keeps in close touch with the boy to evaluate the progress made on the job. Again the boy is graded on his work.

When a youth reaches 16 or 17 (legal school-leaving age), it is anticipated that he may want to return to the regular academic or vocational high school program. Providing he has passing grades in the work program and is deemed mature enough, help will be extended to enable him to do so. It is felt that most boys will neither be willing nor able to handle the regular school program and will continue in the work-study program.

Work Stage III. At this stage, when the youth are between 16 and 18, and in their fifth or last year of the program, they would leave school for a full-time job. The dividing line between Stage II and Stage III is purposely left fluid to allow for an easy transition whenever each individual youth is ready. The boys will be assisted in finding full-time jobs, and while no longer under close supervision by the school personnel, the work supervisor would maintain some contact to enable the youths to change their jobs or get new ones. Progress in this stage will be evaluated on the basis of employers' reports and personal interviews until the youth reach 18 years of age. At this point, a final evaluation will be made of their "initial adult competence" and they will have officially completed the program. Comparisons will be made with the control groups.

The program, which is due to end in June 1969, is budgeted at $650,900. Of 87 boys enrolled in Stage I in 1961, 63 were still enrolled, and six had moved on to Stage II by the end of 1962. The group started in 1962 has 106 boys enrolled in Stage I. The first group (1961) was chosen from four junior high schools. The second group (1962) was selected from the same four junior high schools plus one senior high school with an eighth grade.

Just as the Kansas City Work-Study Program sees work experience as a means to prevent delinquency for in-school youth, certain other programs use work experience as a rehabilitative device for adjudicated delinquents, whether in-school or out-of-school. Here, too, the feeling is that work has intrinsic value and can be used to steer wayward youth onto the right track.

Accent on Work—In-School and Out-of-School Youth. *Hamilton County (Cincinnati, Ohio) Juvenile Court Work-Therapy Program.* This program was inaugurated in 1958 by the Juvenile Court Judge under the theory that if a child works, he will not get into trouble. He established a new department in the probation section of the Juvenile Court, calling it the Job Placement and Work Therapy Department, to put into practice the "rehabilitation through work" program. Using on-the-job work experience, the program attempts to establish a "milieu-therapy" situation to provide positive experiences for the problem adolescent. A graduated scale of earnings is used to motivate youth to change their work attitudes and performance. The program has a number of different phases through which a youth might move. Although originally concerned with the out-of-school adjudicated delinquent, the program has been expanded to include in-school youth who are classified as "potential dropouts" and therefore "potential delinquents."

Boys and girls between the ages of 15 and 18 who show no mental or emotional difficulties that might interfere with learning (the court psychologist administers a test battery for screening), may be referred to the program by the Juvenile Court Judge, probation officers, and court referees, if they show lack of salable work skills, responsibility, self-discipline, or personal pride. Youth referred to the program are placed in screening groups for periods of five to ten weeks, depending upon individual progress. These groups meet at least once a week in a public agency where they work together on such tasks as leaf-raking, grass-cutting, painting, dusting, mopping, etc., under the direction of a work counselor. During this period, in which the youth receive lunch and carfare money but are not paid a salary or hourly wage, the work counselor and the probation officer determine which phase of the program the youth will enter next. This depends upon each one's degree of readiness.

Phase I. This is a structured subsidized program where the youth do the same type of work they had done in the screening groups, but for which they are now paid at the rate of $5 per day for not more than one day's work per week. The staff attempts to guide the spending of this money, and encourages the purchase of appropriate clothing, haircuts, and whatever else is necessary to improve appearance and arouse pride. Placement in this phase is part of the youth's probation and he must keep his assignments.

Phase II. For those youth who succeed in the screening group and the subsidized work phase, attempts are made at full-time placement in the community. These jobs are solicited by the staff of the program, but the youth are hired on their own merits—they go through the regular application and interview sessions established by each employer. The employers are informed as to the problems of the youth. Youth are paid by the employer at the going wage.

Phase III. For those youth deemed ready for full-time employment, but for whom no jobs are available, an interim step is placement for one day a week in private homes doing domestic work.

Phase IV. Those youth who demonstrate aptitudes in particular directions may be placed in training programs which exist in the community. Welding school, art school, modeling school, and other training facilities are utilized. The Court, at times in cooperation with other agencies and private industry, pays the tuition for these programs.

A youth may go through all of the above phases or merely one, depending upon how staff interprets his needs and readiness.

While the program has many other facets—a summer program, an informal remedial program, supportive counseling, job guidance, psychological services, etc.—the major emphases are job placement and work therapy, with actual work experience as the prime tool in rehabilitating delinquent youth. There is no research being done in the program, but it is felt by staff that rehabilitation can best be measured in terms of "human interest factors."

The program is financed entirely by Court funds, through fees received from speaking engagements by the Juvenile Court Judge, the Chief Probation Officer, and by private donations. The budget may run from $12,000 to $20,000 a year. The numbers of youth handled depend to a great extent on the amount of money which can be raised. In 1962, in all the programs, approximately 500 youth received some type of assistance: 288 youth were involved in the special summer programs; 45 were involved in the "after-school dropout program;" 150 in the subsidized work programs. In addition, 75 "graduates" of various phases of the program were placed in permanent part-time or full-time jobs in the community.

Accent on Work and Job Guidance. The majority of general preparation programs using work experience differ from the Kansas City Work-Study Program and the Hamilton County Juvenile Court Work-Therapy Program in that they combine work experience with what we have termed "job guidance." [2] They give about equal weight to these elements, assuming that they are mutually dependent and that to use one without the other would not provide a meaningful learning experience. Other elements—remedial services, occupational practice—may be added as supplements, but it is work experience and job guidance that are considered fundamental in preparing the unemployable for employment.

Help for School Dropouts: Detroit Job Upgrading Program. Since 1949, the Detroit Job Upgrading Program has been the prototype for most other job preparation programs throughout the country. During the war, Detroit's youth had little trouble getting jobs at fairly good pay. When World War II ended, returning veterans began to compete for jobs with youth who were dropping out of school. The upgrading program was initiated to meet the problem. Starting slowly, the program gradually expanded, until today there are 11 job-upgrading centers operating in ten high schools and one junior high school.

[2] Called in some programs "group guidance," "job skills," "job upgrading," or "job conditioning."

The program is jointly sponsored by the Detroit Board of Education and the Detroit Council for Youth Service, Inc., which was the originating agency. It offers a short-term job-guidance course combined with a subsidized work experience to aid school dropouts in preparing for employment or returning to the regular school program.

Youth aged 16 through 20 who are out of school and unemployed are referred to the program by community agencies, interested individuals, and the schools. They are interviewed by the specially selected job-upgrading teacher (who also tries to interview the parents) before they are enrolled. The program is designed to run for 12 weeks and has two closely related and overlapping phases.

Phase I. The first six weeks are devoted to an informal job-guidance class that meets with the upgrading teacher three hours each morning, five days a week. Instruction and assignments are given largely on an individual basis, according to each student's rate of progress. These sessions are devoted to the problem of how to get and keep a job, and instruction in basic skills, including reading and arithmetic. In addition to these morning sessions, youth are encouraged to attend one or two regular classes in the afternoon —an individual program is worked out by the upgrading teacher, and they take such projects as typing, remedial reading, welding, etc. If a youth indicates a desire to return to the regular school program, arrangements are made for him to take credit subjects as part of his morning program.

Phase II. After six weeks in the program, the youth who will not be returning to school may be placed in a part-time, subsidized training job. He continues to attend the job-guidance course in the morning and works in the afternoon. The part-time jobs are located in city departments, social agencies, and in private industry. Wages vary from 60 cents to 75 cents an hour for such jobs as clerical and maintenance helpers, counter work, sales, and stock work—jobs that are basically unskilled. Youth are supervised on the job by the employer who reports regularly to the teacher.

It is hoped that after 12 weeks in the program, the youth will be ready to find full-time jobs. Attempts are made to help them get placed. There is a follow-up period of six months after a youth has completed the 12-week program.

The program, which serves more than 1,000 youth a year, is budgeted at over $140,000 (1960–61 figure). Because of limited funds, only about a third of the youth can be given the subsidized work experience. There is no formal research or evaluation included in the program; in reporting, the program leans heavily on numbers and anecdotal material.

Training For Specific Occupations. Youth employment programs that stress occupational training derive from vocational education. Work, when it is used, becomes on-the-job training to teach youth specific occupational skills, not to impart general understanding of the work world, or to improve attitudes, motivation or behavior alone.

Bedford YMCA (Brooklyn, New York) Youth and Work Program. The Bedford program is another of the eight pilot programs co-sponsored by the New York State Division for Youth for reaching the unemployed dropout. While the Youth and Work Program cosponsored by the Vocational Advisory Service (as previously described) emphasizes guidance, the Bedford YMCA program focuses on mechanical skill training. It includes a number of other elements—work experience, counseling, and remedial services—used to complement or enhance the skill training.

The program is deliberately aimed at the more capable dropouts, to obviate competition with youth of less ability for the unskilled entry jobs. It provides training to prepare a youth for entry into a trade area as a helper or apprentice. Boys between the ages of 16 years, 10 months and 18 years, who have been identified as official dropouts by the Board of Education and who reside within the Bedford-Stuyvesant, Fort Green, or Bushwick communities, are eligible for the program. After testing and interviewing, the staff determines which youth meet minimum standards for admission to available mechanical trade courses. From the pool of youth so identified, a control group and an experimental group are selected randomly. (The New York State Division for Youth conducts the research.) Youth in the control group are referred to Youth Employment Service counselors in the community who try to place them. Youth who are selected for the experimental group are given a week of orientation, counseling, and job preparation before participating in the regular program.

Once a trainee is enrolled in the regular program, his day is spent in the following manner: mornings are devoted to a subsidized work experience in a nonprofit social agency; there is a short period devoted to lunch, travel, and some informal individual counseling; in the afternoon the youth takes trade training in the Bedford YMCA Trade School shops; remedial services, and individual and group counseling take place after the shop work.

Phase I, Work Experience. The work experience is not directly related to the specific skill training which the youth receives later on in the day. It is offered to the trainee to teach him some positive work habits in a real work setting. It also provides him with maintenance money for the training period and with a job recommendation for the future. Part-time jobs as helpers are provided in New York branches of the YMCA where the trainee assists plumbers, electricians, painters, or food service managers. The trainee is paid $1.00 an hour from funds provided by the Division for Youth, and works a maximum of 20 hours a week.

On-the-job supervision is provided by the building superintendent or his representatives. The project's work supervisor visits each work station weekly. He observes each trainee, counsels with the appropriate branch supervisor, and is available at the project office with other staff personnel to discuss with each youth the concerns or problems of his work experiences.

Phase II, Trade Training. The Bedford YMCA has operated its own trade school since 1908. Located next door to the YMCA, it consists of three floors of well-equipped shops for teaching auto mechanics, welding, machine shop practice, refrigeration, oilburner servicing, and radio and TV repair. Only those which are taught in the day school are available to project trainees. These are: auto mechanics, refrigeration mechanics, and machine shop practices. The youth take a maximum of 225 hours of shop work in the trade area in which they have indicated interest and aptitude. Stress is placed on those aspects of the regular curricula which have been found to be necessary for early entrance into the trade areas. Each phase of laboratory or shop work is preceded by basic theory classes in rooms adjacent to each shop. Tools and tuition are provided by the program. At the completion of training, a successful participant keeps his set of tools as an aid in his search for employment.

Remedial reading and mathematics sessions meet for four hours each week and are conducted by certified teachers who relate the material to the individual needs of each trainee and the trade-training course.

Group counseling sessions are held once a week. In general, they deal with problems relating to project behavior, work experience, and expectations of the world of work. In addition, special conferences are arranged to introduce the youth to YES procedures, the way to dress and approach a prospective employer, and the possible post-project training opportunities that are available.

The first training class began in September 1962. Within a year from that date, the project proposed to train 60 youth in three 16-week cycles (20 youth per cycle). Actually, 66 youth were exposed to training during this period; 35 have successfully completed training and were referred to YES interviewers for full-time placement, hopefully in the area of their trade-training courses. Twelve of those who did not complete the training have been unemployed since they dropped out. Only two of those who successfully completed the training have been idle.

The project staff maintains its contacts with all trainees for three months after their termination of training. The Division for Youth is responsible for follow-up for two years after training. In comparing the trainees who completed the program with those who dropped out, results indicate that the project has a positive effect on attitudes and potential success for those able to complete the course.

. . .

Implications for Programing

Program evaluation is most difficult to carry out in rigorous research terms. Life tends to be more complex than art; yet the categories we use to describe youth employment problems are still more like art than like life. We may have some notion of what it means to be unemployed, but we still know relatively little about the implications of unemployability.

Nor are we very clear on the meaning of various program elements. We still lack knowledge, for example, of the general value of work experience; of how the effects of general work experience differ, if at all, from the effects of the part-time jobs which many high school students find for themselves; of the comparative value of different types—individual placement, versus group work projects, versus contract services.

With the development of larger youth programs, there should be improvement of research techniques for meaningful assessment of programs. It may be that refining measurement and scaling techniques and the scrupulous application of statistical methods are secondary to the posing of appropriate questions and the refinement of criteria of success. On this latter point, program makers need to be far more aware of the success goals they project for their clients, and how well these match the aspirations of youth themselves.

·   ·   ·

23   Boys, Blisters, and Behavior— The Impact of a Work Program in an Urban Central Area

JAMES C. HACKLER

In January 1964 the Opportunities for Youth Project was launched in Seattle.[1] The purpose of this paper is to discuss the thinking that guided the action program and to present a preliminary evaluation of the experimental portion of the project. Our material has been organized into four sections: (1) the theoretical framework which guided the action program; (2) a description of the research design; (3) problems in carrying out the proposed design; and (4) the impact of the program on the boys.

The Theoretical Framework

A basic assumption shared by many students of social behavior is that we internalize sets of norms and values which in turn guide our actions. Therefore human behavior is described as being normatively regulated. Deviant

Reprinted from *The Journal of Research in Crime and Delinquency*, 3 (July 1966), 155–164, with permission of the National Council on Crime and Delinquency, and the author.

A modified version of a paper presented to the Society for the Study of Social Problems, Chicago, August 1965.

[1] This program was supported jointly by the Ford Foundation, the Seattle Housing Authority, and the Boeing Employees United Good Neighbor Fund. The author would like to express his thanks to Richard Jones, Richard Nagasawa, Dave Campbell, Herbert Costner, Walt Hundley, Maryan Neal, and many others who worked with the Opportunities for Youth Project in Seattle and contributed to this paper.

behavior is commonly perceived to be the result of ineffective internalization of conventional norms or of effective internalization of deviant norms.

This basic assumption has had an effect on action programs designed to curb juvenile delinquency. These programs frequently include a deliberate attempt to modify the value orientations, attitudes, or norms of delinquent boys. The goal of the program may be explicitly stated in such terms, and a variety of techniques is utilized in the attempt to achieve this goal. One approach involves detached workers who deal directly with gangs of delinquent boys. The expectation is that the boys will identify with a person who has conventional attitudes and norms.[2] Other approaches attempt to restructure the normative orientation of the entire group.[3] Although the action program may vary considerably, it makes the tacit assumption that (1) it can change attitudes or norms and (2) if attitudes and norms are changed, a modification of behavior will result.[4]

We are not attempting here to present and defend a causal theory of deviant behavior. Instead we will focus on a few of the assumptions inherent in such theory and their implications for an action program. This study makes no attempt to deny an association between the endorsement of deviant norms and involvement in deviant behavior. We do propose, however, that the developmental processes leading to deviant behavior, and not simply the association between deviant behavior and various factors, should be taken into account if action programs are to have the intended impact.

The perspective presented here is that the self-concept develops out of the responses of others, or, more accurately, out of the ego's *perception* of those responses. These self-relevant responses constantly indicate to ego the type of person he is and what is expected of him. These self-categorizations and the concomitant perceived expectations, in turn, influence the roles he will seek to play in an effort to behave in ways compatible with his imagined characteristics and capacities.

This perspective further proposes that such self-relevant responses include the responses not only of significant others who stand in a primary relation to the boy, such as parents and peers, but also of persons who represent community institutions crucial to his future goal attainment, such as teachers and employers.

It is assumed, further, that the boy tends to choose those activities which

[2] New York City Youth Board, *Reaching the Fighting Gang* (New York: Youth Board, 1960); Paul L. Crawford, Daniel I. Malamud, and James R. Dumpson, *Working with Teen-Age Gangs* (New York: Welfare Council of New York City, 1950).

[3] H. Ashley Weeks, *Youthful Offenders at Highfields: An Evaluation of the Effects of the Short-Term Treatment of Delinquent Boys* (Ann Arbor: University of Michigan Press, 1958); Lloyd W. McCorkle, Albert Elias, and F. Lovell Bixby, *The Highfields Story* (New York: Holt, 1958); LaMar T. Empey and Jerome Rabow, "The Provo Experiment in Delinquency Rehabilitation," *American Sociological Review*, October 1961, pp. 679–96.

[4] In his presidential address to the Society for the Study of Social Problems in August 1965 at Chicago, Irwin Deutscher pointed out the frequent discrepancy between what people say they will do and what they actually do. This raises an even broader question than the one discussed here: How valid are statements of intent or expressions of values as indicators of actual behavior? See Irwin Deutscher, "Words and Deeds: Social Science and Social Policy," *Social Problems*, Winter 1966, pp. 235–54.

are compatible with his evolving self-image and that finally, through dis-sonance-reducing mechanisms, ego may be expected to endorse selectively those normative prescriptions and values that are compatible with his ac-tivities and with his self-image. Following these assumptions, we hypothesize that values and attitudes *follow* behavior and are the *product* rather than the *cause* of deviant activities. Deviant activities are seen as the result, not of internalized values, norms, or attitudes, but of a self-image that emerges in the context of social interaction. We suggest that concentrating on the role of values held by delinquents in order to understand the etiology of deviant behavior is inappropriate. If this viewpoint is correct, we would do well to · reorient our attention to those factors that *precede* deviant acts and the development of a deviant self-concept.[5] In the Opportunities for Youth Project the major efforts are directed at modifying a boy's perceptions of the way others expect him to behave. A boy who believes that others in the society expect him to conform should, then, behave accordingly.

Research Design

The four public low-cost housing projects in Seattle, in areas with rela-tively high rates of official delinquency, served as the experimental commu-nities.

Within each housing project, four experimental groups of approximately ten boys were formed. (See Table 1.) Two of these groups worked at part-time jobs either in the housing project or in the city parks. Experimental Group 1 worked under a supervisor who was "informal"—that is, he at-tempted to make the boys believe that he anticipated capable, responsible work characteristics. Experimental Group 2 worked under a "formal" super-visor who acted as a conventional foreman and exercised fairly rigid control over the boys. In essence the two types of supervisors were to play roles called for by the theoretical scheme. The "informal" supervisors provided responses which would tell the boy that he was a nondeviant—a normal, adequate boy. The "formal" supervisors didn't attempt to provide such responses to the boys in their groups.

Members of the third experimental group worked independently at jobs in the surrounding community, with the Opportunities for Youth Project acting as an employment agency. In practice we found that, when the sum-mer season was past, it was impossible to maintain a meaningful indepen-dent work program.

Before examining Experimental Group 4, let us turn to those experimen-tal variables that apply to the community as a unit rather than to the in-dividual boys. Attempts to create a positive community attitude toward youth were to be made in Communities A and C (see Table 1). Our idea was to develop community-wide programs which would cause adults to view adolescents in a more favorable light. We considered using such techniques as false surveys which would ask the residents leading questions like, "Don't

---

[5] This argument is presented in greater detail in James C. Hackler, "A Sequential Model of Deviant Behavior," unpublished Ph.D. dissertation, University of Washington, 1965.

Table 1

Experimental Design of Opportunities for Youth

	Attempt to Create a Positive Community Attitude toward Youth		No Attempt to Modify Community Attitudes Toward Youth
	Community A	Approx. No. of Boys	Community B
Teaching Machine Testing Program	Exp. Group 1—Work as group; informal supervision.	10	Same experimental and control groups as in Community A.
	Exp. Group 2—Work as group; formal supervision.	10	
	Exp. Group 3—Work individually; minimal supervision.	10	
	Exp. Group 4—No work; remedial teaching offered.	10	
	Control Group—No work; no remedial teaching.	20	
	Total number	60	
	Community C		Community D
No Teaching Machine Testing Program	All experimental and control groups the same as in Community A except Exp. Group 4. This group received no remedial teaching but was placed on an "active waiting list," which would give the members more perceived access to jobs than the control group.		Same experimental and control groups as in Community C.

you think the boys are doing a good job working here in the project?" or "Don't you think this will keep all of the boys out of trouble?" or "Have you noticed how responsible the boys have become?" "Communities B and D would not be involved in such programs. Actually, we found that some communities were already more favorably disposed than others toward the boys and decided simply to classify them according to this attitude rather than attempt to modify existing attitudes.

In Communities A and B, a teaching machine testing program was established. One could think of this program as remedial education, but the boys were also asked to help decide whether the machines would be useful in a classroom setting. Although the persons who supervised these groups were professional teachers, they were asked *not* to give the impression that they were helping the boys but instead were to assume that the boys were able to succeed in the task at hand. In keeping with our theoretical perspective, the supervisors of the teaching machine program were to convince the boys that they anticipated behavior which was in keeping with an academically capable person.

Boys in Experimental Group 4 did not work on any part-time job. In Communities A and B, they took part in the teaching machine testing program along with those boys who did have jobs; in Communities C and D, they were only on a waiting list.

We tried *not* to be selective but rather to involve *all* the 13- to 15-year-old boys who lived in the housing projects. The boys were *not* told that we were trying to help them. Instead they were told that we had jobs that needed to be done.

Everyone took the initial questionnaire; then the boys were randomly assigned to the various work and control groups.

Problems in Carrying Out the Proposed Design

Originally, we had planned to make tests for second- and third-order interaction by using two-way analysis of variance techniques. However, teen-age boys do not respond exactly like white rats in the laboratory. The size of some of our groups varied; in fact, two of the twenty groups in the original plan disappeared completely. For interaction we finally used the chi-square test for a 2 x 2 x 2 table. This method is not as demanding as two-way analysis of variance.[6]

The experimental variable involving a "formal" and an "informal" supervisor probably was not meaningful. The boys saw both in a favorable light. However, distinctions between the two groups were maintained. The previous week's pay was picked up at the beginning of the work session by boys in the informal group and at the end of the session by the formal group. The informal group was more involved in selecting work tasks, etc.

We had hoped that the teachers who were guiding the teaching machine testing program would be able to avoid giving the impression that they were

[6] A two-way analysis of variance design would have dealt more effectively with the small number of boys assigned to the various experimental and control groups. The design permitted the 200 boys to be distributed over 20 unique groups. It was not possible, however, to maintain equal cell frequencies. In addition, our data did not meet the requirements of an interval scale and it seemed more reasonable to dichotomize the variables in order to handle the large quantity of data. Our tests for interaction utilized the chi-square test for the 2 x 2 x 2 table suggested by M. S. Bartlett, "Contingency Table Interactions," *Supplement to the Journal of the Royal Statistical Society*, 1935, pp. 248–52. This has been described as a test for "second-order interaction"; see George W. Snedecor, *Statistical Methods* (Ames: Iowa State College Press, 1946), pp. 200–04. Herbert L. Costner and L. Wesley Wager, "The Multivariate Analysis of Dichotomized Variables," *American Journal of Sociology*, January 1965, pp. 455–66, suggest that this test has an operational interpretation in asking whether there is a significant difference between two Qs. This would be appropriate only if the variables in the 2 x 2 tables are ordinal. We can conceive of all of our variables as ordinal. Even race, for example, can be viewed as a status-ascribing factor, with Caucasians ranking higher than Negroes.

helping or that they were pleased if a child did well on a particular lesson. It is probably unreasonable to expect any teacher to ignore a child's academic accomplishment and merely praise his task of rating the teaching machine itself.

In general, the main theme of the program was carried out. Boys were placed in positions where it would be difficult for them to fail; success was practically guaranteed. We hoped that these boys would begin to see themselves as capable and adequate.

The Impact of Certain Phases of the Program

The perspective presented earlier suggests that if the experimental program was successful, boys would perceive others as anticipating socially desirable behavior on their part and would begin to see themselves as behaving in a socially adequate manner. It also suggests that norms or values would change to a lesser degree than the boys' perception of others' anticipations of their behavior. In other words, changes would take place first in the way boys believe the world sees them, and then in the way that they see themselves. This would be reflected later in the activities in which they are involved and, finally, in the values they hold. Since the boys were involved in the program for only a few hours each week, we did not expect major changes in any of these areas but felt that if a change did take place it would be seen first in their perception of others' anticipations.

Thirty-nine variables were used to assess the impact of the program. These included police records, referrals to the school counselor, ratings by the teacher, and questionnaire items answered by the boys. Obviously, it is awkward to deal with 39 separate criteria; therefore, we organized these items into three groups. The 16 items in Group I are those that would be most likely to change if the experimental program were a success according to the rationale behind the entire project. They include the boy's perceptions of others' anticipations for him, measures of the self-image, and similar items. Group II items are made up of nine factors that one would reasonably expect to change in a successful program even though they are not specifically stated in the theoretical rationale; for example,. the boys might become less alienated. (The 25 items included in Groups I and II will be the main focus of interest in deciding whether or not the program was effective.) Group III is made up of 14 items that would be *unlikely* to change in such a short time according to the rationale. It would be unreasonable, for example, to expect a work program to reduce the official delinquency rate. Group III items, then, may be valid criteria; but, if changes appeared in Group I and II items, a lack of change in Group III items would still permit us to claim success for the project.

Did the type of work group make a difference? To see whether there was a differential impact as a result of membership in the formal work group, the informal work group, the independent work group, the waiting list, or the control group, we examined the percentage of boys who changed in a favorable direction from the beginning to the end of the program. Averaging the percentage of boys who changed in a favorable direction for the 16 items making up Group I criteria gives us a rough composite score that can be easily interpreted when compared for all five groups. (No change at all on a given item was classified as an unfavorable change.)

Table 2 compares the five groups. The control group seemed to show more change in a favorable direction than the four experimental groups. The differences are not large, but they show, clearly and painfully, that the action program had no impact on the boys.

Table 2

	Average Percentage Change in a Favorable Direction				
Criteria Used	Formal Work Group	Informal Work Group	Independent Group	Waiting List	Control Group
I	31	32	31	32	37
II	31	35	32	31	37
III	26	27	30	24	39

Next, we grouped the formal and informal work groups together and compared the resultant group with the waiting list and the control group added together. When we dichotomized the criterion variables into changes in a favorable direction and changes in an unfavorable direction or not at all, we were able to generate a series of 2 x 2 tables. With Yule's Q, a relationship of approximately .50 would have been significant at the .05 level. On each set of 39 criterion variables, then, the "shotgun" approach to finding significant measures of relationships should have revealed, by chance alone, about two tables with measures of .50 or above.[7] When we compared the work groups with the controls, one relationship reached .46 and another reached .48. The second relationship, however, was in the opposite direction. Hence, we find no meaningful difference between the work groups and the controls.

Of the 39 criterion variables used, about 14 measures (Group III) were ones which we had predicted would not change—values, for example, and police records. By focusing on only those 25 variables (Group I and II) which measured such concepts as self-image, alienation, and the like, we hoped that our batting average would improve. It didn't. Actually, we had not anticipated statistically significant results, but we had hoped for consistent patterns of relationships in a predicted direction for selected variables. As a general rule, this hope was not realized.

Faced with these disappointing results, the researcher is forced to utilize less demanding criteria if he is to retrieve some useful information from the data. In the steps that follow, the reader should be aware that patterns which

---

[7] Leslie Kish, "Some Statistical Problems of Research Design," *American Sociological Review*, June 1959, p. 336.

appear are suggestive rather than conclusive. They should be considered worthwhile hypotheses to be tested more rigorously at a future time.

Since 39 separate criteria were used to evaluate the program, we can conceive of 39 distinct evaluations. By merely examining each criterion separately and ignoring any relationship with a Q of less than .10, we can devise a box score of the number of tests favoring the work group compared with the number of tests favoring the control group. For example, one can see (Table 3) that eight of the criteria changed in favor of the work group,

Table 3

Criteria Used	Number of Criteria Which Changed in Favor of the Work Groups	No Difference (less than .10)	Number of Criteria Which Changed in Favor of the Control Groups
I	2	6	8
II	3	4	2
Total (I & II)	5		10
III	3	4	7
Total	8		17

while 17 changed in favor of the control group. For our purposes we will focus on the 25 criteria in Groups I and II—those pertinent to the theoretical rationale. Here again the box score is 5 to 10 against the program.

Did some portions of the program have an impact? Although we have no evidence that the program in general modified the boys' behavior in any way, it is possible that those who were involved in both the work program and the teaching machine testing program changed in some way. In Table 4 we note that the score is 13 to 6 in favor of those boys who were involved in the teaching machine program, but 5 to 12 against those who

Table 4

Criteria Used	Boys Who Took Teaching Machine Testing			Boys Who Did Not Take Teaching Machine Testing		
	Changes Favoring Work Group	No Difference	Changes Favoring Controls	Changes Favoring Work Group	No Difference	Changes Favoring Controls
I	6	5	5	2	5	9
II	7	1	1	3	3	3
Total, I & II	13		6	5		12
III	5	5	4	2	4	8
Total	18		10	7		20

were not involved in machine teaching. The combined effects of the work and teaching machine program or the teaching machine program by itself may have had some favorable impact on the boys.

Did the program have an impact on a particular group? A work program and a teaching machine testing program could be viewed with suspicion by boys with a background of unpleasant experiences in school. Therefore we posed the question: Do "good" boys respond to such opportunities to a greater degree than "bad" boys? [8] We have defined boys as "good" if they had not been referred to the counselor at school and as "bad" if they had been referred. In Table 5 we notice that our score favored "good" boys (10

Table 5

Criteria Used	Boys Not Referred to Counselor			Boys Referred to Counselor		
	Changes Favoring Work Group	No Difference	Changes Favoring Controls	Changes Favoring Work Group	No Difference	Changes Favoring Controls
I	5	7	4	3	3	10
II	5	2	2	2	4	3
Total, I & II	10		6	5		13
III	7	2	5	2	2	10
Total	17		11	7		23

to 6) but was against "bad" boys (5 to 13). Interaction is a possibility. The program could have been more successful (or less unsuccessful) for the boys who were already getting along with authority figures. Such a finding is compatible with other efforts to work with the underprivileged—those who have been a problem often get little out of attempts to do something with or for them. These are the boys of most concern. Boys who get into trouble at school are quite often those who seem to have less ability. It is also possible that those with ability will take advantage of a work program to a greater degree than those with little ability. Therefore, in Table 6 we have looked at the results separately for boys with high IQ's and those with low IQ's. The score is 9 to 13 against the boys with high IQ's and 6 to 9 against boys with low IQ's. Neither category seemed to respond to the program. These data would not support the suggestion that the relationship found in Table 5 was spurious because of ability. The avoidance of trouble may be an important conditioning factor for an action program, while the ability of the boys may be less relevant.

Opportunities for Youth seemed to have greater support from the Negro population in the housing projects. There were 403 boys aged twelve to

[8] David Campbell, research assistant on the project, provided the rationale and predicted the results in Table 5 despite the author's original skepticism.

Table 6

Criteria Used	Boys with High IQ			Boys with Low IQ		
	Changes Favoring Work Group	No Differ-ence	Changes Favoring Controls	Changes Favoring Work Group	No Differ-ence	Changes Favoring Controls
I	3	2	11	3	7	6
II	6	1	2	3	3	3
Total, I & II	9		13	6		9
III	3	5	6	1	9	4
Total	12		19	7		13

fifteen in the projects in October 1964. Of these, 37 per cent were Negro and 54 per cent were Caucasian. An attempt was made to involve all boys in this age group in work or control groups. Of the 200 boys who took part, 57 per cent were Negro and 36 per cent were Caucasian. In two of the housing projects boys were solicited from the surrounding area as well, and these areas had a concentration of Negroes; however, it seems that Negro boys and their parents were more responsive than the Caucasians.

In Table 7 we consider the hypothesis that Negro boys would exhibit

Table 7

Criteria Used	Negro Boys			Caucasian Boys		
	Changes Favoring Work Group	No Differ-ence	Changes Favoring Controls	Changes Favoring Work Group	No Differ-ence	Changes Favoring Controls
I	5	6	5	2	4	10
II	5	1	3	1	4	4
Total, I & II	10		8	3		14
III	3	5	6	1	2	11
Total	13		14	4		25

more favorable changes in the action programs than the Caucasians. The score is 10 to 8 favoring the Negro boys and 3 to 14 against the Caucasians. Such findings suggest a differential impact on the two races. However, other data, not discussed here, suggested just the opposite—that Caucasian boys responded better than Negroes. We have been unable to resolve this inconsistency or to uncover errors which would explain such results. While our staff has the definite impression that Negro boys benefited most from the program, our data present a confusing picture.

We asked the boys this final question on the last questionnaire: "Do you think that Opportunities for Youth has been a good thing for boys like you?" They were asked to circle a number on a seven-point Likert scale with "Yes" on one end, "It doesn't matter" in the middle, and "No" on the other end. As one would expect, the boys were favorably disposed toward the project. Using just the two extreme choices on the "Yes" end of the seven-point continuum, we get the pattern shown in Table 8.

Table 8

	Percentage Who Rated Opportunities for Youth Very Favorably
Work Groups	
Negro Boys (59)	83%
White Boys (37)	65%
Total (96)	76%
Control Groups	
Negro Boys (43)	77%
White Boys (17)	47%
Total (60)	68%

The difference between the boys in the work program and in the control groups is small. Everyone seems to approve of the project, but the work program boys approve just a little more than those in the controls. The same pattern holds when we look at the Negro and white boys separately. However, the Negro boys in the *control groups* are more favorably disposed toward the project than white boys in the *work program*—by 77 per cent to 65 per cent. We notice also that Negro boys in the control group are only slightly less well disposed toward the program than Negro boys in the work groups. On the other hand, there is a greater difference between the white boys who were in the work program and those in the control groups. Our comments earlier about the Negro support for this type of activity seem to be verified.

Impact of the Work Program

When we examined the change scores for 39 different evaluation criteria for the formal, informal, and independent work groups, the waiting list, and the control groups, we found that, though the differences were small, the controls changed more than any other group. Tests of statistical significance do not show any meaningful differences between work and control groups. When we look for evidence of any impact of the work program on various sub-groupings, we also find no differences large enough to be considered clear support for the effectiveness of the work program. There are, however, patterns which suggest some possible changes. These suggestions are weak and possibly in error but they are worth considering for future research.

1. The work program may have had an impact when combined with the teaching machine testing program.

2. The teaching machine testing program may have had some impact by itself.

3. The program may have had more impact on boys who had not been in trouble at school.

4. Negro boys and Negro mothers seemed to support the program to a greater degree than white boys and white mothers. Negro boys rated the project higher than white boys; however, our data do not indicate that the program had a greater impact on Negro boys. One set of data favors the white boys, another the Negro boys.

The general lack of impact for the overall program makes it impossible to use the action program as a test of the theoretical framework presented earlier. Further analysis is planned at a later time.

Implications for Other Programs

This preliminary analysis of the Opportunities for Youth Project counsels caution to other programs using employment as a means of delinquency control. Perhaps a more intensive effort would have had a measurable impact. But it is also possible that work programs have not chosen the correct target. The assumption is that *boys* can be changed, and if *they* change the rest of the world will treat them differently. But the world may not recognize any change and may, therefore, not treat the boys differently, and the boys may know it. In New York, Mobilization for Youth may be following a more promising line of action by changing the community structure itself. Perhaps we should stop working so hard on the boys themselves and focus on the way they interact with the rest of society. In a sense, Opportunities for Youth did try to modify the interaction patterns which surrounded the boys. It attempted to modify the way a boy thinks the world sees him. We tried to provide a set of mirrors that would reflect a favorable image. Our results do not tell us what was lacking: Were the ideas incorrect? Or were we unable to manipulate the environment successfully?

24 Goals for Gang Workers

DAVID M. AUSTIN

The big-city street-corner group, lounging in front of the candy store—blue jeans, cigarettes, Presley haircut, and a chip on the shoulder—has be-

Reprinted with permission of the National Association of Social Workers and the author, from *Social Work*, Vol. 2, No. 4 (October, 1957), pp. 43–50.

AUTHOR'S NOTE: This paper is based upon two delinquency control projects which

come a standard part of the American culture and a favorite subject of discussion or harangue at any community gathering. In communities that have started to tackle this "gang-problem," one of the popular methods being tried is the use of the so-called "gang-worker," "street-corner group worker," or "detached worker." Such programs have been under way now for ten to fifteen years in a few cities, not counting the cellar-club work in the 1930's, but many programs have been started in the early 1950's, and many more are being considered at this time. In nearly all cases professional social workers are intensely involved in planning for such programs, in administering them, and in some instances in direct service to street-corner groups.

It is time now to begin to clarify what this service is, what the process includes, and what can legitimately be expected in the way of accomplishment. The following discussion attempts to do this on the basis of two programs that have been in operation for more than three years. The focus is on work with the relatively large male street-corner group (fifteen to twenty-five or more members) which shows some evidence of group identity and structure. This is the group most frequently labeled the "teen-age gang." Not covered by this term are smaller groups of more uniformly disturbed boys who are frequently in trouble but do not make the papers as often, or girls' groups which are a significant aspect of the general delinquency problem. No effort is made to describe the related work with families, community organization work with adult community groups, and the network of relationships with other agencies that are an integral part of an effective area approach to the general problem of delinquent behavior.

These two programs differ in many details. The first one—the Special Youth Program of the Greater Boston Councils for Youth—has an independent budget and uses full-time, professionally trained social workers, who work intensively in one area of the city as part of a diversified approach to the problem of delinquency, and who concentrate on a single group for periods ranging from one to nearly three years. The other program, the Unreached Youth Program of the Cleveland Group Work Council, is a city-wide program with a central co-ordinator and a central fund of money to provide part-time staff (for the most part not trained social workers) who work with a single group and who are supervised by professionally trained staff in existing agencies. This program covers many different areas of the city and different neighborhoods and is not tied into any comprehensive or area approach to delinquency. With all of their diversity, it is still possible to abstract from the two programs the essential elements and to construct

---

were initiated in 1954 in Boston and in Cleveland. The paper was prepared in 1957 based on the first two-and-one-half years' experience in each project. The conclusions presented in the paper are based on the pattern of adolescent groups found in central city areas at that time. In most American urban areas the pattern of adolescent groups and the neighborhood situation within which they function has changed in significant ways during the past decade.

an outline of a professional service for which a given process and certain goals can be specified.

The first and perhaps most essential element is that it is a professional community *service*, not a membership program. Nearly all the traditional leisure-time programs, whether Scouts, YMCA's, settlements, or public recreation centers, offer an adult organized program which individuals and occasionally groups can choose to use or become part of by paying a fee and becoming a "member." In contrast, a client or a patient does not become a member of a child welfare agency, a family casework agency, or a hospital. These adult-organized youth programs have activity content already worked out by adults, frequently with a great deal of thought and study. This type of program has in the past and will in the future continue to be a major aspect of the social institutions of a large city. The approach being described here, however, is not just a modification of the content of such existing programs (the modifications in existing program services required by contemporary adolescents is a separate topic). The focus of this paper is on a service that starts with a *problem*, not a *program*. The content of this professional service is determined by the peculiar nature of a particular problem. Moreover, the service is made available at the point of greatest need rather than at the point where those most eager for a program have paid a fee, become members, and created an organizational structure.

The second essential element is that the heart of this professional service to aggressive delinquent street-corner groups is an *individual* worker. The key to success is not to be found in a type of building, a set of activities, a structured program, or even in a set of group techniques. The essential tool is the individual worker and his network of relationships with the group. His skills in personal relationships, his preparation for the job, his understanding and sensitivity are not only important, they are essentially the only things that will achieve success. This is not a team operation in the same sense that a medical team in a hospital brings a series of professional skills to bear on a patient one at a time, or sometimes jointly. While the skills and understanding of many professional persons may be used through supervision and consultation and may be required more directly for supplemental help in individual and family situations, the street-corner group worker is essentially a lone operator in working with groups. All the skills and knowledge of the team must be incorporated within his practice if they are to be of any assistance.

A third essential element is that this professional service is carried on in the *community*—not in an institution, and not primarily within the four walls of a building owned by an organization. By certain formal standards an institution can select its clientele who live in an essentially artificial and controlled situation with opportunity for the professional worker to control such variables as the size and criteria of group membership or the circumstances of personal interviews. Even in a building-centered youth program, many formal controls on membership and time and type of program are used by professional workers to create the best possible situation for effective work. But the street-corner group worker controls very few of the circumstances under which he works. The time and place of a personal interview are often beyond his control. Other community forces, such as schools, police, and the courts are also beyond his formal control, and often beyond his powers of prediction as well. He is constantly presented with immediate and demanding ramifications of the group situations in which he is involved. He is working with individuals who are under constant and unrelenting pressure from damaging environmental conditions, family and otherwise. It may be nearly impossible for the worker to change these conditions for a single individual, but it may seem equally impossible for the worker to wait for the changes needed affecting whole groups and communities.

The fourth essential element is that this service is *not initially requested* by the group. It is a "reaching-out" service, an assertive service. Therefore, an entire range of considerations and actions are involved in establishing the first contact with a group. Yet it is not an authoritative or protective service. It is not presented on an either/or basis—either you play football by my system of a single-wing back, or you can play T-formation at the state training school. It is a reaching-out service because the community through the worker takes the first step, takes the initiative to break through the fear and suspicion and hostility that are blocking positive communication between this group and the community.

Finally, a fifth essential element is that this is a professional service to *groups*, groups who have at least unconsciously made their own decision to be a group, who control their own membership, and the time, place, and content of group activity. Even though the worker may have a number of individual contacts with the families, essentially he is involved in, and working with, the interactions and forces within the group, and the relationships between the group as a whole and many aspects of its community environment. The street-corner group worker is not doing casework with a series of individuals who happen to be in the same neighborhood at the same time. He is working with a group which these individuals have created and which continues to function even as individuals come and go or even as individual behavior changes.

Putting all these essential elements together, then, we have a nonmembership, community-located professional service provided through a single worker who works in an environmental situation over which he has limited control and who extends service to a group without prior request from them for service.

Street-Corner Groups

In order to formulate objectives and goals of a professional service to the street-corner group, it is necessary also to consider the contemporary situation in which the group exists and the role it plays in the lives of street-corner adolescents.

We have in contemporary American life a large number of peer, single-sex, teen-age groups. They are found in all strata of society and probably in nearly every ethnic grouping. Because of current cultural factors involving the undefined and changing role of adolescence, the separation of the world of adults from the world of adolescents, the discrepancies between the public rules of behavior and the private practice of living, the conflicts in values between major groups of adults in the community, and the adjustments required by factors of discrimination—for all these reasons the adolescent looks to his close friends for guidance in values and behavior.

These adolescent groups often play a major role in determining the behavior, values, and aspirations of their members. This is true of adolescent groups in all ethnic, social, and economic groupings. Certain groups in any one neighborhood or community or social situation have an undue influence on a wide range of their immediate peers and those boys and girls immediately younger. Each neighborhood has its own way of defining who are the "big wheels."

In the intercity neighborhood the strong male street-corner group, generally between fourteen and eighteen years of age, is the group of primary influence. It influences even those boys and girls who reject it. The values and attitudes of the street-corner group are the results of several forces. The behavior and attitudes of the immediate adult community, and particularly of those persons just a little older, are a primary source of guidance. Some values and behavior are related to the desire of the group to protect itself from adult pressure or from other teen-age groups. Still other guides to specific behavior emerge from the group reinforcement of feelings of hostility toward the adult, middle-class, institutional, and major group communities. Some behavior reflects the particular mixture of individuals with individual needs and characteristic patterns of action found in the group at a particular moment. This is not to say that there are no appreciable influences on the group and the group members which might result in non-hostile, community-approved behavior. There are, of course, in nearly every group, but for the moment the concern is with those forces which result in law-violating, socially disapproved behavior.

There are a wide variety of such acts. Some are clear-cut violations of the law—murder, theft, breaking and entering. Some are acts of constant and sizable community disturbance such as gang fighting or drunken brawls. Some are disapproved in primarily moral terms, such as casual sex activity; some are acts of omission, such as not going to school. Others are incidents of hostility toward adults in positions of authority, such as insolence to a teacher, and still others are activities allowed or tolerated on the part of adults but disapproved of or forbidden to children—the use of liquor, private gambling parties, being out extremely late at night. Some are acts of racial hostility reflecting adult attitudes and even adult acts in their own community. Within a typical street-corner group all these types of actions may occur; in fact a single individual may be involved in this total variety of acts. These acts cannot be viewed as single and unrelated incidents. They are the reflection of a set of attitudes, of a code of values which brings a group and its individual members again and again into formal conflict with the law or with the formal moral code of the community. The adult community fears this group behavior more than just the occurrence of a single act of theft or vandalism, which is all too often excused with the comment that "boys will be boys." It is the unpredictableness of individual acts, the feeling of violence behind the simplest of incidents such as a scuffle on a bus, the overwhelming quality of group acts of violence, the sense of hostility toward all adults and all institutions that have brought on much of the public outcry. The feeling that this behavior has a widespread influence on adolescents in general and may even affect one's own child creates almost a sense of panic in many parents.

These many acts of delinquent behavior must be viewed as related to the broader picture of contemporary urban adolescent behavior rather than as scattered sparks from a fire to be put out by being stepped on one at a time. These acts do not occur because of an absence of formal moral or legal knowledge. The adolescent, delinquent or nondelinquent, knows what is illegal or immoral. He knows that legally and morally he is not supposed to stab someone with a knife, or take another person's money, or have sex relations with his girl friend. He knows these are wrong in the eyes of the larger adult community, and yet spontaneously, impulsively, foolishly, or angrily he does them. If much of the delinquent behavior of adolescents including the more serious, though occasional, acts of major law violation are impulsive and unplanned, then we cannot expect that approaches emphasizing logic or punishment are likely to accomplish the desired effect with the members of the typical street-corner groups though they may affect other types of adolescents in the general community.

Goals and Activities of Worker

Based on the concept that the delinquent behavior of members of a street-corner group grows out of a network of individual and group forces which include the pattern of group values, the goal of the street-corner group worker is to modify these forces in such a way that law violations and socially disapproved behavior will occur less frequently and that community-approved behavior will occur more frequently. Such changes in the forces within the group will take place over a period of time; they will affect various individuals in the group in different ways, and they will also affect individuals beyond the group. A long-range goal is the modification of the forces within the significant groups in the adolescent community in such a way that the general community pattern of adolescent values is affected. In turn, the patterns of imitation for the young adolescent and preadolescent are changed so the effect will be cumulative over a period of time and will result in a less delinquent-producing community.

This may appear to be a very large, perhaps speculative, statement of goal, but it is not if the resources that are available are clearly seen and understood. The most important resources the worker has in trying to achieve such a goal are the very forces which created the group in the first place. In fact, it is probably true that the stronger the forces creating the group and the stronger the group cohesion resulting, the better the chance of success for the street-corner group worker—regardless of the extent of major law violation found in the group initially.

When a boy moves into the street-corner group, it becomes a major source of guidance for his daily behavior. A major goal of group members is to achieve prestige and status, "to be someone instead of nobody." Failure to achieve status by middle-class institutional standards for many reasons causes group members to seek status through "toughness." Such toughness includes many characteristics including the imitation of many adult behavior patterns. The effort to prove that one is tough and grown-up, that is, not a "fag," "a square," or "chicken," lies back of many individual delinquent acts.

How does a professional worker use the forces which bring the group together in the first place and cause it to use delinquent and aggressive behavior as one way of achieving status? The method chosen is that of introducing into the street-corner group situation a completely new element —an adult community agent who has an assignment to work with this particular street-corner group. A great deal can be presented about the specific activities of the worker, the steps he takes in working with the group, and the effects on the worker himself. Some of this is described in detail in other reports of the Special Youth Program and in reports from other programs.

The major steps in process for the professional worker appear to be as follows:

1. An initial period of exploration in the community.

2. A first major verbal contact with members of a specific teen-age street-corner group.

3. A period of varied and often intense testing.

4. Establishment of a contract through which the group defines the form of structure within which the worker will have continued contact with them —frequently a club.

5. An extended period of mutual interaction during which the significant activity of the worker takes place.

6. A period of termination.

Particularly during the fifth step there will be intensive individual contact with some group members, involvement with families and work with other community agencies, as well as active program work with the group. But this is not just an unrelated series of events or a program of activities. In fact, if the worker only sees it as a series of program activities, then it becomes difficult to find a focus or to establish priorities among the endless demands upon his time. If the worker sees that his focus is the group and its values, and that modification of these values may have a greater effect within the group and on the community than he can have through a series of individual contacts, then he can put his work with a single individual or his response to a particular emergency situation into perspective.

The appearance of the worker in the neighborhood situation and his initial efforts to become acquainted with the group are a first and significant step. By his behavior he seeks to break down certain stereotypes the group has created about adults which form a convenient rationale for much of their attitude and behavior. This stereotype is that adults are against us, they don't understand us, they don't like us, they are afraid of us, if they pretend to be interested in us it is for their own purposes, and even if they are really sympathetic with us they are inconsistent and undependable. To the degree that the worker is successful in refuting these stereotypes through his own behavior, he opens the door for possible communication between himself and the group members and ultimately between the group members and other adults. His response to the group strikes at some of its basic values. He is neither impressed by nor fearful of the tough behavior of the group; he is not impressed by how bad they are nor does he panic when they threaten to be bad. He does not lecture or threaten when confronted with delinquent behavior, but he is concerned about the consequences for the group members. He demonstrates this concern—not by protecting individuals from the consequences when the community apprehends them but by demonstrating his concern while they are in court and, if necessary, while they are in an institution. He tries to be consistent— consistent in his concern for them, consistent in his refusal to be a chaperone and thus relieve the group members of the necessity of facing up to the consequences of their behavior, and consistent in demonstrating in his own behavior that one can act like and feel like a "somebody" without proving how tough and bad he is.

Thus the early relationship of the worker and group begins to break down the base upon which a fairly simple and unified set of group-supported values have been constructed, i.e., that adults are bad and why should we be any better, or that adults don't care about us and therefore why should we do what they want us to do? Moreover, a new type of person has come into the situation who can serve as an object of identification during this period of adolescence when identification is such an important process.

How Behavior is Influenced

As important as these two processes are, breaking down stereotypes about adults and provision of a new person for identification, they are not enough because they do not deal with the prestige problem. Old forms of behavior are not given up easily, particularly if there is no corresponding gain in another direction. Therefore, once the period of initial testing has been completed and a more stable framework of relationship has been worked out (frequently taking the shape of a formal athletic and social club), the worker faces the job of helping the group find new ways of gaining status and prestige and of breaking down the barriers between the group and those community forces which the adolescent group members see as hostile as well as those they see as potential objects of exploitation. This is not easy. A group that is convinced of its inability to be successful in any group activity but a fight, or whose pattern of participation in an organized activity, whether athletics or a dance, has traditionally involved heavy doses of alcohol, finds that it takes a great deal of group discussion—and loud arguing and cursing at each other—and a great deal of support and work and time from the worker before there can be success. Success need not be a victory at the first football game or a profit at the end of the first dance. Success means carrying through to the end on a planned activity as an organized group at a level of performance somewhat better than anticipated. It means ending a football game even in defeat without a riot and with the feeling that as a group they have actually made a game of it. Using another term, the group begins to develop a new kind of internal morale, a new perception of itself, and the individual members get a new perception of themselves, too. At this point a number of forces come to bear on the situation with a cumulative effect.

First, success in organized public group activities begins to draw public attention; such public attention may be sought by requests to merchants for financial support or news items in the local weekly. This public attention for community-approved activities begins to bring pressure from within the group for behavior to support the new community perception of the group. The more elements that identify the group publicly—such as jackets, a name, or a meeting place—the stronger the pressure on individual members to make their behavior support this new public attitude.

Second, the requirements of having a club business meeting, an effective football team, or a well-run dance mean a certain amount of self-discipline within the group, a willingness to accept direction, to curb or defer the expression of aggressive or disruptive behavior. This is only true, however, when the activity (whether a club meeting or a football team) is a genuine expression of the interests of the group. Structure or program introduced before the initial testing is worked through may become only another area for testing.

Third, through individually satisfying group experiences as well as through the relationship with the worker, individual tensions and hostile feelings may be reduced so that acting-out behavior on the part of individuals may decrease.

Fourth, through the individual efforts of the worker in some cases, and through new community attitudes toward the group as a result of their effective group activities, new lines of communication may develop between the group as a whole or individual members and adult institutions in the community. The group may receive more of a welcome at the neighborhood community center both because the worker has been able to interpret their situation and feelings and because they are ready to exercise somewhat more control over their own behavior. These, then, are four of the ways through which the pattern of values and activities of the group are modified. Individual behavior is modified as a consequence.

This rosy view needs some qualification, however. Some individuals and cliques within a particular group may move faster or slower than the group as a whole. In both cases, the individuals or cliques may leave the group or take on a fringe relationship to it. The cliques that cannot move as fast in giving up hostile attitudes and behavior—and generally they have and are experiencmg the greatest deprivations and damage—may include individuals who are quite likely to continue to come to the attention of the police and courts. What is important is that they no longer set the pace for the entire group. There may be community factors that the worker alone cannot modify and that interfere with the movement of the group. The presence of other hostile and attacking teen-age groups who do not have a worker may make it difficult or even unsafe for a group to give up its psychological readiness to fight. Overt community racial discrimination or extremely punitive attitudes on the part of the police may also delay changes in a group. A relatively weak group with little leadership may move very slowly and require more time and active support from the worker than a cohesive group.

The ultimate goals toward which the worker and the agency aim must be evaluated realistically. There will be no miracle changes in most cases, e.g., few of the aggressive acting-out boys will be chosen as the best all-round representatives of American youth, few school drop-outs will reenter school to continue into professional or business administrative fields. But certain definite achievements can be expected if the job is done right. The type of behavior that responds most readily to the treatment described above is *public group behavior*—the behavior of the football team, participation in gang fights, and group vandalism. The street-corner group worker approach, if used effectively with the several groups in a fighting network, can substantially diminish gang fighting. Also, a readiness may emerge to use existing community youth agency programs and to re-establish participation in local church activities.

Another aspect of behavior hopefully affected is *public individual behavior*, that is, behavior on the street corner, on public transportation facilities, and participation in theft, illegal behavior, and truancy, whether as individuals or in cliques. Although complete improvement for all members of the group should not be expected, the total amount of such behavior involving group members should decrease.

The area of behavior that may be least affected is *private individual behavior*, that is, social drinking, gambling, and sex behavior when only a single couple is involved. The evidence to date indicates that in this area changes come more slowly. Most of this behavior reflects general patterns of behavior in the immediate adult community and is not acted on by law enforcement agencies. Interpretations about goals to the general public should be realistic about what can be accomplished given the facts of contemporary society and the nature of urban community living.

Conclusion

Essentially, a worker must begin by accepting a group of street-corner boys not as a collection of perverse and bad individuals or as a group of innocent but misunderstood children, but as a group of individuals *operating within a framework of values which reflects their view of the world and the view of much of the community around them*—a framework of values that brings them into frequent and often harsh conflict with the larger community. This framework of values may be opposite to that which the worker uses to guide his own life, but he must, nevertheless, accept its reality and the validity it has for the group members. His goal is to modify that framework of values, not by directly attacking it but by helping to create a series of real experiences for the group as a result of which their view of the world and its possibilities for them will be modified and the standards by which they judge their own behavior and that of their friends will be modified. This calls for two qualities in the worker in great measure —patience and faith—faith in the potentialities of socially positive behavior on the part of the group members, and faith that our society has a place for them.

25   The Effectiveness of a Boys'
         Club in Reducing Delinquency

ROSCOE C. BROWN, JR. and DAN W. DODSON

The rise of juvenile delinquency has prompted many youth-serving agencies to re-assess their role in the prevention of this most challenging problem. This article deals with an attempt to assess the impact of one of the 450 Boys' Clubs on the delinquency rates of the neighborhood it serves. The particular club involved in this report is the Louisville Red Shield Boys' Club of Louisville, Kentucky.

The National Boys' Clubs of America national staff selected this Club for evaluation for several reasons. First, its establishment was fairly recent, 1946; its operation is in an area where incomes are generally low and housing comparatively poor; the delinquency rate was high when the club began operation; and lastly, the Boys' Club was the only major youth-serving agency operating in the area in the interim studied.

Although periodic reports which had been prepared by the Louisville Division of Police tended to show that the delinquency rate in the club area had decreased sharply between 1946 and 1954, the Boys' Club officials wanted an impartial study of the change in the club area of Louisville as contrasted to comparable areas within the city and with the city as a whole.

Reprinted from *The Annals of the American Academy of Political and Social Science,* 322 (Mar. 1959), 47–52, with permission of the Academy and the authors.

They wished to determine whether the pattern of decline was real, and if so, whether it was explainable on alternate bases to that of the impact of the youth-serving institution. The authors participated in the study as members of the staff of the New York University Center for Community and Field Services, the agency engaged to do the evaluation.

Some Methodological Considerations

Social scientists will readily recognize the pitfalls of studies of this type. The public is anxious to find the simple "pat" solution to the handling of youth. All youth-serving agencies would like to maintain that they have a role in the prevention of delinquency. In fact, many base a major portion of their fund-raising campaigns upon this type of claim. Yet respected social agencies have a right to come to universities and ask that they assist in evaluating the impact of a program on those they claim to serve. The research technician is caught in the dilemma of the limitations of his methods, which preclude definitive answers, and his desire to be useful. He is caught between the risks of having his limited findings used adversely against the agency, if they are not complimentary to it, and having his limited findings used as "endorsement of science" if they do turn out to be complimentary to the program.

The first methodological consideration involved establishing the usefulness of a statistical study in determining the effectiveness of the Boys' Club program in preventing delinquency. The staff of the Center pointed out that a statistical study could not provide definitive evidence on the Club's actual role in the prevention of delinquency. Even if the delinquency rate has declined, there are several factors other than the Boys' Club that might have brought about the changes. Since there is usually some feedback between happenings in a community, changes in a large-scale social phenomenon such as delinquency would probably be the result of the interaction of several factors. Further, since the study was of necessity an ex post facto design, it would be impossible to provide for the controls necessary for a true test. Nevertheless, the Boys' Club and the authors felt that knowledge of changes in the delinquency rate in the Club area and in other comparable areas of Louisville would be helpful in establishing a point of departure for future studies.

The next consideration was the definition of delinquency, and the legal concept of juvenile delinquency in Louisville was used. Thus, in this study, delinquency was considered as "those offenses defined by the Crime Prevention Bureau of the Louisville Division of Police as being delinquent acts." Children between 5 and 16, from 1944 to 1952, and between 5 and 17, since 1953, committing delinquent acts in Louisville were processed by the Crime Prevention Bureau if apprehended. Some of the types of offenses classified as delinquent acts were: auto thefts, destruction of property, unlawful entry of property, offenses against persons, larceny, and truancy. In all, sixteen different categories of delinquent acts were identified by the authors.

Selection of Comparable Areas. Data on delinquency rates for a two-year period previous to the opening of the Boys' Club were collected so that a base line might be established. The data covered the period 1944–1954 inclusive. Then permission had to be obtained to utilize the Crime Prevention Bureau's records and to develop a method of computing delinquency-rate statistics. The Assistant Chief of Police, who was a leader in the Boys' Club movement in Louisville, was quite helpful in obtaining permission for us to gain access to their records. The only limitation was that the boys' names were not to be used. Since there were some delinquents who were repeaters, it was decided that the delinquent rates should be based on the number of individuals. Thus, the rates were based on the comparison of the number of boys committing delinquent acts in a given year to the total number of boys residing in the area during that year. It was necessary to use the 1950 United States Census data as a base and extrapolate back to 1944 and forward to 1954 because there were no accurate data on the number of boys in each age bracket dating back to 1944. Although this method was approximate, the data followed a pattern of changes in the number of boys in each age group which was consistent with the over-all population trend in Louisville.

The most significant methodological problem was the selection of similar areas of Louisville for comparison with the Boys' Club area. This selection was the most crucial phase of the study because of the ex post facto nature of the design. When such a design is used for making comparative judgments, it is assumed that all factors other than those being compared are equal. Therefore, it was necessary to identify some basic ecologic factors that could be used to select areas comparable to the Club area. The criteria of median income, median rental, median education, type of housing, percentage of nonwhite population, and absence of a youth-serving agency building were used to select areas. These data were obtained from the 1950 census and from reports of the Louisville Planning and Zoning Commission and Health and Welfare Council of the Community Chest. Fortunately, neighborhood areas had been identified by the Planning Commission so that it was possible to compare neighborhoods of which the Club area was one and to select two other areas that were most comparable to the Club area. Unfortunately, they were not similar on all the selection criteria.

A summary of the basic comparative data follows:

Area	Median Income	Median Rental	Median Education Years	Population	Per Cent Nonwhite
Area A (Club Area)	$2703	$23.82	8.5	28,044	1.7
Area B	2423	24.83	8.6	10,088	11.05
Area C	2743	33.44	8.7	31,703	9.27
City of Louisville	$2723	$33.22	8.9	319,077	15.7

These data are indicative of the difficulty of matching neighborhoods even in a community the size of Louisville. It is necessary that the findings of the type of study reported here be carefully evaluated in terms of the similarities or differences of the areas being compared.

The Boys' Club Program

Since this study was primarily concerned with the comparison of the delinquency rates in areas that were comparable to the Club area, we did not study the Club program extensively. However, a brief description of the Boys' Club program is given so that the reader can see the type of emphasis the Club placed on various activities and the age groups of boys being served by them.

The program philosophy of the Boys' Club emphasizes an all-around program for boys working in small groups. Through working with each group, program activities that are most acceptable to the boys are developed. The program attempts to provide training in citizenship and to promote the development of the boys through constructive activity. Some of the activities included in the Club program were: clubs, athletics, woodwork, crafts, dramatics, swimming, Boy Scouts, and a summer camp program.

The Club began its activities in 1944 in an older area in the western section of Louisville. The Club was originally located in a two-story frame building until 1952 when a new, modern building was opened. The Club's activities were restricted to the white population of the area. It is interesting to note that 55 per cent, 1,540 out of 2,822, of the white boys in the Club area were members of the Club in 1954–55. Seventy-one per cent of the 10 to 14 age group were members of the Boys' Club. This is a significant fact because there was a large decline in the delinquency rate for this age group. Also, the Boys' Club philosophy places a great deal of emphasis on programs for this age group.

The Actual Findings

The delinquency rate for the Club area decreased rather steadily from 1 in 19 boys in 1946, when the Boys' Club opened, to 1 in 39 in 1954. The decrease in the delinquency rate in the Club area was in contrast to an increase in the rate for the City of Louisville from 1 in 29 boys in 1946 to 1 in 18 in 1954. The delinquency rates for the two other areas in Louisville also increased. The increase in area B was from 1 in 44 boys in 1946 to 1 in 16 in 1954; the increase in area C was from 1 in 28 to 1 in 21 in the same period. The complete findings are summarized in Table 1.

Delinquency Pattern.   Such a clear difference in delinquency rate statistics between the Club area, other comparable areas in Louisville, and the city as a whole could easily lead to the conclusion that the Boys' Club was responsible for the decline of delinquency in one area of the city while delinquency was increasing in other similar areas. Since the study was not an experimental controlled study, it is necessary to look at other factors. The first step was to find what was different in the Club area when compared

Table 1

Delinquency Rates [a] for Boys' Club Area, Area B, Area C
and the City of Louisville, Kentucky

Year Age Group	'44	'45	'46	'47	'48	'49	'50	'51	'52	'53	'54
				The Boys' Club Area							
5–9	55	251	365	87	234	173	179	1347	143	779	0
10–14	7	10	15	17	27	21	19	27	23	31	42
15–17	4	5	7	8	10	9	9	10	11	11	11
Total Area	10	14	19	21	33	27	26	35	30	35	39
				Area B							
Year Age Group	'44	'45	'46	'47	'48	'49	'50	'51	'52	'53	'54
5–9	340	133	421	225	0	501	144	535	136	138	122
10–14	18	21	37	35	31	42	29	35	20	15	12
15–17	16	13	13	13	16	9	11	16	27	7	7
Total Area	40	30	44	42	48	30	26	50	36	18	16
				Area C							
Year Age Group	'44	'45	'46	'47	'48	'49	'50	'51	'52	'53	'54
5–9	93	133	424	892	156	119	205	536	399	321	342
10–14	34	23	21	34	23	20	32	34	35	18	20
15–17	13	12	13	22	16	17	15	9	9	6	6
Total Area	30	26	28	50	33	24	42	32	38	18	21
				City of Louisville							
Year Age Group	'44	'45	'46	'47	'48	'49	'50	'51	'52	'53	'54
5–9			331	299	157	58	62	78	69	75	79
10–14	Data not		24	32	30	18	19	18	16	18	15
15–17	available		11	10	10	7	8	7	6	8	7
Total		16	21	29	35	33	21	22	21	19	21	18

[a] To be read as one of "x" boys as delinquent (e.g., 55 = 1:55).

to other areas of the city. There are several factors, all of which were not
studied, that might have influenced delinquency in the Club area: the leadership structure of each area, the influence of religious organizations, the type
of family units, the relationship between the races, economic stability, and
the effect of commercial expansion. For example, there was a difference
in the number of industries in the areas studied. There were 30 in the Club
Area, 50 in Area B and 65 in Area C.

A closer look at the actual delinquency pattern seems to indicate that while the Boys' Club probably had some influence on the delinquency problem, several other factors were also operating to produce social stability in the Club area and social instability in the other areas. The delinquency pattern for both areas B and C fluctuated a great deal between 1944 and 1952 and then increased greatly in 1953 and 1954. This increase coincided with the inclusion of 17-year-olds in the delinquency statistics. In contrast to this pattern, the delinquency rate for the Club area declined sharply from 1946 to 1948 (1 in 19 to 1 in 33) and then remained rather stable until 1954. Thus, the rate of the Club area did not increase when the 7-year-olds were added to the delinquency statistics. The rather stable pattern of decline in delinquency statistics in the Club area despite the unstable pattern of increase in two other areas of Louisville might have been caused by the presence of the Boys' Club. Another interpretation, however, might be that the social forces in the community that led to the establishment and expansion of the Boys' Club were lacking in the other areas. The absence of such community-oriented social forces might then be associated with a general pattern of social disorganization which is conducive to delinquency. This analysis is similar to that of Bernard Lander in his discussions of the relationship of anomie to delinquency.

The results of this study should be comforting in one respect. Namely, the presence of an active, well-organized Boys' Club in an area where delinquency had been high and in a city where delinquency was increasing was associated with a decline in delinquency rate statistics while these rates were increasing in other areas of the city. Although specific cause and effect relationships cannot be determined, the results of this study indicate that in at least one major community in this country, the Boys' Club was a significant part of the community's arsenal in the battle against delinquency.

Considerations for Future Research

The authors feel that this type of ex post facto study has some merit in establishing a base line from which further studies can begin. Although it is not possible to generalize from this study of one community to other communities, the design of this study provides evidence of the limitations of the statistical approach to studying the effectiveness of any procedure in preventing delinquency. There is a fairly general feeling among social scientists, which is shared by the authors, that studies to obtain definitive answers to the prevention of delinquency should involve both the study of community process and case studies of large numbers of delinquent and nondelinquent boys. Whereas a study of the type that is reported here is comforting in its confirmation that the program of an agency such as the Boys' Club contributes to the alleviation of the delinquency problem, it adds little to basic knowledge on the prevention of delinquency.

26 Does Recreation Prevent Delinquency?

BERTRAM M. BECK Assisted by DEBORAH B. BECK

The difficulties in analyzing recreation as a system and defining the field of interaction between it and the offender have not deterred partisans of organized recreation from glib proclamations concerning the way in which recreation might reduce crime and delinquency. Behind these claims is a simplistic view of criminal behavior which sees the offender as resorting to crime simply because he has nothing better to do. According to Mabel Elliott, "the scientific backing for these assertions was supplied by H. W. Thurston, author of the 1918 study, 'Delinquency and Spare Time,' which concluded that 2,587 delinquents in Cleveland (Ohio) were delinquent because of the habitual misuse of their leisure." [1]

While, as previously noted, some forms of criminal or delinquent behavior are in fact misuses of leisure, one cannot automatically conclude that conventional character-building or recreational activities can offer an alternative attractive to the offender.

Often, behind the "glib assertions" is a struggle for organizational existence that has little to do with the prevention of delinquency. A number of character-building and recreational organizations secure public or voluntary funds on the assumption that their presence is necessary to combat crime and delinquency. Such organizations have a bread and butter stake in the question of whether or not socially destructive behavior can be curbed through the expansion of recreational resources.

A number of studies have been done seeking to establish the relationship between recreation and crime or delinquency. Most, however, have not actually dealt with the relationship between play behavior and criminal acts. Rather, they have concerned themselves with the relationship between a specific organization or organizational behavior and the behavior of individuals. A notable exception is Thrasher's sociological classic, "The Gang." [2] In "The Gang," Thrasher, some 30 years ago, wrote about the criminal be-

Reprinted from "Recreation and Delinquency," by Bertram M. Beck, assisted by Deborah B. Beck, in Task Force Report: Juvenile Delinquency and Youth Crime, The President's Commission on Law Enforcement and the Administration of Justice, Washington, D.C., U.S. Government Printing Office, 1967, pp. 333–334.

[1] Elliott, Mabel A., "Group Therapy in Dealing with Juvenile and Adult Offenders," Federal Probation, XXVII:3 (September 1963), p. 49.

[2] Thrasher, Frederic M., The Gang: A Study of 1,313 Gangs in Chicago (second revised edition, University of Chicago Press, 1936).

havior of the group. He reached the conclusion that only through a system-atic community-wide approach encompassing all phases of the predelinquent's experience could an attempt at delinquency prevention be made. This method included sifting all children to find the group most likely to become delin-quent and concentrating all manner of institutional supports and programs in its behalf. He also noted that since this group is most prevalent in the blighted, declining and interstitial areas of cities, action should be con-centrated there. Of recreation facilities in particular, Thrasher noted,

> The common assumption that the problem of * * * delinquency will be solved by the multiplication of playgrounds and social centers in gang areas is entirely erroneous. The physical layout of gangland provides a realm of adventure with which no playground can compete. The lack is not of this sort. The real problem is one of developing in these areas or introducing into them leaders who can organize the play of boys, direct it into wholesome channels and give it social significance * * * . Ganging is merely one symptom of deepening community disorganization.[3]

In this particular study, Thrasher was not concerned with determining how play could be used to prevent or treat delinquency; rather, his stance was that of the scientist trying to describe interrelationships, and recreation or play was one part of the total life experience of the gang. In that sense, his study was the precursor of Albert Cohen's seminal work, "Delinquent Boys," [4] which accented the role of the peer group as crucial in the genesis of delinquent behavior. Thrasher (in the above-mentioned study), Cohen, and others who have concerned themselves with the relationship between group behavior and criminal acts merely emphasize for us the potential for organized recreation as a crime deterrent. They leave substantially untouched the issue of how to structure opportunities for play and pleasure so as to have an impact on antisocial behavior.

Studies closer to operational issues include another by F. M. Thrasher in which he analyzes the impact of a boy's club on delinquency. Here he found that more delinquents than nondelinquents were members of their organized recreational group and that composed as such, these groups did not necessarily deter delinquency.[5]

Since the first Thrasher study there have been a number of surveys which have attempted to examine delinquency rates before and after the establish-ment of a boy's club in a particular area. These studies universally found a decrease in recorded delinquency subsequent to the introduction of the boy's club program.[6] Such studies suffer from the chronic problem of determining

---

[3] *Ibid.*, p. 494.

[4] Cohen, Albert K., *Delinquent Boys, The Culture of the Gang* (Glencoe, Ill.: Free Press, 1955).

[5] Thrasher, Frederic M., "The Boys' Clubs and Juvenile Delinquency," *American Journal of Sociology*, 42 (July 1936), pp. 61–80.

[6] See, for example, Brown, Jr., Roscoe C., "A Boy's Club and Delinquency," Monograph No. 2, New York University Center for Community and Field Service (1956); "Studies in Population and Juvenile Delinquency," Oakland, California: Community Chest Survey (1944–45); "Agency Contacts with Membership of Boys' Clubs of Cincinnati, Inc., Older Unit" (Cincinnati, Ohio: Joint Study With Boys' Clubs of Cincinnati, Citizens Committee on Youth and Police Department, Community Health and Welfare Council Research Department, April 1960) (mimeographed).

a cause and effect relationship between a particular program and the number of recorded delinquencies. There are methodological difficulties in such an endeavor that make any findings, negative or positive, suspect.

Other studies include those of the Gluecks. In "Unraveling Juvenile Delinquency," [7] the Gluecks compared the life history of 500 adjudicated delinquents committed to two Massachusetts training schools with a control group of 500 youngsters with no official police records who were from the same types of neighborhoods and were then attending Boston public schools. The nondelinquent youngsters showed significantly higher involvement in organized recreational and character-building activities, but one could hardly view this as a cause of their social conformity, since crime and delinquency by their very nature suggest an exile from organized society.

In addition to the studies already mentioned, there have been other efforts to assess the relationship between the provision of recreation and the incidence of delinquency. These studies neither demonstrated in any conclusive fashion that recreation prevented delinquency nor were they able to demonstrate conclusively that recreation was without value in delinquency prevention. The reader is left with the conclusion that recreation is good or at least not harmful and might be of some value in crime prevention.[8]

The picture then is a cloudy one. It would appear that certain types of recreational opportunities may deter youngsters from delinquency, but this effect is largely dependent on the nature of the activity and cannot be attributed to recreation as an entity. There is practically no data pertaining to the deterrent effect of recreation with respect to adults.

27 Urban Planning and Prevention: Fantasy or Reality?

JANE JACOBS

Among the superstitions of planning and housing is a fantasy about the transformation of children. It goes like this: A population of children is condemned to play on the city streets. These pale and rickety children, in

Reprinted from "The Uses of Sidewalks: Assimilating Children," in *The Death and Life of Great American Cities*, by Jane Jacobs, New York, Random House, 1961 with permission of the publisher.

[7] Glueck, Sheldon and Eleanor, *Unraveling Juvenile Delinquency* (New York: The Commonwealth Fund, 1950), p. 399.

[8] See, for example, Truxall, Andrew G., *Outdoor Recreation Legislation and Its Effectiveness* (New York: Columbia University Press, 1929), p. 218; Shanas, Ethel B. and Dunning, Catherine C., "Recreation and Delinquency" (Chicago, Ill.: Chicago Recreation Commission, 1942), p. 284; Reed, Ellery, "How Effective Are Group Work Agencies in Preventing Delinquency?" *Social Service Review*, 22:1948, pp. 340–48.

their sinister moral environment, are telling each other canards about sex, sniggering evilly and learning new forms of corruption as efficiently as if they were in reform school. This situation is called "the moral and physical toll taken of our youth by the streets," sometimes it is called simply "the gutter."

If only these deprived children can be gotten off the streets into parks and playgrounds with equipment on which to exercise, space in which to run, grass to lift their souls! Clean and happy places, filled with the laughter of children responding to a wholesome environment. So much for the fantasy.

Let us consider a story from real life, as discovered by Charles Guggenheim, a documentary-film maker in St. Louis. Guggenheim was working on a film depicting the activities of a St. Louis children's day-care center. He noticed that at the end of the afternoon roughly half the children left with the greatest reluctance.

Guggenheim became sufficiently curious to investigate. Without exception, the children who left unwillingly came from a nearby housing project. And without exception again, those who left willingly came from the old "slum" streets nearby. The mystery, Guggenheim found, was simplicity itself. The children returning to the project, with its generous playgrounds and lawns, ran a gauntlet of bullies who made them turn out their pockets or submit to a beating, sometimes both. These small children could not get home each day without enduring an ordeal that they dreaded. The children going back to the old streets were safe from extortion, Guggenheim found. They had many streets to select from, and they astutely chose the safest. "If anybody picked on them, there was always a storekeeper they could run to or somebody to come to their aid," says Guggenheim. "They also had any number of ways of escaping along different routes if anybody was laying for them. These little kids felt safe and cocky and they enjoyed their trip home too." Guggenheim made the related observation of how boring the project's landscaped grounds and playgrounds were, how deserted they seemed, and in contrast how rich in interest, variety and material for both the camera and the imagination were the older streets nearby.

Consider another story from real life, an adolescent gang battle in the summer of 1959 in New York, which culminated in the death of a fifteen-year-old girl who had no connection with the battle, but happened to be standing at the grounds of the project where she lives. The events leading to the day's final tragedy, and their locales, were reported by the *New York Post* during the subsequent trial, as follows:

> The first fracas occurred about noon when the Sportsmen stepped into the Forsyth St. Boys' turf in Sara Delano Roosevelt Park [1] . . . During the

[1] Forsyth St. borders Sara Delano Roosevelt Park, which extends for many blocks, the Rev. Jerry Oniki, pastor of a church on the park border, has been quoted in the *New York Times*, with reference to the park's influence on children, "Every sort of vice you can think of goes on in that park." The park has had its share of expert praise, however; among the illustrations for a 1942 article on Baron Haussmann, the rebuilder of Paris, written by Robert Moses, the rebuilder of New York, Sara Delano Roosevelt Park, then newly built, was soberly equated as an achievement with the Rue de Rivoli of Paris!

afternoon the decision was made by the Forsyth St. Boys to use their ultimate weapon, the rifle, and gasoline bombs . . . In the course of the affray,
also in Sara Delano Roosevelt Park . . . a 14-year-old Forsyth St. boy was
fatally stabbed and two other boys, one 11 years old, were seriously wounded
. . . At about 9 P.M. [seven or eight Forsyth St. boys] suddenly descended on
the Sportsmen's hangout near the Lillian Wald housing project and, from the
no-man's land of Avenue D [the project grounds' boundary] lobbed their gasoline bombs into the group while Cruz crouched and triggered the rifle.

Where did these three battles occur? In a park and at the parklike grounds
of the project. After outbreaks of this kind, one of the remedies invariably
called for is more parks and playgrounds. We are bemused by the sound
of symbols.

"Street gangs" do their "street fighting" predominantly in parks and playgrounds. When the New York Times in September 1959 summed up the
worst adolescent gang outbreaks of the past decade in the city, each and
every one was designated as having occurred in a park. Moreover, more
and more frequently, not only in New York but in other cities too, children
engaged in such horrors turn out to be from super-block projects, where
their everyday play has successfully been removed from the streets (the
streets themselves have largely been removed). The highest delinquency belt
in New York's Lower East Side, where the gang war described above occurred, is precisely the parklike belt of public housing projects. The two
most formidable gangs in Brooklyn are rooted in two of the oldest projects.
Ralph Whelan, director of the New York City Youth Board, reports, according to the New York Times, an "invariable rise in delinquency rates"
wherever a new housing project is built. The worst girls' gang in Philadelphia has grown up on the grounds of that city's second-oldest housing
project, and the highest delinquency belt of that city corresponds with its
major belt of projects. In St. Louis the project where Guggenheim found
the extortion going on is considered relatively safe compared with the city's
largest project, fifty-seven acres of mostly grass, dotted with playgrounds and
devoid of city streets, a prime breeding ground of delinquency in that city.[2]
Such projects are examples, among other things, of an intent to take children
off the streets. They are designed as they are partly for just this purpose.

The disappointing results are hardly strange. The same rules of city safety
and city public life that apply to adults apply to children too, except that
children are even more vulnerable to danger and barbarism than adults.

In real life, what significant change *does* occur if children are transferred
from a lively city street to the usual park or to the usual public or project
playground?

In most cases (not all, fortunately), the most significant change is this:
The children have moved from under the eyes of a high numerical ratio
of adults, into a place where the ratio of adults is low or even nil. To think
this represents an improvement in city child rearing is pure daydreaming.

City children themselves know this; they have known it for generations.

[2] This too has had its share of expert praise; it was much admired in housing and architectural circles when it was built in 1954–56 and was widely publicized as an exceptionally
splendid example of housing.

"When we wanted to do anything antisocial, we always made for Lindy Park because none of the grownups would see us there," says Jesse Reichek, an artist who grew up in Brooklyn. "Mostly we played on the streets where we couldn't get away with anything much."

Life is the same today. My son, reporting how he escaped four boys who set upon him, says, "I was scared they would catch me when I had to pass the playground. If they caught me *there* I'd be sunk!"

A few days after the murder of two sixteen-year-old boys in a playground on the midtown West Side of Manhattan, I paid a morbid visit to the area. The nearby streets were evidently back to normal. Hundreds of children, directly under the eyes of innumerable adults using the sidewalks themselves and looking from windows, were engaged in a vast variety of sidewalk games and whooping pursuits. The sidewalks were dirty, they were too narrow for the demands put upon them, and they needed shade from the sun. But here was no scene of arson, mayhem or the flourishing of dangerous weapons. In the playground where the nighttime murder had occurred, things were apparently back to normal too. Three small boys were setting a fire under a wooden bench. Another was having his head beaten against the concrete. The custodian was absorbed in solemnly and slowly hauling down the American flag.

On my return home, as I passed the relatively genteel playground near where I live, I noted that its only inhabitants in the late afternoon, with the mothers and the custodian gone, were two small boys threatening to bash a little girl with their skates, and an alcoholic who had roused himself to shake his head and mumble that they shouldn't do that. Farther down the street, on a block with many Puerto Rican immigrants, was another scene of contrast. Twenty-eight children of all ages were playing on the sidewalk without mayhem, arson, or any event more serious than a squabble over a bag of candy. They were under the casual surveillance of adults primarily visiting in public with each other. The surveillance was only seemingly casual, as was proved when the candy squabble broke out and peace and justice were re-established. The identities of the adults kept changing because different ones kept putting their heads out the windows, and different ones kept coming in and going out on errands, or passing by and lingering a little. But the numbers of adults stayed fairly constant—between eight and eleven—during the hour I watched. Arriving home, I noticed that at our end of our block, in front of the tenement, the trailor's, our house, the laundry, the pizza place and the fruit man's, twelve children were playing on the sidewalk in sight of fourteen adults.

To be sure, all city sidewalks are not under surveillance in this fashion, and this is one of the troubles of the city that planning ought properly to help correct. Underused sidewalks are not under suitable surveillance for child rearing. Nor are sidewalks apt to be safe, even with eyes upon them, if they are bordered by a population which is constantly and rapidly turning over in residence—another urgent planning problem. But the playgrounds and parks near such streets are even less wholesome.

Nor are all playgrounds and parks unsafe or under poor surveillance, as we shall see in the next chapter. But those that are wholesome are typically in neighborhoods where streets are lively and safe and where a strong tone of civilized public sidewalk life prevails. Whatever differentials exist in safety and wholesomeness between playgrounds and sidewalks in any given area are invariably, so far as I can find, in the favor of the much maligned streets.

People with actual, not theoretical, responsibility for bringing up children in cities often know this well. "You can go out," say city mothers, "but stay on the sidewalk." I say it to my own children. And by this we mean more than "Don't go into the street where the cars are."

Describing the miraculous rescue of a nine-year-old boy who was pushed down a sewer by an unidentified assailant—in a park, of course—the *New York Times* reported, "The mother had told the boys earlier in the day not to play in High Bridge Park . . . Finally she said all right." The boy's frightened companions intelligently raced out of the park and back to the evil streets where they enlisted help quickly.

Frank Havey, the settlement-house director in Boston's North End, says that parents come to him time and again with this problem: "I tell my children to play on the sidewalk after supper. But I hear children shouldn't play on the street. Am I doing wrong?" Harvey tells them they are doing right. He attributes much of the North End's low delinquency rate to the excellent community surveillance of children at play where the community is at its strongest—on the sidewalks.

Garden City planners, with their hatred of the street, thought the solution to keeping children off the streets *and* under wholesome surveillance was to build interior enclaves for them in the centers of super-blocks. This policy has been inherited by the designers of Radiant Garden City. Today many large renewal areas are being replanned on the principle of enclosed park enclaves within blocks.

The trouble with this scheme, as can be seen in such already existing examples as Chatham Village in Pittsburgh and Baldwin Hills Village in Los Angeles, and smaller courtyard colonies in New York and Baltimore, is that no child of enterprise or spirit will willingly stay in such a boring place after he reaches the age of six. Most want out earlier. These sheltered, "togetherness" worlds are suitable, and in real life are used, for about three or four years of a small child's life, in many ways the easiest four years to manage. Nor do the adult residents of these places even want the play of older children in their sheltered courts. In Chatham Village and Baldwin Hills Village it is expressly forbidden. Little tots are decorative and relatively docile, but older children are noisy and energetic, and they act on their environment instead of just letting it act on them. Since the environment is already "perfect" this will not do. Furthermore, as can also be seen both in examples already existing and in plans for construction, this type of planning requires that buildings be oriented toward the interior enclave. Otherwise the enclave's prettiness goes unexploited and it is left without easy surveillance and access. The relatively dead backs of the buildings or, worse still, blank end walls, thus face on the streets. The safety of the unspecialized sidewalks is thus exchanged for a specialized form of safety for a specialized part of the population for a few years of its life. When the children venture forth, as they must and will, they are ill served, along with everyone else.

I have been dwelling on a negative aspect of child rearing in cities: the factor of protection—protection of children from their own idiocies, from adults bent on ill, and from each other. I have dwelt on it because it has been my purpose to show, by means of the most easily understood problem, how nonsensical is the fantasy that playgrounds and parks are automatically O.K. places for children, and streets are automatically not O.K. places for children.

But lively sidewalks have positive aspects for city children's play too, and these are at least as important as safety and protection.

Children in cities need a variety of places in which to play and to learn. They need, among other things, opportunities for all kinds of sports and exercise and physical skills—more opportunities, more easily obtained, than they now enjoy in most cases. However, at the same time, they need an unspecialized outdoor home base from which to play, to hang around in, and to help form their notions of the world.

It is this form of unspecialized play that the sidewalks serve—and that lively city sidewalks can serve splendidly. When this home-base play is transferred to playgrounds and parks it is not only provided for unsafely, but paid personnel, equipment and space are frittered away that could be devoted instead to more ice-skating rinks, swimming pools, boat ponds and other various and specific outdoor uses. Poor, generalized play use eats up substance that could instead be used for good specialized play.

To waste the normal presence of adults on lively sidewalks and to bank instead (however idealistically) on hiring substitutes for them, is frivolous in the extreme. It is frivolous not only socially but also economically, because cities have desperate shortages of money and of personnel for more interesting uses of the outdoors than playgrounds—and of money and personnel for other aspects of children's lives. For example, city school systems today typically have between thirty and forty children in their classes—sometimes more—and these include children with all manner of problems too, from ignorance of English to bad emotional upsets. City schools need something approaching a 50-percent increase in teachers to handle severe problems and also reduce normal class sizes to a figure permitting better education. New York's city-run hospitals in 1959 had 58 percent of their professional nursing positions unfilled, and in many another city the shortage of nurses has become alarming. Libraries, and often museums, curtail their hours, and notably the hours of their children's sections. Funds are lacking for the increased numbers of settlement houses drastically needed in the new slums and new projects of cities. Even the existing settlement houses lack funds for needed expansions and changes in their programs, in short for more staff. Requirements like these should have high priority on public and philanthropic funds—not only on funds at the present dismally inadequate levels, but on funds greatly increased.

The people of cities who have other jobs and duties, and who lack, too, the training needed, cannot volunteer as teachers or registered nurses or librarians or museum guards or social workers. But at least they can, and on lively diversified sidewalks they do, supervise the incidental play of children and assimilate the children into city society. They do it *in the course of carrying on their other pursuits.*

Planners do not seem to realize how high a ratio of adults is needed to rear children at incidental play. Nor do they seem to understand that spaces and equipment do not rear children. These can be useful adjuncts, but only people rear children and assimilate them into civilized society.

It is folly to build cities in a way that wastes this normal, casual manpower for child rearing and either leaves this essential job too much undone—with terrible consequences—or makes it necessary to hire substitutes. The myth that playgrounds and grass and hired guards or supervisors are innately wholesome for children and that city streets, filled with ordinary people, are innately evil for children, boils down to a deep contempt for ordinary people.

In real life, only from the ordinary adults of the city sidewalks do children learn—if they learn it at all—the first fundamental of successful city life: People must take a modicum of public responsibility for each other even if they have no ties to each other. This is a lesson nobody learns by being told. It is learned from the experience of having *other people without ties of kinship or close friendship or formal responsibility to you* take a modicum of public responsibility for you. When Mr. Lacey, the locksmith, bawls out one of my sons for running into the street, and then later reports the transgression to my husband as he passes the locksmith shop, my son gets more than an overt lesson in safety and obedience. He also gets, indirectly, the lesson that Mr. Lacey, with whom we have no ties other than street propinquity, feels responsible for him to a degree. The boy who went unrescued in the elevator in the "togetherness"-or-nothing project learns opposite lessons from his experiences. So do the project children who squirt water into house windows and on passers-by, and go unrebuked because they are anonymous children in anonymous grounds.

The lesson that city dwellers have to take responsibility for what goes on in city streets is taught again and again to children on sidewalks which enjoy a local public life. They can absorb it astonishingly early. They show they have absorbed it by taking it for granted that they, too, are part of the management. They volunteer (before they are asked) directions to people who are lost; they tell a man he will get a ticket if he parks where he thinks he is going to park; they offer unsolicited advice to the building superintendent to use rock salt instead of a chopper to attack the ice. The presence or absence of this kind of street bossiness in city children is a fairly good tip-off to the presence or absence of responsible adult behavior toward the sidewalk and the children who use it. The children are imitating adult attitudes. This has nothing to do with income. Some of the poorest parts of cities do the best by their children in this respect. And some do the worst.

This is instruction in city living that people hired to look after children cannot teach, because the essence of this responsibility is that you do it without being hired. It is a lesson that parents, by themselves, are powerless to teach. If parents take minor public responsibility for strangers or neighbors in a society where nobody else does, this simply means that the parents are embarrassingly different and meddlesome, not that this is the proper way to behave. Such instruction must come from society itself, and in cities, if it comes, it comes almost entirely during the time children spend at incidental play on the sidewalks.

Play on lively, diversified sidewalks differs from virtually all other daily incidental play offered American children today: It is play not conducted in a matriarchy.

Most city architectural designers and planners are men. Curiously, they design and plan to exclude men as part of normal, daytime life wherever people live. In planning residential life, they aim at filling the presumed daily needs of impossibly vacuous housewives and preschool tots. They plan, in short, strictly for matriarchal societies.

The ideal of a matriarchy inevitably accompanies all planning in which residences are isolated from other parts of life. It accompanies all planning for children in which their incidental play is set apart in its own preserves. Whatever adult society does accompany the daily life of children affected by such planning has to be a matriarchy. Chatham Village, that Pittsburgh model of Garden City life, is as thoroughly matriarchal in conception and in operation as the newest dormitory suburb. All housing projects are.

Placing work and commerce *near* residences, but buffering it off, in the tradition set by Garden City theory, is fully as matriarchal an arrangement as if the residences were miles away from work and from men. Men are not an abstraction. They are either around, in person, or they are not. Working places and commerce must be mingled right in with residences if men, like the men who work on or near Hudson Street, for example, are to be around city children in daily life—men who are part of normal daily life, as opposed to men who put in an occasional playground appearance while they substitute for women or imitate the occupations of women.

The opportunity (in modern life it has become a privilege) of playing and growing up in a daily world composed of both men and women is possible and usual for children who play on lively, diversified city sidewalks. I cannot understand why this arrangement should be discouraged by planning and by zoning. It ought, instead, to be abetted by examining the conditions that stimulate minglings and mixtures of work and commerce with residences, a subject taken up later in this book.

The fascination of street life for city children has long been noted by recreation experts, usually with disapproval. Back in 1928, the Regional Plan Association of New York, in a report which remains to this day the most exhaustive American study of big-city recreation, had this to say:

> Careful checking within a radius of ¼ mile of playgrounds under a wide range of conditions in many cities shows that about ⅕ of the child population from 5 to 15 years of age may be found on these grounds . . . The lure of the street is a strong competitor . . . It must be a well administered playground to compete successfully with the city streets, teeming with life and adventure. The ability to make the playground activity so compellingly attractive as to draw the children from the streets and hold their interest from day to day is a rare faculty in play leadership, combining personality and technical skill of a high order.

The same report then deplores the stubborn tendency of children to "fool around" instead of playing "recognized games." (Recognized by whom?) This yearning for the Organization Child on the part of those who would incarcerate incidental play, and children's stubborn preference for fooling around on city streets, teeming with life and adventure, are both as characteristic today as they were in 1928.

"I know Greenwich Village like my hand," brags my younger son, taking me to see a "secret passage" he has discovered under a street, down one subway stair and up another, and a secret hiding place some nine inches wide between two buildings, where he secretes treasures that people have put out for the sanitation truck collections along his morning route to school and that he can thus save and retrieve on his return from school. (I had such a hiding place, for the same purpose, at his age, but mine was a crack in a cliff on my way to school instead of a crack between two buildings, and he finds stranger and richer treasures.)

Why do children so frequently find that roaming the lively city sidewalks is more interesting than back yards or playgrounds? Because the sidewalks are more interesting. It is just as sensible to ask: Why do adults find lively streets more interesting than playgrounds?

The wonderful convenience of city sidewalks is an important asset to children too. Children are at the mercy of convenience more than anyone else, except the aged. A great part of children's outdoor play, especially after they start school, and after they also find a certain number of organized activities (sports, arts, handcrafts or whatever else their interests and the local opportunities provide), occurs at incidental times and must be sandwiched in. A lot of outdoor life for children adds up from bits. It happens in a small leftover interval after lunch. It happens after school while children may be pondering what to do and wondering who will turn up. It happens while they are waiting to be called for their suppers. It happens in brief intervals between supper and homework, or homework and bed.

During such times children have, and use, all manner of ways to exercise and amuse themselves. They slop in puddles, write with chalk, jump rope, roller skate, shoot marbles, trot out their possessions, converse, trade cards, play stoop ball, walk stilts, decorate soap-box scooters, dismember old baby carriages, climb on railings, run up and down. It is not in the nature of things to make a big deal out of such activities. It is not in the nature of things to go somewhere formally to do them by plan, officially. Part of their charm is the accompanying sense of freedom to roam up and down the sidewalks, a different matter from being boxed into a preserve. If it is impossible to do such things both incidentally and conveniently, they are seldom done.

As children get older, this incidental outdoor activity—say, while waiting to be called to eat—becomes less bumptious physically and entails more loitering with others, sizing people up, flirting, talking, pushing, shoving and horseplay. Adolescents are always being criticized for this kind of loitering, but they can hardly grow up without it. The trouble comes when it is done not within society, but as a form of outlaw life.

The requisite for any of these varieties of incidental play is not pretentious equipment of any sort, but rather space at an immediately convenient and interesting place. The play gets crowded out if sidewalks are to narrow relative to the total demands put on them. It is especially crowded out if the sidewalks also lack minor irregularities in building line. An immense amount of both loitering and play goes on in shallow sidewalk niches out of the line of moving pedestrian feet.

There is no point in planning for play on sidewalks unless the sidewalks are used for a wide variety of other purposes and by a wide variety of other people too. These uses need each other, for proper surveillance, for a public life of some vitality, and for general interest. If sidewalks on a lively street are sufficiently wide, play flourishes mightily right along with other uses. If the sidewalks are skimped, rope jumping is the first play casualty. Roller skating, tricycle and bicycle riding are the next casualties. The narrower the sidewalks, the more sedentary incidental play becomes. The more frequent too become sporadic forays by children into the vehicular roadways.

Sidewalks thirty or thirty-five feet wide can accommodate virtually any demand of incidental play put upon them—along with trees to shade the activities, and sufficient space for pedestrian circulation and adult public sidewalk life and loitering. Few sidewalks of this luxurious width can be found. Sidewalk width is invariably sacrificed for vehicular width, partly because city sidewalks are conventionally considered to be purely space for pedestrian travel and access to buildings, and go unrecognized and unrespected as the uniquely vital and irreplaceable organs of city safety, public life and child rearing that they are.

Twenty-foot sidewalks, which usually preclude rope jumping but can feasibly permit roller skating and the use of other wheeled toys, can still be found, although the street wideners erode them year by year (often in the belief that shunned malls and "promenades" are a constructive substitute). The livelier and more popular a sidewalk, and the greater the number and variety of its users, the greater the total width needed for it to serve its purposes pleasantly.

But even when proper space is lacking, convenience of location and the interest of the streets are both so important to children—and good surveillance so important to their parents—that children will and do adapt to skimpy sidewalk space. This does not mean we do right in taking unscrupulous advantage of their adaptability. In fact, we wrong both them and cities.

Some city sidewalks are undoubtedly evil places for rearing children. They are evil for anybody. In such neighborhoods we need to foster the qualities and facilities that make for safety, vitality and stability in city streets. This is a complex problem; it is a central problem of planning for cities. In defective city neighborhoods, shooing the children into parks and playgrounds is worse than useless, either as a solution to the streets' problems or as a solution for the children.

The whole idea of doing away with city streets, insofar as that is possible, and downgrading and minimizing their social and their economic part in city life is the most mischievous and destructive idea in orthodox city planning. That it is so often done in the name of vaporous fantasies about city child care is as bitter as irony can get.

VI Prevention Through Community Reorganization

With a number of notable exceptions, most of the specific prevention efforts outlined in this volume have focused on preventing delinquency among specific individuals who have been identified in one manner or another as potential delinquents. One of the assumptions underlying these efforts has been that the sources of delinquency are located primarily within the individual and hence successful prevention requires manipulation of individuals either singly or in group contexts in order to modify their values, attitudes, and behavior. An objective evaluation of programs of this kind must lead to the conclusion that they have been demonstrated to be not particularly effective, although this does not imply that they have no utility. Part of their lack of success appears to be caused by such factors as the failure to differentiate between those individuals whose background and experiences would lead them to respond to "treatment" and those who would not, or to the inability to successfully put rigorous programs into actual practice. We think that the major problem, however, is the failure to recognize that much delinquent behavior is not the result of individual pathologies, defects, disturbances, or inadequacies, but may actually be a rational means of dealing with problems for which other kinds of solutions are less readily available.

A relatively large body of research indicates that delinquency is concentrated in certain social categories and in certain geographical areas. The works of Shaw and McKay and others document the persistence of high delinquency rates over a period of time in certain parts of cities, even though the composition of the population has changed. This evidence is consistent with those theories locating the causes of delinquency "outside" the individual and suggests that prevention efforts should be concerned with modifying social and cultural variables rather than personal characteristics. Because delinquency rates and social and cultural conditions vary from community to community in consistent ways, it would seem that the logical unit on which to focus prevention efforts would be the community. This does not require, however, that other approaches be abandoned. Individualistically oriented programs as well as extracommunity efforts can at least be supplementary to community reorganization.

The community reorganization orientation has served as the basis for a number of delinquency prevention programs. These programs have varied in their specific approaches, although they are generally attempting to accomplish prevention through a similar orientation. Some have relied heavily upon professional personnel and have attempted to modify only a limited number of factors (for example, the Boston Midcity Project), while others have included a large number of components in an effort to produce changes in many segments of the community simultaneously (for example, New York's Mobilization for Youth). Still others have attempted to prevent delinquency by establishing a sense of community, developing indigenous leadership, and rebuilding inadequate social institutions (for example, Chicago's Area Project). Recognizing that the type of community and the form of delinquency will influence the strategies and programs that are most appropriate, and that the variations are numerous, we have chosen not to present illustrations of the range of variations evident in this approach, but some theoretical and empirical justification for it. We have therefore included only one type of program that we think provides a representative illustration of the general community reorganization approach.

The first article is concerned with the prevention of delinquent subcultures in urban communities. Richard A. Cloward discusses the importance of regulating access to legitimate and deviant opportunity structures as a means of social control. He points out that by themselves agencies of formal social control cannot eliminate deviance unless socially approved alternatives are provided to prevent the deviance from reappearing in some other form. Cloward discusses the different kinds of community organization (or disorganization) that theoretically exist and how they are related to the forms of deviance that emerge. He concludes by arguing that social control is more effective when it is internal to the community than when it is imposed from outside. He suggests that effective prevention involves generating new institutions in the community.

Eleanor E. Maccoby, Joseph P. Johnson, and Russell M. Church report the results of a study assessing the impact of community integration upon the social control of delinquency. Two different areas of Cambridge, Massachusetts, that were similar in socioeconomic status but that had divergent delinquency rates, were compared on degree of community integration, permissiveness toward delinquent acts, and willingness to take remedial action toward children who committed delinquent acts. The authors conclude that social integration apparently has direct effects on the degree of social control exerted over juvenile misbehavior.

Solomon Kobrin presents an assessment of the Chicago Area Project, a program that had been in effect for twenty-five years at the time of his analysis. The article presents the philosophy underlying the project as well as a description of its operation. He points out the difficulties of measuring the impact of large-scale prevention programs, while suggesting that the project achieved positive results in both delinquency prevention and other socially significant areas of concern. Kobrin concludes that the project has demonstrated that the residents of high-delinquency areas are capable of successfully dealing with their own delinquency problems if given the appropriate impetus and resources.

In the final article, John M. Martin evaluates three approaches to delinquency prevention. He discusses their advantages and disadvantages and indicates that both individual treatment and general prevention are necessary. He concludes, however, that long-term success in preventing delinquency is basically dependent upon successful social organization or reorganization.

28   The Prevention of Delinquent Subcultures: Issues and Problems

RICHARD A. CLOWARD

Delinquency has many forms. In this paper, I shall be concerned solely with delinquent subcultures—that is, with groups in which some type of law-violating activity is required in the performance of group roles. It is not the commission of collective delinquent acts that distinguishes the delinquent subculture from other groups; this definition excludes the many groups that occasionally commit collective delinquencies but do not construe such activities as required forms of role behavior (4). I shall also limit my remarks to delinquent subcultures composed of lower-class, adolescent males.

There appear to be three more or less distinct types of delinquent subculture among male adolescents in the slums of large urban areas. One is essentially a "criminal subculture," a type of gang devoted to theft, extor-

Reprinted from *Role of the School in Prevention of Juvenile Delinquency,* ed. by William R. Carriker, Washington, D.C., U.S. Dept. of Health, Educ. and Welfare, 1963, pp. 69–84.

tion, and other illegal methods of obtaining income. Another is the "conflict subculture," a type of gang in which the manipulation of violence predominates as a way of winning status. The third is the "retreatist subculture," a type of gang in which the consumption of drugs and other illicit experiences are stressed. Although these subcultures are rarely found in pure form, they generally exhibit sufficient differentiation to warrant being classified separately.

In this paper, I am concerned with some of the issues and problems which face us in trying to construct programs for the prevention of delinquent subcultures, and I shall try to identify some of the related problems calling for research. Unfortunately, there is little research to draw upon. Previous studies have generally focused on the individual delinquent or on particular types of delinquent act rather than on the delinquent subculture.

Choice of Targets for Action

One of the first problems in constructing programs of prevention is to avoid the tendency to equate deviance indiscriminately with evil and conformity with good. Even if it were possible to completely eliminate deviance in all its varied forms, it is doubtful that this would be desirable. Deviant behavior is often functional for a society, contributing to the stability of existing institutional forms or exerting pressure for useful changes (3). In defining targets of action, then, we cannot simply disavow deviance and support conformity. Rather, we must systematically discriminate among various types of aberrant behavior on the basis of the social costs they exact and the positive functions they perform for the society. Resources for combatting deviance are always limited. In practice, then, choices among forms of deviance are implicit in every program of action. If we decide to devote our resources to modifying one type of deviance, then clearly we are saying that other forms are less dangerous to society. Unfortunately, such decisions sometimes rest upon premises that are of doubtful validity.

In the field of delinquency, for example, there seems to be much more public concern about conflict subcultures than about drug-using groups. Indeed, gang delinquency is equated in the public mind with conflict behavior; warfare in the streets has become the dominant symbol of lower-class adolescent male delinquency. The highly visible nature of conflict behavior may in part account for its notoriety. One may ask, however, whether the emphasis on conflict subcultures rather than on drug-using subcultures is realistic. Without examining systematically the various social costs and functions of these two forms of deviance, we may note that conflict behavior is invariably abandoned with approaching adulthood, whereas drug use often persists throughout adult life. Furthermore, offenses against property and persons are committed with greater frequency by members of drug-using groups than by members of conflict gangs, for drugs are so expensive that the addict usually turns to crime as a source of funds.[1] Ad-

---

[1] Police officials informally estimate that at least 50 percent of the property crimes committed by juveniles in New York City are related to drug use.

diction also has more negative consequences for family life and for educational and occupational stability than conflict behavior. Furthermore, drug use probably causes no fewer deaths among addicts than does conflict behavior among participants. In these and other ways, then, the current focus upon conflict behavior is open to question.

These definitions greatly influence the form and allocation of resources in the fight against delinquency. It is generally easier to obtain funds and to recruit personnel when the target is a conflict group rather than a drug-using group. Furthermore, social agencies are to some extent controlled by these definitions and thus are forced to allocate more of their resources to fight the conflict type than the retreatist type of delinquency. In many communities, for example, the settlement house is severely criticized if it fails to stem violence among the young but is not nearly so likely to be blamed if rates of addiction mount.

A second problem inherent in identifying targets for action has to do with what it is we want the deviant to become. Some definition of conformity is embedded in every program of action, but too often we have neglected to specify and justify our definitions. The term "conformity" does not refer to a single mode of behavior. In a society as complex as ours, conformity embraces a spectrum of behavior ranging from the prescribed to the tolerated. Just as we must discriminate among types of deviance, so we must discriminate among types of conformity. Our failure to do so has sometimes led us to espouse unduly restricted goals for the nonconformists we are seeking to change. In our work with lower-class delinquents, for example, many of us have acted as if the only acceptable outcome were the adoption of middle-class values and models, despite the fact that conforming with such models often precipitates intense conflict with persons in the delinquent's immediate social milieu.

Social research has a vital role to play in the process by which we make choices among alternative forms of deviance and alternative forms of conformity. We have yet to identify systematically the functions and dysfunctions of various modes of deviant behavior; hence we cannot rank types of aberrant behavior in terms of their relative costs and contributions to the social order. Similarly, we have yet to identify systematically the types of conformity which prevail in different sectors of the social structure (e.g., in different social-class groupings, ethnic groups, and the like); hence we are unable to make intelligent judgments about the appropriate goals toward which we might orient deviants who come from different segments of the social order. Here, then, are two areas in which research can help us to construct a more rational program of action.

Regulating Access to
Legitimate Adaptations

What we do about a particular type of deviance depends, in part, on our assumptions about the forces that give rise to it. The theory of culture conflict, for example, states that delinquent groups arise either as a way of managing conflicting identifications resulting from the simultaneous internalization of two divergent cultural codes (14) or as a consequence of internalizing a cultural code which so deviates from the prevailing middle-class values that conformity with it creates tension and conflict (6, 8, 10). If we accept this theory in either form, then the school, depending on its approach, can either heighten the conflict or help young people develop skills in managing it. According to another theory delinquent subcultures are a response to barriers in the transition from adolescence to adulthood (1). Our society, according to this theory, encourages the young to want to achieve adult status but places obstacles in the way of their achieving this goal. The gang arises to perform the functions served by *rites de passage* in more ordered societies. This theory also has implications for the school; it suggests, for one thing, that the school may have to be reorganized in order to afford young people better channels of integration with adult roles. Still another theory suggests that delinquent gangs in our society arise in response to barriers to masculine identification among boys. These barriers are said to be particularly strong in female-centered households, such as those prevailing among lower-class Negroes. The delinquent group, which is said to arise by a process of reaction formation, represents a "protest" against the femininity of these households; it serves as a structure within which masculine modes of adaptation can be tested and adopted (9). This theory also has implications for education, for there is a tendency in many sectors of our society to regard the school and those who are successful in school as "unmasculine." Thus we might want to be concerned with the sex distribution in school faculties and the relative masculinity of the curriculum.

My own view of the origins of pressure toward delinquent subcultures stems principally from what I call, together with Lloyd E. Ohlin, the theory of differential opportunity systems (4). This theory states that deviance is a result of the systems of forces governing the accessibility of culturally approved goals by legitimate means (7) and by illegitimate means (2). Limitations on the accessibility of cultural goals by legitimate means are, in this theory, the principal source of pressures toward deviance; the relative accessibility of cultural goals by *illegitimate* means is the principal determinant of the *content* of the resulting deviant adaptation. In this section, I shall briefly discuss the availability of legitimate opportunity in our society and the pressures which it exerts toward deviance. In the next section, I shall consider illegitimate opportunity systems and their impact upon types of delinquent subculture. In both instances, implications for prevention will be noted.

Discrepancies between definitions of success-goals and access to opportunities for achieving these goals create great pressure for the emergence of delinquent subcultures. In Western democratic societies, people are universally enjoined to orient themselves toward making marked improvements in their social and economic position. The ideology of equality of opportunity buttresses these high aspirations and gives hope to the dispossessed that a better way of life can be achieved. Difficulties arise in the pursuit of this goal, however, because of the differential distribution of opportunities and resources for achievement. In other words, for many people there is no connection between the ends to which they orient themselves and the means at hand for achieving those ends. This disjunction is greater at some points in the social structure than at others. It appears, for example, that lower-class youngsters are at a disadvantage in the competitive struggle to improve their social and economic position by legitimate means. Access to higher educational facilities—one of the most widely sanctioned routes for upward mobility—is partly dependent upon economic resources. Even in the primary and secondary grades, it costs several hundred dollars a year to send a child to school, for he must have adequate clothes, transportation, lunches, and pocket money for extracurricular activities. Those in the lower strata of society therefore experience acute frustration, which may lead to delinquency among adolescents and other forms of deviance among adults.

I am not saying here that delinquent subcultures are a product of poverty. Quite the contrary: responses to poverty vary considerably, according to the way in which people define this state. In American society, poverty is defined as a temporary condition from which the individual can reasonably expect to rise. Channels of mobility are said to be available to every aspirant, regardless of his social origins. But when people find that such factors as socioeconomic background and racial affiliation *do* materially influence the possibility of becoming mobile, discontent and frustration result. It is not poverty as such that produces these frustrations but objective discrepancies between culturally induced aspirations and socially structured possibilities of achievement.

Coupled with objective differentials is the accessibility of success-goals. There are cultural patterns which hinder lower-class young people from making effective use of the opportunities they do have. It appears, for example, that academic skills are more closely integrated with middle-class than with lower-class socialization; the middle-class child is encouraged to develop verbal fluency, a capacity for deferred gratification, a sustained attention span, and other attributes which facilitate academic achievement. The result is that many lower-class young people eventually compare themselves invidiously with middle-class youngsters, who are more likely to succeed in school. Lower-class adolescents may subsequently become estranged from the school and join the ranks of the dropouts (11).

Members of the lower class are doubtless aware of the general importance assigned to education in our society and of the relationship between education and social mobility. But they are doubtless also very much aware of economic barriers in access to educational facilities. It is my view that social-class differences in the value placed on education in large part reflect objective differentials in the availability of educational opportunities. Educational attainment and related forms of goal-striving are eschewed not so much because they are inherently devalued as because access to them is relatively restricted. And once these adaptive patterns arise in a particular community, young people may be exposed to them directly and thus exhibit little interest in education from an early age.

Although I have been focusing upon *class* differentials in pressures toward deviant behavior, it should also be noted that these pressures affect males more than females and adolescents more than younger or older people. It is primarily the male who must go into the marketplace to seek employment, make a career for himself, and support a family. Adolescence is a time when preparation for these roles is greatest. The adolescent male in the lower class is therefore particularly vulnerable to pressures toward deviance arising from discrepancies between aspirations and opportunities for achievement. These pressures are especially acute among adolescents in slum communities, which are populated largely by adults who have themselves failed to become mobile. Delinquent subcultures represent specialized forms of adaptation to this problem of adjustment. The criminal and conflict subcultures provide illegal avenues to success-goals that are unavailable by legitimate means. The retreatist subculture is a loosely structured group of persons who have withdrawn from the competitive game, who anticipate defeat and seek escape from the burden of failure.

Some of the implications stemming from this theory seem clear. First, efforts must be made to expand the structure of legitimate opportunity for those segments of the population which now suffer from restrictions. Education in particular must be made more accessible regardless of race or socioeconomic status. We must also be concerned with the restrictions on access to skilled vocations. Perhaps we should re-examine our laws governing work among minors in order to permit lower-class adolescents to earn the money they need for future training. Methods of overcoming traditional adaptive responses to limited opportunity, such as apathy and hedonism, must also be found and put into effect. An approach involving both the provision of greater opportunity and the modification of adaptive, defeatist attitudes should have an important impact upon the problem of delinquent subcultures.

This theory implies, further, that we must be concerned with the social regulation of aspirations. The task is not, however, to persuade lower-class young people to lower their levels of aspiration but to induce them to join in efforts to expand legitimate opportunities for people in their social category as a whole. Excessive individualism has always been the greatest deterrent to the development among dispossessed groups of organized efforts to improve their lot in life, and the case of our lower classes certainly constitutes no exception. The task is one of demonstrating, as in the case of labor movements, that the likelihood of one's social advancement is partly dependent upon the elevation of the whole social category to which the individual belongs. But now I am intruding upon a subject which should more properly be discussed in connection with the special problem of social alienation and delinquent subcultures, one of the subjects to which I shall now turn.

Regulating Access to
Illegitimate Adaptations

Pressures toward deviance can probably be reduced; however, it is doubtful that they can or should be completely eliminated. Stress between various parts of the society (i.e., between adolescent and adult, between different socioeconomic groups, etc.) is inherent in every society and often performs useful functions. Thus, the task of prevention is not simply to enlarge opportunities for legitimate adaptations but, as I shall now try to show, to restrict access to certain illegitimate adaptations as well. Most attempts to explain delinquency stop once the sources of pressure have been identified, and most programs of prevention are limited to trying to modify these forces. But the forces that lead people to violate social norms do not necessarily determine the *content* of the violations. A given problem of adjustment can have a variety of deviant outcomes. Thus one cannot predict the outcome of pressures toward deviance simply by identifying these pressures. New variables intervene to channel pressures toward deviance into one or another form of deviant behavior.

To illustrate this point, consider two people who occupy the same position in the social structure except that one is male and the other female. Despite the similarity in their positions, we would not ordinarily expect them to respond in the same way to equivalent problems of adjustment. Types of deviant behavior, like types of conforming behavior, are differentiated along a dimension of masculinity-femininity. Some forms of deviance, such as armed robbery, are characteristically masculine; others, such as prostitution, are characteristically feminine. We would consider it "inappropriate" for a female to become an armed robber or for a male to become a prostitute. When people become deviant, in other words, the selection of deviant adaptations is partly controlled by cultural values. This, then, is one sense in which the social structure regulates the outcome of pressures toward deviance.[2]

The crucial regulatory function of the social structure has been overlooked not only in the development of etiological theories but in the construction of programs of action as well. Yet it represents an area of research which, in my opinion, is of paramount importance. To explain any form of deviance, we must know not only why pressures toward deviance arise but also why these pressures result in different outcomes throughout the social structure. And to prevent any form of deviance, we must not only reduce pressures toward deviance but also modify the social forces that channel these pressures into a given type of deviance.

Alienation and Deviant Behavior. One of the crucial ways in which the social structure regulates the outcome of pressures toward deviance is by influencing the actor's definition of his problems of adjustment. This is an important determinant of his response to these problems (4). Some

[2] For a further example of this regulatory influence see Cloward's discussion of inmate adaptations (3).

persons who experience disjunction between their aspirations and the possibilities of achievement look outward, attributing their dilemma to unjust
and arbitrary institutional practices, such as racial discrimination. Others
look inward, attributing their difficulties to personal deficiencies, such as a
lack of discipline, zeal, intelligence, or persistence. Whether the "failure"
blames the social order or himself is of central importance to the understanding of delinquent conduct (if not of all forms of deviance), for the
one form of attribution leads to alienation from the social order and the
other to self-depreciation. Once he is alienated from conventional rules and
ideologies, the deviant is free to experiment with illegitimate ways of securing access to success-goals—for example, searching for status through
conflict behavior or for money through participation in groups organized
for thievery.

In our society, success and failure are explained in essentially individualistic
terms. Success is formally attributed to ambition, perseverance, talent, and
the like; failure, on the other hand, is said to result from a lack of these
traits. In explaining occupational achievement or failure, we do not ordinarily refer to "life chances" or "objective opportunities"; we tend, rather,
to ask whether people have made the most of their chances, whether they
have been diligent, industrious, and imaginative in the pursuit of success-
goals. This tendency to equate success with individual merit and failure
with individual inferiority contributes to the stability of existing social
arrangements by deflecting criticism from the institutional order. Those who
attribute failure to their own shortcomings in effect accept the prevailing
ideology of the society. They explain their adjustment problems on the
basis of socially accepted criteria. Such persons are not at odds with society;
on the contrary, self-blame is an important index of attitudinal conformity,
for it is essentially an affirmation of the fairness and moral validity of the
prevailing ideology. Individuals who explain failure in this way then have
the problem of coping with the psychological consequences of regarding
themselves as unworthy or inferior. It is unlikely, however, that they will
join with others to develop collective solutions, for they see their adjustment problems as essentially personal.

Those who feel that they are victims of arbitrary institutional arrangements, however, are at odds with the social order. This alienation generates
a great deal of tension in their dealings with the carriers of the dominant
ideology, such as teachers, policemen, and judges. To some extent, tension
can be relieved if alienated persons gain support from others who are in the
same position and who share the view that their misfortunes are due to
unjust social arrangements. Collective support can provide reassurance, security, and validation for a frame of reference toward which the world at
large is hostile and disapproving.

If alienation is an important factor in the development of delinquent
subcultures, then the implication for prevention is clear. Approaches to
lower-class youth generally and to participants in delinquent subcultures
particularly must entail a frank recognition of the objective barriers to op-

portunity which they face. Too often we act as if our object is to lead dissident adolescents to account for their circumstances by questioning their own adequacy rather than by questioning the adequacy of institutional arrangements. Indeed, this seems to be the implicit goal in many current clinical approaches to delinquent subcultures.[3] The tendency is to explore the motivations underlying the individual's membership in a deviant group, and to assess the ways in which he has learned to satisfy his needs through such deviant activity. The result, whether intended or not, is often to define the delinquent subculture as the product of individual maladjustment, without acknowledging the influence of the social order. The projected remedies are thus of a psychological nature, and the ideological and structural bases of the social order are left unchallenged.

I believe, however, that our approach to the management of delinquent subcultures would be much more successful if we did not so often focus upon personality issues to the exclusion of issues of social justice. Many participants in delinquent subcultures are bright and alert; they may be underachievers, poor readers, or school failures, but they are not lacking in basic intelligence. In Negro neighborhoods in large urban centers adolescents are aware not only that many legitimate economic channels are restricted or closed to them but that even the various stable illegitimate economic channels (e.g., the "rackets") are controlled exclusively by other racial and socioeconomic groups. This situation would pose somewhat less of a problem in a society which sought to make a virtue of poverty or which otherwise controlled the aspirations of its participants. But in a society which systematically inculcates discontent with one's social position and which emphasizes the doctrine of equality of opportunity, barriers to opportunity based on race, nationality, or socioeconomic status create a pervading sense of defeat and despair among the dispossessed.

I contend, in short, that we must give much greater attention to problems of social structure and social justice than has generally been the case in previous approaches to prevention. Dispossessed young people are entitled to have their views of the world given a fair appraisal by professionals. We should acknowledge to them that there *are* marked inequalities in access to opportunity in our society and that one's life chances are materially affected by the vicissitudes of birth. Unless we can convince them that we understand what it is to live in despair, without goals and without hope, large numbers of these young people will be disaffected from the outset.

Further, it seems to me that we must offer these young people an ideology of hope based on the assumption that people can do something about their social conditions. The major institutions with which the urban lower-

---

[3] A considerable amount of clinical opinion holds that many of the participants in delinquent subcultures, unlike most "lone" delinquents, are not distinguished by personality disorganization or pathology. Perhaps for this reason, the problem of delinquent subcultures has not generally attracted the attention of clinicians, although they have had much to do with individualistic delinquents. This may also account for what I believe to be a fact; namely, that there is no systematic psychological theory of the origins, evolution, and maintenance of delinquent subcultures.

class adolescent comes in contact—the school, the church, the settlement house—have been greatly at fault in failing to make available programs in which adolescents can come to grips with the issues that affect their lives and can develop skill in collectively acting upon these issues. The school and settlement house and church tend, for the most part, to insulate lower-class young people from any channels through which they might express legitimate grievances against the social order. The problem of dealing with delinquent subculture is not simply to reduce pressures toward deviance or to dissuade individual delinquents, by therapeutic and other means, to relinquish deviant ways of behaving. If they are to be asked to give up forms of adjustment that they find satisfying, they must be given functional alternatives. If they harbor a deep, inarticulate sense of resentment against existing institutional arrangements, they must be shown not that their alienation is without basis but that there are nondeviant, though perhaps controversial, ways of expressing such sentiments. This may mean that those of us working in schools, churches, settlement houses, and other institutional spheres of lower-class life will have to reorganize our programs in order to create realistic opportunities for collective efforts against racial discrimination, slum housing, and the like. The task is not to subtly persuade these young people that their grievances are imaginary or to help them adjust to unfortunate social realities but to provide legitimate ideologies and channels for the collective expression of alienation and discontent and to teach them how to use these channels. This may be one of the most crucial ways in which the social milieu can be altered to prevent delinquent subcultures. To put such an approach into practice, however, it will be necessary to make some basic changes in the organization of services and in our concept of power and its uses.

Limiting Access to Deviant Adaptations. Attempts to regulate the outcome of pressures toward deviance by providing the young with functional alternatives, such as opportunities for collective social action, should be coupled with efforts to reorganize the social milieu to remove the social supports and resources for various forms of deviance. As I have observed, public concern today focuses largely upon conflict subcultural behavior as distinct from other types of delinquency. For this reason, I shall use this form of behavior to illustrate the proposition that access to deviant adaptations is controlled by the social milieu.

To understand the emergence of conflict subcultures as opposed to other types of delinquent subculture, let us compare the social conditions under which the fighting gang develops with those that give rise to criminally oriented subcultures. Criminal and conflict subcultures do not arise in the same types of urban neighborhood. Where the criminal adaptation prevails, one finds strong counter-pressures against conflict behavior, and where the conflict adaptation prevails, one finds that the social milieu is unfavorable to stable criminal forms of adaptation.

Slum communities, a number of observers have noted, are not necessarily disorganized simply because they are slums (13). Sometimes they exhibit forms of social organization which, although different in many respects from middle-class forms of organization, are extremely stable and give unity, direction, and cohesion to community life. Slum communities, like other communities, can therefore be placed on a continuum ranging from a high degree of organization to little or none (5). Such differences are of great significance, for different types of delinquent subculture tend to be associated with variations in slum organization.

It should be noted that the successful performance of deviant social roles, like that of conforming social roles, requires more than the volition of the actor. One cannot simply decide to make a career of crime and then do so, any more than one can merely *will* a successful career in law; in both instances, certain social supports must be present. For the development of a criminal, two types of social support are essential. One is integration between the carriers of conventional and criminal values: patterns of accommodation and cooperation among police, politicians, racketeers, professional criminals, businessmen, and other local residents. The second is integration among offenders of different age-levels: close relationships among criminal apprentices, semisophisticated young adult criminals, and mature members of the underworld (4).

These two features of social organization exert a crucial influence upon the evolution of delinquent subcultures. Unless the society seeks the services performed by the occupants of a social role, the role will not be likely to persist. Criminals, especially those engaged in organized crime, provide many services which are more or less in demand—gambling, sexual outlets, narcotics, strong-arm squads, and the like. If these services are to be provided in an orderly, continuous way, the activities of criminals must be protected from scrutiny by elements in the society who would like to suppress them. Thus coalitions of groups who have an interest in the preservation of these services grow up to defend them. In communities where these coalitions exist, we have the integration of carriers of criminal and of conventional values. Such integration is a functional ·prerequisite for the existence of stable, organized criminal enterprises. Communities which exhibit this form of integration can provide illegitimate career opportunities for young people who feel that legitimate channels to success-goals are restricted or closed to them. Because integration of the carriers of both the criminal and the conventional values produces a stable criminal opportunity structure, the young in such communities may orient themselves toward careers in crime as alternatives to the inaccessible legitimate careers which might otherwise have commanded their allegiance.

The opportunity to engage in a criminal career does not account for the actual emergence of such a career. Persons who orient themselves toward criminal careers must be inducted into criminal groups; they must be exposed to situations in which the prerequisite criminal values and skills can be acquired. This learning function is performed by the integration of different age-levels of offender. In slum communities which exhibit such integration, a young man finds older offenders after whom to pattern himself and from whom to learn the ways of crime. Each age-level is connected to a higher level so that young offenders are, through intervening age-grades, ultimately linked to the adult criminal system. Knowledge, values, skills, and attitudes are transmitted through this age hierarchy. For those who excel in learning, upward passage is assured, and a position in a stable adult criminal enterprise may be the eventual reward (12). These are communities, then, which provide both criminal learning and criminal opportunity; they are characterized by the criminal type of delinquent subculture, a subculture composed of adolescents gradually coming to occupy positions of apprenticeship in organized or professional crime.

Purposeless, undisciplined, aggressive behavior is not sanctioned in communities which exhibit these particular forms of integration. This is not to say that violence has no place in their scheme of life; there are occasions when violent behavior is appropriate, but street combat between gangs in search of status is generally discouraged. What intergang conflict occurs in these areas is generally defensive, as when local gangs defend their territory against "invasion" by foreign, marauding gangs. The young are made aware by their elders that street warfare not only has little point but tends to bring unfavorable public scrutiny to the neighborhood and thus endangers the various illegitimate community enterprises. Thus the social groups of the community, *illegitimate as well as legitimate*, constantly exert pressure to restrain aggressive behavior among the adolescents. In effect, illegitimate norms support and buttress the conventional prohibitions.

These norms against violence are known to dissident adolescents and are enforced by powerful community sanctions, controlled by various adults in the distribution of illegitimate rewards. In criminal opportunity systems, as in opportunity systems in general, there is a surplus of contenders for positions; not all who orient themselves toward a place in these structures can succeed. A process of selection takes place at every age level. Control of this selection process gives adults in the community enormous influence over the behavior of adolescents, for the adults are in a position either to make great rewards available or to withhold them. Thus the behavior of the young is encompassed within a system of social controls that originates in both legitimate and illegitimate sectors of the community. This point has been developed by Kobrin (5). This type of slum community, in short, is not a favorable environment for the emergence of the fighting gang.

The conflict subculture is principally a product of unstable communities. High rates of vertical and geographic mobility, massive housing projects, and changing patterns of land use (as in the case of residential areas that are encroached upon by adjacent commercial or industrial areas) are among the factors that keep a community off balance and check tentative efforts to develop social organization of any kind. Transiency and instability thus become the overriding features of social life.

Disorganized communities tend to produce a conflict form of delinquency for several reasons. They cannot provide alternative channels to success-goals, legitimate or criminal. Although there may be a good deal of criminal activity in these areas, it is sporadic, unorganized, and poorly protected. Because stable criminal opportunity structures do not exist, stable criminal careers cannot develop. To the extent that the adolescents also experience discrepancies between aspirations and legitimate avenues of social ascent, the absence of illegitimate channels heightens their frustration in these communities.

Furthermore, disorganized neighborhoods have virtually no means of controlling the expression of impulses to deviate. Not only the conventional institutions but also the illegitimate activities of the communities are disorganized. Hence social controls do not originate in either legitimate or illegitimate segments of community life. The combination of heightened frustration and simultaneously weakened social controls appears to give rise to the conflict form of subcultural behavior. Lacking institutionalized channels of social ascent, legitimate or illegitimate, and without effective patterns of social control, dissident adolescent groups seize upon violence as an avenue to status which is available and which *can* be utilized by them. Thus there grows up a network of gangs which compete for status on the basis of skills in street combat and other forms of violence.

This analysis has a number of implications for the prevention of conflict subcultures. Above all, the degree of community solidarity must be heightened in order to reduce conflict behavior. In this sense, the target in a program of prevention should be not the individual delinquent or even the conflict subculture but, rather, the community. If relationship patterns among adults can be strengthened, access to conflict behavior can be gradually restricted. The problem of prevention is therefore partly a problem of social control and partly a problem of reorganizing the social milieu so as to reduce the availability of a particular form of deviant behavior.

I am aware that it is not fashionable in professional circles today to speak of social control as a component of prevention. An emphasis on social control is generally regarded as punitive, primitive, and unresponsive to the needs of young people. I would agree if social control is the exclusive emphasis; the delinquency field has provided some dramatic illustrations of the futility of programs based solely on control. For example, it has been observed in a number of communities in New York City that when access to violence as a means of securing status is abruptly closed to delinquents, drug use increases sharply. Many areas in which organized, systematic harassment and suppression by the police and other agencies have forced conflict groups to relinquish violence have subsequently exhibited a disconcerting rise in drug use and other forms of passive, retreatist delinquency. The point is that by restricting access to one form of deviance *without providing functional but conforming alternatives*, we run the risk of simply converting one form of deviance into another. But where conforming alternatives are provided, where the social milieu is reordered so that the means and resources for conforming adaptations are made more accessible, various measures of social control will also be useful.

It should be noted that social control is probably more effective when it is an internal feature of a community than when it is externally imposed, and when access to the conflict subcultural adaptation is restricted by building indigenous institutional forms in a slum community, by increasing the observability of community prohibitions against violence and by enhancing the capacity of a community to impose sanctions. In the long run, young people will be far more responsive to an adult community which exhibits the capacity to organize itself, to manage its problems, and to mobilize indigenous resources than to a community which must have these functions performed by external agents.

The task of generating institutions in disorganized communities poses a variety of problems. Among other things, we need new concepts of the institutional forms most appropriate in an age of rapid social change. Some of the older forms—such as the nationality or ethnic organizations characteristic of the traditional but disappearing immigrant ghettos—may not be suitable in contemporary lower-class urban communities. Once we have decided upon appropriate models, we face a host of questions concerning the way in which to involve the residents of a community in the process of reconstruction. We need to know much more about concepts of leadership in the lower class and in different ethnic groups, about patterns of interpersonal relationships which are compatible to various groups, about the organization and use of power. We may, for example, have to become much more concerned about the role of indigenous groups in large urban communities with respect to the formulation of school policies and practices.[4] We cannot speak of reconstructing community organization without involving the school in this process. These, then, are some of the issues and problems that face us in the prevention of delinquent subcultures.

.   .   .

REFERENCES

1. BLOCH, HERBERT, and NIEDERHOFFER, ARTHUR. *The Gang: A Study in Adolescent Behavior.* New York: Philosophical Library, 1958.
2. CLOWARD, RICHARD A. "Illegitimate Means, Anomie and Deviant Behavior," *American Sociological Review*, Vol. 24, No. 2, 1959.
3. ———. "Social Control in the Prison," *Theoretical Studies of the Social Organization of the Prison*, Bulletin No. 15, New York: Social Science Research Council, 1960.
4. ——— and OHLIN, LLOYD E. *Delinquency and Opportunity: A Theory of Delinquent Gangs.* Glencoe, Ill.: Free Press, 1960.
5. KOBRIN, SOLOMON. "The Conflict of Values in Delinquency Areas," *American Sociological Review*, Vol. 16, 1951.
6. KVARACEUS, W. C., and MILLER, W. B. *Delinquent Behavior: Culture and the Individual.* Washington, D. C.: National Education Association, 1959.

[4] The control of school systems in many urban areas has become so bureaucratized and centralized that local residents no longer feel that they can have any important role to play in school affairs. This is especially true in low-income areas where school officials often have virtually no contact with adult residents.

7. MERTON, ROBERT K. *Social Theory and Social Structure*, (Rev. and Enl. Ed.) Glencoe, Ill.: Free Press, 1957.
8. MILLER, WALTER B. "Lower Class Culture as a Generating Milieu of Gang Delinquency," *Journal of Social Issues*, Vol. 14, No. 3, 1958.
9. PARSONS, TALCOTT. *Essays in Sociological Theory*, (Rev. Ed.) Glencoe, Ill.: Free Press, 1954.
10. SELLIN, THORSTEN. *Culture Conflict and Crime*, New York: Social Science Research Council, 1938.
11. SKLARE, MARSHALL (ed.); Toby, Jackson. "Hoodlum or Businessman: An American Dilemma," *The Jews: Social Patterns of an American Group*, Glencoe, Ill.: Free Press, 1958.
12. SUTHERLAND, EDWIN H. *The Professional Thief*. Chicago: University of Chicago Press, 1937.
13. WHYTE, WILLIAM. *Street Corner Society: The Social Structure of an Italian Slum.* Chicago: University of Chicago Press, 1955.
14. WIRTH, LOUIS. "Culture Conflict and Misconduct," *Social Forces*, 9:484–92, June 1931.

29   Community Integration and
the Social Control of
Juvenile Delinquency

ELEANOR E. MACCOBY, JOSEPH P. JOHNSON,
RUSSELL M. CHURCH

The important role that community integration and social control are assumed to play in the prevention of delinquency is highlighted by Shaw, in his discussion of the differences in delinquency rates in various parts of Chicago. In the famous Chicago studies, done more than 25 years ago, it was found that delinquency was highest in the center of the city, areas marked by physical deterioration and declining population. Shaw offered the following hypothesis:

Reprinted from *The Journal of Social Issues*, 14 (No. 3, 1958), 38–51, with permission of the Society for the Psychological Study of Social Issues.

This article reports some of the findings from a study done as a class project in a seminar on field research methods in the Department of Social Relations, Harvard University, during the fall of 1954. Members of the seminar, who participated in the design of the study and the field work were: Abraham Black, Louis Cervantes (S.J.), Elizabeth Cohen, Eugene Gallagher, J. B. Hefferlin, Dean Peabody, Bernard Portis, Molly Potter, Paul J. Reiss, R. Cuyugan Santos, Paul Sawyer, Nancy Waxler, and Henry Wechsler. The authors would like to express their gratitude to Peter F. Rossi, who encouraged members of his class in urban sociology to participate as interviewers, and who made available the delinquency rate statistics which were used in the choice of areas. We also wish to thank Leroy Gould and Barbara Ullman, who helped to classify the incidents reported in tables 6 and 7.

Under the pressure of the disintegrative forces which act when business and industry invade a community, the community thus invaded ceases to function effectively as a means of social control. Traditional norms and standards of the conventional community weaken and disappear. Resistance on the part of the community to delinquent and criminal behavior is low, and such behavior is tolerated and may even become accepted and approved.

Moreover, many of the people who come into the deteriorating section are European immigrants or southern Negroes. All of them come from cultural and social backgrounds which differ widely from the situations in the city. In the conflict of the old with the new the former cultural and social controls in these groups tend to break down. This, together with the fact that there are few constructive community forces at work to re-establish a conventional order, makes for continued social disorganization.[1]

If community disintegration is indeed a factor producing juvenile delinquency, how precisely are the effects produced? In an attempt to devise an empirical study of the effects of community integration, we reasoned that something like the following process might occur: a child who, for a variety of reasons, has an interest in deviating, tries out one or two deviant acts in a tentative way, to see what the reaction of the community will be. If he lives in a disorganized community (where the rate of moving in and out will be high and where neighbors are not closely bound by social, religious, or kinship ties) there will be relatively little chance that he will be seen by someone who knows him or knows his parents, so long as the act is committed outside the walls of his own dwelling. The people who do see him may be deviants themselves, and may not consider the behavior especially reprehensible. But even if they do disapprove, they may nevertheless choose not to interfere, being reluctant to mention the incident directly to the child or his parents since they do not know them, and being afraid to attract the attention of the police to themselves by reporting the act to the authorities.

Our basic hypothesis is then, that in disorganized neighborhoods individual adults will feel less responsibility for guiding other people's children into the paths of "good" behavior, and will ignore deviant acts when they see them being committed, unless they themselves are directly involved. Under these circumstances, the children who are making their first tentative explorations into delinquency will find that they have a good chance of escaping any painful consequences of their antisocial activities, and will be emboldened by this knowledge, with the result that delinquency will increase in the disorganized neighborhoods.

To test whether this hypothetical picture represents what actually occurs, we compared two areas of Cambridge, Mass. The areas were chosen to be as similar as possible with respect to socio-economic status of residents, but still highly different in delinquency rates. We set out to test the following specific hypotheses:

---

[1] Clifford R. Shaw and collaborators, *Delinquency Areas*, University of Chicago Press, 1929, pp. 204–5.

1. The high delinquency area will be less "integrated" than the low, in the sense that people living in the "high" area will be less homogeneous with respect to ethnic and religious background, will be more transient, will be less well acquainted with their neighbors, and have fewer perceived common interests with them.

2. In the high delinquency area, values about pre-delinquent acts will be more "permissive" than in the low delinquency area. That is, there will be a tendency for residents to believe that youthful acts such as fighting, drunkenness, minor shoplifting, and minor vandalism are not especially reprehensible, are "natural" and sometimes to be condoned. Attitudes toward such behavior in the low delinquency area, on the other hand, should be relatively severe.

3. In the high delinquency area, private citizens will be less likely to take remedial action when they see other people's children engaging in some kind of delinquent or pre-delinquent activity.

We interviewed a sample of adults in each of our two neighborhoods, and our questions covered (a) the respondent's attitudes toward several categories of juvenile misbehavior, (b) the degree of the respondent's integration in his community, and (c) reports of incidents of juvenile delinquent or pre-delinquent behavior in the neighborhood. We asked each respondent to tell us exactly what action (if any) had been taken by people who observed or knew about the incident.

Before we report our findings, let us describe our criteria for choosing the two neighborhoods, and our methods of obtaining the information we required.

The Two Neighborhoods

It is well known, of course, that delinquency rates are higher in neighborhoods where the residents have low socio-economic status. We were not interested in studying this factor, however, we wanted to hold it constant. We therefore selected two census tracts from the city of Cambridge, one with a high delinquency rate and one with a low rate, with socio-economic factors constant as nearly as possible. We were not able to achieve as close a match on all factors as would have been desirable. Table 1 shows how the two areas compared with respect to delinquency and with respect to socio-economic factors. It will be seen that the areas were well matched on education, fairly well matched on occupation, with a difference of over five hundred dollars in median income. The differences in delinquency rates were quite dramatic.[2]

We were unable to find areas which were closer than these two in socio-economic level and which still differed significantly in delinquency rates. It is impossible to tell, of course, whether the differences which exist between the two areas in socio-economic status are sufficient to produce the differences in delinquency rate. All that we can say is that considering the

[2] It will be noted that in the high delinquency area a higher proportion of the cases which are reported to the police are brought into juvenile court. This may mean either that the offenses committed by juveniles in this area are more serious, or that families in the low delinquency area are able somehow to keep their children's cases out of court after they have come to the attention of the police.

whole socio-economic range in Cambridge, these neighborhoods are fairly similar on such items as rent, occupation, education, and even income, while they differ by a considerably greater part of the range in delinquency rates.

The Survey Method

Having selected our two areas, we chose dwelling units from these areas by probability sampling methods (area sampling) and within households, selected for interview 50 per cent of the adults in the selected households.[3] We defined as adults all individuals who were married plus all unmarried people of 21 or over. Since our interview concerned a "sensitive" topic, and

Table 1

The Two Sample Areas Compared

	High Delinquency Area	Low Delinquency Area
Juvenile Delinquency		
Average annual rate per 1000 children in 7–16 age group from 1948 through 1950, based on number of cases brought before the juvenile court.	15.2	4.9
Cases handled by Crime Prevention Bureau		
Average annual incidence per 1000 in the 7–16 age group from 1950 through 1952, based on number of cases reported to the Cambridge police dept.	34.0	22.1
Truancy		
Rate per 1000 in 7–16 age group for five-month period Sept. 1952–Jan. 1953, public and parochial elementary and high schools, as reported by the City Attendance Supervisors.	34.1	4.1
Education		
Per cent adults without high school diplomas 1950 census, computed for those over 25 years of age.	76.1	71.2
Occupation		
Per cent employed males in occupation group, 1950 census:		
Professional, managerial, clerical, and sales	26.5%	27.3%
Craftsmen, foremen	17.9	25.8
Operatives, service workers, laborers.	55.6	46.9
Median Income (1950 Census)	$2630	$3176
Mean Rent (1950 Census)	$25.72	$30.48
Population (1950 Census)	3976	3818
Percent of population between 7–16 yrs.	14.8	14.2

[3] Residents of each household were listed by the interviewers in pre-determined order. Each household listing sheet was marked to indicate whether it was the first and third, or the second and fourth, occupants listed who were to be interviewed.

respondents were asked to tell us about certain incidents of delinquent behavior in the neighborhood which may not have come to the attention of the police, we took great pains to try to convince the respondents that we had no connection with any official agency. Even so, there were a number of families who clearly did not want to confide in us; we encountered more suspicion in the high delinquency area, where we suspect that some of our potential respondents believed we had come in connection with some delinquent act of their own children. Altogether 11 per cent of the people approached for interview refused to be interviewed. An additional 16 per cent could not be reached, because they could not be found at home after several call-backs, because of illness, etc. We did not include in the sample anyone who had lived at his present address less than six months, because we felt such people would not be in a good position to give us accounts of neighborhood incidents. In the high delinquency area we interviewed 129 people, in the low delinquency area 107. Our sample contained a somewhat higher proportion of women than census figures would lead us to expect in a complete probability sample.

The interview took between 25 minutes and an hour, and consisted of a standard list of open-ended questions plus a list of probes that were to be used whenever the respondent mentioned a specific incident of juvenile delinquency occurring in the neighborhood. At the end of the interview, the interviewer filled out an "incident report sheet" recording the age and sex of the children involved in the incident, the relationship of the witness to the deviating children, and the nature of the control action (if any) taken by the respondent or other individuals in the neighborhood. The kinds of delinquency inquired about in the interview were: major and minor thefts, truancy, vandalism, street fighting, drunkenness, and the use of insulting, abusive language.

Results

Community Integration. Our high delinquency area was clearly less integrated in terms of the criteria of integration we employed. First of all, the low delinquency area was highly homogeneous with respect to religion: 93 per cent were Catholic, as contrasted with 53 per cent in the high delinquency area. Furthermore, those who were Catholics were more frequent church-goers in the low delinquency areas than in the high. Thirty-five per cent of the Catholics in the high delinquency area said they attended church less than once a week, while in area "low" only 15 per cent report this. Area "low" was also more homogeneous ethnically: Here our sample shows a fairly high concentration (32 per cent) of people of Canadian origin, quite a few of these being French Canadian, with virtually no Negroes, or people of Eastern European origin. In contrast, our sample from the high delinquency area had 18 per cent Negroes, and 16 per cent East Europeans, with only 9 per cent Canadians.

We expected that the high delinquency area would contain more people who were "transient"—who had lived in the community only a short time.

We found a slight tendency for this to be true, but both areas were highly stable. Sixty per cent of the respondents in the high delinquency area and 71 per cent in the low area had lived in their present neighborhood for ten years or more.

Despite the fact that most of the people in the high delinquency area had lived in their neighborhoods a substantial length of time, they were less integrated in their communities. As Table 2 shows, they knew fewer of their neighbors by name, did not know many people intimately enough to borrow something, less often felt they had common interests with their neighbors, and more often disliked the neighborhood.

These differences between the areas in attitudes toward the neighborhood and relations with neighbors are still found, even if one considers only the people who have lived in the neighborhood ten years or more. Therefore, the differences in "integration" of individual citizens into their communities cannot be attributed primarily to differences in length of residence. We might point out parenthetically that the lower level of integration in our high delinquency area need not reflect a progressively deteriorating situation. This particular low level of social interaction might remain stable for many years.

Table 2

Area Differences in Measures of Integration

Per cent who:	High Delinquency Area	Low Delinquency Area
Report liking the neighborhood	64%	85%
Know more than ten of their neighbors by name	52%	63%
Know more than five neighbors well enough to borrow something ("Like a hammer or a cup of sugar")	28%	50%
Feel they have "pretty much the same interests and ideas" as the other people in the neighborhood	33%	59%
Number of cases:	129	107

We do, then, find evidence for the first of our hypotheses. In the high delinquency area, residents do not know each other as well as in the low delinquency area, and do not feel as much a part of the community. Does this mean that they withdraw from playing any role in the informal control of children's deviant actions in their community? Before we examine the answer to this question, let us take up one other factor that might lead the residents of a high delinquency area to avoid controlling delinquent or pre-delinquent actions; perhaps they do not take such actions as seriously as do the residents of a low delinquency area. Do the two areas differ in their values about certain actions that the larger society defines as "delinquent"?

Attitudes Toward Deviant Behavior. Measuring attitudes toward deviant behavior is a difficult matter. One clearly cannot ask "Do you think excessive drinking is a good or bad thing? How about theft? Assault?" In our first formulations of questions in this area, we found we were getting universally righteous answers, in which everybody reported (at least to our primarily middle-class interviewers!) being "against sin." In pretesting question wording, we found that the only way we could differentiate among respondents in this area was to ask, not whether certain actions were "right" or "wrong," but *how serious* actions were. That is, while all respondents might agree that stealing a candy bar from the dime store was "wrong," some expressed the view that it was not a very serious matter—that it was the sort of thing all children might be expected to do at some time or another, and that they would outgrow it if no issue were made of it; others regarded such actions as the first step toward more serious criminal actions, and felt that drastic disciplinary action was called for. We inquired about seven different kinds of pre-delinquent behavior. Two of our questions are presented below to illustrate the way we approached these issues:

> Every neighborhood has a certain amount of fighting between groups of children. Some people think it's very important to stop these fights, other people think the youngsters are just learning to stand up for themselves and should be left alone. How do you feel?
>
> Sometimes we hear of children damaging the property of people who live in the neighborhood—for instance, bending over car aerials or letting the air out of tires or ripping up fences. If children do this sort of thing, do you think it's anything to worry about, or are they just letting off steam?

Table 3 shows the proportion of respondents in each area who thought each of the seven kinds of act was "serious," who qualified their answers, or who thought the actions were "not serious." The striking thing about the table is the similarity of the attitudes in the two areas. In both areas, drinking is considered the most serious juvenile offence, fighting the least. People in the low delinquency area took a slightly more serious view of minor thefts from stores, damage to public property, and drinking than did their high-delinquency-area counterparts; but this trend was counter-balanced by a tendency for the high-delinquency-area respondents to take a more serious view of abusive remarks and fighting.

Our findings, then, are not consistent with the point of view that the adults in a high delinquency area take a tolerant or indifferent attitude toward delinquent and pre-delinquent activities on the part of children. We see no evidence that "delinquent values" about the "wrongness" or "seriousness" of these actions prevail in the high delinquency area. This issue will be discussed further below.

Informal Social Control. We have seen that while the two areas did not differ in their views about how serious various kinds of delinquent behavior are (at least if their verbal reports to our interviewers may be trusted), the high delinquency area was less integrated, and we reasoned that this lack of integration might result in individual residents being unwilling to take

Table 3

Area Differences in Attitude Toward Types of Pre-delinquent Acts *

		Seri-ous	De-pends	Not Seri-ous	No An-swer	
Abusive remarks	High Delinquency Area	57	30	12	01	100%
	Low Delinquency Area	47	33	12	08	100%
Minor thefts	High Delinquency Area	36	50	12	02	100%
from stores	Low Delinquency Area	49	46	05	01	100%
Damage to public	High Delinquency Area	57	26	10	06	100%
property	Low Delinquency Area	64	22	08	07	100%
Damage to private	High Delinquency Area	40	32	22	07	100%
property	Low Delinquency Area	41	36	15	08	100%
Fighting	High Delinquency Area	28	48	23	02	100%
	Low Delinquency Area	22	50	27	02	100%
Drinking	High Delinquency Area	79	17	03	01	100%
	Low Delinquency Area	87	08	01	04	100%
Truancy	High Delinquency Area	42	42	12	04	100%
	Low Delinquency Area	41	42	11	06	100%

* The percentages in this table are based upon 129 cases in the high delinquency area, 107 in the low. In none of the seven instances are the two neighborhoods significantly different in the proportion reporting a "serious" attitude.

action if they observed their neighbors' children engaged in some sort of deviant behavior. We asked our respondents hypothetical questions about whether they *would* step in and try to do something about it if they observed abusive language, property damage, fighting, or drunkenness. Table 4 shows that the respondents in the low delinquency area report themselves somewhat more ready to "do something about it," significantly so in the case of fighting and drinking.

The actual controlling behavior in real incidents reported by the respondents showed some area differences in the same direction, although the differences are not large. To study the kinds of action that had been taken in actual incidents of neighborhood delinquency, we first recorded all the incidents from the "incident report sheets" in which action by the respondents was both "possible and necessary," and in which the respondent's own children were not involved. If someone else had already taken remedial action about the incident, we did not regard it as necessary for the respondent to do so, even if the respondent observed the incident. And if the respondent knew about the incident but had not actually seen it and/or did not know the identity of the culprits, we did not regard it as possible for the respondent to act. On the other hand, if the respondent heard about the incident without actually witnessing it, and *did* know the identity of the delinquent children, we included the incident in our list of incidents in which some controlling action by the respondent would have been pos-

Table 4

Area Differences in Percentages Who "Would Do Something About It" in Hypothetical Instances of Delinquency

Child's Hypothetical Act	High Delinquency Area	Low Delinquency Area
Open rudeness, insulting language	26%	31%
Property damage	32%	42%
Fighting	12%	25%
Drinking	8%	21%
Number of cases	129	107

sible. For example, an incident of vandalism in a parochial school was reported, in which a gang of boys had entered the school by breaking windows, and had thrown ink on the floors and slashed furniture. The police had been unable to learn the identity of the vandals. One of our respondents knew who the boys were, having learned the details through her own sons, who were ostensibly not involved. She could have told either the police or church authorities, but had not done so. This incident would be included in the list of incidents in which action by our respondent was both "necessary and possible."

In all, 206 such incidents were reported by the respondents in our high delinquency area, and 130 were reported by the respondents in our low delinquency area. Of course, some respondents reported no such incidents, while others reported several.

Having listed the incidents in which control by the respondent would have been possible, and in which no one else had already taken remedial action, we wished to determine the number of these incidents in which the respondent actually had taken action. Before doing this, however, we divided the incidents according to whether the respondent had or had not been the *victim* of the delinquent act. Our hypothesis about greater social control in the low delinquency area applies especially to acts of delinquency in which the observer is *not* the victim. That is, in both areas, we might expect that when the respondent himself has been stolen from or had his property damaged, he will be motivated to catch and punish the offenders. But we have hypothesized that in well-integrated neighborhoods, individual citizens will act to stop deviant juvenile behavior even if they themselves are not involved.

Table 5 shows that, as expected, when the respondent is himself the victim of an anti-social act on the part of a juvenile offender, he is very likely indeed to take action, and this is true in both the high and low delinquency areas. The kinds of action taken included calling the police, reproving the child directly, or getting in touch with the child's parents. When the respondent is not the victim, there is a somewhat greater tendency for an observer to take action in the low delinquency area than in the

Table 5

Area Differences in the Number of Incidents in Which
the Respondent Took Controlling Action

	Number of incidents reported	Respondent took action	R. did not take action	% of incidents in which R. acted	Number of respondents reporting at least one incident
Respondent the victim:					
High delinq. area	86	72	14	84%	62
Low delinq. area	78	69	9	88%	47
Respondent not the victim: (but control possible)					
High delinq. area	120	48	72	40%	68
Low delinq. area	52	31	21	60%	41

high. In 60 per cent of the non-victim incidents reported from the "low" area in which the respondent was in a position to take action, he did so; in the high delinquency area, the comparable figure is 40 per cent. It is difficult to evaluate the statistical significance of the differences between these last two figures, since they are based upon the number of *incidents* reported, rather than upon the number of respondents reporting them. The fact is that, out of the 68 respondents in the high delinquency area who reported at least one incident in which they could have taken action but were not the victim, 30 took no action and 38 took action in at least one of the incidents he reported. In the low delinquency area, out of the 41 people reporting at least one non-victim incident, 16 took no action and 25 took action in at least one instance. These proportions are quite similar (and not statistically different). The difference between the two areas appears to lie in the fact that in the high delinquency area, each respondent reports more non-victim incidents, and his tendency toward controlling action is not proportional to the number of incidents he reports. That is, the more incidents a respondent reports, the lower the proportion of them he will have attempted to control. And 44 of the respondents in the high delinquency area had *ignored* at least one non-victim incident in which they could have taken action; only 21 respondents in the low delinquency area did this.

One explanation of this fact is that in the high delinquency area, more of the delinquent acts are committed by *gangs* of children (rather than by individual offenders), and the deviant children are older, on the average. Naturally, when an observer sees a delinquent act being committed by a group of five or six boys in their middle or late "teens," the observer will hesitate to interfere because of the physical danger to himself. Several of our respondents told us of people who had been beaten up when they attempted to stop gangs of boys who were engaged in delinquent activity. But the greater frequency of older offenders in the high delinquency area does not fully account for the lower proportion of controlling actions on the part of residents who are not directly involved. Even when the deviant child is young enough so that it would not be dangerous to try to control him, his deviant action is somewhat less likely to meet with a controlling action in the high-delinquency area (see Table 6).

Table 6

Area Differences in Controlling Action in Relation to the Age of the Deviant Child. (Including Only Incidents in Which the Respondent Was Not the Victim)

	No. of incidents (action necessary and possible)	Action taken by R.	No action taken by R.
Child under 13 yrs. old *			
High delinq. area	51	29	22
Low delinq. area	29	20	9
Child 13 or over			
High delinq. area	62	16	46
Low delinq. area	23	11	12

* When several children were involved in delinquent activity together, the median age of the group was taken as the age for this tabulation. The number of incidents included is less than the number reported in Table 5, since for some incidents the respondent did not report the age of the child or children involved.

In both areas, many of our respondents expressed reluctance to interfere in the control of other people's children. We asked: "We're interested in how you feel about whether it's all right to correct somebody else's child. When somebody else's child gets into mischief, and you see it, do you think it's up to you to say anything, or do you think it's better to stay out of it?" One third of the respondents in each area said that they thought it was all right for them to do something, but the majority expressed strong doubts about the propriety of interference, and many said categorically that a child's misbehavior is his parents' responsibility and others ought not to interfere. One respondent expressed this reaction as follows:

> We generally keep out of other people's business with their kids. They just don't want us to do anything about them. Definitely—even if I knew them —I'd just go on and not pay any attention. People wouldn't like it—they'd say what does he know about my kids! We get along fine with everybody and I wouldn't want it to change by sticking my nose somewhere where it's not wanted.

It is interesting that while we found no area differences in respondents' *own* opinions about whether it was all right to interfere with other people's children, we did find some differences when we asked whether *other people in the neighborhood* felt it was all right. In the high delinquency area, people more often said that their neighbors believed one ought to mind one's own business (22 per cent said this, as contrasted with 9 per cent in the low delinquency area).

There are a number of reasons, then, why an individual might choose not to interfere. One is the desire to maintain harmonious relations with neighbors. Perhaps one reason why respondents in the high delinquency area ignored more of the incidents they saw is that they did not want to get the reputation of being interfering busybodies; so they therefore took action only in the most serious cases or in the cases where they had hope of being effective. Another concern, mentioned primarily by respondents in the high delinquency area, is that of avoiding retaliation from either the deviant child or his parents. We were told of instances in which an individual had tried to go to the parents of a child who had committed a delinquent act, and had been met with abusive language or even physical violence from the parent. Finally, in our high delinquency area, eight respondents said they had decided not to speak to a delinquent child or his parents because they already knew that the family would be unresponsive to pressure—that the parents themselves were alcoholic or criminal or indifferent to the activities of their children.

Summary and Discussion

We compared two areas of Cambridge which were similar in socio-economic status, one having a high rate of juvenile delinquency and the other a low rate. We interviewed a sample of residents in these two communities concerning "community integration," attitudes toward delinquent behavior, and the social control of such behavior. We took 129 interviews in the high delinquency area, 107 in the low, and reached 73 per cent of the people initially designated for interview in a probability sample. Our major findings were:

1. The high delinquency area was less "integrated" than the low. That is, residents of the "high" area, as compared with residents of the low delinquency area, did not like their neighborhood as well, did not know their neighbors as well, and did not so often feel that they shared interests and points of view with their neighbors. This was true despite the fact that both areas had fairly stable residence patterns. The low delinquency area was also somewhat more homogeneous with respect to the religious and ethnic backgrounds of the residents.

2. The areas did not differ in their attitudes toward the "seriousness" of different kinds of deviant juvenile behavior.

3. Residents of the low delinquency area, when they saw a child engaged in deviant behavior in which the observer was not directly involved, were somewhat more likely than residents of the "high" area to take some action—either interfering directly with the child's activities, or informing the police or the child's parents. Area differences in this respect were not great, however, and an attitude of reluctance to interfere prevailed in both areas.

Some of our initial speculations about the processes of social control are supported, and some are not. We found, as expected, that people in the

high delinquency area do tend to ignore children's pre-delinquent and delinquent actions somewhat more often, and this provides an atmosphere in
which delinquency can grow more easily.

We originally thought that one of the reasons residents in a high delinquency area might be slow to take controlling action when they observed incidents of delinquent behavior was that they hold delinquent values
themselves, and feel that actions of delinquent children are actually quite
acceptable. We did not find this to be the case; residents of the high delinquent area were just as quick as the residents of the "low" area to tell
us that minor vandalism and small thefts from stores, etc. were serious and
should be dealt with severely. How shall we interpret this finding? One
possibility is that the respondents did not reveal their real conscious attitudes
to our interviewers. We do not know; we can only point out that while a
number of respondents *did* express indulgent attitudes about juvenile misbehavior, in response to our particular question-wording, these respondents
were found equally often in the two areas, so that the attitudes they expressed do not appear to be differentially related to a high delinquency rate.

Assuming for the moment that most of our respondents told us the
truth about their conscious attitudes, how are we to explain the fact that
the residents of a high-delinquency area appear to share the values of the
larger society about the "wrongness" and "seriousness" of such activities
as stealing, damaging property, juvenile drunkenness, etc.? We may be dealing here with the ticklish problem of different "levels" of attitudes—perhaps
these people are ambivalent, and while they consciously hold pro-social attitudes, they simultaneously have strong anti-social impulses, so that when
they see a child deviating they may consciously disapprove but at the same
time experience enough vicarious pleasure in the child's anti-social actions
that they do not take steps to stop the child. Or perhaps, while sharing
the general values about specific criminal activities, they may hold *other*
values which interfere. For example, a strong belief in the value of individual autonomy, or the importance of immediate impulse gratification, might
run counter to the effective implementation of anti-criminal values.

Another possible explanation is that the "delinquent values" which have
been assumed to prevail in high-delinquency areas actually characterize, not
the entire delinquent neighborhood, but only the actual families in which
the delinquent children are found. We encountered some evidence that
when a family of children got the reputation of being "bad," the neighborhood would withdraw from the family and isolate them. Other children
would be forbidden to play with the deviant children, and the parents of
the neighborhood, who might have made previous efforts to deal with the
parents of the delinquent children, would give up such efforts and leave
the family alone. Thus the pro-social values of the larger neighborhood might
cease to affect delinquent children.

Within the families themselves in which delinquent children grow up, do
"delinquent values" prevail? We have little evidence on this point, but
would like to argue against an uncritical assumption that they do. There

may, of course, be a few cases in which, for instance, a father is a skilled pickpocket or safe-cracker, and trains his son in these skills while the mother smiles proudly to see her boy growing up "just like daddy." It is equally possible however (and, we suspect, much more common) that the parents in delinquent families do not want to see their children become criminals. Granted that the reasons why the children do in fact become criminals may lie in parent-child interaction; nonetheless, they may be centered in other processes than the direct transmission of values. The literature is full of suggestions as to what these processes may be—e.g., the parents may be too inconsistent, too rejecting, or too brutal in their punishment to transmit values effectively. In our own study, we interviewed a woman one of whose children was already in a reformatory, and whose younger children were notorious in the neighborhood for stealing and property damage. This woman strongly expressed values about the "wrongness" and "seriousness" of juvenile thievery and vandalism. Yet we learned from her neighbors, who we also interviewed, that she was helping her children to conceal stolen goods. Neighbors also said that the children were forcing their mother to abet their activities in this way, by threatening to tell their father about the male visitors she occasionally entertained during his absence. It appears, then, that the lack of maternal control over these particular delinquent children stemmed, not from their mother's failure to adopt the values of the larger society about the "wrongness" of theft and vandalism, but from the special circumstances which gave these children freedom to reject their mother's efforts to inculcate these pro-social values.

Our study suggests that a neighborhood pattern of social isolation of families may be an important factor in delinquency. We see no evidence that this social pattern is either the cause or the result of lack of homogeneity of values *about delinquent activities as such*. But the lack of social integration appears to have certain direct effects in a lowered level of social control of delinquent and pre-delinquent activities.

30   The Chicago Area Project—
A 25-Year Assessment

SOLOMON KOBRIN

       .   .   .

The Chicago Area Project shares with other delinquency prevention programs the difficulty of measuring its success in a simple and direct manner.

Reprinted from *The Annals of the American Academy of Political and Social Science*, 322 (Mar. 1959), 20–29, with permission of the Academy and the author.

At bottom this difficulty rests on the fact that such programs, as efforts to intervene in the life of a person, a group, or a community, cannot by their very nature constitute more than a subsidiary element in changing the fundamental and sweeping forces which create the problems of groups and of persons or which shape human personality. Declines in rates of delinquents —the only conclusive way to evaluate delinquency prevention—may reflect influences unconnected with those of organized programs and are difficult to define and measure.[1]

For two reasons the simple and satisfying laboratory model of the controlled experiment is difficult to achieve in measuring the effects of a program. First, it is virtually impossible to find groups which are identical in all major respects save that of participation in a given program. Second, there exists a widespread and understandable reluctance to deny to systematically selected segments of homogeneous groups the putative benefits of programs, a procedure which does produce an approximation to a control group.[2]

The present assessment of the Chicago Area Project will have to rest, therefore, on an appraisal of its experience in carrying out procedures assumed by its founders and supporters to be relevant to the reduction of delinquency. To this end, the theory of delinquency causation underlying the Area Project program will be presented. This will be followed by a description of the procedures regarded as essential to the modification of conditions which produce delinquency. Finally, the adaptations and modifications of these procedures will be described and evaluated.

Conception of the Delinquency Problem

A distinctive feature of the Area Project program is that at its inception it attempted explicitly to relate its procedures in a logical manner to sociological postulates and to the findings of sociological research in delinquency. Under the leadership of the late Clifford R. Shaw, founder of the Area Project and its director during virtually all of its existence, a series of studies completed between 1929 and 1933 brought to the investigation of this problem two heretofore neglected viewpoints: the ecological and the sociopsychological. The first was concerned with the epidemiology of delinquency in the large city; the second with the social experience of the delinquent boy in the setting of his family, his play group, and his neighborhood.[3]

---

[1] For example, rates of delinquents among nationality groups whose children at one time figured prominently in juvenile court statistics declined as these groups improved their economic and social position and moved out of neighborhoods of high rates of delinquents. See Clifford R. Shaw and Henry D. McKay, *Juvenile Delinquency and Urban Areas* (Chicago: University of Chicago Press, 1942), pp. 151–57.

[2] See Edwin Powers and Helen Witmer, *An Experiment in the Prevention of Delinquency* (New York: Columbia University Press, 1951), as a distinguished and solitary example of one program which, in the interest of advancing knowledge, denied hypothesized benefits of a program to a control group.

[3] Studies in the first category include Clifford R. Shaw and others, *Delinquency Areas* (Chicago: University of Chicago Press, 1929); certain sections of Clifford R. Shaw and

With respect to the first problem, it was found that certain areas of the large city produced a disproportionately large number of the delinquents. The high rate areas were characterized as "delinquency areas" and subsequently an effort was made to define their major social features. In the American city of the period, the populations of these communities were made up of predominantly recent migrants from the rural areas of the Old World. As a group they occupied the least desirable status in the economic, political, and social hierarchies of the metropolitan society and in many ways showed an acute awareness of their position. Their efforts to adapt their social institutions to the urban industrial order were at the most only partly successful. The generation of immigrants, in their colonies in the decaying heart of the city, adapted with moderate success only those institutions which preserved customary forms of religious practice, mutual aid, and sociability.

However, the immigrant generation was notably unable to preserve the authority of the old institutions, including the family, in the eyes of the rising generation and was quickly confronted with a problem of conflict with their children. Disruption of cross-generational control produced the conditions for the emergence of a variant species of youth subculture in these communities marked by a tradition of sophisticated delinquency. At the same time this tradition was sustained and fostered by the anonymity of much of the population of slum areas, by the presence of a young adult element which engaged in crime both as an occupation and a way of life, and by the extraordinary harshness of the competitive struggle which arises when the controls of social usage decay. The distribution of official delinquents pointed firmly to the conclusion that the high-rate areas constituted the locus of the city's delinquency problem, both as to number of delinquents and seriousness of offenses.

The Delinquent as a Person

With respect to the second problem, these investigations suggested that, given the conditions of social life in the delinquency areas, delinquency in most cases was the product of the simple and direct processes of social learning. Where growing boys are alienated from the institutions of their parents and are confronted with a vital tradition of delinquency among their peers, they engage in delinquent activity as part of their groping for a place in the only social groups available to them. From investigations of the type re-

Henry D. McKay, *Social Factors in Juvenile Delinquency* (Washington: U. S. Government Printing Office, 1931); and a final volume in which the geographic distribution of rates of delinquents in a number of American cities was analyzed in great detail, Clifford R. Shaw and Henry D. McKay, *Juvenile Delinquency and Urban Areas*. While the last volume was published a decade after the earlier ones much of its data were available to the authors at the time of the founding of the Area Project. Studies of the social experience of delinquent boys include Clifford R. Shaw, *The Jack-roller* (Chicago: University of Chicago Press, 1930); Clifford R. Shaw, *The Natural History of a Delinquent Career* (Chicago: University of Chicago Press, 1931); and Clifford R. Shaw, Henry D. McKay, and James F. McDonald, *Brothers in Crime* (Chicago: University of Chicago Press, 1938).

ported in *The Jack-roller, Natural History of a Delinquent Career,* and *Brothers in Crime,* the conclusion was drawn that with significant frequency, delinquency in the slum areas of our cities reflects the strivings of boys in a social rather than an antisocial direction. These studies focused attention on the paradoxical fact that no matter how destructive or morally shocking, delinquency may often represent the efforts of the person to find and vindicate his status as a human being, rather than an abdication of his humanity or an intrinsic incapacity to experience human sentiment.

This view formed something of a contrast to notions of human nature and delinquency which were, and still are, somewhat more widely accepted. These beliefs, which generally represent delinquent conduct as a manifestation of pathology or malfunction of personality, rest implicitly on an image of man as quick to lose his distinctively human capacities under adverse conditions. The image implied in the Area Project conception of the delinquency problem is that man tends always to organize his behavior in the service of his human identity. To what extent this view is supported by the research of Shaw and his associates, and to what extent the research proceeded from this view is, of course, a difficult question to answer. The fact remains, however, that from the beginning the Area Project program rested on a conception of human nature which was optimistic concerning the prevention of delinquency and the rehabilitation of the delinquent. Delinquency was regarded as, for the most part, a reversible accident of the person's social experience.

Thus, the theory on which the Area Project program is based is that, taken in its most general aspect, delinquency as a problem in the modern metropolis is principally a product of the breakdown of the machinery of spontaneous social control. The breakdown is precipitated by the cataclysmic pace of social change to which migrants from a peasant or rural background are subjected when they enter the city. In its more specific aspects, delinquency was seen as adaptive behavior on the part of the male children of rural migrants acting as members of adolescent peer groups in their efforts to find their way to meaningful and respected adult roles essentially unaided by the older generation and under the influence of criminal models for whom the inner city areas furnish a haven.

Socialization and Community Action

Research in the problem of delinquency formed one of two major sources of suggestion for the Area Project program. The second was furnished by what may best be regarded as a set of sociological postulates concerning, first, the processes by which persons come under the influence and control of social groups and take over their values; and, second, those affecting communal or collective action in the solution of social problems.

It is a commonplace of sociological observation that the source of control of conduct for the person lies in his natural social world. The rules and values having validity for the person are those which affect his daily nurturance, his place in primary groups, and his self-development. He is responsive as a person within the web of relationships in which his daily existence as a human being is embedded.

The inference seemed unavoidable, therefore, that to succeed delinquency prevention activities must somehow first become activities of the adults constituting the natural social world of the youngster. Or, put another way, a delinquency prevention program could hardly hope to be effective unless and until the aims of such a program became the aims of the local populations. Thus, an indispensable preliminary task of delinquency prevention is to discover effective methods of inducing residents of the disadvantaged city areas to take up the cause of prevention in a serious manner. The disposition of the founders of the Area Project was to regard this element of the program as so indispensable that if these populations proved unable to act in relation to the problem, the prevention of delinquency was a lost cause.

A second postulation concerned the problem of developing collective action toward delinquency. Here another commonplace of sociological observation suggested that people support and participate only in those enterprises in which they have a meaningful role. The organized activity of people everywhere flows in the channels of institutions and organizations indigenous to their cultural traditions and to the system of social relationships which defines their social groups. Consequently one could not expect people to devote their energies to enterprises which form part of the social systems of groups in which they have no membership. The relevance of this observation is that there had always existed an expectation that people residing in the high delinquency rate areas could somehow be induced to support the welfare agencies established there. A basic assumption of the Area Project program was that under prevailing conditions it was illusory to expect this to happen.

Thus, in view of the primacy of the local social life in the socialization and control of the young person, all effort, it was felt, should be devoted to helping residents of high delinquency rate areas to take constructive action toward the problem. The interest of the wider society in winning the rising generation of these communities to orderliness and conformity had first to become a vital interest of the local society.

Organization of the Delinquency Area

A final assumption necessary to the rationale of the Area Project program had to do with the social and institutional organization of the high delinquency rate neighborhood and with the related issue of the capacity of residents of these areas to organize and administer local welfare programs. It was observed that despite the real disorder and confusion of the delinquency area, there existed a core of organized communal life centering mainly in religious, economic, and political activity. Because the function of the slum area is to house the flow of impoverished newcomers and to furnish a haven of residence for the multitudes who, for various reasons, live at the edge of respectability, the nucleus of institutional order actually present is sometimes difficult to discern. There seemed further to- be strong evidence that the residents most active in these local institutions were, in terms of interest, motivation, and capacity, on their way up the social class ladder. With respect to these elements of the population it was assumed, therefore, that they represented forces of considerable strength for initiating delinquency prevention activities.[4] There being no evidence of a deficiency of intelligence among them, it was taken for granted that with proper guidance and encouragement they could learn how to organize and administer local welfare programs.

In summary it may be said, then, that the Area Project program regards as indispensable to the success of welfare activity in general and delinquency prevention in particular the participation of those who form a significant part of the social world of the recipients of help. This is seen not as a prescription or a panacea, but as a condition for progress in finding a solution. The program has remained experimental in the sense that it has continued to explore the question: What kind of participation is necessary on the part of which kinds of persons in terms of social role in the local society? But it has rested firmly and consistently on the conviction that no solution of a basic and lasting character is possible in the absence of such participation.

Procedures in Neighborhood Organization

It follows that the basic procedure in the program is the development of local welfare organization among residents of high delinquency rate neighborhoods. This undertaking called for skill in the organizer in identifying the residents holding key positions of influence and the ability to arouse their interest in youth welfare activities. The first phase requires a knowledge of the local society; the second a capacity for sympathetic identification with the local resident. Knowledge of the local society implies familiarity with its culture and history, in the case of ethnic groups; with the local institutions; with the structure of power through which decisions are made and executed; and with the conflicts and cleavages which orient and align the population.

Initial organization in several of Chicago's delinquency areas was undertaken by sociologists employed jointly by the Behavior Research Fund, now dissolved, the Chicago Area Project, and the Illinois Institute for Juvenile Research. The Institute, an agency of state government, until recently has furnished a major share of the salaries of the staff engaged in this program.[5]

It became quickly evident, however, that, for cogent reasons, the employment of qualified local residents offered advantages in the establishment of such programs. In the first place the indigenous worker usually possessed a natural knowledge of the local society. Second, he was hampered by none

---

[4] It should be observed in passing that some of the economic and political leadership of these communities did not always fit phillistine specifications of respectability, and that on this score the Area Project program came under criticism during its early days.

[5] A recent reorganization of these services shifted much of this staff to the administrative jurisdiction of the Illinois Youth Commission.

of the barriers to communications with residents for whom the nonresident, especially those identified with "welfare" enterprise, tended to be an object of suspicion and hostility. Third, his employment was a demonstration of sincere confidence in the capacity of the area resident for work of this sort. Fourth, he was more likely than the nonresident to have access to the neighborhood's delinquent boys and therefore to be more effective in redirecting their conduct. Fifth, his employment represented a prime means of initiating the education of the local population in the mysteries of conducting the welfare enterprise. Hence, virtually from the first, one of the most distinctive features of Area Project procedure was the employment, in appropriate categories and under the tutelage of staff sociologists of the Institute, of local residents to aid in the organization of the approximately dozen community or civic "committees" which were established in Chicago over the course of two decades.[6]

A second major procedural feature of the Area Project program is represented by efforts to preserve the independence of the neighborhood groups after they become established as functioning units. This turned out to be mainly an exercise in self restraint, for the easier and in many ways more natural course would have been to maintain a close supervision and control of their activities. However, since it was the aim of the program to foster the development of knowledge and competence in the conduct of youth welfare activities and to encourage among residents of delinquency areas confidence in their own capacities to act with respect to their problems, the policy was followed of insisting upon a formal, structural autonomy of the organization. The problem in this connection was to maintain full support and help without rendering the independence of the group an empty formality.

Maintaining Autonomy

Three devices were found to be useful in dealing with this problem. First, neighborhood groups either exercised the power of veto in the assignment of Area Project staff to function as their executives; or, more frequently, nominated a qualified local resident as their executive who was then employed as an Area Project staff member. Second, staff members were required to function as representatives and spokesmen of the local groups rather than as representatives of the Area Project central office or of the Sociology Department of the Institute for Juvenile Research. This served to foster an identification of the worker with the point of view and the needs of the local group. Third, policy decisions of neighborhood groups which appeared to Area Project staff to be unsound were nonetheless accepted and

---

[6] Sharp question has been raised by leaders of the social work profession regarding the competence of such persons, whose qualifications rested on assets of character and personal trait rather than on formal training and education. Leaders of the Area Project have always encouraged talented workers in this field to obtain as much training in the group work and social work fields as they could. However, they have regarded the talent for this work as the primary value.

acted upon by them. Since staff members exercised much informal influence with the groups to which they were assigned, this problem arose infrequently. However, when it did arise, the autonomy of the neighborhood group was scrupulously respected.

These, then, are the procedural principles of the Area Project program: development of youth welfare organizations among residents of delinquency areas; employment of so-called indigenous workers wherever possible; and the fostering and preservation of the independence of these groups.

Types of Neighborhood Groups

Before moving to an evaluation of the Area Project as a delinquency prevention program, some indication ought to be made of the specific activities and forms of organization found among these neighborhood groups. The founders of the Area Project were always mindful of variety in the forms of social life and of the necessity, therefore, of adapting the approach to problems of organization as well as the content of program to conditions existing in each work location. In consequence each neighborhood organization within the Area Project differs somewhat from the others in both these respects.

Generally these differences are related to the patterns of social organization existing in their areas of operation and to the degree of unity and coordination among local institutions. On this axis, delinquency areas may be classified as structured and stable, structured but unstable, and unstructured and unstable.[7]

In the structured and stable communities, Area Project neighborhood organizations reflect a direct expansion in interests and functions of established neighborhood institutions. In some cases in this category, the dominant local church sponsors the organization, encouraging influential lay leaders to assume responsibility in the development of its program. However, there are few urban neighborhoods in which a single institution exercises complete dominance of the life of the residents. The more usual case in this class is represented by the local organization in which a number of important neighborhood institutions participate. These may include one or more churches, local political bodies, businessmen's groups, and lodges and fraternal groups. However, the representation is always informal, and membership belongs to participating persons as individuals. This informal mode of representation has come to be preferred, probably because it permits the inclusion of important groups which are not formally constituted. Such, for example, are extended kinship groups, friendship cliques, and aggregations of persons temporarily unified around specific problems or issues. In unstructured or unstable communities the member usually represents only himself.

---

[7] These terms are relative. From the vantage point of an orderly and integrated middle-class residential community the structured and stable delinquency area might appear to be both excessively disorderly in terms of delinquency, crime, and other social problems and excessively controlled and dominated by religious or political organizations.

Reasons for Joining Groups

Differences of this order among Area Project groups seem also to be accompanied by differences in motivation for participation. Members of all Area Project groups share a responsiveness to slogans of youth welfare. However, members of groups operating in the relatively well-organized neighborhoods tend to find in this activity a means for realizing their aspiration for upward mobility. A related need is served in those communities where the framework of institutional life fails to furnish a satisfactory place for certain age or sex groups. In these situations young adults and women, for example, may find in the Area Project neighborhood organization a means of gaining recognition.

The second major motivation is found most frequently in communities with few or no organizations (unstructured), and in those that have no fixed pattern of integration of the activities of organizations which may exist (unstable). Here the dominant motives for participation in the Area Project group are, first, a simple concern with the tragedies attending youthful law violation; and second, a desire to break down social isolation through organized contact with neighbors. These constitute the motivations most frequently sanctioned in official representations of Area Project doctrine because they are most apt to evoke a positive response to promotional appeals.

Variety in Program Content

Area Project neighborhood organizations all include, with varying emphasis and elaboration, three elements in their programs. The first is the sponsorship of a standard kind of recreation program for the children of the neighborhood, including in some instances programs of summer camping of considerable scope. Such recreation programs are likely to have two distinctive features: the use of residents, usually active members of the Area Project group, as volunteers assisting in carrying on the recreation program; and the improvisation of store-front locations or unused space in churches, police stations, and even basements of homes for recreational use.

The second element of the program is represented by campaigns for community improvement. These are usually concerned with such issues as school improvement, sanitation, traffic safety, physical conservation, and law enforcement.

The third element of the program is reflected in the activity directed to the delinquent child, gangs of boys involved in delinquency, and, in some cases, adult offenders returning to the neighborhood from penal institutions. The activity includes helping police and juvenile court personnel develop plans for the supervision of delinquent youngsters; visiting boys committed to training schools and reformatories; working with boys' gangs in the informal settings of the neighborhood; and assisting adult parolees in their problems of returning to the community.

Specific program content in each of the local groups varies in relation to a number of factors. Among these are the facilities available for recreation

or camping; the character and intensity of problems of safety, physical maintenance, or law enforcement in the area; and the staff's ability to arouse
enthusiasm and effort from the leaders of the local organization in carrying
on direct work with delinquents. Some groups are committed to an extensive program of recreation, including the development and operation of
summer camps. Others, located in neighborhoods well equipped with such
facilities, carry on no recreation work at all.[8] Some have labored strenuously
in programs of neighborhood conservation; others have not concerned themselves with such issues. All have been continuously encouraged and helped
by state employed Area Project staff to maintain direct work with delinquent children and with street gangs, and with virtually no exception all
local groups have done so.

Achievements of the Area Project

The achievements of the Area Project may best be assessed in relation to
its theory of delinquency causation in the social setting of the high-rate
neighborhoods. In this theory, delinquency is regarded as a product of a
local milieu (a) in which adult residents do little or nothing in an organized public way to mobilize their resources in behalf of the welfare of the
youth of the area; (b) in which the relative isolation of the adolescent male
group, common throughout urban society, becomes at its extreme an absolute isolation with a consequent absolute loss of adult control; and (c) in
which the formal agencies of correction and reformation fail to enlist the
collaboration of persons and groups influential in the local society. Leaders
of the Area Project assume that progress in the prevention of delinquency
cannot be expected until these three problems are well on their way to solution. Since progress in the solution of these problems comes only slowly,
permanent declines in delinquency are not expected even after years of effort.

First among the accomplishments claimed by the Area Project is its demonstration of the feasibility of creating youth welfare organizations among
residents of delinquency areas. Even in the most unlikely localities capable
persons of good will have responded to the challenge of responsibility and
have, with help and guidance, operated neighborhood programs. On the
whole these organizations have exhibited vitality and stability and have
come to represent centers of local opinion regarding issues which concern
the welfare of the young. Above all, they have justified the assumption
made by Clifford Shaw and his associates that persons residing in these
localities have the capacity to take hold of such problems and contribute
to their solution.

The Area Project has made an equally distinctive contribution respecting
the problem of the isolation of the male adolescent in the delinquency area.
From the beginning it called attention to the fact that the recreational and

[8] Contrary to popular impression those of our big city neighborhoods which have been
centers of social problems, including delinquency, for many decades sometimes acquire
more than a just share of recreational facilities. This has resulted, quite simply, from
their long-time status as objects of society's solicitude and philanthropy.

character-building agencies in these areas were unable, through their established programs, to modify the conduct of boys caught up in gang delinquency. In all probability the Area Project was the first organized program in the United States to use workers to establish direct and personal contact with the "unreached" boys to help them find their way back to acceptable norms of conduct. The adoption of this pattern in many cities during recent years may be regarded as in part, at least, a contribution of the Area Project to the development of working methods in the delinquency prevention field. At the same time, it should be indicated that from the viewpoint of Area Project assumptions and procedures such work, to be effective, must be carried on as an integral part of a more general program sponsored by residents of the locality.

Finally, the Area Project has pioneered in exploring the problem of tempering the impersonality of the machinery which an urban society erects to control and correct the wayward child. Leaders of the Area Project have tended to regard the procedures of juvenile courts, school systems, police departments, probation and parole systems, training schools, and reformatories as inescapably bureaucratic. That is, the procedures of these organizations tend to become set ways of dealing with persons as members of categories. While it is both rational and efficient as a way of processing human problems, of doing something about and hence disposing of cases, this mode of operating results in serious loss of control of the conduct of the young person. The young person in particular is regarded as responsive mainly to the expectations of his primary groups. Thus, to enhance the effectiveness of the corrective agencies of society, it is necessary to enlist the disciplining power of such groups. This is a difficult and complex undertaking, since the customary primary groups for the child, namely family and peers, are often, in the disorder of the delinquency area, unable or undisposed to exercise the needed discipline.

However, it has been found that in no area is the disorder so unmitigated as to be devoid of persons, whether residents or staff employees of the local organization or both, who staunchly represent the values of conformity, many of whom have or can gain the trust of the wayward. Such relationships capture the essential element of the primary group. The Area Project effort has been to discover an effective pattern through which the good offices of these persons may be used by teachers, police, social workers, and court officials to formulate and execute for the supervision of delinquent children jointly conceived plans designed to meet the specific problems and needs of the person. In this exploration the Area Project has found that there are natural primary relationships with delinquents which may be used effectively for delinquency prevention and that they are best utilized in collaboration with the agencies having formal responsibility for the welfare of the children and the protection of the community.

Concluding Observations

In all probability these achievements have reduced delinquency in the program areas, as any substantial improvement in the social climate of a community must. However, the extent of the reduction is not subject to precise measurement. The effects of improvement in the environment of children are diffuse, cumulative, and intertwined with trends and forces which have their origin outside of programs of this character. In the final analysis, therefore, the Area Project program must rest its case on logical and analytic grounds.

No assessment of this program can be complete without defining its historically unique character. The genius of its founder, Clifford Shaw, lay in his sharp perception of delinquency as human behavior and in his sense of the naturalness or inevitability of violative activity in the youngster who, whether singly or in groups, is neglected, despised, or ignored as a person. This is the spirit which has animated the Area Project program and which has made it distinctive among delinquency prevention programs. This image of the delinquent and this notion of the delinquency-making process have led to the program's insistence on centering the operation within the milieu directly productive of delinquency, upon drawing into the operation as many as possible of the persons involved in the basic socializing experiences of youngsters, and upon dealing with delinquents or incipient delinquents as persons worthy of consideration and respect.

Not uncommonly, programs of prevention, whatever their initial intention or resolve, understandably tend to move away from direct contact with the delinquent and his milieu. Distance is achieved by interposing institutional forms between workers and delinquents, as in programs of formal and official treatment, or by dealing with the delinquent as a person arbitrarily abstracted from his social environment, as in programs based on individual therapy. This kind of evolution is comprehensible in the former type of retreat because the delinquent arouses anger and resentment in the law-abiding person, who consequently is hard put to form a sympathetic identification with him. Retreat from the milieu of the delinquent is even more understandable, for nothing would seem more unrewarding than to attempt to put aright the social disorder of the delinquency area.

It may well be that in perspective the Area Project's distinctive contribution to delinquency prevention as a field of practice and technique will be seen in its development of a method designed to keep preventional work focused upon its proper object, the delinquent as a person in his milieu. Central to this method is not only a view of the problem which stubbornly refuses to uncouple the delinquent from the social world which has created him, but a set of procedures which have demonstrated a capacity to draw into the preventional process itself the inhabitants of this world.

31   Three Approaches to Delinquency Prevention: A Critique

JOHN M. MARTIN

Aside from punishment and strict repression, delinquency prevention is usually defined in these three different ways:

1. Delinquency prevention is the sum total of all activities that contribute to the adjustment of children and to healthy personalities in children.

2. Delinquency prevention is the attempt to deal with particular environmental conditions that are believed to contribute to delinquency.

3. Delinquency prevention consists of specific preventive services provided to individual children or groups of children.[1]

General Description

The logic underlying preventive activities of the first type is disarmingly simple: anything that contributes to the adjustment of children and to their healthy personality development prevents delinquency. Basically this approach links delinquency prevention with general improvements in the institutional fabric of our society, particularly as these affect child welfare. In large part this approach rests on a continuation and extension of measures, now commonplace on the American scene, which are designed to reduce the economic inequities of our social system. Such activities include procedures for raising the income levels of poverty stricken families, better low-rent housing, improving job tenure and work arrangements, and other means for reducing the rigors of poverty and economic insecurity. The approach also embraces attempts to reduce prejudice and discrimination against minority group people, increase the educational achievements of oncoming generations, improve marital relations by premarital counseling and family social work, and increase the impact of religious doctrines on both adults and children.

Reprinted from *Crime and Delinquency*, 7 (Jan. 1961), 16–24, with permission of the National Council on Crime and Delinquency, and the author.

Adapted from the author's book, *Juvenile Vandalism: A Study of Its Nature and Prevention*, to be published by Charles C. Thomas, Springfield, Ill.

[1] H. A. Bloch and F. T. Flynn, *Delinquency: The Juvenile Offender in America Today*, New York, Random House, 1956, p. 512.

Preventive activities of the second type, by and large, aim to overcome factors in the immediate environment of children that seem to contribute to their delinquency. Such activities include attempts at community organization, such as the Chicago Area Projects (to be discussed later in this article); work by "coordinating councils" for harmonizing the efforts of welfare and child care agencies in delinquency prevention; the work of recreational and character-building agencies of all types; and attempts to reduce the commercial activities of adults which are clearly illegal and detrimental to the welfare of children who may get caught up in such traffic as, for example, the sale of liquor to minors, dope peddling, and receiving stolen goods.

Preventive activities of the third type include probation and parole services to children and youths, the programs of residential institutions and special schools for delinquents, child guidance clinics insofar as they are concerned with the diagnosis and treatment of delinquents, direct work with antisocial street gangs, and a variety of other services whose principal purpose is the adjustment of individual children or groups of children.

Relative Merits

It would be enormously difficult, if not impossible, to measure the effectiveness of these three types of preventive activities in terms of their ability actually to reduce delinquency, and no attempt will be made to do so here. However, general comment will be made about the relative merits of the three approaches.

In the main it is correct to conclude that improvement in the collective welfare, particularly in the welfare of depressed minority people will reduce delinquency. In areas such as metropolitan New York the reduction of juvenile delinquency is most intimately linked with the successful assimilation of low-status groups, in particular the ever increasing number of migrant and uprooted Negroes and Puerto Ricans.[2] Whatever contributes to the welfare and assimilation of these people reduces the delinquency rate among their children and, correspondingly, in the communities in which they live; conversely, whatever impedes their progress inflates the delinquency rate in those areas.

But the relationship between delinquency and improvement in the general welfare is more complicated than it appears at first glance. For example, although it is tempting to claim that improved housing and the reduction of poverty will reduce both crime and delinquency, evidence that delinquency is highest during periods of extreme prosperity and *not* during depressions, as well as awareness of the variety and number of offenses committed by middle- and upper-class persons, should warn us against the facile assumption that the elimination of poverty is the Rosetta stone of crime prevention.

The relationship between delinquency, at least in terms of official sta-

[2] For an excellent discussion of this point, see O. Handlin, *The Newcomers*, Cambridge, Mass., Harvard University Press, 1959, especially chap. 4.

tistics, and poverty and poor housing has, of course, long been noted by students of social problems. However, it is erroneous to conclude that the abolishment of these living conditions will also abolish delinquency among low-status children. As Bernard Lander pointed out in his study of differential juvenile delinquency rates by census tracts in Baltimore,[3] delinquency appears to be fundamentally related to social instability or *anomie* and not basically to poverty and poor housing.

It is within this context that we can best understand the disillusionment of those who expected too much by way of delinquency prevention from public housing. Their disappointment is well reflected in the pungent remark reportedly made by one student of New York's slums: "Once upon a time we thought that if we could only get our problem families out of those dreadful slums, then papa would stop taking dope, mama would stop chasing around, and Junior would stop carrying a knife. Well, we've got them in a nice apartment with modern kitchens and a recreation center. And they're the same bunch of bastards they always were."[4]

Emphasis upon *anomie* or social disorganization as a basic contributing factor to the high delinquency rates characteristic of some urban areas, with a concomitant de-emphasis of the obvious poverty of these areas as the underlying factor in their high delinquency rates, would, then, appear to be of cardinal importance for understanding and preventing delinquency in such places.

Anomie and Delinquency

Useful as Lander's statistical analysis of census tracts in Baltimore may be for destroying the myth that poverty and inadequate housing are the root causes of delinquency, the relationship between *anomie* and delinquency may also be more complicated than it seems. Lander emphasized the "internal" disorganization characteristic of high delinquency areas. Yet relatively *stable* neighborhoods may also be characterized by comparatively high rates of delinquency. A good example of just such a neighborhood is the tightly knit Italian slum of "Eastern City" examined by William Foote Whyte in his classic, *Street Corner Society*.[5]

The existence of stable but delinquent neighborhoods suggests that there are at least two kinds of areas that produce delinquency:

One is the rapidly changing and thoroughly chaotic local area of the kind isolated by Lander, perhaps best illustrated by New York City's racially mixed and tension-ridden Spanish Harlem so well described by Dan Wakefield in *Island in the City*.[6]

The other is the rather well-organized neighborhood such as the Italian

---

[3] See B. Lander, *Towards an Understanding of Juvenile Delinquency*, New York, Columbia University Press, 1954, especially p. 89.

[4] D. Seligman, "The Enduring Slums" in The Editors of Fortune, *The Exploding Metropolis*, Garden City, N.Y., Doubleday, 1958, pp. 111–132.

[5] W. F. Whyte, *Street Corner Society*, enlarged edition; Chicago, University of Chicago Press, 1955.

[6] D. Wakefield, *Island in the City*, Boston, Houghton Mifflin, 1959.

ethnic community studied by Whyte, "disorganized" primarily in the sense that the way of life there is judged "out of step" when contrasted with the essentially middle-class culture of the greater society.[7]

It is in the second kind of area particularly that well-developed relationships are likely to exist between criminally precocious adolescents, corrupt politicians, and the seemingly inevitable racketeers. These relationships go far in explaining the easy transition many delinquents make from juvenile misbehavior to the more sophisticated forms of adult criminality. It is in this type of area, too, that personality and family structures are less likely to split and disintegrate under the stresses and strains characteristic of more chaotic and tension-ridden neighborhoods.

But distinctions of this sort, important as they may be for understanding differences in the social structure of delinquency areas, must not obscure a more basic fact: quite aside from the stability or instability of social relations in delinquency-prone areas, the traditions, standards, and moral sentiments of such areas are notoriously delinquent and criminal in "complexion" and "tone." This peculiar cultural climate has long been recognized by students of urban life, particularly by the ecologists and social psychologists of the "Chicago School" of American sociology.[8]

Recently this recognition has linked up with a more general discussion of social class subcultures and particularly with more detailed analyses of lower-class culture as a breeding ground for delinquency. A good example of this is found in an article by Walter B. Miller which called attention to the delinquency proneness of lower-class culture in a discussion of the "focal concerns" of the urban lower-class way of life.[9] Miller's emphasis is not upon the so-called "subculture of the delinquent gang" as discussed by Albert K. Cohen,[10] but upon the content of the whole mode of existence of urban lower-class people. Miller believes that in the lower class, in contrast with the middle class, people are likely to have commitments to focal concerns such as physical "toughness," "smartness" interpreted as the ability to "con" or dupe others, and "excitement" in terms of seeking thrills, taking risks, and courting danger. When these commitments are combined with the intense need for "in-group" membership and status or "rep" so characteristic of lower-class adolescents, Miller feels that conditions are especially ripe for the development of juvenile misconduct, particularly gang delinquency.

Thus the concept of social disorganization can be used to describe both stable and unstable delinquency areas. If we accept such disorganization as basic to an understanding of law violation in both kinds of areas, then

[7] For a further discussion of these two kinds of delinquency areas, see W. F. Whyte, "Social Organization in the Slums," *American Sociological Review*, February, 1943, pp. 34–39.

[8] For an excellent survey of studies in the "social ecology" of crime conducted during the past 150 years, see T. Morris, *The Criminal Area*, London, Routledge and Kegan Paul, 1958, chaps. I–VI.

[9] W. B. Miller, "Lower Class Culture as a Generating Milieu of Gang Delinquency," *The Journal of Social Issues*, Vol. 14, No. 3, 1958, pp. 5–19.

[10] See A. K. Cohen, *Delinquent Boys: The Culture of the Gang*, Glencoe, Ill., The Free Press, 1955.

we must question the value of other delinquency prevention methods besides those aimed at the reduction of poverty. In particular we should examine the limitations inherent in current attempts to prevent delinquency by the use of "individual-centered" techniques, such as social casework and related psychological-psychiatric services.

"Individual-centered" Techniques

Practitioners of such techniques work toward individual adjustment, not social change. Seldom do they try to reduce the delinquency-producing features of the delinquent's environment, especially his extrafamilial environment; instead they emphasize adjustment to prevailing environmental conditions. For most delinquents, who are generally without emotional disturbance and who reflect the patterned deviancy so often found in their lower-class neighborhoods, [11] this means that they are expected to make a nondelinquent adjustment to a highly delinquent life situation. Our recidivism rates testify that at best this adjustment is precarious. Furthermore—and this is perhaps the more basic point—because such efforts fail to come to grips with the underlying social and cultural conditions giving rise to delinquency, they do little to prevent the outcropping of delinquency in the first instance. Most try to take hold only after maladjustment, even delinquency itself, has become manifest in the lives of the youngsters they seek to help.

This, however, should not be taken as a rejection of probation and parole, of training schools and reformatories, of child guidance clinics, and of other kinds of institutions and agencies given over to the care and "correction" of delinquents. Far from abandoning this line of approach, we must work hard at improving existing facilities of this sort and act imaginatively regarding the "invention" of new ones. Furthermore, we must, as we have seldom paused to do in the past, rigorously test and verify the effectiveness of various approaches aimed at the rehabilitation of individual delinquents. In this regard the basic question still to be answered is: To what extent and under what conditions do our correctional agencies really correct?

But despite all of this, we must not be so carried away by our desire to rehabilitate delinquents that we fail to see individual treatment in a proper perspective, lose sight of its limitations, and ignore the fundamental proposition that *the prevention of delinquency should include both individual treatment and general or social prevention.* Unfortunately this is just what has happened. To a truly remarkable degree public and private delinquency-prevention agencies have spent comparatively little money or energy on community-centered programs of social prevention. For decades most of these agencies have put their effort into establishing various kinds of facilities for rehabilitating delinquents on a case-by-case basis, with the "model" and most prestigeful approach in recent years being that of the psychiatrically oriented child guidance clinic.

---

[11] For a recent discussion of this crucial point, see W. C. Kvaraceus, *et al., Delinquent Behavior: Culture and the Individual,* Washington, National Education Association of the United States, 1959, chap. 7.

In sum, if we grant the primary role social disorganization plays in the development of delinquency, then the prevention of delinquency is not fundamentally a problem of bettering the general welfare of children or rehabilitating individuals, although the wisdom of continuing our attempts at both seems obvious. Nor for that matter is delinquency prevention essentially a problem of coordinating the activity of welfare agencies, although, like the application of "individual-centered" techniques, this too has an important role to play in prevention. (The coordination of agency activity is particularly valuable insofar as it enables accurate statistics on reported delinquency to be gathered in various jurisdictions, for it is only on the basis of such statistics that a community can determine the trend of its delinquency and measure the effectiveness of its preventive efforts. Agency coordination is even more valuable when it serves to bring various preventive programs and techniques to bear on potential delinquents before their deviancy becomes well established.)

Basically, the problem of delinquency prevention is a problem of social organization or reorganization and other approaches have merit only to the degree that they contribute to such reorganization.

Social Reorganization

How can social reorganization best be accomplished? Although we may be both unable and unwilling to reduce substantially the drift toward *anomie* that Robert K. Merton [12] and others have suggested is a pervasive characteristic of American society, we may be able to make partial inroads upon such disorganization, particularly insofar as it is related to the problem of juvenile delinquency, if we focus directly on the local areas in which delinquency is most pronounced. The logic underlying this proposal is that a local area "does not need to control the entire culture of a nation (which would be impossible) in order to control its delinquency rate. The things that need to be done are local and relate to personal interaction rather than to the larger institutions." [13] The essence of this approach to social reorganization, then, is to stimulate social change in delinquency-prone neighborhoods.

Unfortunately we have no rich arsenal of tried and proven techniques for accomplishing such change. Much needs to be learned and many innovations need to be developed toward this end. Despite these difficulties, however, we do know much about stimulating change in delinquency areas. The framework within which the reorganization of such neighborhoods can be accomplished has been well described by Frederic M. Thrasher in his outline of a proposal for coordinating neighborhood activity for delinquency prevention. [14]

This proposal envisions that any attempt to prevent delinquency in local

---

[12] See R. K. Merton, *Social Theory and Social Structure*, Glencoe, Ill., The Free Press, 1949, chap. IV.

[13] E. H. Sutherland, "Prevention of Juvenile Delinquency" in A. Cohen *et al.* (eds.), *The Sutherland Papers*, Bloomington, Indiana University Press, 1956, pp. 131–140.

[14] F. M. Thrasher, "Some Principles Underlying Community Co-ordination," *The Journal of Educational Sociology*, March, 1945, pp. 387–400.

areas must fix responsibility for social change at the neighborhood level where such changes can be implemented by local community leaders assisted by experts. Implicit in this approach is the assumption that in even the most delinquency-prone neighborhoods not all the residents are crimi-nals or delinquents, and that in such areas there is actually a duality of conduct norms—one favoring law-abiding behavior, the other favoring delinquency.[15]

Although Thrasher's plan utilizes, as subsidiary techniques, the best services offered by the usual community agencies—especially those of school, court, training institutions, and child guidance clinic—his proposal "represents a radical departure from the methods of social work and community organization as formerly conceived." [16]

This comment made almost three decades ago is nearly as applicable now as it was then. When one surveys current social work efforts at community organization, it becomes abundantly clear that, far from being focused in local areas, this activity is largely county- or city-wide in scope. Furthermore, all too often "community organization" in social work means that professional social workers meet with one another and with upper- and middle-class laymen for the purposes of mapping fund-raising campaigns, educating the public, coordinating agency activity, and similar objectives. Even when particular neighborhoods are the targets for such organization, seldom is the basic responsibility for such work placed in the hands of leaders who are truly representative of the people living in such areas.

Fundamentally the difference between the kind of plan outlined by Thrasher and traditional social work proposals for community organization is that in the former the real work is done by local residents who, banded together in a committee or council, act to (1) get the facts about delinquents and delinquency in their neighborhood; (2) organize existing preventive forces serving their neighborhood; (3) stimulate the development of new programs and services as required; and (4) in cooperation with professional agencies, look to the adjustment of their own delinquents, organize the leisure-time activities of their own children and young people, and improve the neighborhood environment, particularly by encouraging the enforcement of laws outlawing the activities of "slum landlords," petty racketeers, and other adults that are clearly detrimental to the welfare of their neighborhood and their children.

Other sociologists besides Thrasher have also foreseen the urgency of organizing the local community for delinquency prevention. Thus Edwin H. Sutherland, for example, endorsed local community organization as the most effective means for preventing delinquency, emphasized the need for placing responsibility for such organization in the hands of those whose children are the most likely to become delinquent, and cited the necessity

[15] For a discussion of the duality of conduct norms in delinquency areas, see S. Korbin, "The Conflict of Values in Delinquency Areas," *American Sociological Review*, October, 1951, pp. 653–661.

[16] F. M. Thrasher, *The Gang*, second revised edition; Chicago, University of Chicago Press, 1936, p. 538.

of including juveniles themselves as participants in such organization.[17]

The inclusion of children and youths in neighborhood organizations for delinquency prevention is most vital. Too often they are simply left out of the planning and management phases of such activity. As a result, the isolation of their adolescence is compounded and a real opportunity for establishing closer ties between the generations is overlooked.

Chicago Area Project

Perhaps the best known of the relatively few delinquency-prevention programs predicated on local community organization that are actually in operation are the Chicago Area Projects developed by Clifford R. Shaw and his associates.[18] Basically these projects aim at producing internal cohesiveness and conventional behavior in delinquency areas through the development of *indigenous leadership*. Outside professional leadership is minimal. Chiefly it is used to interest and develop local talent. Program activities are not ends in themselves but are used to achieve local unity. Some direct work is done with children and adolescents on a one-to-one counseling basis, and psychiatric and other types of referrals are made when needed. But the central aim is to draw local youngsters into various project activities so that they will identify with conventional rather than with delinquent groups and cultural patterns.

Outside leaders have a definite but limited role. This approach to area reorganization places principal emphasis on the role of natural community leaders who are carriers of conventional conduct norms. Not only do such leaders serve as nondelinquent models for emulation by youngsters attracted to programs offered by projects of this type, but because these indigenous leaders have prestige in the local area, they easily attract adults, as well as children and youths, to project programs in the first instance. It is around natural community leaders, then, that legitimate social structures can be germinated and multiplied in delinquency-prone areas. And it is in relationship with such leaders and within such structures that youngsters can develop the close and intimate attachments with conventional models, achieve the satisfactions, and acquire the sense of personal worth and purpose necessary to counter the drift toward delinquency characteristic of their life situations.

Some Basic Questions

Two basic questions arise relative to preventive programs like the Chicago Area Projects: First, *can they be established, and once established will they last?* Second, *do they actually prevent delinquency?*

In regard to both parts of the first question, the answers seem to be defi-

---

[17] Sutherland, "Prevention of Juvenile Delinquency," *op. cit.*

[18] For detailed descriptions of the Chicago Area Projects, see A. Sorrentino, "The Chicago Area Project After 25 Years," *Federal Probation*, June, 1959, pp. 40–45; S. Kobrin, "The Chicago Area Project—A 25-Year Assessment," *The Annals of the American Academy of Political and Social Science*, March, 1959, pp. 19–29.

nitely affirmative. Thus, in their recent evaluation of the Chicago Area Projects, Witmer and Tufts found that:

1. Residents of low-income areas can organize and have organized themselves into effective working units for promoting and conducting welfare programs.
2. These community organizations have been stable and enduring. They raise funds, administer them well, and adapt the programs to local needs.
3. Local talent, otherwise untapped, has been discovered and utilized. Local leadership has been mobilized in the interest of children's welfare.[19]

A definite answer to the second question is much more difficult to obtain. However, two types of evidence tentatively suggest that it too may be affirmative. First, statistics from 1930 to 1942 indicate that delinquency rates declined in three out of four of the communities in which projects were then being carried on; second, in some of the projects, work with men and boys on parole from institutions has been very successful, with one project noting that out of forty-one parolees worked with between 1935 and 1944, only one was recommitted to an institution.[20] However, evidence such as this, without comparable controls, must obviously remain inconclusive. As has been remarked elsewhere, "the role of any preventive agency is likely to be most difficult to assess." [21] The Chicago Area Projects are no exception.

Another question that arises with respect to delinquency prevention programs geared to local leadership is: *How can they best be originated?* In this regard Walter C. Reckless has warned against waiting for the "spontaneous generation of experimental action"; outside help must get such programs started by stimulating local leaders to action.[22] Likewise it seems necessary that outside assistance should also include sufficient money, at least in the beginning, to help defray costs. Again and again programs of this type have foundered because the few hundred dollars raised by raffles, cake sales, thrift shops, and local donations were simply not enough to meet day-to-day expenses.

Who should provide such assistance? To this there are a number of answers. The potential role of private foundations, boards of education, fraternal organizations, and private industry and labor unions in supporting or initiating such activity is enormous. Of special significance is the potential but presently underdeveloped role urban churches can play in this field. The force of organized religion in the prevention of delinquency will be more fully realized if, and only if, more churches make realistic financial appropriations for such purpose and if, on the personal level, more churchmen base their approach to delinquency on love, direct service, intimate

---

[19] H. L. Witmer and E. Tufts, *The Effectiveness of Delinquency Prevention Programs,* Children's Bureau, United States Department of Health, Education, and Welfare, Publication 350, Washington, Government Printing Office, 1954, p. 15.

[20] *Ibid.,* p. 16.

[21] Bloch and Flynn, *op. cit.,* p. 514.

[22] W. C. Reckless, *The Crime Problem,* New York, Appleton-Century-Crofts, 1950, pp. 524–525.

communication, and example, instead of on benign indifference, social distance, and exhortation.[23]

Assistance should also be available from other sources. For example, communities in states with Youth Authority plans might well call upon such authorities for help insofar as these state agencies actually make provision for realistic assistance to local communities; and in New York the new State Youth Division, one purpose of which is to stimulate communities to take action with regard to delinquency, should be a prime source of both money and advice, as should the Youth Board in New York City. Although the Federal Youth Corrections Act makes no provision for rendering assistance to local communities, the capacity of the federal government in this and other facets of community programs for delinquency prevention is tremendous. Finally, professional social workers themselves, as citizens, as agency representatives and educators, and as spokesmen for their highly influential professional associations, might become less remiss about endorsing, inaugurating, and experimenting with community-centered crime prevention programs.

In any event, if neighborhood programs run by residents are to develop to their full potential, it seems almost axiomatic that outside assistance must be provided.

In Summary

Students of delinquency are becoming increasingly aware of the necessity of reaching out beyond the child and his family in their efforts at prevention. It is submitted that the most efficacious approach for modifying the operating milieu of the bulk of our delinquents is through the widespread establishment of community-centered programs of prevention. Supported by continued improvement in the collective welfare—particularly in terms of the successful assimilation of low-status groups—and incorporating the best of "corrections" and individual treatment, the community-centered approach offers the most hope for reducing law-violation by our children and adolescents.

---

[23] For excellent descriptions of religious programs in which churchmen have established intimate relationships with gang members and other residents of delinquency-prone neighborhoods, see C. K. Myers, *Light the Dark Streets*, Greenwich, Conn., Seabury Press, 1957, and H. J. Rahm and J. R. Weber, *Office in the Alley: Report on a Project with Gang Youngsters*, Austin, University of Texas, Hogg Foundation for Mental Health, 1958.

DATE DUE

DEC 3 94	DEC 0 2 1994		